Palgrave Studies in Compromise after Conflict

Series Editor
John D. Brewer
Queen's University Belfast
Belfast, UK

This series aims to bring together in one series scholars from around the world who are researching the dynamics of post-conflict transformation in societies emerging from communal conflict and collective violence. The series welcomes studies of particular transitional societies emerging from conflict, comparative work that is cross-national, and theoretical and conceptual contributions that focus on some of the key processes in post-conflict transformation. The series is purposely interdisciplinary and addresses the range of issues involved in compromise, reconciliation and societal healing. It focuses on interpersonal and institutional questions, and the connections between them.

More information about this series at
http://www.palgrave.com/gp/series/14641

Kim Wale
Pumla Gobodo-Madikizela
Jeffrey Prager
Editors

Post-Conflict Hauntings

Transforming Memories of Historical Trauma

palgrave
macmillan

Editors
Kim Wale
Stellenbosch University
Stellenbosch, South Africa

Pumla Gobodo-Madikizela
Stellenbosch University
Stellenbosch, South Africa

Jeffrey Prager
Department of Sociology
University of California Los Angeles
Los Angeles, CA, USA

New Center for Psychoanalysis
Los Angeles, CA, USA

Palgrave Studies in Compromise after Conflict
ISBN 978-3-030-39076-1 ISBN 978-3-030-39077-8 (eBook)
https://doi.org/10.1007/978-3-030-39077-8

Cover illustration: Alistair Macrobert

This Palgrave Macmillan imprint is published by the registered company Springer Nature Switzerland AG.
The registered company address is: Gewerbestrasse 11, 6330 Cham, Switzerland

Foreword[1]

The legacy of what has come before us and is still unresolved is unremittingly with us. Whether it goes by the name of 'postmemory' (Hirsch 2012) or 'trans-generational transmission of trauma' (Salberg and Grand 2017) or we use the trope of 'haunting' (Gordon 1997), what is being referred to is the perpetuation of injustice. This is in relation to both *historical* injury—what has been left unacknowledged and unremedied from the past—and *continuing* oppression. Just as in the cases of people suffering from 'post-traumatic stress disorder' (a diagnostic category developed only in the last couple of generations) the most intractable problem is when the trauma is repeated and the conditions of privation are not ameliorated; so too with social and political oppression—the conditions of suffering carry on, as they did after the Holocaust for many people and as they continue to do in post-apartheid South Africa and elsewhere, as so many of the chapters in this book evidence. Sexual abuse, for example, is rarely a one-off event; more commonly it is sustained over time as a prolonged pattern of abuse and then continues as a failure of recognition (a failure of listening and hearing rather than speaking, as one chapter in the book notes). Institutional abuse is even more likely to be sustained and to be uncovered only once social conditions change sufficiently for the survivors to speak out, gaining support in solidarity but also revealing just how little 'post-ness' there is to suffering. On the broader scale, as the editors of this collection note, 'the violence of the past continues to play out in times that are deemed as post-conflict.' The politics of post-conflict societies are marked by *continuing* conflict that does not allow rest to anyone, living or dead, and often the only hauntings that are recognised are those that promote retaliatory and/or defensive violence rather than those that achingly reach towards reconciliation.

Yet hauntings are of different kinds. Some of them plague a guilty conscience; these hauntings perhaps trouble perpetrators most and often lead them to recast themselves as victims (e.g. the discourse of German victimhood that characterised much of German society in the 1950s—Frie 2017), but they can also disturb the sleep of later generations who were patently not responsible for their ancestors' crimes and yet feel implicated in them. And who can say for sure that they are wrong in feeling implicated, in the sense that they are not free from the responsibility to respond in some ways to the post hoc necessity for justice to be done, even if the result of this is that those who own up to the crime are not the criminals but those who either might have benefitted from it (in other contexts, this might be called the patriarchal or the colonial 'dividend') or feel that their inheritance is stained by the continuity of a name, a society, a history that drips blood across the generations? Other hauntings are of the violence that one generation has suffered and somehow passes down to the next. The Holocaust is the most worked example, but it is important to recognise the limitations of this literature as well as what can be learnt from it, especially the question of whether the Western 'literary' models for considering trauma that have arisen out of some of the Holocaust work make assumptions that are inappropriate for the situation of post-colonial societies and others in the global south (Craps 2013). The editors note, 'these assumptions are seen to reproduce relations of epistemic hegemony by applying Western Eurocentric conceptions of the self to post-colonial experience. These experiences have rarely been treated on their own terms and in relation to the socio-historical conditions out of which post-colonial suffering emerges.' This is undoubtedly the case and the chapters of this book set out in many instances to confront this issue. Nevertheless, there may also be lessons that generalise across the terrain. This involves acknowledging the relevance of 'multidirectional memory' (Rothberg 2009), which means that what is learnt in one place or from one set of phenomena is also relevant to others.

Post-Conflict Hauntings deliberately steps away from the Holocaust-centred literature, but in a way that shows its power as the lessons learnt from there—lessons of continued denial and culpability and the damage it does on both sides, to the generations of the victims and those of the perpetrators too—are applied to these other contexts, South African and Rwandan, Northern Irish and American, Korean, Zimbabwean and Australian. One could have added many other places too, particularly in Latin America (the failures of the Truth Commissions in Brazil are exemplary, but so too is the memorialisation work and the resistance to it in Argentina, Chile, Venezuela, Mexico, Guatemala, Ecuador and almost everywhere one chooses to look), but this merely emphasises the point: these ghosts of unrequited victimhood are everywhere to be found and are still waiting to be put to rest.

Part of the urgency here is marked by what may be another difference between the case of the Holocaust and many of these other cases. After the Nazis, there were relatively few Jews left in Europe; those that remained had to find ways to rebuild their lives and in many cases left afterwards, sometimes (as in the case of Poland) because of further anti-semitic attacks and even pogroms. The consequence was the post-war separation of victims from perpetrators, which allowed the victims some kind of painful space in which the response to the emerging 'new' Germany (which had far too many echoes of the 'old' one, not least in the continuity of ex-Nazis in positions of civil and judicial power—Fulbrook 2018) could be worked out, however haltingly and passionately, in ways full of uncertainty and ambivalence, and allowing for the possibility of refusing any kind of contact at all. For most of the populations described in this book, the issue is different; it is more on the model of the post-apartheid situation in which, as Pumla Gobodo-Madikizela (2016) has noted elsewhere, the oppressed and the oppressors, the victims and the perpetrators, have to find ways to continue to live together. 'That victims, perpetrators and bystanders live in the same country,' write the editors, 'and in some cases (for example in Rwanda), closely together as neighbours after violent conflict, is one of the fundamental issues in the chapters in this book.' The alternative to reconciliation is too dangerous, though it might nevertheless have some justification—the 'no hope' feelings of some black South Africans about the future for their country is one that has to be taken seriously (Hook 2014). Under such circumstances, it is imperative to find ways to reconcile, or at least to move 'forwards' together—remembering for the future, as one contributor puts it, rather than being haunted by the past. Actually, as I have pointed out elsewhere (Frosh 2013), the future often haunts us, containing a worry or threat, the anxiety over something coming back in a return (the return of the repressed being perhaps the central trope of Freudian psychoanalysis). It is not a terrain of unlimited possibility, as imagining the future almost always involves drawing out from the past one's fears as well as hopes. We will become what we have been; what we fear, based on the past, may come true; is there any escape from this? There has to be, if the hopes of reconciliation are to be realised and if there is ever to be an end to cycles of violence, if there ever is to be peace.

This profoundly important book deals with the issue of the future every bit as much as it deals with the past. Its subtitle, *Transforming Memories of Historical Trauma*, looks forward to possibilities: the idea of 'transformation' is crucial to the prospects for building societies that have *memories* in place of ghostly hauntings because, as Yerushalmi (1989) tells us, without memory there cannot be justice. Yet these ghosts cannot be simply exorcised; they are also crucial provocations to memory, which means that in the present we cannot do without them. Silencing them is exactly the way to maintain their restlessness, to ensure that the next generations, as individuals and as whole societies, continue to be possessed by the unreconciled violence of the past. The injustice is what makes the ghosts haunt us; and being possessed we either act out their own unfinished trauma or, quite commonly, we defend against their presence by enacting new forms of violence ourselves, the violence of, for instance, competitive victimisation ('only one can live' is what Jessica Benjamin (2018) calls it). This is why we need the ghosts, but we also have to hope we can act in their name in such a way as to lay them to rest—which does not mean forgetting them. Adorno and Horkheimer (1947, p. 216) claim, 'In reality, the dead suffer a fate which the Jews in olden days considered the worst possible curse: they are expunged from the memory of those who live on.' This is precisely the condition of haunting and why the laid-to-rest ghost needs also to be remembered. In the discussions in this book, we can see this idea recurring: remembering for the future is essential to make a less tainted future possible at all; but for it to work, the past has to be put conscientiously in its place.

The urgency of this acknowledgement agenda is enormous; everywhere one looks, the violence of the past recurs. One can even see it in the impulse of so many chapters of this book to find a way forward: there is a danger that we are deceiving ourselves, that the belief in a better future is a messianic belief, useful only to cover over the reality of the past. Remember Kafka (1961): 'The Messiah will come only when he is no longer necessary; he will come only on the day after his arrival; he will come, not on the last day, but on the very last.' And even more violently: 'There is an infinite amount of hope in the universe … but not for us.' No one is to blame for this; without the hopefulness, the hope can never be realised; utopian projects are necessary too. This book also has important suggestions about how to put this into action—what strategies of reconciliation to take, how memorialisation can be made to work. It is also not naïve: plenty of the authors note the difficulty, and some even the likely failure of all such work. Yet the importance of these reconciliatory attempts is not to be underestimated nor should the necessary cynicism that might keep us sane when faced with failure be used to undermine the ethical imperative to make the attempt. This might be linked even to the ethical impulse of psychoanalysis, which offers a frame for much of this work: psychoanalysis might be an 'impossible profession' (Freud 1937, p. 248) and the difference it might make to anyone could be small, but that does not mean it is free to give up. The messiah comes only when called.

London, UK Stephen Frosh

Note

1. Foreword to *Post-Conflict Hauntings*, edited by Kim Wale, Pumla Gobodo-Madikizela and Jeffrey Prager.

References

Adorno, T., & Horkheimer, M. (1947). *Dialectic of Enlightenment*. London: Verso, 1997.

Benjamin, J. (2018). *Beyond Doer and Done to: Recognition Theory, Intersubjectivity and the Third*. London: Routledge.

Craps, S. (2013). *Post-colonial Witnessing: Trauma Out of Bounds*. Basingstoke: Palgrave Macmillan.

Freud, S. (1937). Analysis Terminable and Interminable. *The Standard Edition of the Complete Psychological Works of Sigmund Freud, Volume XXIII (1937–1939): Moses and Monotheism, An Outline of Psycho-Analysis and Other Works*, 209–254.

Frie, R. (2017). *Not in My Family*. Oxford: Oxford University Press.

Frosh, S. (2013). *Hauntings: Psychoanalysis and Ghostly Transmissions*. London: Palgrave.

Fulbrook, M. (2018). *Reckonings: Legacies of Nazi Persecution and the Quest for Justice*. Oxford: Oxford University Press.

Gobodo-Madikizela, P. (2016). *What Does It Mean to Be Human in the Aftermath of Historical Trauma? Re-envisioning The Sunflower and Why Hannah Arendt was Wrong*. Uppsala: The Nordic Africa Institute and Uppsala University.

Gordon, A. (1997). *Ghostly Matters: Haunting and the Sociological Imagination*. Minneapolis: University of Minnesota Press.

Hirsch, M. (2012). *The Generation of Postmemory: Writing and Visual Culture after the Holocaust*. Columbia University Press.

Hook, D. (2014). Antagonism, Social Critique and the Violent Reverie. *Psychology in Society, 46*, 21–34.

Kafka, F. (1961). *Parables and Paradoxes*. New York: Schocken.

Rothberg, M. (2009). *Multidirectional Memory: Remembering the Holocaust in the Age of Decolonization*. Stanford: Stanford University Press.

Salberg, J., & Grand, S. (eds) (2017). *Wounds of History: Repair and Resilience in the Trans-Generational Transmission of Trauma*. London: Routledge.

Yerushalmi, Y. (1989). *Zachor: Jewish History and Jewish Memory*. Seattle: University of Washington Press.

Series Editor's Preface

Compromise is a much used but little understood term. There is a sense in which it describes a set of feelings (the so-called spirit of compromise) that involve reciprocity, representing the agreement to make mutual concessions towards each other from now on: no matter what we did to each other in the past, we will act towards each other in the future differently as set out in the agreement between us. The compromise settlement can be a spit and a handshake, much beloved in folk lore or a legally binding statute with hundreds of clauses.

As such, it is clear that compromise enters into conflict transformation at two distinct phases. The first is during the conflict resolution process itself, where compromise represents a willingness amongst parties to negotiate a peace agreement that represents a second-best preference in which they give up their first preference (victory) in order to cut a deal. A great deal of literature has been produced in Peace Studies and International Relations on the dynamics of the negotiation process and the institutional and governance structures necessary to consolidate the agreement afterwards. Just as important, however, is compromise in the second phase, when compromise is part of post-conflict reconstruction, in which protagonists come to learn to live together despite their former enmity and in face of the atrocities perpetrated during the conflict itself.

In the first phase, compromise describes reciprocal agreements between parties to the negotiations in order to make political concessions sufficient to end conflict; in the second phase, compromise involves victims and perpetrators developing ways of living together in which concessions are made as part of shared social life. The first is about compromises between political groups and the state in the process of statebuilding (or re-building) after the political upheavals of communal conflict; the second is about compromises between individuals and communities in the process of social healing after the cultural trauma was provoked by the conflict.

This book series primarily concerns itself with the second process, the often messy and difficult job of reconciliation, restoration and repair in social and cultural relations following communal conflict. Communal conflicts and civil wars tend to suffer from the narcissism of minor differences, to coin Freud's phrase, leaving little to be split halfway and compromise on, and thus are usually especially bitter. The series therefore addresses itself to the meaning, manufacture and management of compromise in one of its most difficult settings. The book series is cross-national and cross-disciplinary, with attention paid to inter-personal reconciliation at the level of everyday life, as well as culturally between social groups, and the many sorts of institutional, inter-personal, psychological, sociological, anthropological and cultural factors that assist and inhibit societal healing in all post-conflict societies, historically and in the present. It focuses on what compromise means when people have to come to terms with past enmity and the memories of the conflict itself, and relate to former protagonists in ways that consolidate the wider political agreement.

This sort of focus has special resonance and significance for peace agreements are usually very fragile. Societies emerging out of conflict are subject to ongoing violence from spoiler groups who are reluctant to give up on first preferences, constant threats from the outbreak of renewed violence, institutional instability, weakened economies and a wealth of problems around transitional justice, memory, truth recovery and victimhood, amongst others. Not surprisingly, therefore, reconciliation and healing in social and cultural relations is difficult to achieve, not least because inter-personal compromise between erstwhile enemies is difficult.

Lay discourse picks up on the ambivalent nature of compromise after conflict. It is talked about in common sense in one of two ways in which compromise is either a virtue or a vice, taking its place among the angels or in Hades. One form of lay discourse likens concessions to former protagonists with the idea of restoration of broken relationships and societal and cultural reconciliation in which there is a sense of becoming (or returning) to wholeness and completeness. The other form of lay discourse invokes ideas of appeasement, of being *compromised* by the concessions, which constitute a form of surrender and reproduce (or disguise) continued brokenness and division. People feel they continue to be beaten by the sticks which the concessions have allowed others to keep; with restoration, however, weapons are turned truly in ploughshares. Lay discourse suggests, therefore, that these are issues that the Palgrave Studies in Compromise After Conflict series must begin to problematise, so that the process of societal healing is better understood and can be assisted and facilitated by public policy and intervention.

No issue is more important to societal healing and to compromise after conflict than that of trauma. Trauma is both individual and collective at the same time, suffered by people and by groups or societies as a whole. As such, it is an inter-disciplinary space where many subjects meet and is a topic that can really be understood only from multiple disciplinary and theoretical perspectives. Trauma narratives in the public sphere often medicalise the experiences of its victims and sufferers. Trauma does have medical consequences, but to medicalise it as an issue neglects its other dimensions. What is characteristic of this latest volume in the Series is its multi-disciplinarity and thus its whole roundedness when considering the topic. Sociology, theology, psychoanalysis, law, jurisprudence, anthropology, history and social psychology are amongst the disciplines represented in this volume. Moreover, contributions come from amongst the world's best scholars on trauma, as well as post-doctoral fellows and practitioners. It is a hallmark of the Series that early career researchers are published alongside senior academics, allowing for the freshness and engagement of young scholars to combine with the experience and wisdom of older generations. This mix is wonderfully represented in this volume.

The commitment of the Series to career development and to interdisciplinarity is matched in this volume with a consideration of traumatic hauntings in many former or ongoing conflicts across the globe, from Israel-Palestine, Northern Ireland, South Africa, Australia, Korea,

Rwanda, Zimbabwe and the United States of America. Those experiencing traumatic hauntings, or who are exposed to its risk, thus vary from indigenous peoples in Australia, Afro-Americans in the USA, and victims of apartheid, of 'the Troubles' in Northern Ireland, and genocide in Rwanda, amongst many more. The perfectionist will never be satisfied; there is always one more conflict, another set of victims or an extra-disciplinary approach that can be represented. The pragmatist in me sees the coverage here as impressive, whether in terms of disciplinary spread, case countries and types of victim.

The major contribution of the volume, however, is the intellectual attention it gives to intergenerational trauma. Many recent conflicts address the traumatic hauntings of first-generation victims, but some conflicts addressed in this volume are long enough ago for intergenerational trauma to affect subsequent generations. Even the recent conflicts, however, confront risks to cultural trauma at the societal level that can be passed on through social and individual processes of dissemination that affect the future. Traumatic hauntings are thus not only about the past atrocities that define the victimhood experience, fundamentally they are about the future. The idea of post-traumatic repair, for individuals, groups and societies is a strong theme that connects the chapters and gives them coherence.

The chapters address this future orientation at both the individual and societal levels through many processes that encourage post-traumatic repair, ranging from psychoanalysis to new forms of remembrance, from narrative and story-telling to art, drama and performance. Indeed, the whole of Part III is devoted to artistic interventions into healing haunted memories. This makes an important contribution that challenges the medical model of trauma. By foregrounding the social and cultural ways of repairing, transforming and working through the traumatic memories of the past, this volume is a very important addition to the Series and, as Series Editor, I very warmly welcome it.

Belfast, UK
November 2019

John D. Brewer

Acknowledgements

Firstly we would like to thank the contributors who committed their time and energy to writing the chapters that comprise this book. It has been a pleasure and honour to work with this group of inspired scholars, activists and practitioners. Our gratitude also goes to the chapter reviewers for their thoughtful, critical reviews of earlier drafts of these chapters. Special thanks go to Series Editor Professor John Brewer for his support of this project. We also owe much gratitude to Professor Stephen Frosh for contributing the Foreword to this volume. Thank you to the editorial team at Palgrave Macmillan, Josie Taylor and Liam Inscoe-Jones, for their professional handling of the manuscript as well as their support, encouragement and patience. We are grateful to Alistair MacRobert for the image design on the front cover.

We would also like to express our gratitude to Professor Eugene Cloete for supporting our vision for this project. It has been a great privilege to have the space for our research and administrative teams at Studies in Historical Trauma and Transformation. We gratefully acknowledge the generous financial support of the Andrew W. Mellon Foundation that made the work on this volume possible. We are grateful for the funds made available by the National Institute for Humanities and Social Sciences for providing the initial grant that made this project possible, and for their continued support, including the costs associated with the production of this book. Finally, we wish to acknowledge the research support of the National Research Foundation through its support of the South African Research Chair Initiative (SARChI) Chair in Violent Histories and Transgenerational Trauma.

Praise for *Post-Conflict Hauntings*

"This sparkling collection of essays explores the pressing question of how societies emerging from conflict can deal with the haunting legacies of the past in such a way as to prevent recurrence and lay the ground for a just and lasting peace through a dazzling array of case studies from around the world. Resolutely international as well as interdisciplinary in its scope and ambition, *Post-Conflict Hauntings* can be seen to respond to recent calls for memory and trauma studies to become more diverse, pluralistic, culturally sensitive, and future-oriented. Building on the pioneering work of the editors in this area, and paying ample attention to the role of artistic and creative practices in mediating and transforming historical trauma, this rich and stimulating volume stresses the importance and intertwining of psychological healing and material redress. It models precisely the kind of scholarship needed to understand the spectral presence of the past in an increasingly globalized and troubled world, which is not only haunted by memories of past violence, but in which the violence of the past also continues to play out in the present and, unless addressed, compromises the future. Anyone interested in issues of memory, trauma, and justice in post-conflict settings will find this book an invaluable resource".

—Professor Stef Craps, *Director of the Cultural Memory Studies Initiative at Ghent University, Belgium*

"Wale, Gobodo-Madikizela and Prager, the editors of *Post-Conflict Hauntings: Transforming Memories of Historical Trauma*, have created and compiled an indispensable aggregate of master narratives that scholars, public policy analysts, clinicians and artists, among others, will forever treasure. The authors provide us with myriad epistemic conversations and manifestations of psychologically-charged "post" external world trauma outside the Jewish Holocaust. Settings of such traumata include South Africa, Rwanda, Zimbabwe, United States of America, Korea, Palestine and Northern Ireland. If and when ghosts (revenants) return, in what form do they quietly and insidiously reappear? What are metonymic or metaphorical forms of their return? The editors and authors provide rich accounts of hitherto unarticulated forms of rememory in the form of structured and repeatable injustice, quotidian and post-traumatic forms of historical injury. They succinctly and successfully challenge us to come to grips with historical precepts, new texts and new contexts so that when we are able to recontextualize our histories, we may be able to have hope in the face of irreparable large-scale and as yet unmetabolized injury".

—Professor Maurice Apprey, *Dean of African American Affairs, University of Virginia, USA*

Contents

Notes on Contributors

Judy Atkinson is Emeritus Professor at Southern Cross University, NSW, Australia, and patron of We Al-li. She is the author of *Trauma Trails – Recreating Songlines: The Transgenerational Effects of Trauma in Indigenous Australia.* In retirement Atkinson chooses to work on the ground with traumatised populations, particularly children and youth caught in the generational violence-trauma vortex. Her tools of choice are expressive art therapies in ceremonial healing circles. She is documenting outcomes from working within an indigenous therapeutic framework in *the Ancient University.*

Jaco Barnard-Naudé is Research Professor in the Free State Centre for Human Rights at the University of the Free State, Bloemfontein, South Africa. He is a recipient of the UCT Fellows' Award and of the British Academy's Newton Advanced Fellowship in the Westminster Law & Theory Lab, Westminster University, London. Other affiliations include Honorary Visiting Research Fellow, Birkbeck Institute for the Humanities, University of London, and the Trame Institute at the University of Bologna, Italy. He has published widely on the jurisprudential aspects of post-apartheid justice, including transitional justice, sexual minority freedom, spatial justice in the post-colony; post-apartheid rhetoric; and psychoanalytic jurisprudence in the context of protest after apartheid.

Andrea Bieler is Professor of Practical Theology at the University of Basel in Switzerland. She is the author of five monographs and nine edited volumes. Most recently she has published the following: with Isolde Karle, HyeRan Kim-Cragg and Ilona Nord (eds.) *Migration and Religion: Negotiating Hospitality, Agency, and Vulnerability* (2019); *Verletzliches Leben. Horizonte einer Theologie der Seelsorge (Arbeiten zur Pastoraltheologie, Liturgik und Hymnologie Bd. 90)* (Vandenhoeck and Ruprecht 2017); with Christian Bingel und Hans-Martin Gutmann (eds.), *After Violence. Religion, Trauma and Reconciliation* (2011).

John D. Brewer is Professor of Post Conflict Studies at Queen's University Belfast and Honorary Professor Extraordinary at Stellenbosch University. He was awarded an honorary doctorate from Brunel University in 2012 for services to social science. He is Member of the Royal Irish Academy, Fellow of the Royal Society of Edinburgh, Fellow in the Academy of Social Sciences and Fellow of the Royal Society of Arts. He has held visiting appointments at Yale University, St John's College Oxford, Corpus Christi College Cambridge and the Australian National University. He has been President of the British Sociological Association and is a member of the United Nations Roster of Global Experts. He is the author or co-author of 16 books and editor or co-editor of a further 6.

Shari Eppel is Director of Ukuthula Trust in Bulawayo, Zimbabwe. She is completing her Doctorate in Anthropology at the University of Cape Town, while also training an exhumation team in Zimbabwe. The team will be exhuming victims of the *Gukurahundi* massacres in alliance with Zimbabwe's National Peace and Reconciliation Commission.

Pumla Gobodo-Madikizela is a professor in the Faculty of Arts and Social Sciences and holds the SARChI Chair (South African National Research Foundation Chairs Initiative) on 'Violent Histories and Transgenerational Trauma' at Stellenbosch University. She has published extensively on victims and perpetrators' responses to historical trauma. Her books include the award-winning *A Human Being Died That Night: A South African Story of Forgiveness*, *Narrating Our Healing: Perspectives on Healing Trauma*, as co-author; *Memory, Narrative and Forgiveness: Perspectives on the Unfinished Journeys of the Past*, as co-editor; *Breaking*

Intergenerational Cycles of Repetition: A Global Dialogue on Historical Trauma and Memory, as editor. She has been awarded honorary doctorates from Rhodes University (2019), the Friedrich-Schiller University, Germany (2017), and from Holy Cross College in Massachusetts (2002).

Grace Kagoyire is a PhD candidate in the faculty of Arts and Social Sciences, under the Chair for Historical Trauma and Transformation, Stellenbosch University. She is conducting her doctoral research on genocide memory construction among second-generation Rwandan youth. She has extensive individual and group counselling experience working with Rwanda's post-genocide population, as well as with Congolese refugees living in Rwanda, and has conducted training of community mental health workers. With Annemiek Richters, she co-authored a special issue of *Torture: Journal on Rehabilitation of Torture Victims and Prevention of Torture*, entitled: 'Of Death and Rebirth: Life Histories of Female Genocide Survivors'.

Irit Keynan is Associate Professor of History and Humanities. She is Dean of the School of Education at the College of Management, Rishon Le'Zion, Israel. Her research interests, where she has published extensively, are collective memory, war trauma, reconciliation, democracy, multiculturalism and social justice. Keynan is the author of two award-winning books on the survivors of the Holocaust and on war trauma and is the co-editor of two essay collections on multiculturalism and on civil and cultural aspects of security. Her monograph *Memories from a Life I Never Lived*, narrating the story of Jewish-Yugoslav prisoners of war in Nazi German hard-labour camps and the fate of Macedonian Jewry, is forthcoming (in Hebrew, Pardes Publishers, Haifa). Keynan is also active in reconciliation initiatives and on overcoming the psychological barriers of collective memory. Keynan holds a PhD from Tel Aviv University.

Cheryl Lawther is Senior Lecturer in Law, School of Law, Queen's University Belfast. She is working on a number of funded research projects looking at the construction and politicisation of victimhood; reparations, responsibilities and victimhood in transitional societies; and representations of victimhood at dark tourist sites. Lawther's article '"Securing" the Past: Policing and the Contest over Truth in Northern

Ireland,' in *British Journal of Criminology* (2010), was awarded the Brian Williams Article Prize by the British Society of Criminology in July 2011. Her monograph *Truth, Denial and Transition: Northern Ireland and the Contested Past* was published by the Routledge Transitional Justice Series in 2014. Lawther's most recent book *Research Handbook on Transitional Justice* (co-edited with L. Moffett and D. Jacobs) was published by the Edward Elgar Research Handbooks in International Law series in 2017.

Borislava Manojlovic is Assistant Professor of Conflict Analysis and Resolution at George Mason University Korea. She is an expert in peacebuilding, transitional justice, peace education and atrocities prevention. As a peacebuilding practitioner, she worked on minorities- and reconciliation-related issues with the United Nations and the Organization for Security and Co-operation in Europe in both Croatia and Kosovo for over seven years. Her book *Education for Sustainable Peace and Conflict Resilient Communities* was published by Palgrave Macmillan in 2017.

Marietjie Oelofsen is a post-doctoral fellow at Studies in Historical Trauma and Transformation at Stellenbosch University in South Africa. Since 2016, she has been a researcher on a project that explores the intergenerational effect of apartheid trauma in three communities in South Africa's Western Cape Province. In 2019, she co-edited the book *These Are the Things That Sit with Us,* with Pumla Gobodo-Madikizela and Friederike Bubenzer. This book features stories from participants in the research on intergenerational trauma. The analysis of this body of research is ongoing. She has previously written articles on the relationship between journalism and citizens' sense of being and belonging in post-apartheid South Africa.

Jeffrey Prager is a research professor at University of California Los Angeles and a training and supervising analyst at the New Center for Psychoanalysis in Los Angeles. He is the author of the award-winning *Presenting the Past, Psychoanalysis and the Sociology of Misremembering* (Harvard) and co-editor (with Anthony Elliott) of *The Routledge Handbook of Psychoanalysis in the Humanities and Social Science.* He publishes articles at the intersection of sociology and psychoanalysis, including 'Healing from History, Psychoanalytic Considerations on Traumatic

Pasts and Social Repair.' His research concerns the reparative impulse in social relations and the intrapsychic and institutional mechanisms intended to thwart them. Prager regularly collaborates with Professor Gobodo-Madikizela and teaches psychoanalysis in China.

Annemiek Richters is an MD and anthropologist, Emeritus Professor of Culture, Health and Illness at Leiden University Medical Center, and a staff member of the Amsterdam Institute for Social Science Research, University of Amsterdam, the Netherlands. From 2005 onwards she has contributed in a number of leadership capacities to the development of community-based sociotherapy in Rwanda. The majority of her publications over the past years focus on research addressing themes that emerged from the practice of sociotherapy in a post-conflict society.

Marianne Vysma is a Jungian psychoanalyst and medical anthropologist, as well as a lecturer at Webster University Leiden (the Netherlands) in psychodynamic therapy and group processes. Her theoretical interests have focused on how intrapsychic healing requires social connection. In that context she has participated in various training activities of community-based sociotherapy in Rwanda since 2012. She is the co-editor of a book, *Roads and Boundaries: Travels in Search of Reconnection* (2011).

Kim Wale is a Senior Researcher at Studies in Historical Trauma and Transformation at the Stellenbosch University. She is leading the analysis of a large dataset on memories of violence and transgenerational transmission of trauma in South Africa, a research project led by Professor Pumla Gobodo-Madikizela and funded by the A. W. Mellon Foundation. Her first major book titled *South Africa's Struggle to Remember: Contested Memories of Squatter Resistance in the Western Cape* was published by Routledge. She has co-edited the book *Class in Soweto* published by UKZN Press. She has published a number of articles and book chapters on collective memories of violence and trauma, as well as on issues of race, class and whiteness in post-apartheid South Africa.

List of Figures

1

Introduction: Post-Conflict Hauntings

Kim Wale, Pumla Gobodo-Madikizela, and Jeffrey Prager

This book deals with the haunting power of histories of mass violence. In the aftermath of political conflict and following transitions to peace and democracy, countries attempt to rebuild political structures and shape social relationships in the hope of creating more peaceful futures. Yet, the memory of past violence does not stay neatly in the past. It troubles and disrupts—haunts—our best efforts to move forward. Along with important social and political efforts, it is crucial that peace-building processes also grapple with and respond to the individual and collective memory ghosts of past violence. And so, at a time when many nations are struggling against their own injustices and attempting to acknowledge their own violent pasts, this volume is dedicated to assessing the many forms of memory

K. Wale (✉) • P. Gobodo-Madikizela
Stellenbosch University, Stellenbosch, South Africa
e-mail: kwale@sun.ac.za

J. Prager
Department of Sociology, University of California Los Angeles, Los Angeles, CA, USA

New Center for Psychoanalysis, Los Angeles, CA, USA
e-mail: jprager@soc.ucla.edu

K. Wale et al. (eds.), *Post-Conflict Hauntings*, Palgrave Studies in Compromise after Conflict, https://doi.org/10.1007/978-3-030-39077-8_1

traces that are left behind in the wake of violent histories and what it means to respond to these legacies ethically, contextually and creatively.

The starting point for the story of this book was the South African context, a country known both for its painful histories of racist violence and oppression, as well as its celebrated transition to liberation and democracy. Yet, a quarter of a century following this transition, many South Africans who suffered under apartheid, continue to suffer under democracy. The lack of transformation is particularly striking for the millions who continue to live in dehumanising "township" spaces, originally created by the apartheid state to house South Africans classified as "black" by this racially oppressive system. As these spaces grow in the post-apartheid era, so too does the sense of social, political and economic exclusion from the promised, hoped-for, liberation. Cities such as Cape Town, add further insult to injury, as the stark juxtaposition between wealth, beauty and luxury confront those who suffer with conditions entirely unfit for human lives. For these South Africans the haunting power of the past is not simply a memory of past violence, but a lived, everyday experience of continued suffering and exclusion.

For many of the people who live through this painful reality, they experience it through a heavy mix of confusion, anger, betrayal and despair. Where there was a moment of hope for the future in the lead up to transition, today their future feels dark seeped in a growing sense of despair. This haunted condition is not simply the burden of the victims of apartheid, in many ways its weight falls more heavily on the generation that came after apartheid, the so-called "born-free" in popular South African parlance. On the one hand, they carry the hopes and dreams of liberation on their shoulders, yet they continue to live in conditions of oppression and exclusion. This haunted hope recently gave way to the student movements #RhodesMustFall and #FeesMustFall, which again saw the youth take up the banner of struggle against the intersecting race and class injustice which permeates South African society, and particularly university spaces. Day by day these young South Africans are re-living the memory of the past, not simply as memory but also as concrete reality.

The metaphor of haunted memory has been used to describe the nature of psychic trauma and its intergenerational transmission (Abraham and Torok 1994). From this South African example, however, it is clear that we need to rethink this conceptualisation in ways which include the social, economic and political forms of haunting that are entangled with the intergenerational psychic realm. Similarly, Stephen Frosh's (2013) book *Haunting, Psychoanalysis and Ghostly Transmissions* demonstrates how the ghosts of the past are not simply a metaphor for psychic trauma. They are also materially expressed through the external, material and structural factors at work in remembering the past. As Frosh (2013, 167–8) explains:

> This is to say that the symbolic structures of culture – practices, traditions, rituals, class divisions, racialisations, gender discrimination, media representations, literary heritages and so on and so forth, all with their counterpoints in other structures that are hidden, denied and delegitimised – are themselves modes of remembrance.

For countries like South Africa this understanding of haunting—as an intertwining of the psychic and the material—is central to how we understand and deal with memories of violent past/presents. This conceptualisation means that dealing with the ghosts of the past is not only important for collective psychological healing but also crucial for processes of doing justice to the legacy of the past (Derrida 1994; Gordon 1997/2008; Frosh 2013). This is the justice that emerges in the ethical act of tending to and repairing the entangled wounds of the past that call out in the present and towards the future.

It is the complicated condition of "haunted freedom" in South Africa, and particularly the burden it places on future generations, that sparked our desire to understand the issue of post-conflict memory in global perspective. We wanted to explore locally relevant practices of transforming the haunting power of the past from the perspective of different country case studies to think through the following questions: How might we promote new and deeper understandings of the relationship between memories of violence and on-going violence, in South Africa and elsewhere as well? What does it mean to transform this legacy that haunts us? How does the South African experience provide insight to better understand contemporary hauntings around the world? How do experiences in other national settings shed clearer light on better resolving South Africa's on-going struggles?

Post-Conflict Hauntings is a result of our exploration into these questions from two complementary directions. The first reports on a locally focused five-year research project designed to deepen our understanding of the nature of post-conflict hauntings in the South African context. Chapters eight and nine of this volume draw on an analysis of this data. Other chapters, however, are globally focused and seek to generate spaces for conversations with scholars and practitioners from a variety of different post-conflict settings. Many of the chapters are products of a number of conferences held at the University of Stellenbosch, over the last three years, and one at a symposium "Living with the Haunting Power of the Past", held in 2018 in Kigali, Rwanda.

How we deal with legacies of past violence speaks to one of the most pressing global issues of our time. The concern is urgent precisely because we have witnessed, all too many times, the cyclical nature of violent conflict. The *history* of violence has often been identified in the peace-building literature as key to understanding obstacles to the economic, political and legal processes of rebuilding society. Collective or haunted memories of past violence have the power to shape the path of political transitions and world politics (Bell 2006; Assmann and Shortt 2012), they also hold the potential to derail traditional peace-keeping and conflict resolution methods (Cairns and Roe 2003; Bar-Tal 2007; Tint 2010) and are passed down through generations (Volkan 2001; Lorey and Beezley 2002; Argenti and Schramm 2010). This haunted memory often becomes the site of repetition. However, chapters in this volume consider as well particular sites and various practices where the goal has explicitly been to transform memory to overcome various presents pre-occupied with their violent pasts.

This book backgrounds the violence per se and aspires to contribute to the emerging work that seeks to understand what it means to deal with the psychosocial effects of contemporary legacies of mass violence (Hamber and Gallagher 2015). More specifically, it places at the centre of analysis memory and the many ways it can trouble the process of reconciliation; the various contributors build into their analyses the challenges implicit in transforming the haunting power of post-conflict memory instead to positive good. The following chapters, in sum, draw together insights from diverse theoretical, empirical and practical approaches to further understand how *memories* of mass violence continue to haunt present-day politics, society and culture and ways to mitigate their potency.

There have already been important theoretical and practical strides made in this area. Theoretically the "trauma theory" that sought to understand the aftermath of the Holocaust provides a crucial starting point for many of the chapters to engage with, contest and contribute to. Practically, the South African Truth and Reconciliation Commission (TRC), which immediately followed the end of apartheid, was designed to do the work of dealing with collective memories of violence by creating national spaces of healing and social repair. It has become a model of social innovation that other countries have followed. At the same time, South Africa continues to struggle with what has been referred to as the "unresolved business" of the TRC (Swart 2017, 2). While the TRC opened the door and set the ethical tone for a global, collective imperative to deal with the collective trauma of memories of violence, this process was also inevitably haunted by exclusions, assumptions and limitations. This book aims to deepen and expand this important work of collective and intergenerational repair in the aftermath of violence. Drawing from different contexts across the globe, these chapters offer alternative, culturally relevant and creative/artistic practices that move beyond the Western psychoanalytic frameworks of trauma and healing.

This introductory chapter seeks to conceptually frame the work of the following chapters within the over-arching notion of *Post-Conflict Hauntings*. It demonstrates how this concept asks us to open up new ways of understanding *time* in relation to post-conflict processes of peacebuilding. It argues that the present-day condition of our global age, requires us to take seriously Jacques Derrida's shift in perspective from "ontology" to "hauntology" and what this means for processes of collective repair in the aftermath of violence (Derrida 1994). It then hones in on the psychoanalytic concept of trauma which has historically come to frame the way in which post-conflict states deal with haunted memory. It unfolds some of the theoretical developments and contestations that have emerged in relation to the trauma concept and locates this book within this terrain. Finally, it outlines the structure of the volume, and the contributions of its chapters which draw on, challenge and expand the trauma concept to propose more contextually relevant frameworks for transforming haunted memory in the aftermath of historical trauma which include embodied, artistic and culturally located forms of wisdom.

1 Conceptualising Post-Conflict Hauntings

"A spectre is haunting Europe" is the opening sentence of Marx and Engels' *The Communist Manifesto*, published in 1848. And Jacques Derrida in 1994 entitles his book *The Spectres of Marx* to characterise the sense of his time as distorted, due to enduring ghosts or traces from the past. In the opening passage of the third chapter Derrida repeats a phrase "the time is out of joint" from Shakespeare's play *Hamlet* which is about ghosts. He alerts us to an experience of haunted time in a world that is "going badly". Derrida writes this book at the time of transition from apartheid to democracy in South Africa and dedicates it to the memory of Chris Hani, an anti-apartheid liberation fighter assassinated in the lead up to the transition to democracy:

> *The time is out of joint.* The world is going badly. It is worn but its wear no longer counts… *The time is out of joint.* The age is off its hinges. Everything, beginning with time, seems out of kilter, unjust, dis-adjusted. The world is going very badly, it wears at it grows. (Derrida 1994, 77)

Measured in time, South Africa is well into its post-conflict process but the country remains deeply troubled by the past reverberating in ways that defy full understanding. Many of the chapters in this book grapple with "post" conflict contexts struggling with a similar sense of hauntedness, where the violence of the past continues to trouble the present. This returns us yet again to this feeling expressed by Derrida that the "age is off its hinges" with things "out of kilter, unjust, dis-adjusted". This experience of a post-conflict "time out of joint" asks us to search again for new pathways and imaginations to listen and tend to the ghosts of our painful past and the messages they may have for us in the present and for the future. It is towards this searching that the chapters in this book contribute.

"*Time out of joint*" must be approached, Derrida proclaims, not ontologically but through the lens of "hauntology". Whereas the former refers to our being-in-the-world in relation to what is present, hauntology is rather concerned with absent presences that haunt our being-in-the-world—from the past and from a future not yet brought into being. Derrida's repetitive play on the phrase "*the time is out of joint*" captures an awareness of a haunted being-in-the-world in two respects. The first describes the troubling flow of temporality from past to present (to future), when spectral traces from our past disturb our easy relationship to the present and the presence of things. The second relates to "the age" that is "off its hinges" with the forms of injustice that haunt as they grow and wear our world down with time.

The concept of post-conflict hauntings is similar to what Avery Gordon defines as an eerie disruption in our sense of being-in-time (1997/2008, xvi). Gordon describes these as "instances of haunting":

> those singular yet repetitive instances when home becomes unfamiliar, when your bearings on the world loose direction, when the over-and-done-with comes alive, when what's been in your blind spot comes into view. Haunting raises specters and it alters the experience of being in time, the way we separate past present and future.

The topic this book addresses is in itself haunted in the sense that it captures the contradiction implicit in our use of the term "post" when in many ways the violence of the past continues to play out in times that are deemed as post-conflict. Connecting the post-conflict concept to the notion of haunting draws immediate attention to the trouble with our conceptualisation of time in post-conflict studies, which imagines that there can be a clear sense of *post* or *after* mass violence. The troubling of time in relation to the notion of "post-conflict" is engaged in some of the recent scholarship dealing with the aftermath of the Northern Ireland Troubles. For example, the way in which violent pasts live on in the present is interrogated through Graham Dawson's (2016) notion of the "temporal afterlife of emotion" or through Cillian McGrattan's (2012) imagination of "belatedness" that he proposes might replace the discourse of transition in order to highlight the way in which "the past" of mass violence is never really past. Nicolas Argenti (2019) articulates a similar challenge in his ethnography of memories of massacre on the Greek Island of Chios. Here, a Western progressive and linear concept of time fails to capture important different experiences of being-in-time, especially in the aftermath of violence, as in Chios, that is both cyclical and recurring. The concept of post-conflict hauntings, explored in the various chapters that follow, similarly seeks to disrupt the notion of time.

Hauntology also raises the question of justice because troubled memories alert us to the forms of injustice that continue to unsettle our attempts to move forward with our "weary" and "out of kilter" world. Avery Gordon (1997/2008, pxvi), again, describes it well:

> haunting is one way in which abusive systems of power make themselves known and their impacts felt in everyday life, especially when they are supposedly over and done with (slavery, for instance) or when their oppressive nature is denied (as in free labor or national security).

For Derrida, the importance of paying attention to the haunting traces that trouble our world is in order to speak about justice and what justice means in relation to the "ghosts" of "certain others who are not present" (1994, xix). Justice, he insists, entails not so much "doing right", the act of making good or "restitution", but finding remedies for past inequity (1994, 23). Following Levinas, Derrida rather emphasises presently attending to our "relation to others" as we all reconcile with the ghosts of the past and their haunting in the present (Levinas 1961, 62 cited in Derrida 1994, 23).

In Stephen Frosh's (2013, 169) "manifesto for sensitively dealing with ghosts" he offers a practice of care, justice and reparations to acknowledge the "ghosts that haunt". Point number five of his "manifesto" reads:

> We should seek out ceremonies of reparation, rituals of recovery. We will note their insufficiency but acknowledge that engaging in them may be all we can do. We must understand that if a ghost keeps troubling us, it may

> mean that we have missed the point; but it may also mean that we are the only hope the ghost has left. (Frosh 2013, 170)

Frosh's "manifesto" highlights an important task for post-conflict and peace studies, to which this book contributes. This is the consideration of how we develop ethical cultures, "ceremonies of reparation" and "rituals of recovery" to enable us to "sensitively" connect, listen and respond to the haunting memories that trouble the present.

In his more recent work on "implicated witnessing", Frosh 2019 highlights the importance of being able to "slow time down" and develop "endurance" with haunted memory. He describes this as "the capacity to endure with others, to acknowledge their suffering without trying to wish it away… remaining with a situation until it organises itself under the pressure of its own desire" (Frosh 2019, xvi). In doing so, he alerts us to the risks of memory work that we may too quickly move to resolve the haunted memory of others and foregrounds instead the sustained capacity to be-present with the memories that haunt allowing them to resolve in their own way and time.

All of this signals the importance of paying attention to, and moving with (not ahead of) the haunting of post-conflict time, allowing it to slow us down and draw our attention to the forms of injustice within ourselves, our relationships, our politics and our social structures. Our historical obsession with progress and the forms of violence committed in the name of this progress, have led us into this "world going badly" this "age off its hinges". While the creation of something new out of the ashes of the old is important, the denial of the ghosts which haunt those ashes will only seek to ensure that the old becomes entangled with and repeated in the new. To begin to create something new, will also require the careful and attentive slowing down, to listen and transform the haunted presences of the past. Towards this end, this book draws on examples of such efforts from across Africa, America, Europe, Australia and Asia. Some chapters focus on particular country case studies while others draw comparative insights across different cases.

2 Haunting Beyond the Trauma Frame

Current debates on historical trauma and its transgenerational legacies came into prominence in the late 1980s with the rise of studies investigating the repercussions of the Holocaust among descendants of survivors, the second and third generation of survivors of the Holocaust. At the same time, the popularity of studies on historical trauma in the 1990s in the Humanities and Social Sciences was linked to the rise of memory studies and the various ways in which past trauma, and especially historical trauma, is represented among descendants of survivors and their communities. The reference point for the canonical texts on historical trauma and memory—the lingering legacies of mass violence—has mainly been the Holocaust or other perspectives inspired by Euro-American case studies. The collection in this book seeks to shift the lenses to focus on the global south in order to explore new avenues of inquiry in this field. That victims, perpetrators and bystanders live in the same country, and in some cases (e.g. in Rwanda), closely together as neighbours after violent conflict, is one of the fundamental issues in the chapters in this book. It would seem to have a considerable impact on how memories of the traumatic past are framed by survivors and their descendants, as well as on the kinds of narratives that emerge in the post-genocide and post-conflict period. Therefore, going beyond the individualistic focus that has provided the framework for trauma studies, and beyond the denial of memory and the "pact of forgetting" (Assmann 2009) that characterised earlier studies on historical trauma and memory, this book volume is interested in how societies confront the past. It seeks to provide a more social and relational account of the repercussions of the past as a fulcrum for explaining the human action that unfolds in the post-conflict contexts discussed in the chapters.

Psychoanalytically informed trauma theory has been influential in describing the obduracy and persistence of earlier trauma on the everyday life experiences of those who endured it. In his collection of oral histories from surviving victims of the Holocaust, Lawrence Langer demonstrated how this overwhelming experience of suffering continues to exist like a living presence or "parallel existence", in the everyday lives of victims

(Langer 1991, 95). The traumatised "carry an impossible history with them" (Caruth 1995a, 5). They are overwhelmed with memories that are "inaccessible" to, and "unclaimed" by, narrative memory, yet the memories continually "return" as flashbacks to haunt the trauma sufferer who relives the experience as if it was happening in real time (Freud 1939; Caruth 1995b, 155; 1996).

van der Kolk and van der Hart (1995, 146) interpret the Holocaust survivor's narratives collected by Langer through the lens of psychoanalytic trauma theory as follows: "Traumatic memories are unassimilated scraps of overwhelming experiences, which need to be integrated with existing mental schemes, and be transformed into narrative language". Thus, the haunting nature of painful pasts are seen here as the return of the un-integrated "scraps of overwhelming experience" that need to be returned to, and their story shared and assimilated within, normal experience. These writers argue that the haunted nature of traumatised memory requires ways of careful and creative listening to not only what is said but also what is communicated in the space where "understanding breaks down" (Caruth 1995b, 155).

The ghosts of the past, if not laid to rest by the generation who experienced the violence, become inherited as "urgent mandates" appropriated by future generations (Apprey 2014, 2019). How traumatic memory is transmitted to those who are not the immediate victims of that violence has become the object of increased attention. Much of this literature draws on the Freudian informed theoretical developments of Maria Torok and Nicolas Abraham, who conceptualise intergenerational traumatic memory as a "psychic crypt" that holds a shameful secret that haunts the psyches of future generations (Abraham and Torok 1994; Prager 2003; Schwab 2004). In work with Holocaust survivors and their descendants, scholars have emphasised the "conspiracy of silence", "cocoon of silence" and shame that surrounds memories of the Holocaust and contributes to the transgenerational transmission of trauma (Danieli 1984; Hoffman 2004; Richter 2017). Through her concept of the hinge generation, or the generation that "comes after" the Holocaust, Eva Hoffman demonstrates the sense of "guardianship" and responsibility that the descendants of Holocaust survivors feel towards this historical memory (Hoffman 2004, xv). Drawing on Hoffman's work, Marion Hirsch (2008) develops the concept of "post-memory" to highlight the personal and creative connection that the second generation feels towards memories of the first that preceded their birth. This connection to painful pasts is transferred not only inter-psychically but also through cultural objects such as photographs and everyday household objects from the past that continue to be imbued with significance in the present (Hirsch 2008; Kidron 2009).

Other scholars and writers move beyond the family unit to explore the enduring power of memories of violence. Colonial violence, for example, becomes etched in the present among subsequent generations through various forms of social discourse and significantly shapes social relationships long after the physical violence itself has ended. Toni Morrison, the Nobel Prize winning author, explores violence's enduring significance, its inscription, in other ways as well. In her *Beloved*, the main character is a ghost—a child murdered by her mother as an act of love to ensure that she not be sold into slavery. Or, in her work on memories of the Maji Maji resistance war against colonialism in Tanzania, Nancy Rushohora (2017) foregrounds the way in which this history is present in the material memory of battlefield landscapes and the role archaeology has played in memory work. In the Democratic Republic of Congo (DRC), Emery Kalema demonstrates how memories of violence enacted during the Mulele "rebellion" are inscribed into wounded bodies in ways that reproduce suffering in the present and annihilate a sense of "future time" (Kalema 2018, 263). The research on trauma and memory in post-apartheid South Africa, presented in this volume through the two chapters by Marietjie Oelofsen and Kim Wale, demonstrate the entanglement of past and present violence and how this is experienced and interpreted by the generation born after apartheid. What is clear across these various treatments is that past violence re-plays out in the present. The very much alive presence of past violence in the landscapes, structures, relationships and wounded bodies confronts the descendants of violence, not as an absent presence, but as a visceral and violent present, an intensely lived reality of everyday suffering.

While the trauma theory which framed interpretations of post-Holocaust memory played a vital role in calling the humanities, and especially literary scholarship, to play closer attention to the haunted dimensions of post-conflict memory, and what it means to listen to the unspoken in the aftermath of mass violence, it also placed as front and centre a psychoanalytically informed, Western Eurocentric experience of trauma and healing. This has emerged as one of the main critiques of trauma theory—that the assumptions of Western psychotherapy, which underpins trauma theory, are inappropriate to understand the nature of post-colonial suffering (Bennet and Kennedy 2003; Craps and Buelens 2008; Rothberg 2008; Craps 2013). Instead, these assumptions are seen to reproduce relations of epistemic hegemony by applying Western Eurocentric conceptions of the self to post-colonial experience. These experiences have rarely been treated on their own terms and in relation to the socio-historical conditions out of which post-colonial suffering emerges.

Moving beyond the critique of trauma theory, Craps (2013) calls for trauma theory's rethinking in ways that are more applicable to a post-colonial context, taking these experiences of suffering on "their own terms". Further, such post-colonial experiences of suffering do not simply result from a single event that disrupts identity, but rather they are a continuous wounding that is part and parcel of quotidian life, and that creates rather than disrupts identity (Andermahr 2015). Everyday life itself is the traumatic experience and not outside of normal awareness; it creates normal awareness. A notion of racial trauma that more adequately captures this continuous and everyday identity structuring trauma of colonial violence can be found in Maria Root's (1992) concept of insidious trauma. While there have been important responses within the literary field to Craps' call to rethink trauma in post-colonial contexts (see Andermahr 2015; Ward 2015) these typically neglect an engagement with the everyday meaning making narratives of ordinary people struggling with memories of violence in post-colonial contexts.

Another critical intervention into trauma theory emerges through a body of work that attempts to move its focus from the individual to the collective. As the seminal theorist of social memory, Maurice Halbwachs (1992) demonstrated, it is not simply individuals who remember but also collectives and they do so through socially shared "frameworks of meaning". In relation to memories of trauma, the sociological work of Jeffrey Alexander and his colleagues theorised "cultural trauma" as a "sociological process that defines a painful injury to the collectivity, establishes the victim, attributes responsibility, and distributes the ideal and material consequences" (Alexander 2004, 22). As such, the collective memory of trauma is theorised as a socially constructed system of meaning or discourse through which collectivities create a shared sense of identity (Eyerman 2004). Further critical work has demonstrated the contested nature of the trauma concept, the role that discourses of trauma come to play within a broader social and political landscape and the impact this has on those who are constructed as victims within this discourse (Young 1997; Leys 2000; Fassin and Rechtman 2009; Wale 2017).

The essays included in *Post-Conflict Hauntings*, while part of this on-going exploration of the efficacy of memory in shaping contemporary social relations, nonetheless reject a reduction of collective memory to mere social construction or political efficacy. Trauma, too, may be a concept too broadly applied to too varied of settings; many of our authors are mindful of not drawing conclusions too broadly from specific sites and practices. Even so, memories of violence across societies remain very much alive, and promote on-going suffering, in the lived experiences of those living in the present. The haunted traces of the past rise up, trouble and call out in loud and visceral ways from places beyond the present meanings that we may collectively ascribe to historically traumatic events.

Speaking to this dynamic within the field of historical studies, Dominick LaCapra shows how distanced efforts to represent historical traumatic events tend to reproduce the logics of trauma effects. He highlights the way in which a constructivist approach to traumatic histories may "eliminate or overly alleviate" the "after effects of trauma, by seeing the past only in terms of contemporary uses and abuses, for example, as symbolic capital in memory politics" (LaCapra 2001/2014, 39). He identifies a potential "numbing" or "splitting-off" from the affective content of traumatic memory that inhibits the scholars capacity to represent the power of the past that haunts present and future generations. He argues for the importance of developing the historian's capacity for "empathic unsettlement" in relation to the affective power of traumatic pasts (LaCapra 2001/2014). In so doing, the scholarly representation of trauma may become part of a process of connecting to and "working through" the haunting power of traumatic affect.

Representing painful pasts in a way that enables the working through of haunted memory is delicate work. It involves the capacity to become "empathetically unsettled" while at the same time not "transferring" oneself into the memories of others. The following chapters each confront the challenges faced as various collectivities seek to "work through" collectivised forms of traumatised memory. This collection builds upon the previous work of the editors: Gobodo-Madikizela's work on efforts to transform trauma instead of repeating it (2008, 2009), what she has referred to as "disrupting intergenerational cycles of repetition" (2016a, b); Prager's work on "social repair" in the aftermath of violence (2011); and Wale's (2016) findings that the younger generation of anti-apartheid fighters are haunted by a sense of betrayal by the older generation of political leaders in the post-apartheid era. Trauma is a powerful trope for post-conflict work but one that carries with it problematic assumptions and epistemological power dynamics. Through this book, we aim to harness its explanatory power for post-conflict memory work. At the same time, we aim to draw from the insights of our global case studies to challenge the unconscious reproduction of some of the problematic assumptions that haunt the trauma frame.

3 Structure of the Book

3.1 Part One: Towards an Ethics of Haunted Memory

The opening set of chapters address ethical questions faced by every post-conflict collectivity: in relation to its violent past, what "ought to be remembered" and what "ought to be forgotten" (Margalit 2002, 17). Paul Ricouer describes memory as not simply an action but also a "perception, imagination, understanding" (1999, 5). For Ricouer (1999) memory can be used in the work of mourning as well as justice but also can be abused in the service of power to repeat the wounds and scars of history in the state of melancholia (see, e.g. Prager 2014). The ethical process of working through traumatic and humiliating memories is to find in them the dimensions that may guide us towards the future and the goal of "evolving a culture of just memory" (Ricouer 1999, 11).

In the opening chapter, John Brewer highlights the importance of remembering without "living in" the past through the question: "How can we not live in a past that is ever present?" He develops the notion of "remembering forwards" to balance the haunting burden of the past with a sense of hope, imagination and commitment to the future. He offers five pillars upon which this is built: (1) truth as an act of consciously putting the past back together again (re-membering) should be tempered with (2) tolerance for competing versions and multiple victims of the past, to achieve a sense of (3) togetherness in both the act of remembering and in what is remembered. These pillars should also include a commitment to the (4) transformation of enduring forms of structural inequalities and socio-economic redistribution and a sense of (5) trajectory towards the kind of shared future we wish to inherit.

Irit Keynan's chapter asks how it might be possible for groups from opposite sides of the conflict to do the work of remembering together. Drawing on both Emmanuel Levinas and the African Humanism of Ubuntu, she asserts that memory be framed as a relational way of being with the other, not simply a framework for how to remember. Keynan rejects a more conventional understanding of memory in post-conflict societies as individualistic and organised around victimhood, she emphasises instead the interpersonal character of memory noting that subjectivity "is inextricably intertwined with that of others in one's community" (Gobodo-Madikizela 2016b, 115). Keynan argues that this recognition of others also allows societies to move beyond the repetitive melancholic loop of traumatised societies. She draws on the example of two Palestinian-Israeli dialogue groups to demonstrate how this practice of remembering together across conflict lines emerges spontaneously in the context of the safe space of mutual empathic connection. Only then, the surrender of the self to the openness of the other becomes possible.

Jaco Barnard-Naudé considers the link between haunting, justice and the possibility of hope in relation to Giorgio Agamben's concept of "the irreparable". In this chapter, Barnard-Naudé argues that reparations are a necessary component of any programme for transitional justice. The failure to realise a programme of reparations describes the spectre that haunts post-conflict/still-conflict societies that have applied the TRC model. These include South Africa and Rwanda. He argues that "reparation is impossible and necessary at the same time" and it is this internal contradiction that gives rise to its spectral quality. Nonetheless, without reparation, there can be no hope. He writes, "hope is generated in the negotiation between the impossible reparation and the reality of the irreparable".

Jeffrey Prager's contribution further unpacks the necessity for reparations in those societies where memory haunts. In his chapter, he makes his case by demonstrating the centrality of reparations to overcoming the current racial impasse in the United States. American racism, he argues, exists as a powerful defence thwarting the reparative impulse in contemporary America. The asymmetric relationship between blacks and whites can only be addressed through what he describes as a "politics of love", where the American collectivity acknowledges the necessity for explicit measures of social repair. For Prager, the restoration of a reparative impulse relates not only to an ethical obligation but also as a national psychological imperative.

The final chapter in this part by Pumla Gobodo-Madikizela reflects on the powerful role that the body plays in the trauma testimonies captured in the South African Truth and Reconciliation Commission. Re-reading these in the light of the present she argues that their embodied expressions can be interpreted as both addressed to the violence of the past and as a "prophetic foretelling" of the violence that would continue into the future "post" conflict era. In the second part of her chapter she highlights the problem of perpetrator "denial of responsibility for the past" and proposes that we move beyond the language of "forgiveness" and "reconciliation" because it does not leave enough room for the "complicated, enigmatic, muddy, elusive, and unpredictable" lived experience of victim-perpetrator processes. She reflects on an alternative way of framing dialogue about the past as "empathic repair" and on the role that the arts may play in these processes as an "imagination" that "confronts the living with the haunting presence of the dead".

3.2 Part Two: Local Expressions of Collective Haunting and Healing

The chapters in this second part draw on in-depth qualitative research in Northern Ireland, South Africa, Rwanda and Zimbabwe in ways that expand our understanding of how best to address haunted memories "on their own terms" (Craps 2013, 19), to specify locally relevant practices of "social repair" (Prager 2011), and to "break intergenerational cycles of repetition" (Gobodo-Madikizela 2016a, b). In this part, each of the authors challenge the notion of trauma as solely single event-based and as belonging to individual psyches; each include the intergenerational, geographical, social, political and cultural detail to identify the specific sources that make repair, in their particular case, possible. In each case, the authors of these chapters explore and propose practices of haunted memory work to promote both individual and collective healing.

In Cheryl Lawther's contribution, with Northern Ireland as the backdrop, she offers a useful prism through which to understand the intersection between unresolved pasts, haunted memory and the transmission of trauma after conflict. For her, haunted memory includes memories of the dead mobilised in support of ethnonational and sectarian politics, the landscape—geographical space—frozen as sites of violence, and as a result of the on-going failure to resolve past conflict. Lawther effectively details the multiple dimensions upon which *hauntingness* is constructed and its relevance for the field of transitional justice.

The following two chapters both focus on the South African case, drawing from interview data from the research project on Trauma, Memory and Representations of the Past. Marietjie Oelofsen presents a careful analysis of the narrative of a young woman farm worker who is haunted by "quiet violence"—a form of post-apartheid subjugation which she is unable to articulate within a broader political language. Oelofsen theorises what it would take to foster the kind of "political talking spaces" in South Africa that would enable this quiet violence to be heard and addressed psychologically and politically.

Kim Wale's chapter identifies how nostalgia serves to communicate haunted memory through "intergenerational memory encounters". This chapter deepens our understanding of haunted memory by demonstrating its sensuous and embodied dimensions in contemporary South Africa. Drawing on her analysis of a South African community plagued by multiple histories of mass violence, Wale argues that intergenerational nostalgia serves to bring the silenced traumatic aspects of historical trauma to present-day awareness. It further provides imaginative content through which the youth express their critique of the present and their hopes for the future.

The chapter by Grace Kagoyire, Marianne Vysma and Annemiek Richters adds to our understanding of the various pathways through which haunted memory is transmitted generationally. They report on research conducted with the children of mothers who were rape victims during the Rwandan genocide and subsequently went through a practice described as socio-therapy, a process of intervention to promote both personal and collective healing. They illustrate how it is not only trauma but also forms of healing that are passed down to children. Children benefit from their mother's experience of cultural and community repair, described as a form of re-birth into a new post-genocidal community.

The final chapter of this part, by Shari Eppel, highlights the significance of being especially mindful of the way in which trauma and healing are culturally understood. She highlights the healing power of "bone memory" through describing processes of recovery and reburial of victims of the Gukurahundi massacre in Matabeleland Zimbabwe. Between 1983 and 1987 many Ndebele were tortured and killed by Zanu-PF. Descendants of these victims are at the forefront of political struggles to commemorate the geographical sites of massacre. Eppel warns that the repression of this haunted memory will not silence it, but rather serve to fuel a collective intergenerational identity of pain and anger which could become explosive.

3.3 Part Three: Transforming Haunted Memory Through Artistic Interventions

Societies across the globe remember histories of mass violence through their monuments and memorials, books, and via popular culture, education systems and artistic expressions (Sturken 1997; Assmann 2011; Erll 2011). In the wake of an international concern to remember pasts of mass violence, the museum has emerged and spread across the globe as a dominant cultural mode through which to deal with traumatic pasts (Silberman and Vatan 2013; Sodaro 2018). Artistic and creative modes of remembering violence represent sites through which the haunting nature of historical trauma may be reproduced but they can also serve as powerful agents of transformation. For example, Alieda Assmann has demonstrated the role that the arts has played as both lucid theorist and critic of cultural memory (Assmann 2011). The final chapters of this book explore this power of the arts to intervene in cultural memory in order to validate and elevate those currently alive.

Judy Atkinson demonstrates in the Australian context how Aboriginal women, through processes of memory work that include the use of creativity and art practice, have come to make sense of and respond to the impact of the transgenerational historical trauma of colonial violence. She describes the Kungas Stopping Violence Program run in Alice Springs Correctional Centre Northern Territory. This programme of violence prevention with Aboriginal women was located within an understanding of their own historical trauma expressed over generations and the use of the indigenous concept of Dadirri (deep listening) to draw on the strengths of indigenous culture to facilitate the healing of transgenerational wounds.

Borislava Manojlovic examines the way in which haunted memories of the Korean War are transmitted to future generations of both North and South Koreans. She analyses the history textbooks of both nations to show how they reproduce divisive constructions that blame the other for this violent past. Still, she argues, the education system can also become a site for innovative and creative strategies on behalf of both creative thinking and future peace. She argues that the representation of collective trauma through artistic sources represents a powerful symbolic language capable of illuminating deeper universal knowledge of humanity with the potential to connect students with ways of thinking and feeling about traumatic histories beyond what is presented to them officially.

The final chapter by Andrea Bieler draws on the concept of "travelling memory" (Erll 2011), emphasising the international circulation of mnemonic practices seeking to transform the haunted present through various kinds of memorial and artistic expressions. She describes the importance of these representations, not to solidify an "eternal message" as it is commonly understood, but as a space for contestation, mixed emotions and ambivalent constellations between victims and perpetrators.

References

Abraham, N., & Torok, M. (1994). *The Wolf Man's Magic Word: A Cryptonomy* (N. Rand, Trans.). Foreword: Jacques Derrida. Minneapolis: University of Minnesota Press.

Alexander, J. C. (2004). Toward a Theory of Cultural Trauma. In J. Alexander, R. Eyerman, B. Giesen, N. Smelser, & P. Sztompka (Eds.), *Cultural Trauma and Collective Identity* (pp. 1–30). Berkeley: University of California Press.

Andermahr, S. (2015). Decolonizing Trauma Studies: Trauma and Postcolonialism – Introduction. *Humanities, 4*(4), 500–505.

Apprey, M. (2014). A Pluperfect Errand: A Turbulent Return to Beginnings in the Transgenerational Transmission of Destructive Aggression. *Free Associations: Psychoanalysis and Culture, Media, Groups, Politics, 66*, 15–28.

Apprey, M. (2019). "Scripting" Inhabitations of Unwelcome Guests, Hosts, and Ghosts: Unpacking Elements That Constitute Transgenerational Haunting. *Transactional Analysis Journal, 49*(4), 339–351.

Argenti, N. (2019). *Remembering Absence: The Sense of Life in Island Greece.* Indiana: Indiana University Press.

Argenti, N., & Schramm, K. (2010). Introduction. In N. Argenti & K. Schramm (Eds.), *Remembering Violence: Anthropological Perspectives on Intergenerational Transmission* (pp. 1–40). New York: Berghahn Books.

Assmann, A. (2011). *Cultural Memory and Western Civilization: Function, Media, Archive.* New York: Cambridge University Press.

Assmann, A. (2009). From Collective Violence to a Common Future: Four Models for Dealing with a Traumatic Past. In R. Wodak & G. Auer-Borea (Eds.), *Justice and Memory – Confronting Traumatic Pasts: An International Comparison* (pp. 31–48). Vienna: Passagen Verlag.

Assmann, A., & Shortt, L. (2012). Introduction. In A. Assmann & L. Shortt (Eds.), *Memory and Political Change* (pp. 1–14). Basingstoke: Palgrave Macmillan.

Bar-Tal, D. (2007). Sociopsychological Foundations of Intractable Conflicts. *American Behavioral Scientist, 50*, 1430–1453.
Bell, D. (2006). Introduction. In D. Bell (Ed.), *Memory, Trauma and World Politics: Reflections on the Relationship Between Past and Present* (pp. 1–32). London: Palgrave Macmillan.
Bennet, J., & Kennedy, R. (2003). Introduction. In J. Bennet & R. Kennedy (Eds.), *World Memory: Personal Trajectories in Global Time* (pp. 1–15). New York: Palgrave Macmillan, p. 5.
Cairns, E., & Roe, M. D. (2003). Introduction: Why Memories in Conflict? In E. Cairns & M. D. Roe (Eds.), *The Role of Memory in Ethnic Conflict* (pp. 3–8). Basingstoke: Palgrave Macmillan.
Caruth, C. (1995a). Introduction: Trauma and Experience. In C. Caruth (Ed.), *Trauma: Explorations in Memory* (pp. 3–12). Baltimore: The John Hopkins University Press.
Caruth, C. (1995b). Introduction: Recapturing the Past. In C. Caruth (Ed.), *Trauma: Explorations in Memory* (pp. 151–157). Baltimore: The John Hopkins University Press.
Caruth, C. (1996). *Unclaimed Experience: Trauma, Narrative and History*. Baltimore: John Hopkins University Press.
Craps, S., & Buelens, G. (2008). Introduction: Postcolonial Trauma Novels. *Studies in the Novel, 40*, 1–12.
Craps, S. (2013). *Post-Colonial Witnessing: Trauma Out of Bounds*. Basingstoke: Palgrave Macmillan.
Danieli, Y. (1984). Psychotherapists' Participation in the Conspiracy of Silence About the Holocaust. *Psychoanalytic Psychology, 1*(1), 23–42.
Dawson, G. (2016). Memory, 'Post-Conflict' Temporalities and the Afterlife of Emotion in Conflict Transformation After the Irish Troubles. In M. Corporaal, C. Cusack, & R. van den Beuken (Eds.), *Irish Studies and the Dynamics of Memory* (pp. 257–296). Oxford: Peter Lang. (Reimagining Ireland).
Derrida, J. (1994). *Specters of Marx: The State of the Debt, the Work of Mourning and the New International*. New York: Routledge.
Erll, A. (2011). Travelling Memory. *Parallax, 17*(4), 4–18.
Fassin, D., & Rechtman, R. (2009). *Empire of Trauma: An Inquiry into the Condition of Victimhood*. Princeton: Princeton University Press.
Freud, S. (1939). *Moses and Monotheism* (K. Jones, Trans.). New York: Vintage
Frosh, S. (2013). *Hauntings: Psychoanalysis and Ghostly Transmissions*. London: Palgrave Macmillan.

Frosh, S. (2019). *Those Who Come After: Postmemory, Acknowledgement and Forgiveness*. London: Palgrave Macmillan.
Gobodo-Madikizela, P. (2009). Working Through the Past: Some Thoughts on Forgiveness in Cultural Context. In P. Gobodo-Madikizela & C. van der Merwe (Eds.), *Memory, Narrative, and Forgiveness: Perspectives on the Unfinished Journeys of the Past* (pp. 148–169). New Castle: Cambridge Scholars Press.
Gobodo-Madikizela, P. (2008). Transforming Trauma in the Aftermath of Gross Human Rights Abuses: Making Public Spaces Intimate. In A. Nadler, J. Fisher, & T. Malloy (Eds.), *Social Psychology of Inter-Group Reconciliation: From Violent Conflict to Peaceful Co-existence* (pp. 57–76). London: Oxford University Press.
Gobodo-Madikizela, P. (2016a). Introduction. In P. Gobodo-Madikizela (Ed.), *Breaking Intergenerational Cycles of Repetition: A Global Dialogue on Historical Trauma and Memory*. Opladen: Barbara Budrich Publishers.
Gobodo-Madikizela, P. (2016b). Interrupting Cycles of Repetition: Creating Spaces for Dialogue, Facing and Mourning the Past. In P. Gobodo-Madikizela (Ed.), *Breaking Intergenerational Cycles of Repetition: A Global Dialogue on Historical Trauma and Memory*. Opladen: Barbara Budrich Publishers.
Gordon, A. F. (1997/2008). *Ghostly Matters: Haunting and the Sociological Imagination*. Minneapolis: University of Minnesota Press.
Halbwachs, M. (1992). *On collective Memory*. Chicago/London: University of Chicago Press.
Hamber, B., & Gallagher, E. (Eds.). (2015). *Psycho-Social Perspectives on Peace-Building*. New York: Springer.
Hirsch, M. (2008). The Generation of Post-Memory. *Poetics Today, 29*(1), 103–128.
Hoffman, E. (2004). *After Such Knowledge: Memory, History and the Legacy of the Holocaust*. New York: Public Affairs.
Kalema, E. (2018). Scars, Marked Bodies, and Suffering: The Mulele "Rebellion" in Postcolonial Congo. *The Journal of African History, 59*(2), 263–282.
Kidron, C. A. (2009). Toward an Ethnography of Silence: The Lived Presence of the Past in Everyday the Life of Holocaust Trauma Survivors and Their Descendants in Israel. *Current Anthropology, 50*(1), 5–27.
LaCapra, D. (2001). *Writing History: Writing Trauma*. Baltimore: John Hopkins University Press.
Langer, L. (1991). *Holocaust Testimonies: The Ruins of Memory*. New Haven: Yale University Press.

Leys, R. (2000). *Trauma: A Genealogy*. Chicago: University of Chicago Press.
Lorey, D. E., & Beezley, W. H. (2002). Introduction. In D. E. Lorey & W. H. Beezley (Eds.), *Genocide, Collective Violence and Popular Memory: The Politics of Remembrance in the Twentieth Century* (pp. xi–xxxiii). Wilmington: SR Books.
Margalit, A. (2002). *The Ethics of Memory*. Cambridge, MA: Harvard University Press.
Marx, K., & Engels, F. (1848/1992). *The Communist Manifesto*. Oxford: Oxford University Press.
McGrattan, C. (2012). *Memory, Politics and Identity: Haunted by History*. Basingstoke: Palgrave Macmillan.
Morrison, T. (2005). *Beloved*. London: Vintage.
Prager, J. (2003). Lost Childhood, Lost Generations: The Intergenerational Transmission of Trauma. *Journal of Human Rights, 2*(2), 173–181.
Prager, J. (2011). Danger & Deformation: A Social Theory of Trauma. *American Imago, 68*, 425–448.
Prager, J. (2014). Melancholia and the Racial Order: A Psychosocial Analysis of America's Enduring Racism. In L. Chancer & J. Andrews (Eds.), *The Unhappy Divorce of Sociology and Psychoanalysis* (pp. 284–316). Basingstoke: Palgrave Macmillan.
Richter, J. (2017). Intergenerational Layers of Silence: How the Concealed or the Outspoken Remain Undiscussable or Indescribable. In L. Auestad & A. Treacher Kabesh (Eds.), *Traces of Violence and Freedom of Thought*. London: Palgrave Macmillan.
Ricouer, P. (1999). Memory and Forgetting. In K. Richard & M. Dooley (Eds.), *Questioning Ethics: Contemporary Debates in Philosophy* (pp. 5–11). London: Routledge.
Root, M. P. P. (1992). Reconstructing the Impact of Trauma on Personality. In L. S. Brown & M. Ballou (Eds.), *Personality and Psychopathology: Feminist Reappraisals*. New York: Guilford.
Rothberg, M. (2008). Decolonizing Trauma Studies: A Response. *Studies in the Novel, 40*, 224–234.
Rushohora, N. A. (2017). Theorising the Majimaji – Landscape, Memory and Agency. *Journal of African Cultural Heritage Studies, 1*(1), 19–31.
Schwab, G. (2004). Haunting Legacies: Trauma in Children of Perpetrators. *Postcolonial Studies, 7*(2), 177–195.

Silberman, M., & Vatan, F. (2013). Introduction. In M. Silberman & F. Vatan (Eds.), *Memory and Postwar Memorials: Confronting the Violence of the Past*. New York: Palgrave Macmillan.
Sodaro, A. (2018). *Exhibiting Atrocities. Memorial Museums and the Politics of Past Violence*. New Brunswick: Rutgers University Press.
Sturken, M. (1997). *Tangled Memories: The Vietnam War, the AIDS Epidemic, and the Politics of Remembering*. Berkeley: University of California Press.
Swart, M. (2017). Introduction. In M. Swart & K. van Marle (Eds.), *The limits of transition: The South African Truth and Reconciliation Commission twenty years on* (pp. 1–8). Leiden: Brill-Nijhoff.
Tint, B. (2010). History, Memory and Intractable Conflict. *Conflict Resolution Quarterly, 27*(3), 239–256.
van der Kolk, B. A., & van der Hart, O. (1995). The Intrusive Past: The Flexibility of Memory and the Engraving of Trauma. In *Trauma: Explorations in memory* (pp. 158–182). Baltimore: The John Hopkins University Press.
Volkan, V. D. (2001). Transgenerational Transmissions and Chosen Traumas: An Aspect of Large-Group Identity. *Group Analysis, 34*(1), 79–97.
Wale, K. (2016). *South Africa's Struggle to Remember: Contested Memories of Squatter Resistance in the Western Cape*. London: Routledge.
Wale, K. (2017). Performing and Resisting the Post-TRC 'Trauma-Drama': Survivors Narratives of Past and Present Violence in South Africa. In M. Swart & K. van Marle (Eds.), *The Limits of Transition: The South African Truth and Reconciliation Commission Twenty Years On* (pp. 121–146). Leiden: Brill-Nijhoff.
Ward, A. (Ed.). (2015). *Postcolonial Traumas: Memory, Narrative, Resistance*. Basingstoke: Palgrave Macmillan.
Young, A. (1997). *The Harmony of Illusions: Inventing Post-Traumatic Stress Disorder*. Princeton: Princeton University Press.

Part I

Towards an Ethics of Haunted Memory

2

Remembering Forwards: Healing the Hauntings of the Past

John D. Brewer

1 Introduction

Memory is a problem in conflict transformation because it is concerned only with the present-past relationship, as Dawson (2007, 14) calls it, or, as it is called here, remembering backwards. Soyinka (2000) refers to this as the burden of memory in societies emerging out of conflict. The theoretical problem that provokes this chapter is that remembering backwards distorts the connection between memory and the future. Three problems arise with respect to the future when we only remember backwards. First, continuity between the past, present and future is broken as the actual past is replaced by social and collective memories of the past that are distorted (Reiff 2016, 142–3). Secondly, remembering backward by means of social memory can make the past an arbiter of the future, supposedly

J. D. Brewer (✉)
Senator George J. Mitchell Institute for Global Peace, Security and Justice, Queen's University Belfast, Belfast, UK

Stellenbosch University, Stellenbosch, South Africa
e-mail: j.brewer@qub.ac.uk

K. Wale et al. (eds.), *Post-Conflict Hauntings*, Palgrave Studies in Compromise after Conflict, https://doi.org/10.1007/978-3-030-39077-8_2

with the past first having to be resolved before people and society can move forwards. Specifically, thirdly, the future is shaped by the past as the ghosts and hauntings of the past are carried forward through intergenerational trauma. These three problems define what we can call the burden of the future. By the burden of the future I mean the problem of what Marc Ross, in his account of "the politics of memory and peacebuilding" after conflict, calls the need to focus on a shared society and joint interests (2013, 99). This makes the burden of the future as important as the burden of the past, for societies emerging out of conflict need to heal haunting memories and facilitate people to learn to live together in a shared future *despite* the past. This chapter suggests that a new way of remembering, which it refers to as remembering forwards, offers such a prospect.

Remembering forwards is a challenging idea in memory studies, and thus readily dismissed, but it is not a new term. It has been used by New Age psychotherapists as a way of recovering what is referred to as that inner voice of teacher-guardian we once called intuition (Baron-Reid 2007). A special issue of the public theology newsletter *Comment* was devoted to remembering forwards (see Cardus 2015). Remembering forwards is also much beloved by poets, artists and playwrights who have used their skills to inspire hope to build a better future (for a collection see Keller and David 2009). The Czech playwright, Vaclav Havel, for example, who became his country's first post-Communist president, stressed the importance of rethinking the future for his country's healing (Flatt 2015, 15–19). Remembering forwards as a concept also fits neatly into the emerging discourse in social science on hope (some Christian peacemakers link memory and hope, see Lederach and Lederach 2010, 211; Smith 2015).

In all these diverse and casual references, however, the term is under-theorised and we are given no sense of how remembering forwards operates or how it deals with the problem of divided memories in societies emerging out of conflict. This chapter theorises the process of remembering forwards and by so doing unpacks the complicated relationship between the past, present and the future. In the course of this chapter, I will outline what I mean by remembering forwards and explore its relevance to societies emerging out of conflict. I will suggest that remembering forwards operates on two levels: it defines an approach to memory that places the past in the context of the future, thus managing the burden of the future, and it shows how divided memories might be reimagined in ways that deal with the burden of the past that constitutes the hauntings of memory.

However, we must start by briefly reiterating the problems that can arise in societies emerging out of conflict when we only remember backwards and focus solely on the past-present relationship to the exclusion of the future.

2 Remembering Backwards

There is a prosaic truth central to the field of memory studies that conflict is in part constituted by memory. Divided and contested memories are wrapped up in the process of identity formation, which ends up sculpting mutually exclusive identities. Nations, societies and groups have always been defined in part by their collective memories, which disclose images, narratives and representations of the past that assist in constructing moral boundaries and senses of solidarity. Any collectivity is in large measure defined by its shared memories. Where nations, societies and groups are divided within and between themselves, this division is to some degree always constituted by contested memory.

Collective memories, however, are also personal memories, for where identification with the collectivity is strong, the memory images, narratives and representations that mark the group's collective memory are perceived as personal, part of the individual's past. They may not be personal remembrances—death soon takes those with personal recollections of group events; but these non-experienced representations of the past form part of the individual's social memory. The notion of social memory is a relatively recent concept but with a long history by other names (see Olick and Robbins 1998), and is now a term in wide currency (see Fentress and Wickham 1992; Misztal 2003). It is used by memory studies specialists to capture this idea that collective memories that define the group are simultaneously personal and individual memories, and that these personal and individual memories have consequences at the societal level because of their collective dimension. Social memories involve personal memory and collective memory at the same time.

It is easy to see how social memory connects personal and collective memories, since social memories survive death. Living memory, as it is called, does not limit the effect that social memory has in making group events personal. Some memories are foundational to people today not because people survive who can remember them but for their role in shaping the sense of identity people have now. In surviving death, social memories survive the centuries. People place themselves in historical events of which they have no direct or living memory because these events are experienced as personal as a result of their group loyalties. In this way, people live the present through the past. However, we do not only live the present through the past because of social memory, we also approach the past selectively through the present. Halbwachs made this a central tenet of his conceptualisation of collective memory, which is said to reconstruct the past in the light of the present (see Reiff 2016, 23). Memories have meaning only because of the present. What this means is that social memory selectively appropriates the past in order to speak to the present. We make of memory what the present impels us to.

The idea of social memory, therefore, gives us two maxims for thinking about the relationship between the present and the past. First, the present is lived through the past. People locate themselves in historical events of which they have no direct remembrance because these travails are foundational to the groups with which they identify, resulting in them being perceived as personal. In this way, people can appropriate history to affirm collective affronts and hurts as personal ones, or experience group triumphs as individual achievements and honours. Secondly, the past is understood through the present. People appropriate selectively from the past in order to comment on current events that dominant their personal concerns and group loyalties, making the past a tool for mobilisation.

These maxims are not contradictory. Memory is a lived experience that transcends time. It does not need to be directly experienced in time and space for it to be part of someone's lived experience, for the group's past is perceived as personal and perceived to have continued and enduring personal relevance for group relations in the present. For example, Ignatieff (1996) commented that the past continues to torment "because it is not the past"; it is not over, completed or finished but permeates the present. Dawson (2007, 14) captures this wonderfully in his notion of "present-past". For this reason also therefore, social memory compresses time. Societies emerging out of conflict do not experience the past in a serial order of time but a concurrent one, in which the distance between the past and the present is compressed into a simultaneous experience. As Michael Ignatieff said, yesterday and today are the same (see Ignatieff 1996, 119–21). Present-day circumstances affect how the past is interpreted and events long ago cry to the present as if they were here and now. In these ways, social memory turns memory into a symbolic object, a socially constructed artefact. It is not a collection of actual events; it is a symbolic representation of the past. It is constructed artfully for social purposes. Disentangling the past from the present therefore is not possible because present factors tend to distort recollections of the past.

This defines the "burden of memory" after conflict, as Soyinka (2000) calls it, a term reminiscent of Miroslav Volf's idea of "the end of memory" (2006; also see his earlier work on reconciliation, Volf 1996). The suggestion that remembering painful and haunting memories turns memory into a burden forms the basis of David Reiff's popular argument in praise of forgetting (2016), Connerton's sympathetic distinctions between types of forgetting according to their social functions (2008), and Linden and Rutkowski's (2013) edited collection on the "beneficial forgetting" of hurting memories. However, some forms of memory culture inhibit any consideration of the future.

3 Pathological Memory Cultures and the Burden of the Future

Remembering backwards in societies emerging out of conflict tends to encourage the development of what we might call "pathological memory cultures". These contrast significantly with the "amnesiac cultures" of more socially cohesive societies (I draw this latter term from Flatt 2015, 12). In the context of post-war Europe in 1948 Halévy penned the idea of the acceleration of history, but the fast pace of modern life in contemporary cosmopolitan society has speeded it up to the point where most people pay little attention to the past or the future. Their lives are lived in the heady here and now, the hedonistic and immediate concerns of daily family life. The ubiquity of social media in late modernity intensifies this sense of immediacy, facilitating people to live in the moment since the whole globe comes to their screen as an instantaneous present. Memory is not part of what sociologists like to call the practical habitus of the ordinary person in everyday life: the shallow, lived experience of now, which we call the present, is their primary concern.

We can contrast a healthy regard for the past in normal memory cultures with the pathological memory cultures found in many societies emerging out of conflict, where life is experienced largely through the past and society is thought thus to change little. Memory almost becomes morbid in these pathological memory cultures. If amnesiac cultures have too little memory, pathological memory cultures societies have it in excess.

This argument draws on the familiar criticisms of the collective memory literature that claims that collective memories can enslave rather than liberate humankind (Reiff 2016, 62), lead to abuses of memory (Berliner 2005; Todorov 2003), turn memorialisation sacred (Misztal 2004), and lead to what Reiff dismissively characterises as the fascist-like homage to "the duty of memory" (2016, 63) and the "dictatorship of nostalgia" (Reiff 2016, 93). By contrast, other writers prioritise the past to the neglect of the future. Dawson (2007, 5), for example, argues that the past must first be engaged and reckoned with before the future can be liberated from the past (also see Gready 2003, 2). As Gobodo-Madizikela puts it, South Africans need to face their past in order to find a new future (2014). Many victims, of course, give moral force to this view in their claims for acknowledgement and recognition, summed up well by the late Elie Weisel, writer, Nobel prize-winner and Holocaust survivor, who famously said that a community that does not first come to terms with the dead will continue to traumatise the living. None of these arguments, however, envisaged the past becoming the level of obsession it does in pathological memory cultures.

There are at least two conditions under which societies emerging out of conflict are particularly prone to develop pathological memory cultures. The first is where conservative forms of the Abrahamic faiths dominate. In such circumstances orthodox and traditional religious interpretations invoke an unbroken continuity with ancient times, predisposing covenantal ideas and a "Chosen People" status, preaching an elective affinity between religion, identity and the land, and having conservative forms of religious culture. It is no coincidence that covenantal theology, Chosen People status and the elision of territory, religion and identity feature in a great number of memory conflicts (see Akenson 1992; Elliott 2009). The second condition is when the transition is problematic or challenged, with groups mistrusting the carefully negotiated second-preference peace agreement and remaining loyal to mutually exclusive first preferences. In peace processes where there is no clear winner, erstwhile enemies are better able to sustain their discordant memories and use memory to perpetuate division. Processes of cultural reproduction sustain and disseminate the ancient cleavages and divisions, weakening and slowing the social peace process; relationships remain broken, conflict journalism abounds, communities remain divided, and wounds are deliberately kept open. Injury and offence are hung onto tenaciously as part of their zero-sum identity and the present is thought to have enduring continuity with the past. Erstwhile enemies can share different senses of the past and have little sense of a shared future. People can transfer the physical war of the past into a culture war that involves conflict over, amongst other things, memory, memory symbols and symbolic representations of the past. In such circumstances, the conflict becomes frozen.

At this point we can draw attention to two unfortunate consequences of the neglect of the future in pathological memory cultures. The first is what Ignatieff (1998) calls the warrior's honour of "keeping faith with the dead" or Blustein calls the fidelity and loyalty of the living to the dead (2014, 189). Pathological memory cultures tend to valorise the tradition of the long dead, making the burden of self-sacrifice, spilled blood and martyrdom of previous generations literally a dead weight on the future. These hauntings from the past slow entry into the future by encouraging renewed forms of violence in honour of the spilled blood of the martyrs and by squeezing the space for compromise and flexibility. The second consequence is less obvious. It is that pathological memory cultures lose perspective about the future. If truth is the first casualty of war, perspective is the first casualty of peace, as people lose sight of how far things have changed and how much the peace process has progressed. Pathological memory cultures focus on continuity with the past, on how little has changed, rather than on what little remains to be achieved to realise a shared future. Faithfulness to the past trumps faithfulness to progress.

4 Forgetting and the Burden of the Future

Another detour is necessary at this juncture to discuss the question of forgetting as a way of balancing the future with the present-past. Forgetting is widely advocated as a way of meeting the desperately felt need to transcend and manage the hauntings of the past in order to enter a shared society in the future. Forgiveness is also canvassed as a way of dealing with the hauntings of the past, but because forgiveness does not necessarily implicate the future, it is often isolated from the burden of the future. Forgiveness does not involve forgetting. Forgiveness is a way of managing hurting memories; forgetting a way of obliterating them. Forgiveness carries the memories into the future under a condition that determines those responsible for them are not held to account in the way they deserve; forgetting is about leaving the hurting memories behind. Forgetting thus manages the burden of the future in a different way to forgiveness by eliminating recollection of the past.

This is the entire premise of Reiff's book *In Praise of Forgetting* (2016), where he writes that remembrance is no "reliable friend" of peace (2016, 122), even urging on people to forget the wrongs of the past (2016, 102). Blustein (2014) also writes in support of forgetting, when he warns against "rumination" (2014, 10, 100) and in favour of "rendering memories of wrongdoing difficult to access" (2014, 10), although he sees forgetting as an ingredient and precursor of forgiveness, which is his primary interest. Forgetting, he writes, avoids making one's past into a tyranny (2014, 107). Nietzsche, of course, also urged forgetfulness to avoid being dominated by history (quoted in Blustein 2014, 121).

It bears saying very strongly therefore, that forgetting is impossible and cannot be a way to deal with the burden of the future. Policies of cultural amnesia towards past conflict, as practised in post-independence India, post-Civil War Spain and post-genocide Rwanda, are forms of institutionalised or forced forgetting, but "memory holes" always appear and ghosts resurface, for while victims may be denied legal, political and cultural space to remember, the "shouting silence" inside each victim prevents forgetting. The empty chair at the dinner table, the constraints of the prosthetic limb or wheelchair, the annual painful anniversary, the constant media coverage that makes entertainment or political capital out of victims' pain: these are constant reminders that make forgetting impossible. It is often said that those who forget their past are destined to repeat it. In formulating this aphorism George Santayana obviously had his adopted home of Spain in mind. Even if some might prefer *not* to remember a divided past, forgetting the past is often out of the question because the past lives in us in some way or other as a haunting and ghost. This brings me to the crux of this chapter: how can we *not* live in a past that is ever present? I tender as a solution to the burden of the future the idea of remembering forwards.

5 Remembering Forwards

Hauntings live on in intergenerational trauma, in mistrust, fear and broken relationships; they survive in architecture on the streets and in people's heads, in street artwork that enshrines one group's fidelity and the other's treachery, and they endure in divided memories and contested moral frameworks through which the former violence is understood. It is precisely in this sort of situation that we need to approach the past through the future by remembering forwards.

Remembering forward offers an approach to memory that places the past in the context of the future, thus dealing with the burden of the future, and an approach to reimaging the past in order to deal with the burden of memory. Let me start my depiction of the past-present-future relationship in remembering forwards by pointing out that Santayana said something fundamentally different to how he is forever quoted. He never used the word forget; he used the word remember. Those who fail to *remember* the past are condemned to repeat it. Failing to remember is not the same as forgetting. As we have argued above, to forget is to excise from memory: to wipe out and to destroy. You cannot tell a landmine victim or someone raped by a soldier to forget; it cannot be excised from memory. Nor should it be; and the memory certainly should not be destroyed. To forget victims is to victimise them twice.

The key to contextualising the past, present and future in remembering forwards is to deliberately remind oneself not to recall; it is to remember to cease to remember. In ancient Athens there was an annual ritual in the temple in which worshippers were reminded to continue to cease to recall their defeat in war (Connerton 2008, 61–2). Failing to remember, in other words, involves a conscious act of remembrance in a way that forgetting does not. It involves memory in a future-oriented act: avoiding repetition of the past by remembering to cease to remember the past. This is what I mean by remembering forwards. Miroslav Volf writes of something like this when he refers to what he calls "non-remembrance" (2015). It is not the same as forgetting. He sees it as releasing the memory, not forgetting it; letting go of oppressive and haunting memories so that they no longer have power over the person. It is their haunting hold over us, not the memory itself, which is released by non-remembrance. This is what Simpson means when he writes about "mastering the past" (2009, 106) or Dawson (2007, 77) about "reparative remembering". A Rwandan, having lost 17 relatives in the genocide, when asked if it were better to remember or forget, replied: "we must remember in order to keep it from happening again, but it is only by forgetting that we are able to go on" (cited in Brewer 2010, 147). I take this to mean that forgetting requires continuous remembering in order to be reminded to forget it. This describes the essence of remembering forwards that is encapsulated in Santayana's maxim: we need constantly to remember to put the past behind us by taking a conscious decision to remember to not let the past that lives in us keep us locked in the past. It is about remembering that, in many acts of memory, we are laying down new foundations for the peace our grandchildren will inherit. It is about remembering forwards towards the aspirations, hopes and ambitions that will carry future generations into a shared society. To quote Candice Mama, the daughter of an apartheid victim who eventually met her father's killer, "you robbed me of my dad, I am not going to let you rob me of my tomorrow" (see https://www.britishcouncil.org/voices-magazine/candice-mama-south-africa-forgiveness-reconciliation).

In order to avoid being misunderstood, I want to clarify what remembering forwards is not. First, it is not about developing a common memory. Georges Erasmus, a First Nation leader in Canada, echoed the collective memory literature when once he said that where common memory is lacking, where people do not share the same past, there is no real community. Where community is to be formed, common memory must be created (quoted in Charles 2015, 37). In the immediate aftermath of conflict, where emotions and pain remain very raw, the idea of agreeing the past is illusionary. Remembering forwards is a way in which we can progress to the future while still living *without* common memories. Secondly, remembering forward is not cultural amnesia. Living together in tolerance despite divided memories does not require the sorts of policies of cultural amnesia practised in post-partition India, Franco Spain or post-genocide Rwanda, where public policy in the media, in school history curricula and in the civic sphere omits mention of the past, and where legislators make it illegal even to talk of it. Amnesia is also illusionary. Public repression of social memory like this coexists with many millions of private memories in which the past remains ever present. With cultural amnesia, public repression of the past keeps it alive in countless acts of private memory resistance.

Let me draw out, therefore, the implications of this argument for a popularly canvassed strategy for dealing with the past that advocates drawing a line under it. Living together in tolerance in a shared society despite divided memories, what here I have called the burden of the future, will not happen by drawing a line and forgetting, erasing and wiping away the past. Memory resistance will keep the past alive. Living together in tolerance in a shared society with divided memories will only happen if we transcend the hold that divided memories have on us by remembering to remember not to allow this past to distort our future. I take this to be what Santayana means by remembering in order to avoid the future being a repeat of the past. It is expressed well by Ahmed Kathrada, an Indian Muslim born in South Africa and a former political prisoner, who once said that South Africans should not forget apartheid but remember it selectively in ways that facilitate consensus over a shared future.

Remembering forward, however, is only part of the solution to the burden of the future; we need to rethink the divided memories that will persist into the future. The burden of memory and the burden of the future are inseparable. Remembering to cease to remember memories that oppress and haunt us, takes us only part of the journey into the future. Societies emerging out of conflict need to revisit these divided memories. Blustein (2014, 122), for example, writes of the need to reimagine the past as a way of becoming "comfortable with one's memories", which involves a process of "re-perceiving" and "cognitive reappraisal". By revisiting these ghosts of the past through remembering forwards and reimagining the past, societies emerging out of conflict can at least have the chance of being healed of the hold that haunting memories have.

Remembering forwards involves five features that need to be isolated when reimagining the enduring divided memories that will persist within remembering forwards. In a fondness for alliteration I call them truth, tolerance, togetherness, transformation and trajectory. These virtues define *how* people should remember. They are not necessarily easily practised, but they literally point a way forward.

Change develops at the pace of truth; truth is essential if the burden of the future is to be met and untruth delays the pace of change. Truth, however, is about remembering events as they occurred, not as they are selectively perceived in subsequent symbolic representations of the past. Re-remembering the past is thus imperative. Re-remembering is more than remembering the forgotten events and the unremembered victims; it is about consciously putting things back together again as they actually occurred not as they are misrepresented in social memory. This includes remembering uncomfortable things about the past that do not fit the narrative built up around them. It includes remembering our own acts of commission and omission that disclose our culpability for the past and our contribution to its divisive nature. It means owning up to our own wrongs. Acknowledgement is thus critical to truth. As Ross reminds us, acknowledgement is not the same as acceptance (2013, 98); it recognises differences of opinion and interpretation without necessarily approving them. What is more, untruthful memory actually *dis*members, not *re*members, the past; it keeps it apart and mutilated. Untruthfulness does an injustice to memory, for as Volf puts it, untruthful memory is unjust memory (2015, 48) and, without truth, victims can be peripheralised (Simpson 2009, 123). Accuracy is important for victims, Blustein informs us (2014, 197), because perpetrators and their supporters typically attempt to justify their actions by demeaning victims and falsifying and misrepresenting the past.

Truth, however, must be tempered with tolerance, for evil things actually happen in conflict, as shown in people's torn bodies and torn minds. Tolerance moderates the consequences of truth. Tolerance requires respect for competing narratives and acceptance that others will see these events differently, allowing us to recognise that this selectivity of memory is normal and should not be amplified into sculpting mutually exclusive identities. Tolerance is all the more important because most conflicts involve what elsewhere I have called multiple victimhood (Brewer 2010, 123), where people belong to groups that were victims and perpetrators at the same time. Tolerance is *not* about seeing the past through another's standpoint—near nigh impossible in the aftermath of conflict—but accepting that the other's standpoint is as valid to them as yours is to you. Tolerance is about respecting differences rather than eliminating differences; it is about honouring diversity rather than us becoming all the same. Simpson (2009, 131) comes close to recognising the importance of tolerance when he writes that truth recovery in post-conflict Northern Ireland must be grounded in cross community understandings and moral convictions, arguing further that tolerance is not the same as acceptance (2009, 135). Blustein calls this "respecting persons" and their dignity (2014, 187).

Tolerance in this manner is built on an intellectual development to which the discussion here closely connects—namely, the broadening of the meaning of justice to include respect for the dignity of others (see Wolterstorff 2008, 2013). Human dignity has become part of the lexicon of social science (see Archer 2000; Misztal 2012) as well as of justice theorists, and in this context what it obligates is respect for the other's human dignity even when the other is unable to assert their right to dignity themselves (such as the result of being victimised or culturally marginalised). Respect for the other's human dignity, for human diversity and for human difference is the foundation of tolerance in remembering forwards.

Tolerance balances truth, but truth and tolerance can be accelerated by togetherness. There are two features of togetherness that are relevant to divided memories: togetherness in the act of remembering the past and togetherness in what it is that is remembered. Remembering together is a liberating form of memory, for sharing divided memories *together* facilitates acceptance of the other's standpoint and encourages the tolerance I have just advocated. Karstedt (2016) advocates something similar with respect to the management of post-conflict emotions, where she emphasises the importance of victims and perpetrators sharing their emotions with each other. This is the same principle that underpins Gobodo-Madizikela's approach to traumatic memories, where she emphasises victim-perpetrator dialogue (e.g., see 2012). Togetherness not only supplies the emotional space in which to hear the narrative of the other, it occurs in a physical space in which co-presence facilitates tolerance.

Another part of togetherness, however, also concerns what it is that is remembered. The past can be excavated for "joint remembrances" (a term borrowed from Brewer 2006, 2010); that is, historical events that exemplify togetherness rather than apartness. Joint remembrances describe historical events that we can now see were shared rather than separated, reflecting common experiences rather than divided ones. Joint memories like these are often excised from social memory because they do not fit the mythological past and can emerge only some time later precisely to challenge the divisive narratives; much now as we remember the many Irish Catholics whose blood was spilled on the Somme in 1916 in service of the British Crown, the commemoration of which is an opportunity for togetherness in both the senses used here.

Transformation is another necessary context to remembering forwards because it encapsulates the truism that individuals do not remember within a social vacuum and that the past exists in relationship to the present and the future. Enduring structural inequalities and injustices after conflict retain the hold that haunting memories have over people and society and keep the ghosts alive, such that social betterment and improvement help break the haunting hold that the past has over the future. Post-traumatic growth, for victims and for society generally, is facilitated by social transformation (this is a point Brewer 2018, 234–6 makes with respect to victims' capacity to be moral beacons in Northern Ireland, South Arica and Sri Lanka, which can be easily destroyed in the absence of socio-economic redistribution and social justice).

These four virtues of remembering, however, all need to be contextualised by trajectory. Trajectory is about looking forward rather than backwards. What we remember and how public commemorations are practised should reflect that we all have to inherit a shared society in the future. Remembering in ways that keep us in the past will only delay that future. Trajectory is about remembering to cease to remember the divisiveness and contentiousness of disputed memories, reminding us not to live in the past but to remember the future. It is precisely this trajectory that distinguishes what I have called remembering forwards.

6 Conclusion

In societies emerging out of conflict, where divided memories in part constituted the conflict, social memory privileges remembering backward. Collective and personal memories elide within social memory to perpetuate divided group identities and contested personal narratives. Above all, social memory works to arbitrate the future, by predisposing a pathological memory culture that locks societies emerging out of conflict into the past. This is what is commonly called the burden of memory after conflict. Hauntings thrive in this burden. Forgiving and forgetting are popular strategies advocated for dealing with such hauntings. However, forgetting the past is impossible and undesirable. This impossibility defines what this chapter has called the burden of the future: the problem of how to develop a shared future with a divided past that is ever present. What is needed in societies emerging out of conflict is being released from the hold that oppressive and haunting memories have over people by a form of memory which this chapter has called remembering forwards. This is not a new term, but the diverse and casual references to it have under-theorised it and not explicated how it might operate in post-conflict societies in managing the twin problems of the burden of memory and the burden of the future.

Remembering forwards is not the same as forgetting; and it is more than the simple truisms that we must remember there *is* a future, that we should remember *for* the sake of future (Smith 2015, 3) or place the past at the service of the future (Todorov 2003). Two features mark what this chapter calls remembering forward after conflict: the first is an approach to memory that balances the past with the future; the second is an approach that defines how remembering might be done. These dual characteristics place memory after conflict in a past-present-future relationship that considerably extends the past-present relationship involved when only remembering backwards. The past-present-future relationship under remembering forwards is encapsulated by an approach to memory after conflict that involves remembering to cease to remember oppressive and haunting memories. It does not involve non-remembrance but active remembering: remembering to cease to remember the past. The past lives in us always; remembering forwards assists in us not living in the past. Remembering forwards maximises the prospect of people emerging from conflict living together in tolerance in the future despite the divided memories that endure and live on. It manages, in other words, what this chapter calls the burden of the future. I have suggested that these enduring memories, however, need to be reimagined by the application of truth, tolerance, togetherness, transformation and trajectory. These five virtues of remembering forwards define *how* we should remember under remembering forwards in order to defeat the burden of memory and solve the burden of the future.

References

Akenson, D. (1992). *God's People*. London: Cornell University Press.

Archer, M. (2000). *On Being Human*. Cambridge: Cambridge University Press.

Baron-Reid, C. (2007). *Remembering the Future*. London: Hay House Publishers.

Berliner, D. (2005). The Abuses of Memory. *Anthropological Quarterly, 78*(1), 197–211.

Blustein, J. (2014). *Forgiveness and Remembrance*. Oxford: Oxford University Press.
Brewer, J. (2006). Memory, Truth and Victimhood in Post-Trauma Societies. In G. Delanty & K. Kumar (Eds.), *The SAGE Handbook of Nations and Nationalism* (pp. 214–224). London: Sage.
Brewer, J. (2010). *Peace Processes: A Sociological Approach*. Cambridge: Polity.
Brewer, J. (2018). Afterword on the Sociology of Compromise. In J. Brewer, B. Hayes, & F. Teeney (Eds.), *The Sociology of Compromise After Conflict* (pp. 229–256). London: Palgrave.
Cardus. (2015, Winter). Special Issue on Remembering Forwards. *Comment Magazine*.
Charles, M. (2015, Winter). We Don't Talk About That. *Comment Magazine*, pp. 31–38.
Connerton, P. (2008). Seven Types of Forgetting. *Memory Studies, 1*, 59–72.
Dawson, G. (2007). *Making Peace with the Past?* Manchester: Manchester University Press.
Elliott, M. (2009). *When God Took Sides*. Oxford: Oxford University Press.
Fentress, J., & Wickham, C. (1992). *Social Memory*. Oxford: Blackwell.
Flatt, K. (2015, Winter). Lessons for an Amnesiac Society. *Comment Magazine*, pp. 12–19.
Gobodo-Madizikela, P. (2012). Remembering the Past: Nostalgia, Traumatic Memory and the Legacy of Apartheid. *Peace and Conflict, 18*, 252–267.
Gobodo-Madizikela, P. (2014). *Dare We Hope*. Cape Town: Tafelberg.
Gready, P. (2003). *Political Transition*. London: Pluto Press.
Ignatieff, M. (1996). Articles of Faith. *Index on Censorship, 25*(2), 110–122.
Ignatieff, M. (1998). *The Warrior's Honour*. London: Chatto & Windus.
Karstedt, S. (2016). The Emotion Dynamics of Transitional Justice: An Emotion Sharing Perspective. *Emotion Review, 8*(1), 50–55.
Keller, C., & David, A. (Eds.). (2009). *Remembering the Future*. Eugene: Cascade Books.
Lederach, J. P., & Lederach, A. (2010). *When Blood and Bones Cry Out*. Oxford: Oxford University Press.
Linden, M., & Rutkowski, K. (Eds.). (2013). *Hurting Memories and Beneficial Forgetting*. Amsterdam: Elsevier.
Misztal, B. (2003). *Theories of Social Remembering*. Buckingham: Open University Press.
Misztal, B. (2004). The Sacralization of Memory. *European Journal of Social Theory, 7*(1), 67–84.

Misztal, B. (2012). The Idea of Dignity: Its Modern Significance. *European Journal of Social Theory, 16*(1), 101–121.
Olick, J., & Robbins, J. (1998). Social Memory Studies: From 'Collective Memory' to the Historical Study of Mnemonic Practices. *Annual Review of Sociology, 24*, 105–140.
Reiff, D. (2016). *In Praise of Forgetting*. New Haven: Yale University Press.
Ross, M. (2013). The Politics of Memory and Peacebuilding. In R. MacGinty (Ed.), *Routledge Handbook of Peacebuilding* (pp. 91–101). London: Routledge.
Simpson, K. (2009). *Truth Recovery in Northern Ireland*. Manchester: Manchester University Press.
Smith, J. (2015, Winter) Memory, Forgetting and Hope. *Comment Magazine*, pp. 2–4.
Soyinka, W. (2000). *The Burden of Memory, the Muse of Forgiveness*. Oxford: Oxford University Press.
Todorov, T. (2003). *Hope and History* (D. Bellos, Trans). Princeton: Princeton University Press.
Volf, M. (1996). *Exclusion and Embrace*. Nashville: Abingdon Press.
Volf, M. (2006). *The End of Memory: Remembering Rightly in a Violent World*. Grand Rapids: Eerdmans.
Volf, M. (2015, Winter). The Justice of Memory, the Grace of Forgetting. *Comment Magazine*, pp. 48–57.
Wolterstorff, N. (2008). *Justice: Rights and Wrongs*. Princeton: Princeton University Press.
Wolterstorff, N. (2013). *Journey Towards Justice*. Grand Rapids: Baker Academic.

3

Ethics of Memory, Trauma and Reconciliation

Irit Keynan

The threats of the future may then move beyond our imagination as our memories elude our knowledge
—Samuel Gerson 2009, 1342

In her book *Regarding the Pain of Others*, Susan Sontag (2013) shows how the meaning of a photograph depends on the viewer's collective-national narrative. Presenting a photograph of a slain child, she demonstrates that each side of a persistent conflict interprets it as its own side's child, slain by the adversary. This is an example of the tendency of conflicted societies to automatically attribute violence to the other side, while ascribing pain to one's own group. Most societies believe that "our" side always fights a "just war" and whoever kills on "our" behalf is a hero, while the other side is evil and its warriors are wicked (Meagher 2014). This also applies for war trauma casualties: each side in such conflicts is frequently blind to

I. Keynan (✉)
School of Education, College of Management,
Rishon Le'Zion, Israel
e-mail: iritke@colman.ac.il

K. Wale et al. (eds.), *Post-Conflict Hauntings*, Palgrave Studies in Compromise after Conflict, https://doi.org/10.1007/978-3-030-39077-8_3

the suffering of the rival side's traumatized children and adults, while emphasizing the harm inflicted on its own people (Keynan 2015a).

This viewpoint leads conflicted sides to adopt a competitive victimhood attitude, a contest between opponents about who the "*real*" victim is, who is compelled to defend itself, and who deserves more concessions from the rival (Keynan 2019).

This type of biased attribution of good and evil, right and wrong is quite prevalent as an implication of collective memory and has powerful impact on potential reconciliation between societies in protracted conflicts. In fact, collective memory is known to be a huge barrier to conflict resolution in societies that endure intractable conflicts (Rafferty 2017; Keynan 2014), especially where the conflict involves two traumatized societies (Volkan 2001).

This chapter suggests that there is a way out of this impasse, which requires a novel conceptualization of the ethics of memory that enables members of conflicted groups to remember *with* and not *against*. The new conceptualization is based on two pillars: the first pillar is inspired by Levinas' overarching philosophy of unlimited responsibility for the other (Hansel 2010) and by Ubuntu's view that one's dignity relies on that of the other's.[1] However, when discussing memory in conflicted groups, responsibility for the other also means responsibility for the pain of the other side of the conflict, which is blamed for one's loss and pain. This may cause deep internal rupture in feelings of loyalty to one's own and one's group pain and to the memory of loved ones. The ethics of memory should and can be helpful in resolving such conflicted feelings, especially when bereaved and traumatized people are involved. The second pillar therefore leans on psychoanalytical theories that involve the healing role of a "live third"—in this case, an-other, who—by her/his engaged recognition and concerned responsiveness—generates a livable meaning for the individual's horrible experience (Gerson 2009; see especially pp. 1342; 1353–1354). Based on these two pillars a new definition of the ethics of memory is provided.

The chapter then shows that adopting this definition allows members of conflicted groups to remain loyal to the memory of the suffering of their group and to their own lost loved ones, while at the same time bear responsibility to the pain of the other side. This kind of ethics, as shown below, has the power to reduce animosity and replace the desire for revenge with a wish to put an end to the conflict. Going back to Sontag's photograph, such ethics of memory may prevent the automatic attribution of evil to the "other group" and the immediate interpretation of the slain child as belonging to "my group". Instead it may encourage both sides to take responsibility for stopping the incessant act of war.

The chapter reifies the above conceptualization by looking at the work of two Palestinian-Israeli organizations, The Parents Circle – Families Forum (PCFF) and Combatants for Peace (CFP). These two groups have taken upon themselves ethics of memory in this chapter's definition, creating a shared safe space in its metaphysical meaning of a mutual recognition and empathetic concern, which makes it harmless to get attached to others (Benjamin 2016). In this safe space, they can see each other as singular human beings rather than as a "party in the conflict" who should be blamed for the conflict and its losses. Thus, they can feel empathy for each other's harm and pain, and, in Levinas' terminology, to "think for" instead of "think about" (Meir 1996).

* * *

After explaining the detrimental effects of traumatic collective memory on conflict resolution, the second section expands on how this memory becomes a *closed memory*, a firmly fixed version of the past, with a pernicious grip on society. The third section elucidates relevant ideas from the ethics of Levinas and that of the African *Ubuntu*. The fourth section provides the second pillar for the new conceptualization of the ethics of memory by presenting some psychoanalytic theories that explain the special psychological needs of the bereaved and the traumatized. This pillar paves the way for proposing the new definition of the ethics of memory. The fourth section also provides examples from the work of PCFF and CFP that reify the viability of the new definition as a valuable guide for behaviour. The chapter closes with some conclusions about the ethics of memory in the work of PCFF and CFP, its ability to promote reconciliation, and with some suggestions for further research.

1 Traumatic Collective Memory and Its Detrimental Effects

War leaves emotional scars on all its participants: combatants and civilians, victors and vanquished. Recovery entails overcoming dreadful memories, coping with loss and with issues of meaning, and recomposing the puzzle of one's life, making the pre-and postwar pieces fit together (Keynan 2015a). Most of those exposed to war gradually manage to put the horror behind them. But not all. Many are unable to respond to the demands of daily life after war or terror experiences, or the violent and sudden loss of loved ones. Though they may appear to have returned safe and sound and without injury, they find that their wounds are incurable. These are the psychologically traumatized by war, its bloodless victims, which are possessed by the harm they suffered in war (Caruth 1995).

Genocide and mass national disasters[2] inflict not only individual traumas, but also collective trauma—a blow to the fundamental fabric of the group's social life—through death, injury and humiliation (Erikson 1995), and the dispersion of the previous community. The collective trauma survivors gradually realize that their community no longer exists as a source of support and that a very profound part of their own self has vanished (Erikson 1976).

In persistent conflicts, both kind of trauma have injurious effects, as the circle of individuals afflicted by trauma extend to their children, spouses, families, friends and the entire community (Keynan 2015a). These circles keep growing until the scars merge into a whole that is greater than the sum of the inflicted individuals, producing a group ethos that bears the hallmarks of trauma (Erikson 1995).

Some of personal and social wounds, particularly in collective trauma, are transmitted from generation to generation (Volkan 2006). Moreover, traumatized groups that suffered genocide, massive deportation or drastic loss of land and dignity by others tend to develop what Volkan (2006) calls a "chosen trauma": a mental representation of the historic trauma that imposes upon the group collective feelings of helplessness, victimization and humiliation. The traumatic experience thus becomes the group's prevailing mood and temperament, a sort of culture that dominates the group's sense of self. Such culture creates a sense of kinship within the traumatized members of the group who feel different from others, yet this sense of kinship is misleading, because at the same time, trauma threatens to unravel the threads that hold the community together. Moreover, especially during conflicts, trauma enhances the group's sense of being under siege and of moral superiority and evokes incessant fears of the other side's intentions and of recurrence of past traumas (Keynan 2014).

Some of the lingering effects of collective trauma are the demands that traumatized societies impose on their future generations: to reverse the community's sense of helplessness, humiliation and shame, and to transfigure its weakness and passivity into strength and assertiveness (Volkan 2006). Sometimes, these responsibilities are remoulded as an exaggerated sense of entitlement, which is easily manipulated by political leaders to exacerbate conflicts (Volkan 2006).

Usually, each group perceives its own narrative as the only truth, which morally excludes the narrative of the other side. As Halbwachs (1992) was the first to show, collective memory is not necessarily an accurate historical record, but a self-serving image of the past that helps the group to draw a desirable self-portrait. Nowadays, it is widely accepted that collective memory is a powerful factor in any group's life and it provides a comprehensive narrative that comprises stories, beliefs, aspirations, shared myths and symbols that offer current explanations for the group's situation, development, external relations and the like (Salomon 2004). This combination of history and emotions often prevents adversaries from realizing that a practical solution to the conflict is close at hand (Volkan 2006), driving them to reject possible realistic compromises, and to prefer their old societal beliefs in the wickedness and cruelty of the rival side, and in the impossibility of solving the conflict (Bar-Tal 2012).

2 Collective Memory of Traumatic Memories—A Closed Loop of Memories and Their Grip on Societies in Conflict

In their political, social and public lives, post-traumatic societies "act out" their collective memory in an uncontrolled repetition of post-traumatic symptoms (LaCapra 2014). The term "acting out" is based on Freud's realization in 1917 that victims of unimaginable trauma reproduce the traumatic experience not as a memory but as an action: they act it out, living it again and again (Gerson 2009). Freud's theory has been since developed into the current observation that the common traumatic symptom of repetition is "an unconscious attempt to represent experiences that are simultaneously impossible to forget and impossible to tell" (Gerson 2009, 1344).

Like individuals, post-traumatic societies must "work through" (process) their grief as a pre-condition to a healing process (LaCapra 2014; Volkan 2006). Transposing psychological terms of individuals to the collective level should be used with caution. Accordingly, I use LaCapra's (2014) assertion that the psychological terms of the individual are helpful in explaining social phenomena. This does not mean that they are exactly the same, but that the metaphoric transformation of the psychology of the individual into that of the collective is critical in clarifying the reasons, implications and possibilities for finding a way out of conflicts.

If societies "skip" the phase of mourning, they usually sink into melancholy. According to Freud (2008), the mourning self feels that the world has become meagre and empty, yet in melancholy, the self itself becomes hollow. Melancholy, says Freud, leads the self to an endless exposure of his/her weaknesses and faults, while continuously demonstrating grave suffering and a sense of being victimized by others (Freud 2008). Melancholy goes hand in hand with symptoms of acting out, in which the past keeps returning and the future is blocked. Thus, the individual is trapped in a melancholic loop (LaCapra 2014). One of the outcomes of unprocessed mourning and trauma is a collapsed sense of time, in which the person (or group) cannot distinguish between the past, when the trauma occurred, and the present, which holds a promise of a future (LaCapra 2014). The traumatized, we know today, are haunted by the past, victims of history, which for them is never "subordinated to the present" (Prager 1998, 130).

People or groups with these symptoms tend to develop a "narcissist rage", which is a conspicuous aggression following humiliation (Alexander 1938, cited in Kohut 2007). Kohut (2007) shows that though narcissist rage occurs in diverse forms, all forms share a limitless need for revenge with disregard for reasonable boundaries. This is, I contend, what makes the post-traumatic condition so dangerous in groups' conflicts. The belief that one's group is the *true* victim of the conflict allows each side to also believe that it has a "legitimate right" to attack the other. In such a climate, there can be no dialogue, let alone empathy for the pain of the other side, or understanding of the trap in which both sides are caught. These effects are extremely detrimental to attempts at reconciliation, or even a temporary suspension of the continuous bloodshed.

The effects of traumatic memory are far greater than the effects of horrible recollections, because traumatic memory is not simply a case of devastating memory, but a change in the brain's pattern of memory (Ochberg and Jonathan 2012). In individuals, traumatic memory constitutes an injury that impairs the connectivity between the amygdala (part of the limbic system of the brain that is involved in fear, aggression and identifying dangers) and the anterior cingulate cortex, the part of the brain that is involved particularly in decision making (Keynan and Keynan 2016). The traumatized individual, therefore, is driven to unproportioned responses to any perceived threat (Keynan and Keynan 2016). This observation is relevant for collective trauma as well: trauma is implanted in the minds of the members of groups that suffered genocide or extreme violence as a kind of stigmata. It demands endless melancholy and grieving and determines the group's way of remembering and thinking (LaCapra 2014). Such groups tend to remember and think of the conflict with complete blindness to their own actions or responsibility for the situation, let alone for the pain experienced by the other side. The traumatic memory is considered sacred and any attempt to weaken its grip over the nation's psyche is considered an act of profanity (LaCapra 2014).

Over time, in a transgenerational process, collective memory becomes a "memory of a memory", rather than a memory of an event (Prager 2016). While there may be more than one version of this "memory of memory", it is usually processed by societies into a "closed" unified interpretation of the past (Margalit 2002). By a closed memory, Margalit (2002) refers to the kind of memory in which, there is only one line leading to the event, the one that is authorized by the community's tradition as the canonic version of its history. This is true not only for events in the distant past but also for current events that occur during long persistent conflicts. In the same vein, collective traumatic memory, and especially chosen trauma

(Volkan 2006), becomes with time a firmly fixed version of the representation of the collective fears and humiliations, which tightens its grip on the nation's psyche. When two traumatized groups are involved in a persistent conflict, both tend to melancholy rather than to mourning and both constantly focus on their loss in a way that harms the self, exacerbates hostility towards the other side, and prevents reconciliation.

It thus seems that collective memory and national trauma tend to impede reconciliation. Is this fate or is there a way out? In what follows I explore how the ethics of memory might offer a way out of this impasse.

3 A Revolutionary Approach to Ethics: Levinas and *Ubuntu*

In his book *Totality and Infinity* (Levinas 1969), Levinas suggests that ethics is the first, primary philosophy that stems from unlimited responsibility towards the other. While Western philosophy views the self as the starting point of all perception, Levinas contends that the "face-to-face" relationship precedes the self and demands unlimited responsibility for the other (Hansel 2010). For Levinas, questions about *relations* precede questions about *being* (Lipari 2012): the ethical level precedes the ontological one (Levinas 1969). Even language, Levinas continues, emerges in response to the engagement with the other. Only when reacting to the other does language become a discourse. Levinas' theory "does not ask the ontological question of whether to be or not to be, but the ethical question of whether my relation to others is justified" (Lipari 2012, 228). The responsibility for the other, Levinas (2003a) asserts, is imposed upon the self by the revelation of the face of the other, which transcends the self (subject) from what "there is" (Moses 1993).

The Western perception of the "self-first", which Levinas calls egologia (Meir 2005), totalizes and centralizes the self. This perception has huge implications for ethics, because it allows the subsuming of the other into the self ("the same",[3] in Levinas' terms). It even allows for the elimination of the other, making him/her a mere reflection of the self. In contrast, Levinas (1969) suggests the hospitality approach, in which the other is not *relatively* dissimilar to the self but is *infinitely* different. The face of the other contains the infinity and therefore can never be reduced to being subsumed by the same (Lipari 2012). Hospitality is the basic relation between the subject (the self) and the other, which calls for and even imposes a relation of responsibility and responsiveness to the singularity of each fellow human being (Amiel Houser 2013).

Levinas' approach emphasizes openness to the other's vulnerability, which is signified by the face. Levinas speaks of the naked, defenceless face of the other that calls for the self who cannot seal its ears off to the other's cry (Levinas 1969). The face pressures the self to depart from within and to move to the outside, to infinity, which is the other (Epstein 2005). This is why, according to Levinas, ethics is the gateway to freedom.

Moreover, the face of the other triggers a response of moral consciousness, it is a moral summons (Levinas 1969) that transcends social categories of identity (Lipari 2012). The face of the other evokes a dialogic discourse between the self and the other, which is based on responsibility and releases the self from its egocentricity and narcissism, so it can fulfil its responsibility towards the other (Meir 2005). This *is* ethics.

The importance of this view in the context of this chapter is that it frees the self from a subjugating self-centralism. By this, it negates the idea that the individual is forced to surrender to the forces of history or its inevitability. The self has a choice that is revealed by the infinity in the face of the other. Moreover, this perspective revolutionizes the relations between adversaries, as one has responsibility for the other not only when the other surrenders to one's values, beliefs and views, but especially when the other is distinctively different and does not give into or is included in my morals and principles.

It is remarkable to see the correspondence between aspects of Levinas' theory and the African ethics of *Ubuntu*. *Ubuntu*, a Zulu term that was first used in Zimbabwe (Eickelman 2018), is based on the realization that one's subjectivity "is inextricably intertwined with that of others in one's community" (Gobodo-Madikizela 2016, 115). The concept of *Ubuntu* means that "I am a person because you are a person; that I can't separate my humanity from an acknowledgement of your humanity" (Sachs 2018, x). This view reverberates Levinas' view that the self is "bound in a knot that cannot be undone in a responsibility for others" (Levinas 2003b, 105, cited in Amiel Houser 2013). While some see *Ubuntu* as a moral quality of a person and others define it as ethics (Gade 2012), the different interpretations share a common understanding of human beings relying on each other's dignity. Thus, Levinas' notion that the human spirit is born out of making room for the other (Meir 2005) resembles this concept of African humanism. In both ethics, "A person becomes a human being through the multiplicity of relationships with others" (Gobodo-Madikizela 2016, 116). *Ubuntu* submits the idea of reciprocity as ethics, of being what Desmond Tutu described as a relational subject, "open and available to others" (Gobodo-Madikizela 2016, 116), and it is related to the principle of transformative recognition (Eickelman 2018; Sachs 2018). Both concepts view relations as primary to a subject's autonomy: ethics precedes ontology.

4 The New Definition of Ethics of Memory and the Exposed Face of the Other

Just like ethics itself, the ethics of memory is also subject to different interpretations. Scholars usually identify ethics of memory as regulating questions about what and how individuals and groups should remember or forget, how they should make this remembering and forgetting possible, and how they should address memory's claims (e.g., Margalit 2002; Thompson 2009). This direction of analysis views memory as an action and is compatible with the common concept of ethics as regulating action/behaviour. Yet, as Paul Ricoeur (2002) says, memory is first of all a perception and not an action, which makes reflecting about its ethics "a puzzling task" (Ricoeur 2002, 5). Ricoeur, nonetheless, speaks of ethics of memory, explaining that while memory is related to imagination and understanding, it is also related to action that results from perception, and such action may be subject to abuse. Misuse of memory, he says, is reflected, for example, in an excess of memory, where rituals and myths work to implant memories in a kind of venerable relationship to the past rather than direct it towards a better, just future (Ricoeur 2002). In contrast, an ethical work of memory calls for drawing an "exemplary significance" to past events (Ricoeur 2002, 9), and for remembering that narrative is a choice, and that "it is always possible to tell in another way" and to allow others "tell their own history" (p. 9). This is especially important with respect to memories of the founding events of the community, those that constitute the foundation of a collective memory. "What is considered a founding event in our collective memory may be a wound in the memory of the other" (Ricoeur 2002, 9).

The memory of the 1948 War, after which the state of Israel declared its independence, is a good example of a founding event, whose narrative illustrates Ricoeur's words cited above. For Jewish Israelis, the war was forced upon by the Palestinians, but ultimately paved the way to the fulfilment of a 2000-year dream of the Jewish people to re-establish a sovereign state. For Palestinians, this war means the Nakbah, a national disaster that brought about the destruction of their community as it existed until then, and in which they blame Israel (Keynan 2015b). The way the narrative of the 1948 War is told is a source of growing tension between the two groups, despite ongoing attempts by civil society organizations to agree to a narrative that both communities can live with.

What Ricoeur suggests would, in this case, require the design of a narrative that contains both narratives. As I show elsewhere (Keynan 2015b), this is possible by creating an expanded collective memory, in a manner that acknowledges the conflicting views and emotions. This can be done by following Rorty (1989), who suggested to educate the American children to think of themselves as heirs of traditions of liberty and hope, which grow concurrently with the efforts to overcome conflict and injustice. In other words, Rorty (1989) does not suggest constructing an idealization of the past or to forget slavery or the savagery against Native Americans. Instead, he suggests working on the memory of the conflicted past using a similar idea to that of Ricoeur's (2002)—drawing the past as having a teaching message. This means directing the collective memory towards a promising future instead of remembering it as a closed capsule caught in a melancholic loop (LaCapra 2014).

* * *

Although Ricoeur speaks about ethics as a guide for action, his view shares *Ubuntu* and Levinas' ethics of the other, as his ethics of memory focuses on remembering through mutual empathetic responsibility for the pain of the other. In fact, like Levinas' view, Ricoeur's ethics is more than a guide for action, it is a guide for being, which transcends actual experience into a basis of community between one and the other, despite or even because of the bottomless difference between them (Levinas 2003a). Rivals who adopt this kind of ethics understand that their humanity and dignity are contingent upon the humanity and dignity of their adversaries, and they are committed to each other's exposed face that imposes on them unlimited responsibility, in this case, for their rivals' pain and suffering. To overcome doubts of the feasibility of this suggestion, we should look at the remarkable example of the inclusion of the concept of *Ubuntu* in South Africa's interim constitution of 1993 (Eickelman 2018) and to the unprecedented, inspiring work of the South African Truth and Reconciliation Committees.

All these lead to defining the ethics of memory as a call for remembering and commemorating the injuries of the past with a mutual responsibility for the pain of the other, within the framework of a shared safe space in its metaphysical meaning of a recognition and empathetic concern.

* * *

Two Palestinian-Israeli groups, PCFF and the CFP, are doing exactly this: they feel each other's pain, they take responsibility for each other's agony, and, by feeling non-indifference to each other's loss and unimaginable grief, they bridge the incredibly wide abyss between mothers, fathers, daughters, sons, wives, husbands, brothers and sisters whose loved ones killed each other.

Bushra Awad lost her eldest son, Mahmoud, who was shot by Israeli soldiers on January 24, 2008. "My heart was filled with revenge" she says. For three years she was lost in her grief and angst. "I was consumed by sadness … I wished for death, so I could see him". When a friend suggested she join the PCFF, she firmly refused, "How could I shake the hand of the Israeli side that killed my son?" Then she met Robi Damelin,[4] who lost her only son, David, when a Palestinian sniper shot him in 2002. Bushra says she did not want to speak to Damelin, because the Israeli bereaved mother was nothing more than "the other side" who killed Mahmoud. But

> then the woman got up and … said she would like to hear the story of my son, Mahmoud. … When I showed her his photograph she burst out in tears. She later told me her story and the story of her son, who was killed by a young Palestinian man … I understood that our tears are the same tears. Our pain is the same pain. As mothers who lost their sons, we could share our emotions with each other.[5]

Bushra's description of the moment of her decision to join the PCFF illustrates Levinas' revelation of the face of the other that triggers a shift from one to two, from a "thought about" to a "thought for" (Meir 1996). A link of unindifference has sprung between the two mothers, not on the basis of an ethical guide for action, but rather the very appearance of the other's infinite face with its immeasurable suffering compelled them to take responsibility for the other's pain.

Between the two bereaved mothers a safe space emerged, in which they could walk into together, allowing them to see each other as singular human beings rather than as a "party in the conflict" that should be blamed for their loss. In this space, they are able to recognize each other's humanity and to mourn together instead of feeling empty and acting out their traumatic loss in a melancholic loop. In this safe place, they can now draw the past as having exemplary significance and direct it towards a better future (Ricoeur 2002).

Jessica Benjamin (2016) describes the safe space that the two mothers miraculously produced as an "experience of a co-created space of shared rhythms, attunement and … human cooperation" (p. 72). Benjamin names it the "third" (not to be confused with the third in Levinas philosophy),[6] and more specifically a "moral third" that symbolizes *Ubuntu,* a recognition of the dignity of the other. This, she maintains, is the possibility of dialogue: It allows one to abandon the contest over victimhood and instead recognize the agony of all parties, and become safely attached to others, because recognition has repaired the ruptures (Benjamin 2016).

Bushra and Robi, belong to The Parents Circle – Families Forum. Like many others in this organization and in Combatants for Peace they strive to overcome the detrimental effects of collective memory and war trauma and remember for and not against.[7]

The PCFF, established in 1995, is a joint Israeli-Palestinian organization of over 600 families, all of whom have lost an immediate family member to the ongoing conflict.[8] The members of the organization have concluded that reconciliation between the two nations is an indispensable step for achieving a sustainable peace, a notion that is also supported by researchers (e.g., Hewstone, et al. 2008). Therefore, their main mission is reconciliation. But how is it possible to reconcile with the family or the people who are responsible, even indirectly, for the loss of your loved one? Isn't it more natural to seek revenge? These questions have led the founders and the members of the PCFF to their unique work, which focuses on recognizing the humanity and the pain of the other.

Members of CFP, established in 2006 to uphold the principle of non-violence, are Palestinians and Israelis who were actively involved in the cycle of violence in the region: Palestinians who were combatants fighting against the Israeli occupation and Israeli soldiers who have served in the Israeli Defense Forces (IDF).[9] Although not all of the members are victims in the usual sense of the word, all of them feel victimized by the unfortunate situation imposed on them by the conflict, by what they were forced to endure, and the activities in which they were forced to participate. Many of the members of the organization were mentally or physically wounded during the conflict and quite a few still suffer from PTSD or moral injury. This group, like PCFF, has chosen to transcend each side's original perspective of the other as the enemy and create a new perspective as members of an expanded group who share a common identity of non-violent warriors focusing on ending the conflict (Keynan 2019).

CFP and PCFF join forces in some activities, the most prominent of which is the joint alternative annual Israeli-Palestinian memorial ceremony for Israelis and Palestinians who lost their lives in the conflict (about the ceremony, the objections in raises and the hope it brings, see Keynan 2019).

* * *

Although they will never end "working through" their mourning and grief, the members of these organizations will be able to courageously face the challenge of living with it, without falling into the hollowness imposed by melancholy. To meet this challenge of living with grief, there must be, as a most basic necessity for psychic aliveness, an "active witnessing presence of an other"[10] (Gerson 2009, 1353).

Gerson (2009) writes about survivors of genocide and mass destruction. But his analysis can be applied to other cases of trauma, such as the loss of "live thirds" in an unending violent war. Bereavement may also subject the traumatized individual to "living with the absence of that which made life comprehensible" (Gerson 2009, 1343), thus sentencing him to an everlasting melancholy and continuous "acting out" in an eternal emptiness. However, this endless loop of suffering may be prevented by the presence of a responsive, empathetic witnessing other.

Gerson (2009) did not discuss his idea of a live third in conflicted groups, where the an-other is a member of the rival group; one that the bereaved person blames for her loss. But his ideas prevail in this case too, on condition that the ethics of Levinas and *Ubuntu* are followed. Only then, ethics of memory is carried out and ethical witnessing by a live third who is a member of the rival group, is possible.

The meaning of the third in Gerson (2009) and Benjamin's (2004, 2016) writings is related to the intersubjective mental space that is enabled by recognition; while recognition is seen as letting go and surrender of the self, in the sense of being able to fully accept—to take in—the viewpoint and reality of the other, without attempting to interfere with the other's distinctiveness and otherness (Benjamin 2004). This, according to Benjamin, facilitates sustained attachment to the other and creates a safe space for genuine, secure, respectful dialogue (Benjamin 2016). Although Benjamin's view begins with the self, while Levinas' begins with the other, the two concepts live together at this safe space and moral third that Benjamin tries to build.

5 Conclusion

Looking at CFP and PCFF's work, a captivating phenomenon is revealed: the members of the two groups do not relate to their bereaved counterparts as representatives of the enemy. Rather, they consider group members of both sides as fellow-sufferers, who share a dreadful fate. In fact, they adopt ethics of memory that empowers them to share their sense of victimhood instead of nurturing their mutual animosity.

The two groups naturally adopted ethics of memory in this chapter's definition and their work demonstrates the meeting point of its two pillars. Levinas' responsibility for the other and *Ubuntu's* concept that "a person is a person through being witnessed by and engaging in reciprocal witnessing of other persons" (Gobodo-Madikizela 2016, 116) become reachable in the safe space of mutual empathetic recognition and witnessing by the former enemies, as happened in the enchanting meeting between the two bereaved mothers, Bushra and Robi.

The possibility of this ethics of memory to overcome competitive victimhood is yet to be further explored, especially the question of enlarging the circles of people in the two groups who are ready to adopt it. Can larger circles in the conflicted societies adopt ethics of memory? Can the "we feeling", the sentiment of "we" as a group versus the other group as "they", be overcome by the ethics of memory on a public large scale? What will be the impact of these two groups on the entire population? Although these questions call for further research, it seems that such an ethical behaviour is not utopic. PCFF and CFP have created a community of memory in this spirit, which is growing every year (Keynan 2019). Joining this community is always voluntary and it may be beneficial only when a person is ready to trust the vulnerable bereaved other (not only as an "other" person, but also as a member of the rival group). These requirements are not easy and the large-scale success of this process may be slow. By adopting ethics of memory, however, these two organizations have created a new basis for a dialogic way of coping with the past. Their strenuous, courageous efforts have developed spontaneously into inspirational ethics of memory and witnessing, which helps their members transcend from a victimized positioning of the self to an ethical positioning that makes them responsible for the infinite other. What is so inspiring about their work is that they take upon themselves a commitment to a greater mission than their own relief. They endeavour to extend their ethics of memory to the broader community involved in the conflict in an attempt to prevent the members of the larger community from becoming bereaved as well.

Although this is just the beginning of a process, it shows us all a way towards reconciliation.

Notes

1. Ubuntu is a Zulu term that was first used in Zimbabwe and means that "I am a person because you are a person" (Eickelman 2018).
2. There are other causes of massive trauma, such as natural or technological disasters. In this chapter, I focus on the trauma of war.
3. "Le Même". Levinas claims that Western philosophy conceptualizes any alterity based on sameness and identicality, and thus reduces the "other" to the "same" (Amiel Houser 2013).
4. Robi Damelin joined the PCFF because she wanted to work through her personal pain for the sake of reconciliation rather than revenge. She oversees the PCFF's public relations (Charter for Compassion, https://charterforcompassion.org/robi-damelin).
5. The quotes and Bushra Awad's story are available at the PCFF website, http://theparentscircle.org/en/stories/bushra-awad_eng/
6. In Levinas' theory, the third concerns the limits of one's responsibility to the other, since the "third" is also "my other". For a full explanation of the third and its implications in Levinas' philosophy, See Levy 1993.
7. For an extended exploration of their work see Keynan 2019.
8. For more information see the organization's website: http://theparentscircle.org/en/about_eng/
9. For more information about the group, see the organization's website http://cfpeace.org/
10. Gerson (2009) uses the concept of witness in the sense of a "live third", which he interprets as an an-other, who—by her/his engaged recognition and concerned responsiveness—generates a livable meaning for the individual's horrible experience; an an-other upon whom the individual relies, in whom she puts her trust and who creates a sense of continuity and meaning.

References

Amiel Houser, T. (2013). Margaret Atwood's Feminist Ethics of Gracious Housewifery. *Partial Answers: Journal of Literature and the History of Ideas, 11*(1), 109–132. https://doi.org/10.1353/pan.2013.0008.

Bar-Tal, D. (2012). *Shared Belief in Society: Social Psychological Analysis*. New York: Sage.

Benjamin, J. (2004). Beyond Doer and Done to: An Intersubjective View of Thirdness. *The Psychoanalytic Quarterly, 73*(1), 4–46.

Benjamin, J. (2016). Move Beyond Violence: What We Learn from Two Former Combatants About Transition from Aggression to Recognition. In P. Gobodo-Madikizela (Ed.), *Breaking Intergenerational Cycles of Repetition* (pp. 71–89). Opladen/Berlin/Toronto: Barbara Budrich Publishers.

Caruth, C. (1995). Introduction. In C. Caruth (Ed.), *Trauma, Explorations in Memory* (pp. 3–12). Baltimore/London: JHU.

Eickelman, D. F. (2018). Epilogue: Recognition in Its Place. In Y. Meital & P. Rayman (Eds.), *Recognition as Key for Reconciliation: Israel, Palestine and Beyond* (pp. 168–180). Leiden/Boston: Brill.

Epstein, D. (2005). *Near and Far, on the Philosophy of Emmanuel Levinas* (Hebrew). Tel Aviv: Ministry of Defense.

Erikson, K. (1976). *Everything In Its Path*. New York: Simon and Schuster.

Erikson, K. (1995). Notes on Trauma and Community. In C. Caruth (Ed.), *Trauma, Explorations in Memory* (pp. 183–199). Baltimore/London: JHU.

Freud, S. (2008). *Trauer und Melancholie; Zwangshandlungen und Religionsubungen* (*Sigmond Freud, Selected works in Hebrew IV* (A. Tenenbaum, Trans., pp. 7–44)). Tel Aviv: Resling.

Gade, C. B. N. (2012). What Is Ubuntu? Different Interpretations Among South Africans of African Descent. *South African Journal of Philosophy, 31*(3), 484–503. https://doi.org/10.1080/02580136.2012.10751789.

Gerson, S. (2009). When the Third Is Dead: Memory, Mourning, and Witnessing in the Aftermath of the Holocaust. *The International Journal of Psychoanalysis, 90*(6), 1341–1357. https://doi.org/10.1111/j.1745-8315.2009.00214.x.

Gobodo-Madikizela, P. (2016). Interrupting Cycles Of Repetition: Creating Spaces for Dialogue, Facing and Mourning the Past. In P. Gobodo-Madikizela (Ed.), *Breaking Intergenerational Cycle of Repetition, a Global Dialogue on Historical Trauma and Memory* (pp. 113–134). Oplade/Berlin/Toronto: Barbara Budrich Publishers.

Halbwachs, M. (1992). *On Collective Memory*. Chicago: University of Chicago press.

Hansel, J. (2010). Introduction. In E. Levinas (Ed.), *Totality and Infinity* (Hebrew) (R. Ayalon, Trans., pp. IX–XXIII). Jerusalem: Magnes.

Hewstone, M., Kenworthy, J. B., Cairns, E., Tausch, N., Hughes, J., Tam, T., & Pinder, C. (2008). Steppingstones to Reconciliation in Northern Ireland: Intergroup Contact, Forgiveness and Trust. In A. Nadler, T. E. Malloy, & J. D (Eds.), *The Social Psychology of Intergroup Reconciliation* (pp. 199–226). New York: Oxford University Press.

Keynan, I. (2014). Between Past and Future: Persistent Conflicts, Collective Memory, and Reconciliation. *International Journal of Social Sciences, 3*(1), 19–28.

Keynan, I. (2015a). *Psychological Trauma and Society, Like a Hidden Wound*. London: Routledge.

Keynan, I. (2015b). Collective Memory, Chosen Trauma and Hope. In K. Arar & I. Keynan (Eds.), *Identity, Narrative and Multiculturalism in the Arab Education in Israel* (Hebrew) (pp. 51–72). Haifa: Pardes.

Keynan, I., & Keynan, J. N. (2016). War Trauma, Politics of Recognition and Purple Heart: PTSD or PTSI. *Social Sciences, 5*(57), 1–12. https://doi.org/10.3390/socsci5040057.

Keynan, I. (2019). The Aftermath of Victimhood – Can Victims Share Responsibility for a Better Future? In I. Peleg (Ed.), *Victimhood Discourse in Contemporary Israel* (pp. 137–152). Washington: Lexington Books.

Kohut, H. (2007). *Self psychology and the Humanities, Reflections on a New Psychoanalytic Approach* (Hebrew) (T. Z. Iden, Trans.). Tel Aviv: Tola'at Sfarim.

LaCapra, D. (2014). *Writing History, Writing Trauma*. Baltimore: JHU Press.

Levinas, E. (1969). *Totality and Infinity* (A. Lingis, Trans.) Pittsburg: Duquesne University Press.

Levinas, E. (2003a). *Ethics and the Infinitive, Conversations with Philippe Nemo* (Hebrew) (E. Meir, Trans.) Jerusalem: Magnes.

Levinas, E. (2003b). *Humanism of the Other* (N. Poller, Trans.). Urbana/Chicago: University of Illinois Press.

Levy, Z. (1993). The Concept of the Other and Responsibility in Levinas' Ethics. *Daat: A Journal of Jewish Philosophy and Kabbalah* (Hebrew), *30*, 21–40.

Lipari, L. (2012). Rhetoric's Other: Levinas, Listening, and the Ethical Response. *Philosophy and Rhetoric, 45*(3), 227–245.

Margalit, A. (2002). *The Ethics of Memory*. Boston: Harvard University Press.

Meagher, R. E. (2014). *Killing from the Inside Out, Moral Injury and Just War*. Eugene: Cascade Books.
Meir, E. (1996, October). War and Peace in the Philosophy of Levinas. *The Jerusalem Philosophical Quarterly* (Hebrew), *45*, 471–479.
Meir, E. (2005). Guilt and Responsibility as Characteristics of the Answerable Man in the Thought of Emmanuel Levinas. *Jerusalem Studies in Jewish Thought* (Hebrew), *2*, 851–865.
Moses, S. (1993). Levinas – Ethics as Primary Philosophy. *Daat: A Journal of Jewish Philosophy and Kabbalah* (Hebrew), *30*, 53–61.
Ochberg, F., & Jonathan, S. (2012, April). *Posttraumatic Injury*. http://www.posttraumaticstressinjury.org/letters-endorsing-the-change-from-ptsd-to-ptsi/. Accessed 10 July 2016.
Prager, J. (1998). *Presenting the Past, Psychoanalysis and the Sociology of Misremembering*. Cambridge, MA/London: Harvard University Press.
Prager, J. (2016). Disrupting the Intergenerational Transmission of Trauma: Recovering Humanity, Repairing Generations. In P. Gobodo-Madikizela (Ed.), *Breaking Intergenerational Cycles of Repetition: A Global Dialogue on Historical Trauma and Memory* (pp. 12–26). Leverkusen Opladen/Toronto: Barbara Budrich.
Rafferty, R. (2017). Engaging with the Violent Past to Motivate and Direct Conflict Resolution Practice in Northern Ireland. *Conflict Resolution Quarterly, 35*(2), 197–221.
Ricoeur, P. (2002). Memory and Forgetting. In R. Kearney (Ed.), *Questioning Ethics, Contemporary Debated in Philosophy* (pp. 4–11). New York: Routledge, Taylor & Francis e-Library.
Rorty, R. (1989). Education Without Dogma: Truth, Freedom and Our Universities. *Dissent, 36*(2), 198–204.
Sachs, A. (2018). Foreword. In Y. Meital & P. Rayman (Eds.), *Recognition as Key for Reconciliation: Israel, Palestine and Beyond* (pp. IX–XI). Leide/Boston: Brill.
Salomon, G. (2004). A Narrative-Based View of Coexistence Education. *Journal of Social Issues, 60*(2), 273–287.
Sontag, S. (2013). *Regarding the Pain of Others*. New York: Picador; Farrar, Straus and Giroux.
Thompson, H. (2009). Apology, Historical Obligations and the Ethics of Memory. *Memory Studies, 2*(2), 195–201. https://doi.org/10.1177/1750698008102052.
Volkan, V. D. (2001). Transgenerational Transmissions and Chosen Traumas: An Aspect of Large-Group Identity. *Group Analysis, 34*(1), 79–97.
Volkan, V. D. (2006). *Killing in the Name of Identity, a Study of Bloody Conflicts*. Charlottesville: Pitchstone Publishing.

4

What Pandora Did: The Spectre of Reparation and Hope in an Irreparable World

Jaco Barnard-Naudé

[T]he ghost remains that which gives one the most to think about – and to do
—Derrida 1994, 98

[O]nly if we entertain our ghosts will we have the remotest chance of moving forwards into the next stage of historical time
—Rose 2020

1 The Spectre of Reparation: South Africa, Rwanda, Metonymy

In Volume 5 of the South African Truth and Reconciliation Commission's (TRC) Report, in the ninth chapter entitled 'Reconciliation', the Commission reports as follows: 'After a visit to Rwanda, Archbishop Tutu said: "We must break the spiral of reprisal and counter-reprisal … I said to them in Kigali 'unless you move beyond justice in the form of a tribunal,

J. Barnard-Naudé (✉)
University of the Free State, Bloemfontein, South Africa
e-mail: BarnardNaudeAJ@ufs.ac.za

K. Wale et al. (eds.), *Post-Conflict Hauntings*, Palgrave Studies in Compromise after Conflict, https://doi.org/10.1007/978-3-030-39077-8_4

there is *no hope* for Rwanda'. Confession, forgiveness and reconciliation in the lives of nations are not just airy-fairy religious and spiritual things, nebulous and unrealistic. They are the stuff of practical politics"' (TRC Report 1998a, 351).

These words, with which the TRC reports the Archbishop's visit to post-genocide Rwanda, demand a preliminary analysis. For one thing, they document perhaps the earliest instance of the TRC model's famous 'export' to other post-conflict settings. Second, they appear at the same time to justify the TRC model (encapsulated in the terms 'confession, forgiveness and reconciliation') as an *imperative* for hope in such settings (there will be 'no hope' 'unless' Rwanda follows the TRC model). Third, the logic of these words dictates that the very possibility of such hope turns on an understanding of confession, forgiveness and reconciliation as 'the stuff of practical politics' and from this logic one can draw the conclusion that, on these terms, hope itself is a matter of such 'practical politics'. The two latter points are inter-related, but the last point stresses the politicisation of otherwise 'airy-fairy religious and spiritual things'.

Over the past ten years, I have revisited the Archbishop's words many times in the context of a critical appraisal of the TRC's legacy in South Africa. In this work, I have had reason to focus and insist on a term that does not appear in the aforementioned quotation. That term is 'reparation'. Reparation is by no means absent from the discourse of the TRC as a whole, nor is it missing from the Archbishop's discourse as a whole. Yet, in these words in which the TRC reports the Archbishop's visit to Rwanda, reparation is not mentioned as one of the imperatives if there is to be hope. In other words, reparation as an aspect of the TRC model's export quality, so to speak, is, at best, occluded in this segment from the Report. One may even go as far as arguing that reparation constitutes the unconscious of the TRC model, at least as regards its articulation in these words.

Yet, like the repressed, the case for reparation in post-apartheid South Africa and in Rwanda as the country of its first export, does not fail to return. I do not dispute the Archbishop's words about the critical role of confession, forgiveness and reconciliation in the lives of (post-conflict) nations. I also do not dispute that there have been attempts and efforts to promote reparation in South Africa and, indeed, in Rwanda. The Fund for Neediest Survivors of Genocide in Rwanda ('FARG') is an admirable undertaking and considerable reparation has surely been achieved through FARG and other measures such as the findings of the Gaçaça courts (Bornkamm 2012, 134–136).

On the other hand, nothing more than a quick internet search reveals the numerous media reports since at least 2014 in which the shortcomings of these measures in Rwanda are indicated, along with an increasingly prominent insistence, both in Rwanda and in South Africa, that unity and reconciliation, or truth and reconciliation, cannot be expected to endure in the absence of meaningful reparation (see, for instance, Human Rights Watch 2011; Gasake 2012; De Wet 2018; Yates 2018). This is a conclusion that the TRC itself reached, albeit late, in Volume 6 of its report, when it wrote that its "international legitimacy" (not to mention, presumably, its national legitimacy) depended on "the provision of adequate reparations" (TRC 1998b, 110). The aftermath of that statement is a story of broken promises, corruption and state capture while South Africa ceaselessly capitulated—or was indeed forced to capitulate—to the global neoliberal hegemony.

As for Rwanda, in April 2014, Jean Paul Mugiraneza published an opinion piece in *The Guardian* in which he argued that the government assistance to survivors—through FARG—is 'an obligation for any responsible nation' and that the availability of this form of assistance 'does not remove the right to financial reparations' from other sources (Mugiraneza 2014). In March 2016, *The New Times* reported that 'at least 8,445 cases adjudicated by Gacaca courts have not been executed in terms of paying reparations to the victims' (Rwirahira 2017). A government document on which *The New Times* relied, indicated that '854 court bailiffs have completely failed to execute compensation judgments; 1,016 cases involved genocide convicts who deliberately refused to pay damages, while 1, 277 cases have incomplete files' (Rwirahira 2017).

What these reports tell us is that the question of reparation continues to haunt Rwanda in ways that are similar to and different from the way in which the reparation question returns in various guises in 'post'-apartheid South Africa. I am not going to dwell on the similarities and differences here—for my purposes it is enough to note the haunting quality of the question of reparation in both jurisdictions. In other words, a spectre is haunting both the origin of the TRC *and* one of its most prominent extensions on the African continent. That spectre is reparation.

In what follows, I propose to contribute to the question of reparation by suggesting, first of all, that 'reparation' is and must be understood strictly as the name of a spectre, perhaps *the* spectre that haunts post-conflict societies in which the TRC model played a definitive role in the consolidation of sovereignty. Yet, at the same time, this particular haunting of the spectre of reparation can itself be extended in the manner of a metonymy, so that 'reparation' can be made to name not only that which is haunting the sovereignty of the post-conflict state, but indeed that which is haunting us today on a planetary level and scale. One need look no further than the desperate attempts, now being made all over the planet, to prevent catastrophic climate change. Often enough, these attempts are explicitly articulated in the language of repair (such as the 'repair' of the ozone layer) but even when they are not, a 'drive to make reparation' (Klein 1998, 342) clearly directs them.

To treat 'reparation' strictly as the name of a/the spectre, brings the word into close contact with Jacques Derrida's influential meditations on the spectre in his late work. One name under which Derrida (1994) explicitly treats the spectre is 'justice' and here I shall argue that there is good reason to treat 'reparation' as a synonym for the justice that Derrida expounds. This is the case because both justice and reparation are *aporetic* concepts. Once the aporetic quality of reparation is apprehended (as has been done by Mark Sanders (2007, 115)), what Derrida writes about the spectre in relation to justice, also becomes legible in relation to the spectre of reparation. What is of primary interest in this deconstructive alignment of justice and reparation is the *spectral logic* that attends both.

The question that then emerges pertains to how we are to characterise that which is being haunted. Relying on the work of Giorgio Agamben (1993) and once more on metonymy, I suggest that post-conflict societies—South Africa, Rwanda—could be understood as intense metonymic instances of what Agamben in general calls the world: the Irreparable. The affective point of Agamben's designation here is decidedly not to resign to a pessimistic and hopeless view of the world as such or of post-conflict societies such as Rwanda and South Africa, but rather to acknowledge with Sanders (2007, 116) that reparation in these societies is, strictly speaking, impossible and necessary at the same time. We cannot, as the South African poet, Ingrid de Kok (2006, 121) has written, restore 'an uncut arm, unbruised genital / untroubled sleep, unscarred face, / unweeping mother, children, faith / or wide unwatching private space'. As De Kok's words make clear, the Irreparable is haunted by the spectre of (an impossible) reparation, but precisely because it *haunts,* impossible reparation insists in the Irreparable.

The central contention of this chapter is that what *could* or *may* emerge in this aporetic encounter between the spectre of reparation and the Irreparable is something which I insist on calling 'reparative' (as distinct from 'reparation') and which I have, in previous work (Barnard-Naudé 2016), connected to what Homi Bhabha (2017, 22) calls that troubled 'psycho-affective site' we call citizenship. 'Reparative citizenship',[1] then, concerns the negotiation—here and now, in other words, *in the contemporary*—between impossible reparation and the reality of the Irreparable. It is out of this negotiation with that which is nonetheless not negotiable ('reparation'), that hope can be generated out of the reparative intervention.

I claim that the reparative intervention changes the valency of the Irreparable and, in so doing, generates hope. Well aware of the troubles and vicissitudes of 'citizenship' in the colonial, postcolonial and decolonial context, I must, however leave a discussion of the concept (and of how I think it might be further rehabilitated by reading it through and with the reparative) for another occasion (the groundwork for such a discussion may be found in Barnard-Naudé 2016). Here, I am interested in what is perhaps a prior concern, namely explicitly to articulate and to explore the reparative as it relates to, differs from and arises out of a negotiation with, (the spectre of) reparation.

From this, it should be clear that I do not see the generation of hope as hinging on the exorcism of the spectre of reparation. Rather, I think that the spectral is an indispensable condition of hope. The spectral, in other words, is the often and mostly unspoken, but indispensable, indeed undispensable, ground for the possibility of social transformation. As a relationship to the future, hope *can* be generated when we transform the existing, entrenched ways in which we who inhabit the Irreparable relate to the spectre. One cannot but recall here (as Derrida (1994) also does), Shakespeare's famous instruction to him who is faced with the spectre: 'Thou art a scholar, *speak* to it, Horatio' (Shakespeare 2008, 1925 (emphasis added)). Shakespeare is highly specific here and one cannot but recall in this regard Arendt's characterisation of speech as the quintessential manifestation of politics along with action—words that are 'not empty' and deeds that are 'not brutal', Arendt (1998, 200) writes. For Arendt, 'where words are not used to veil intentions but to disclose realities, and deeds are not used to violate and destroy but to establish relations and create new realities', we find the sites where true transformative power is actualised. The reparative, I argue, is just such a discursive intervention where word and deed do not part company, a way, thus, of becoming conversant with the spectre of reparation in such a way that hope is generated in the active encounter with it.

With 'discourse', then, I do not simply or merely refer to specific forms of speech. Rather, discourse, as Lacan (2007) used it (and as Arendt intimates in the remarks above), is the proper name of the structure of the social link that underlies all forms of communication and is expressed in these forms of communication. To advocate a discursive intervention is thus not simply to advocate a shift in the ways in which we address and respond to one another linguistically. It is, rather, to advocate a shift in the actions that determine the configuration of the dominant social link. Thus, to 'speak' to the spectre (also) includes what one (sometimes indeed silently) does in relation to it and in response to it. Relying on Klein (1998), I argue that changing the ways in which we relate to the spectre of reparation—*relating* to the spectre in a reparative modality—transforms our social relationships, the ways in which we are and are not with each other in the world. For there to be hope, it is accordingly necessary to consort in a reparative way with the spectre.

2 The Name of the Spectre: The Aporia of Justice as Reparation

To suggest that reparation is a spectre is to say that it is always already never fully present, never simply 'here'. As a spectre, reparation is much like the justice that Jacques Derrida (1990, 947) rigorously distinguishes from law and describes in his late work as an *aporia.* An *aporia* is a 'non-road', he writes, 'something that does not allow passage'. For this reason, it is impossible to have what Derrida refers to as a 'full experience' of the aporia. Yet, there is, for Derrida no justice without this experience of the impossible.

We must be careful here not to elide the importance of the fact that the aporia 'does not allow passage', for this implies infinite engagement. The aporia does not let you pass, does not let you go. Thus, it is the very experience of the impossibility of having a full experience of justice that demands ceaseless engagement with it. This is, clearly, the ethical dimension of Derrida's insistence on the aporia of justice—that it demands infinite response-ability. The aporetic nature of justice means that it is always already radically incomplete and thus deficient and absent, never fully over and done. This, in turn, means that justice is intimately related to the idea of the spectre. In the terms of Derrida's engagement with the relationship between law and justice, justice is the name of the spectre that haunts all law: 'Every time that something comes to pass or turns out well, every time that we placidly apply a good rule to a particular case, to a correctly subsumed example, according to a determinant judgment, we can be sure that law (*droit*) may find itself accounted for, but certainly not justice. Law (*droit*) is not justice' (Derrida 1990, 948).

Later in the 'Force of Law' essay, Derrida relates justice explicitly to the notion of the ghost, but he does it through the elaboration of what he calls the 'ghost of the undecidable' (Derrida 1990, 963) as a 'form of the same aporia' (Derrida 1990, 965) of justice. He describes the undecidable as 'the experience of that which, though heterogeneous, foreign to the order of the calculable and the rule, is still obliged [...] to give itself up to the impossible decision, while taking account of law and rules'. It is this experience which 'remains caught, lodged, at least as a ghost – but an essential ghost – in every decision, in every event of decision. Its ghostliness deconstructs from within *any assurance of presence, any certitude* or any supposed criteriology that would assure us of the justice of a decision' (Derrida 1990, 965 (emphasis added)).

In *Specters of Marx,* Derrida (1994) addresses a different but still closely related aspect of the relationship between the spectre and his concept of justice: 'If I am getting ready to speak at length about ghosts, inheritance, and generations, generations of ghosts, which is to say about certain *others* who are not present, nor presently living, either to us, or outside us, it is in the name of *justice*. Of justice where it is not yet, not yet *there*, where it is no longer, let us understand where it is no longer *present*, and where it will never be, no more than the law, reducible to laws and rights [...] No justice [...] seems possible or thinkable without the principle of some responsibility, beyond all living present, within *that which disjoins the living present*, before the ghosts of those who are not yet born or who are already dead, be they victims of wars, political or other kinds of violence, nationalist, racist, colonialist, sexist, or other kinds of exterminations' (Derrida 1994, xix (emphasis added)).

One sees in these later remarks on a different aspect of the relationship between the spectre and justice, nonetheless a convergence that will become important: what joins these quotations, is their references to the present and presence. Derrida's insists that ghostliness/the spectre 'disjoins the living present' and so deconstructs 'any assurance of presence'. Moreover, it is this very disjunctive work of the spectre—its haunting—in the 'living present' that anchors the principle of responsibility, that ensures that no decision can ever be described as fully 'just'.

Sanders (2007, 117) has elegantly shown how the aporia as the ghost of the undecidable attends the question of reparation in the TRC's Report. He shows how the Commission first acknowledges that reparation is impossible, because reparative measures can never 'bring back the dead, nor adequately compensate for pain and suffering' (Sanders 2007, 116), while at the same time the Commission insists that the order of calculation and decision must be entered—the 'quality of life of the victims' must be improved through such measures, which are then elaborated in the details of the individual reparation grants that the TRC recommended to Parliament.

However—and while Sanders is not explicit about this aspect—he also shows (Sanders 2007, 115–119) how this crossing of the aporia, as an assumption of responsibility, eventually broke down. Thabo Mbeki's 2003 speech to Parliament cynically twisted the TRC's engagement with the order of the incalculable, by putting it (the acknowledgement that no monetary value can be placed on life and suffering) in service of, in the form of a justification for, its crude and wholesale surrender to the order of decision based only on calculation and aimed solely at exorcising the ghost of the undecidable: Mbeki unceremoniously announced the decision to pay severely diminished, 'once-off' individual reparation grants, while at the same time making it clear that the government opposed the apartheid reparation litigation in the United States. As regards the individual grants, Sanders (2007, 119) remarks: 'The idea of a "once-off grant," [...] tells one that a debt has been paid and paid off, that things are and can be over, that one ought to think of them as over [...] At worst it restarts the cycle of historical wrong'.

Sanders (2007, 119) relates the fact that the once-off grants were widely considered by victims as grossly inadequate. Since then, the call for reparation in post-apartheid South Africa has reached concert pitch in the midst of a corrupt and captured State, widespread unemployment, a deepening of inequality along racial lines and a marked increase in political polarisation. It is no wonder that, in a crucial correction to its early theory and practice in South Africa, transitional justice responded to the Mbeki-era by turning its attentions much more intensively on the question of reparation as the form of 'justice' to which its name refers (see, for instance, Du Bois and Du Bois-Pedain 2008). Sanders (2007, 119–120) shows that the question of reparation fits transitional justice's reliance on a restorative concept of justice, but my point here is that reparation has not always figured as strongly in transitional *justice* as it does today.

Instead, transitional justice's over-reliance on Tutu's tropes of 'confession, forgiveness and reconciliation' has meant that this formula has often figured as transitional justice all on its own, with the question of reparation on the discursive periphery. This, for instance, is one way of explaining why the reparation debate in South Africa and Rwanda becomes prominent only some years after the formal transition. In this regard, one should not lose sight of the fact that governmental power may well regard the reparation question as a potentially catastrophic threat to the consolidation of the renovated national sovereignty (Salazar 2004, 44) and, for this reason, is interested in managing the discursive field in such a way that the question of reparation is effectively repressed.

It seems, however, that 'reparation' has shifted from the periphery of transitional justice to its very centre, where it is often articulated as 'justice', alongside a term such as 'reconciliation' with the insistence that there can be/is no reconciliation and no forgiveness without justice as reparation (Corlett 2011, 608). By identifying reparation not only as one of the post-conflict forms of justice, but indeed as *the* post-conflict form of justice that is most lacking, transitional justice no longer follows the governmental script and has, perhaps, unwittingly participated in, and supported, the understanding of reparation as the name of the spectre that haunts post-conflict/still-conflict societies. For to assert that it is the form of justice that is most lacking in the postcolony, is to insist that it is the most *spectral*.

Even if it was disputable that reparation is the form of justice that lacks most in the post-conflict setting, would it not be, at all events, responsibly realistic to hold that we are always already and in general *haunted* by reparation, simply because of the fact that, as Sanders clearly shows and this section attempts to underscore, 'reparation' is a form, an instantiation, a name, of the aporetic justice as the spectre that Derrida expounded? As regards the generality of this haunting by reparation, Sanders (2007, 129) quotes Melanie Klein's assertion that '*making reparation* is [...] a fundamental element [...] in all human relationships' and concludes that 'reparation constitutes a basic structure of responsibility'.

While it must be said that I have many doubts about the transposition of Kleinian reparation to the political sphere and especially to the post-conflict sphere, this position supports my sense that the question of reparation in post-conflict societies can be treated as a metonymy. In reference to apartheid, Derrida (1994, xv) describes the work of the metonymy as follows: 'what is happening there translates what *takes place* here, always here, wherever one is and wherever one looks, closest to home'.

3 The Irreparable

This metonymic value of concepts specific to transitional justice can be extended and in this section I want to focus on the term 'irreparable', which has been invoked in transitional justice (for instance, in the title of Doxtader and Villa-Vicencio's 2004 edited collection, *To repair the irreparable*), although not nearly as prominently as 'reparation'. It is telling that when Doxtader and Villa-Vicencio invoke the irreparable in their introduction to the book, they do so with reference to Giorgio Agamben's *The Coming Community* (1993) to argue that the irreparable 'cannot continue' (Doxtader and Villa-Vicencio 2004, xxi). The authors also explicitly rely on the aporetic character of reparation to assert that the impossibility of reparation 'is not a reason to conclude that what's past is past or that legacies imply an inevitability which defies correction' (Doxtader and Villa-Vicencio 2004, xiii). Differently stated, the irreparable as such, does not, according to the authors, militate against reparative work.

Agamben's own formulation of the Irreparable, at first glance, rings much more sceptical: 'The Irreparable is that things are just as they are, in this or that mode, consigned *without remedy* to their way of being. States of things are irreparable, whatever they may be: sad or happy, atrocious or blessed. How you are, how the world is – this is the irreparable' (Agamben 1993, 90 (emphasis added)). For Agamben, then, the world as such and as *thus*, is Irreparable (and this would underscore, once again, the metonymic value of the Irreparable when it is restricted to the post-conflict setting) and there is an overt resonance here with the theological concept of 'Paradisiacal exile' (Willemse 2017, 681).[2]

The formulation of the irreparable as 'without remedy' suggests that Agamben's thought is firmly located in the impossibility of reparation. However, Agamben (1993, 101) also writes—paradoxically, it seems—that 'we can have hope only in what is without remedy' and in so doing, he designates the irreparable as the source of hope. As Bartoloni (2008, 54) has pointed out, this sentiment is echoed in *The Time That Remains* as follows: 'it is the unredeemable that makes salvation possible' (Bartoloni 2008, 54). Prozorov has interpreted this sentiment as the assertion that while '[w]e can never go back on nihilism [...] it does not follow from this that the horizon of salvation is itself to be annulled' (Prozorov 2014, 167).

The reason why the irreparable does not as such annul the horizon of salvation is because, as Bartoloni explains, Agamben invests the Irreparable as such with an infinite worth: 'With the concept of the irreparable, and the category of suchness, Agamben intends to conjure up a mode of being whose exposure to the world, and the things of the world, is no longer postulated by the opposition and separation of subject/object, predicate and pronoun, but on the awareness of *an irreparable belonging based on mutual relations by which the facing of each other as things as such generates an availability that transcends the objectification of the other*' (Murray and Whyte 2011, 109 (emphasis added)). For Agamben, it is thus this very irreparable suchness of beings that is worthy of salvation and to have hope *only* in that which is 'without remedy' is to transform the valence of the Irreparable from despair to hope. It is not that what is being presented here is a simple binary choice between despair and hope, but rather a hope *with* despair, or, indeed, a hopeful despair *as well as* a despairing hope.[3]

This reading is supported by Bartoloni's (2008, 53) remark, elsewhere, that Agamben's thought on the relationship between the Irreparable and hope is indebted to Paul's statement about hope in the letter to the Romans. That statement reads: 'we are saved by hope: but hope that is seen is not hope: for what a man seeth, why doth he yet hope for? But if we hope for that we see not, *then* do we with patience wait for *it*' (Bartoloni 2008, 53). This means, Bartoloni suggests, that 'what is left for us to do [in the face of the irreparable] is to patiently make hope, toil towards it, actively and incessantly' (Bartoloni 2008, 55). Most pertinently for the purposes of this contribution, Bartoloni (2008, 52) writes that for Agamben hope 'needs to be negotiated'. To put it somewhat differently, Agamben's philosophy holds that what is given to us as the living present, as here, is the irreparable world and what is not given to us is hope – we are responsible for 'making' hope, 'actively and incessantly'. As a 'making', hope relies on our capacity as *homo faber* to create out of 'given substance' (Arendt 1998, 139) and in Agamben this given substance is the Irreparable.[4]

These statements neatly return us to the aporia of reparation as a non-road that does not allow passing and that demands 'incessant' responsibility. Indeed, I want to suggest that the 'mode of being' which Agamben 'conjures up', 'whose exposure to the world, and the things of the world, is no longer postulated by the opposition and separation of subject/object, predicate and pronoun' is the mode of being as *haunted* being and *being* haunted. The spectre of reparation—neither object nor subject—haunts nowhere else than in the Irreparable and hope is negotiated—*made*—in the encounter between the Irreparable and the spectre of reparation. In other words, it is in a particular—haunting—encounter with the spectre of reparation that the valence of the Irreparable changes from despair to hope. Bartoloni (2008, 55) is careful to emphasise that '[h]ope is found in what is not seen or possessed, and, as such, hope is beyond us, irreparably unpossessable'—like the spectre.

4 The Reparative, or, What Pandora Did

What, then, would constitute this haunting encounter with the spectre of reparation? How does one *make* hope through a negotiation between the spectre and the Irreparable? In answering these questions tentatively and provisionally, I want to turn now to perhaps the original myth in which hope is made: the tale of Pandora's box. The popular version of the myth is Hesiod's, according to which Pandora originates from Zeus' wish to punish men for the theft of fire from the gods by Prometheus (Hesiod 2009, 73). He accordingly ordered Pandora made (from clay by Haephastus) and sent to Earth with a box, or, rather, a jar which contained 'gifts' from all the gods of Olympus but which were 'a bane to men' (Hesiod 2009, 74). Epimetheus accepted Pandora (whose name of course literally means 'all gifts'), but she opened her jar and out flew all the evils that we have since known in the world. The only thing that remained in the box was hope (*elpis*). With reference to the previous section, Hesiod's Pandora is, clearly, a version of the myth of Paradisiacal exile to which I refer above, and thus of the origin of the Irreparable.

There are many interpretations of this version, but the one that concerns us here, is the radical departure from Hesiod by the classicist, Jane Harrison, upon careful philological reinvestigation of the Pandora myth (Harrison 1900). Harrison's undertaking revealed that Pandora's 'box' was nothing more than a grave and that the evils that Hesiod's 'curious and fatal woman, his Eve', are supposed to have let loose upon the world 'are in fact nothing but ghosts, issuing from a [...] grave' (Harrison 1900, 103). According to Harrison, the popular version of the myth as it is attributed to Hesiod, is grounded in a 'misconception' (Harrison 1900, 100). Time and space does not allow a full discussion here, but suffice it to say that Pandora ended up with evil, as opposed simply to ghosts, as a result of the rise of the monotheistic cult of Zeus in which Pandora became the 'duly subordinate devil' (Harrison 1900, 108).

Harrison reminds her reader that Pandora is in fact none other than the earth-goddess, Gaia, Mother Earth in an anthropomorphic form. It was when Pandora 'emerged in human shape' that she became the natural patron of all ghosts: 'her spirit, the ghosts, were the source of all good and all evil' and her cult was 'a ghost and ancestor cult' (Harrison 1900, 108). Harrison is also, of course, at pains to remind us that it is as this goddess of the Earth and of ghosts and only as the goddess of the Earth and of ghosts, that Pandora remains in charge of hope (Harrison 1900, 109).

Harrison's version of the Pandora myth accordingly reveals that a particular sort of encounter with the spectre generates hope. The first clue as regards the specificities of the encounter is that Pandora in human form is charged with tending to a grave, in other words, to the remains/to what remains. Second, Pandora tends to the grave/the remains in such a way that ghosts are liberated. Third, this tending which liberates ghosts, leaves hope behind *in the grave*. In other words, the remains *become* hope. Now, to return to our terminology, it is not difficult to see that the remains/the grave represents the Irreparable, for that is what the remains in the grave inevitably are 'without remedy'. But, through Pandora's action, the remains are transformed into hope. There is here, then, a close correspondence with Agamben's assertion that the Irreparable – that which is without remedy – is the source of hope.

It is, however, critical to underscore that Pandora *produces/makes hope out of an encounter with ghosts* and that it is a particular encounter, one that *liberates* the ghosts—the liberation of ghosts and the production of hope are thus, in the Pandora myth, two sides of the same coin. In truth, the liberation of ghosts becomes the condition for hope to be left behind. One could therefore argue that the Pandora myth teaches us how to *negotiate* hope in the encounter with the spectral remains. The spectre's one condition is that it be liberated. I would argue that, in this light, Pandora's deed can be recognised as 'reparative'. The etymology of the suffix of the word 'repar*ative*' indicates tending to something, here, most obviously, tending to, or towards, reparation—'without ever fully accomplishing it', is of course the implication. But a tending to also evokes the remains—that which is left in the grave (or taken to a new one, as we shall shortly see).

It was Gillian Rose (1996) who, in *Mourning Becomes the Law*, reinvigorated the sociosymbolic significance of tending to the remains—a significance which we have, of course, known since Antigone. Rose (1996, 23) discusses Plutarch's story (which also forms the subject of Alexander Poussin's painting, *Gathering the Ashes of Phocion*[5]) of the Athenian statesman, Phocion, who was sentenced to his death by a corrupted government on a false charge of treason. As an additional disgrace, Phocion's proper burial inside the city was forbidden. No Athenian was allowed to provide fire for his funeral. Consequently, his body was burnt outside the city by a paid alien who left the ashes untended on the pyre (Rose 1996, 23).

Poussin's painting represents the moment when Phocion's widow and a woman servant—defiant of the decree that his remains be left unconsecrated—venture outside the city to collect his ashes. Upon collecting the ashes, Phocion's widow returns to the city and Rose contends that in this return, she re-engages the ethical and political processes of the city and so comes to challenge—in mourning—the tyranny that culminated in her husband's dishonourable death (Rose 1996, 25–26; 36). Like that of Antigone and like that of Pandora, Phocion's widow's work is a tending and, like Antigone and Pandora, the tending is undertaken/carried out to liberate the spectre. (Pandora and Phocion's widow, I would argue, stand somewhat apart from Antigone, because in the Antigone it is by no means clear that the tending generates hope,[6] whereas this is clear in Pandora and, through Rose's interpretation of Plutarch, also in Phocion's widow.)

The reparative tends to the remains. It is, as such, the name of an intervention. In Arendt's terms, it is undoubtedly action: words that are 'not empty' and deeds that are 'not brutal', deeds that 'are not used to violate and destroy but to establish relations and create new realities' (Arendt 1998, 200).

I want to pause for a moment at speech as reparative action that generates hope. It is, of course, in psychoanalysis that these links are most apparent. In fact, Nicolas Rand (1994, 167), the editor of Abraham and Torok's *The Shell and the Kernel Vol I,* contends that Abraham's concept of the phantom calls for an understanding of psychoanalysis as a 'cult of ancestors' and a form of 'honoring the dead with rightful burial'. He continues: 'in the psychoanalytic realm, laying the dead to rest and cultivating our ancestors implies uncovering their shameful secrets, understanding their nameless and undisclosed suffering. We should engage in this unveiling and understanding of the former existence of the dead not because we may want to appease them or prevent them from perpetrating their nocturnal pranks, but because, unsuspected, the dead continue to lead a devastating psychic half-life in us' (Rand 1994, 167).

There are obvious resonances between this understanding of psychoanalysis and indigenous belief systems and cultural practices in Africa that assign a paramount role to the relationship with the ancestors and in which conversing and consorting with, as well as appeasing, the ancestors, forms a major part of ritual (Kopytoff 1971). Indeed, according to Teffo and Roux (2003, 200) the distinction between the material and the spiritual world 'has no place in African thinking', but ritual is critical in terms of facilitating communication/correspondence between the living and the ancestors.

Against this background, we can understand why this aspect is prominent in both the Rwandan (Major 2015) and the South African national reconciliation processes. Sanders (2007, 40–49) has compellingly drawn attention to the important role that 'according funeral rites to the dead' played in the life of the TRC. Arguing that apartheid should (also) be understood as a 'massive refusal to mourn', Sanders (2007, 40) accounts how witnesses came before the commission with requests for assistance in 'supplying components necessary for completion of those rites'.

In so doing, witnesses asked the TRC to join 'materially and affectively in the work of mourning' and, given that the commission represents the national public, the enlistment of the commission is an enlistment of the whole country. In his extremely sensitive and insightful discussion of the testimony of Joyce Mtimkulu, Sanders (2007, 46) shows how Mrs Mtimkulu's holding up of her dead son, Simphiwo's, hair attached to the scalp, during her public testimony, is 'a reparative symbolic gesture', which accompanies her attempt to 'at least materially' complete 'the required funeral rites'.

It is Sanders' conclusion that brings us back to hope: 'the implication was clear: in order to overcome the divisions of the past, in order to make reparation for the violations of the apartheid era, an equally massive joining in mourning would have to take place. Mourning would make good for the violations of the apartheid era' (Sanders 2007, 49). Stated in the terms of this chapter, the implication is as follows: in order for there to be hope for South Africa, the spectre of reparation had/has to be encountered, a negotiation with the spectre had/has to take place, during which a reparative intervention takes place in relation to the remains. Then, and only then, in this *confluence* of the spiritual and the material, would/will the irreparable remains generate hope.

For this reason, it is also futile to insist, as some commentators still do, that the spiritual and the material dimension of reparation can somehow be neatly separated—the reparative psychic encounter with the remains as spectre has a *necessary* material dimension (as the story of Phocion's widow clearly illustrates), one that is too often under-emphasised in the discourse on and of transitional justice; one that indeed *grounds* the demand for material reparation as an indispensable part of the mourning process where political wrong and violation lies at the root of loss. Interestingly, it is Melanie Klein who succinctly articulates this relationship between hope and the psychic and material confluence of the reparative intervention: 'the drive to make reparation can keep at bay the despair arising out of feelings of guilt, and then hope will prevail, in which case the baby's love and his desire to make reparation are unconsciously carried over to the new objects of love and interest' (Klein 1998, 342).

5 For the Interruptive Discourse of the Analyst: In Politics

In his *Aporias*, Derrida famously remarks that 'there is no politics without an organization of the time and space of mourning, without a topolitology of the sepulcher, without an anamnesic and thematic relation of the spirit as ghost [revenant], without an open hospitality to the guest as ghost whom one holds, just as he holds us, hostage' (Derrida 1993, 61). No politics without mourning, no politics that is not mourning and politics as the work of mourning—this is what we must take from Derrida.

The fundamental reason why this is so, why politics is so intimately bounded up with mourning, is because, as Derrida argues in the same address, the ego is 'constituted in its ipseity in terms of an originary mourning' which means that it 'welcomes or supposes the other within its being-itself as different from itself' (Derrida 1993, 61). And to suppose the other is always already to suppose their mortality. The ego, accordingly, is originally a plurality and, because plurality is, as Arendt (1998, 7) argued, the *conditio* sine qua non and the *conditio per quam* of the political, the ego is as such and from the start 'political'. To put it quite simply: one is always with the mortal other. Sanders does not mention that one other understanding of apartheid is that it was a massive attempt at the destruction of plurality and thus of the political and politics (which is what made it totalitarian and not merely authoritarian); but the analysis that apartheid was a refusal to mourn, clearly implies this.

As for the post-apartheid, I want to draw attention to Arendt's worry about the 'society' of labour and consumption that emerged in the twentieth century, namely that the togetherness one could find in it 'has none of the distinctive marks of true plurality' (Arendt 1998, 212) because it requires 'the actual loss of all awareness of individuality and identity' (Arendt 1998, 213); it rests 'not on equality but on sameness' (Arendt 1998, 213).

Against this backdrop, I would go so far as to suggest that the lack of reparative interventions in post-apartheid South Africa is a symptom of our continued refusal/inability to mourn, which, in the early Freud is designated by the term melancholia (Mitscherlich and Mitscherlich 1975). In his *Postcolonial melancholia*, Paul Gilroy (2005) mounts just such an argument, namely that the melancholia of the postcolonial nation obstructs its capacity for the accommodation of the plurality that sustains authentic politics. Of this denial of plurality in the South African 'post'colony there are signs that are all too visible, from xenophobic violence in townships, to party political fascism, from presentist neoliberal policy that exacerbates inequality, to proliferating hate speech on social media, from the slow pace of transformation in the work place, to the rise of the alt-right movement locally—all of these processes and consequences of South Africa's inscription in the global neoliberal hegemony can be viewed as so many ways of avoiding a reparative encounter with the spectre of reparation, or, to put it in the idiom of the renovated Pandora: they can be viewed as so many attempts to keep the lid on the grave.

This brings me to the question of time. In *Specters of Marx*, Derrida (1994, 99) writes that one can never be sure whether a spectre is coming from the past or from the future and that this means that the spectre creates a disjuncture in time. I have hinted in earlier parts of this chapter at this idea that the ghostly, haunting encounter with the spectre (of reparation) disjoins or dislocates time. For Derrida, the spectre 'disjoins the living present' and so deconstructs 'any assurance of presence, any certitude'. In other words, the haunting encounter depends on the interruption of the flow of 'normal' rectilinear time in what we call the contemporary. This is why the reparative which arises out of such an encounter is an active intervention that takes place in the Irreparable and changes its valence. The reason why the reparative disjoins rectilinear time, is because it introduces both the past (in the form of the spectre) and the future (in the form of hope) in the 'living present' of the irreparable. Without this interruption—which, following Agamben, I have elsewhere called 'rhythm' (Barnard-Naudé 2016, 56)—no hope can be made.

In future work, it will be necessary to explore in much more detail the conditions necessary for such an interruption, but here I would like to conclude by way of stating my sense that one of the major problems of post-apartheid South Africa, of post-genocide Rwanda and—in the spirit of these jurisdictions as intense metonymies—of the world in general, is that we have failed and are failing to institutionalise the interruptive discourse to which Lacan referred to as the discourse of the analyst or 'analytic discourse' (Lacan 2007, 136).

It was not arbitrary whim that led the Nazis to burn Freud's and other psychoanalytic books on a bonfire in Berlin in 1933 (Jones 1961, 496; 498) and once they took power, immediately began liquidating psychoanalysis in Germany. The point of involving these details here is not to hint at a ridiculous and indeed quite ludicrous correspondence between Nazism and neoliberal postcolonial jurisdictions. Rather, it is that fascism, proto-fascism and authoritarianism—wherever they may be—are antithetical to the discourse of the analyst. The reason why this is so, is because the discourse of the analyst is *the inverse* of the discourse of the master (Lacan 2007, 136). As such its aim is not external subjugation (as is the case with the discourse of the master), but freedom.

The discourse of the analyst is by turns described as the discourse of care, of love, of transformation and of revolutionising (Bracher 1988). It is, of course, called the discourse of the analyst in order to call to mind the psychoanalytic setting and the psychoanalytic relation and—recalling the earlier explanation of Lacan's expansive notion of discourse—this tells us much about the qualities of the social link that it aims at. Typically, the patient seeks out an analyst when her life as she knows it has become, for her, in a word, hopeless. This is also why psychoanalysis is interruptive. As Slavoj Žižek (2008, 82) has pointed out, psychoanalysis takes place in a state, and thus in a time, of emergency, or of suspension of the ordinary course of things.

The unbearable, hopeless aspect of life always relates invariably, in one way or another, to the patient's lack. *This* is the fundamental reason why it is the analyst's discourse that must concern those interested in the reparative intervention. In the context of this chapter, it should be clear that the lack which concerns us at the level of the South African nation is the lack of reparative intervention.

In the discourse of the analyst it is in the continuous confrontation with lack that the analysand produces her own master signifier which is Lacan's name for the subject's new primary identification. This master signifier or primary identification is, however, *of a different style* to the master signifier that has hitherto been imposed on the subject from outside (Lacan 2007, 176). This is, as Mark Bracher (1988, 46) writes, 'a style which, we might surmise, is less absolute, exclusive, and rigid in its establishment of the subject's identity, and more open, fluid, processual, constituted, in a word, by relativity and textuality'. To this, Dany Nobus (2000, 97 (emphasis added)) adds the following: 'psychoanalysis is geared towards making discoveries, towards the creation of wonder and surprise at the revelation of the unexpected, in short towards the crystallization of new signifiers that *reduce the painful necessity of repetition* and are therefore *able to change the analysand's life*'. Clearly, this version of the analyst's discourse cannot be further removed from the pernicious, authoritarian public discourse that characterises our dark times.

In this way, psychoanalysis *makes* the new beginning and elicits the natality which Arendt (1998, 247) equated to '[t]he miracle that saves the world, the realm of human affairs, from its normal, "natural" ruin'. It is thus also this natality which is the condition of possibility of the interruptive reparative intervention as a form of action. 'Only the full experience of this capacity [for natality]', writes Arendt, 'can bestow upon human affairs faith and hope' (Arendt 1998, 247) (and, as such, it is natality which militates against the Hesiodic reading of Pandora in which hope counts among 'the evils of illusion' (Arendt 1998, 247)).

I want to be as clear as I can that I am not advocating anything as naïve and simplistic as a wholesale transposition of the discourse of the analyst to the political, although, at the same time, I would reserve a place precisely for the madness which is 'perhaps not so mad', of which Derrida writes—and there are no surprises here—in the context of forgiveness (Derrida 2001, 60). I am interested in a political discourse that bears the ethical features and orientations of the analyst's discourse, because I think that such a discourse provides a conducive matrix for the kind of reparative interventions that can generate hope. First of all, it is useful to re-emphasise that the etymology of the word 'analysis' refers us to the solution of a problem in the manner of the untying of a knot. Žižek (2008, 91) explains that the political value of the discourse of the analyst lies in the way in which it is able to position the political agent as 'the symptomal point, the "part of no part," of the situation', who regains 'the explosive effect of truth' and addresses the subject in a way that confronts it with its lack to the point of hysteria. As a result of this discursive operation, the subject herself produces a master signifier of another style. In her 'Psychoanalysis and the polis', Julia Kristeva (1982, 78) writes about how this discourse is ultimately aimed at counter-weighing the discourse of political authority: 'Psychoanalysis, critical and dissolvant, cuts through political illusions, fantasies and beliefs to the extent that they consist in providing only one meaning, an uncriticizable ultimate Meaning, to human behaviour. If such a situation can lead to despair within the polis, we must not forget that it is also a source of lucidity and ethics. The psychoanalytic intervention is, from this point of view, a counterweight, an antidote, to political discourse which, without it, is free to become our modern religion: the final explanation'.

6 Conclusion: What Will Become of Our World

A spectre is haunting our conflicted societies and that spectre is reparation. The new millennium is already proving to us on a planetary scale what happens when we refuse the spectre its haunting, when we pretend that it is not there, or when we run away from and chase it at the same time (Derrida 1994, 101), in other words, when we repress it: it does only one thing—it returns and, as in Hamlet, it returns to begin. How that beginning ends is ultimately a question of how we relate to the spectre's return. Do we repeat our traumatic flight from it or do we speak to it?

To conclude with an answer to a question that Pumla Gobodo-Madikizela (2014) posed in the form of the title of her recent book: 'Dare we hope?' Tellingly, the subtitle of this book functions as an answer that neatly summarises the concerns of this chapter: 'Facing our past to find a new future'. The answer, then, is yes, we dare hope, if we are prepared, here, in the irreparable world, finally to *make hope* out of the haunting encounter with the spectre. It is such a making of hope that I call reparative and that indeed requires the courage of daring—daring, amongst other things, to act in what Derrida (1990, 967) called 'the night of non-knowledge and non-rule'.

The haunting words of Jean-Luc Nancy (Lacoue-Labarthe and Nancy 1997, 158 (emphasis added)) impose themselves, however, in the final instance: 'What will become of our world is something we cannot know, and *we can no longer believe in being able to predict or command it*. But we can *act in such a way that this world is a world able to open itself up to its own uncertainty* [...] [I]t is *ineluctable to invent a world, instead of being subjected to one, or dreaming of another*. Invention is always without a model and without warranty. But indeed that implies facing up to turmoil, anxiety, even disarray. Where certainties come apart, there too gathers the strength that no certainty can match'.

Notes

1. Once again, I must insist that the signifier 'citizenship' in the phrase 'reparative citizenship' is not meant to designate a site of exclusion grounded in the 'formal', 'official' requirements of a nation-state's citizenship laws. With this word, I have in mind, rather, a designation akin to the way Hannah Arendt invoked the concept to denote political life/the *bios politikos* in general, which readers of Arendt will know is bounded up in Arendt's work with the practice/pursuit of freedom. Of this Arendt writes in the context of the French Revolution that the *citoyen* was a 'new revolutionary concept', a 'new concept of man'. See Arendt (1994, 170).
2. Willemse (2017, 686) uses this term to indicate that, for Agamben, 'all the elements and creatures of the world' are exiled from Paradise and/but, as such, enjoy an 'incorruptible fallenness'. It is in this view of exile and of fallenness as 'incorruptible', that the valence of the Irreparable as a source of hope, arises.
3. One should note here also the contrasting way in which recent critical theory has re-engaged the question of hope. On the one hand, Žižek (2015) insists on the trope of 'hopelessness' in his recent book *The Courage of Hopelessness* while, on the other hand, Terry Eagleton (2015) renders a hope 'without optimism'.
4. It is certainly the case that there is an Arendtian tension that arises here between our capacity as *homo faber* whose work is production and our capacity for politics as the *bios politikos* and describing hope in this way as a political 'making' seems to undermine the very distinction between production and politics that Arendt was at pains to maintain. This is a tension to which future research will attend.
5. The painting can be viewed at http://upload.wikimedia.org/wikipedia/commons/9/90/Nicolas_Poussin_-_Landscape_with_the_Gathering_of_the_Ashes_of_Phocion_by_his_Widow_%28detail%29_-_WGA18326.jpg
6. In fact, in Jean Anouilh's famous adaptation (1946, 95), Antigone positively rails against hope: 'Nous sommes de ceux qui posent les questions jusqu'au bout. Jusqu'à ce qu'il ne reste vraiment plus la petite chance d'espoir vivante, la plus petite chance d'espoir à étrangler. Nous sommes de ceux qui lui sautent dessus quand ils le rencontrent, votre espoir, votre cher espoir, votre sale espoir!' ('We are those who endlessly pose questions, until not even the slightest hope is left to be strangled. We hate your hope, your dear hope, your filthy hope!')

References

Agamben, G. (1993). *The Coming Community*. Minneapolis: University of Minnesota Press.

Anouilh, J. (1946). *Antigone*. Paris: Éditions de la table ronde.

Arendt, H. (1994). What Is Existential Philosophy? In H. Arendt (Ed.), *Essays in Understanding 1930–1954: Formation, Exile, and Totalitarianism*. New York: Schocken Books.

Arendt, H. (1998). *The Human Condition*. Chicago: University of Chicago Press.

Barnard-Naudé, J. (2016). Chapter 3: Towards the Poetic Justice of Reparative Citizenship. In P. Gobodo-Madikizela (Ed.), *Breaking Intergenerational Cycles of Repetition: A Global Dialogue on Historical Trauma and Memory* (pp. 49–70). Leverkusen: Barbara Budrich Academic Press.

Bartoloni, P. (2008). Giorgio Agamben. *Angelaki: Journal of Theoretical Humanities, 13*(1), 51–63.

Bhabha, H. K. (2017). Foreword: Framing Fanon. In F. Fanon (Ed.), *The Wretched of the Earth* (p. 2017). Cape Town: Kwela Books.

Bornkamm, P. C. (2012). *Rwanda's Gacaca Courts: Between Retribution and Reparation*. Oxford: Oxford University Press.

Bracher, M. (1988). Lacan's Theory of the Four Discourses. *Prose Studies, 11*, 32–49.

Corlett, J. A. (2011). Reparations. In J. L. Garfield & W. Edelglass (Eds.), *The Oxford Handbook of World Philosophy*. Oxford: Oxford University Press.

De Kok, I. (2006). *Seasonal Fires: New and Selected Poems*. Roggebaai: Umuzi.

De Wet, P. (2018). These Communities Could Share R500 Million in Apartheid Reparations. https://www.businessinsider.co.za/presidents-fund-regulations-mean-communities-could-get-r30-trc-payouts-2018-7. Accessed 1 Feb 2019.

Derrida, J. (1990). Force of Law: The 'Mystical Foundation of Authority. *Cardozo Law Review, 11*, 921–1045.

Derrida, J. (1993). *Aporias*. Stanford: Stanford University Press.

Derrida, J. (1994). *Specters of Marx: The State of the Debt, the Work of Mourning and the New International*. New York: Routledge.

Derrida, J. (2001). *On Cosmopolitanism and Forgiveness*. London: Routledge.

Doxtader, E., & Villa-Vicencio, C. (Eds.). (2004). *To Repair the Irreparable: Reparation and Reconstruction in South Africa*. Claremont: David Philip Publishers.

Du Bois, F., & Du Bois-Pedain, A. (Eds.). (2008). *Justice and Reconciliation in Post-Apartheid South Africa*. Cambridge: Cambridge University Press.

Eagleton, T. (2015). *Hope Without Optimism*. New Haven: Yale University Press.
Gasake, A. (2012). Reparation. https://survivors-fund.org.uk/awareness-raising/reparation-4/. Accessed 1 Feb 2019.
Gilroy, P. (2005). *Postcolonial Melancholia*. New York: Columbia University Press.
Gobodo-Madikizela, P. (2014). *Dare We Hope? Facing Our Past to Find a New Future*. Cape Town: NB Publishers.
Harrison, J. (1900). Pandora's Box. *The Journal of Hellenic Studies, 20*, 99–114.
Hesiod. (2009). *Theogony and Works and Days*. Indianapolis: Focus.
Human Rights Watch. (2011). Justice Compromised The Legacy of Rwanda's Community-Based *Gacaca* Courts. https://www.hrw.org/report/2011/05/31/justice-compromised/legacy-rwandas-community-based-gacaca-courts. Accessed 1 Feb 2019.
Jones, E. (1961). *The Life and Work of Sigmund Freud*. New York: Basic Books Inc.
Klein, M. (1998). *Love, Guilt and Reparation and Other Works 1921–1945*. London: Vintage.
Kopytoff, I. (1971). Ancestors as Elders in Africa. *Africa, 41*(2), 129–142.
Kristeva, J. (1982). Psychoanalysis and the Polis. *Critical Inquiry, 9*(1), 77–92.
Lacan, J. (2007). *The Seminar of Jacques Lacan Book XVII: The Other Side of Psychoanalysis*. New York: WW Norton & Company.
Lacoue-Labarthe, P., & Nancy, J.-L. (1997). *Retreating the Political*. London: Routledge.
Major, L. (2015). Unearthing, Untangling and Re-articulating Genocide Corpses in Rwanda. *Critical African Studies, 7*(2), 164–181.
Mitscherlich, A., & Mitscherlich, M. (1975). *The Inability to Mourn: Principles of Collective Behavior*. (B. R. Placzek, Trans.). New York: Grove Press
Mugiraneza, J. (2014). Rwanda Genocide: Why Compensation Would Help the Healing. *The Guardian*. https://www.theguardian.com/global-development-professionals-network/2014/mar/04/rwanda-genocide-victims-compensation. Accessed 1 Feb 2019.
Murray, A., & Whyte, J. (Eds.). (2011). *The Agamben Dictionary*. Edinburgh: Edinburgh University Press.
Nobus, D. (2000). *Jacques Lacan and the Freudian Practice of Psychoanalysis*. London: Routledge.
Prozorov, S. (2014). *Agamben and Politics: A Critical Introduction*. Edinburgh: Edinburgh University Press.
Rand, N. (1994). Editor's Note. In N. Abraham & M. Torok (Eds.), *The Shell and the Kernel: Renewals of Psychoanalysis, Volume I*. Chicago: University of Chicago Press.

Rose, G. (1996). *Mourning Becomes the Law: Philosophy and Representation*. Cambridge: Cambridge University Press.
Rose, J. (2020). The Legacy. In J. Barnard-Naudé (Ed.), *Decolonizing the Neoliberal University: Law, Psychoanalysis and the Politics of Student Protest*. London: Birkbeck Law Press.
Rwirahira, R. (2017). Kwibuka23: Kaboneka Warns on Reparations. *New Times*. https://www.newtimes.co.rw/section/read/210447 Accessed 1 Feb 2019.
Salazar, P.-J. (2004). The Joint Sitting of Parliament, 15 April 2003: A Rhetorical View of the Reparation Debate. In E. Doxtader & C. Villa-Vicencio (Eds.), *To Repair the Irreparable: Reparation and Reconstruction in South Africa*. Claremont: David Philip Publishers.
Sanders, M. (2007). *Ambiguities of Witnessing: Law and Literature in the Time of a Truth Commission*. Johannesburg: Wits University Press.
Shakespeare, W. (2008). *Complete Works*. Hampshire: Macmillan Publishers Ltd..
Teffo, L. J., & Roux, A. P. J. (2003). Introduction: Themes in African Metaphysics. In P. H. Coetzee & A. P. J. Roux (Eds.), *The African Philosophy Reader: A Text with Readings*. London: Routledge.
Truth and Reconciliation Commission of South Africa. (1998a). *Truth and Reconciliation Commission of South Africa Report Vol. 5*. Government Printer: Pretoria.
Truth and Reconciliation Commission of South Africa. (1998b). *Truth and Reconciliation Commission of South Africa Report Vol. 6*. Government Printer: Pretoria.
Willemse, A. (2017). The Motif of the Irreparable: Potentiality, Contingency, and Redemption in Agamben's Theology. *Heythrop Journal, 58*(4), 678–691.
Yates, A. (2018). Justice Delayed: The TRC Recommendations 20 Years Later. *Daily Maverick*. https://www.dailymaverick.co.za/article/2018-09-05-justice-delayed-the-trc-recommendations-20-years-later/. Accessed 1 Feb 2019.
Žižek, S. (2008). Lacan's Four Discourses: A Political Reading. In G. Forter & P. Miller (Eds.), *Desire of the Analysts: Psychoanalysis and Cultural Criticism*. Albany: State University of New York Press.
Žižek, S. (2015). *The Courage of Hopelessness: Chronicles of a Year of Acting Dangerously*. London: Penguin.

5

Do Black Lives Matter? A Psychoanalytic Exploration of Racism and American Resistance to Reparations

Jeffrey Prager

The American Negro has the great advantage of having never believed the collection of myths to which white Americans cling….Negroes know far more about white Americans than that; it can almost be said, in fact, that they know about white Americans what parents—or, anyway, mothers—know about their children, and that they very often regard white Americans that way.
—*James Baldwin,* The Fire Next Time

Today I believe in the possibility of love; that is why I endeavor to trace its imperfections, its perversions.
—*Frantz Fanon,* Black Skin, White Masks

Re-publication of an article originally appearing in *Political Psychology* 38, 4 (2017): 637–651.

J. Prager (✉)
Department of Sociology, University of California Los Angeles,
Los Angeles, CA, USA

New Center for Psychoanalysis, Los Angeles, CA, USA
e-mail: jprager@soc.ucla.edu

K. Wale et al. (eds.), *Post-Conflict Hauntings*, Palgrave Studies in Compromise after Conflict, https://doi.org/10.1007/978-3-030-39077-8_5

1 Introduction: Reparations and Racism

Murders of young Black men at the hands of the police, the failure to indict or prosecute those responsible, and the emergence of a formidable movement, *Black Lives Matter*, all within the last several years, have not generated new insights on the doggedness of American racism. In fact, the nation, at this point—even the progressive forces within it—appears exhausted; the intractability of racial division seems to offer the only point of agreement across dissonant perspectives. Yet racism, like the crack in the liberty bell, remains foundational to American democracy. With the current surge of violence against Blacks, the problem is more urgent than ever, requiring fresh thinking.

Psychoanalytic understandings of the human psyche have undeservedly been overlooked in attempts to wrestle with racism's tenaciousness over the course of American history. Yet, racism inhabits the mind; it continues to possess a psychic reality all its own. It operates internally according to its own rules and logic. It remains in place and enacted, in part, because specific mechanisms required to loosen it have remained unconsciously repressed.

This chapter bridges the insights suggested by the comments quoted above by Baldwin (1962) and Fanon (2008) with particular strands of psychoanalytic theory, especially those that highlight the unfolding infant and mother relationship. Mobilizing this body of work, I look anew at American racism, proceeding in five parts. Part I identifies the key role of a *reparative impulse* initiated by the maturing infant toward the mother as it comes to perceive her as existing outside of its own insatiable demands. As the baby recognizes mother's separateness, the need to make amends to mother for his or her self-centeredness is expressed; the mother, in turn, *forgives*. The mutuality of a loving relationship is made possible and deepens. Part II applies this dynamic to the American *body politic* suggesting that racial division can be considered as a condition of *thwarted love*. Here, I characterize an ever-demanding *White baby* resistant to the reparative impulse while the *Black mother* is thereby denied the capacity to forgive. Reconciliation between the two is obstructed. Further, I identify *racism* as the key psychological apparatus that ensures this continuing obstruction; racism, whose core organizing principle is racial *difference,* secures a White supremacist nation without apology.[1]

In light of this psychodynamic approach, Part III emphasizes the limits of reparations conceived as financial compensation. Part IV, in contrast, highlights the powerful recent writings of Ta-Nehisi Coates (2014), who broadens reparations as a foundational moral and ethical obligation of all Americans. Consideration of *the reparative impulse*, I argue, deepens and extends his discussion, redirecting it from political and moral imperative to psychological necessity. Part V casts America's current racial crisis as a *politics of anti-love*, where racism serves to suppress guilt and stifle the possibility for identification by Whites for Blacks. Part VI concludes by exploring the emergence of the *Black Lives Matter* movement and its focus on the most elemental features of American racism. Its critique, I suggest, is consonant with the psychoanalytic insistence that love and mutuality between mother and infant depends on reparative efforts by the baby. This framework of understanding offers a sliver of hope toward the creation of a *politics of love*, with reparations at its core.

2 The Reparative Impulse: A Psychoanalytic Contribution

To acknowledge that wrongs have been done and to apologize, forgive and reconcile with others, psychoanalysts have discovered, are universal human impulses, although in reality achieving them is often frustrated. When the impulse toward repairing significant interpersonal relationships fails whole lifetimes can be affected; in the case of social groups, an inability to acknowledge a rupture in the social bond and collectively apologize for its occurrence often yields harmful consequences that endure (see Gobodo-Madikizela 2016, 2016a; Prager 2008; Volkan 2014). The toll can last generations, even centuries, where the silencing of the reparative instinct yields a distorted, typically hostile and distrustful, set of interactions between the injured parties and their descendants.

In an article "Love, Guilt and Reparation," the British child psychoanalyst and theorist Melanie Klein (1988) describes how each individual at a very early age experiences a reparative impulse (see also Balbus 2004;

Gobodo-Madikizela 2016). It is the baby's own antidote, she explains, to aggressive, demanding, greedy feelings directed toward the object or person upon whom he or she depends. The body can seize up with frustration or excitation when what is wanted is not present soon enough. In time and in most instances, the mother presents herself and the baby calms. As awareness unfolds of total dependence on her care, the infant seeks to please the generous and forbearing mother; mother, in turn, *forgives* the baby's demandingness. She remains reassuring to her child that she continues as a constant and reliable presence.

Should reparation not occur, child and mother fail to achieve the kind of attunement characteristic of a loving relationship. This quintessentially human conundrum of holding the capacity to both love and to hate is solved, Klein argues, through the development of the feelings of *guilt* and the consequent drive to make reparation with others whom you need. The strength of human desires *and* the realization of one's dependence on others yield, for Klein (1988) and psychoanalysis more broadly, *the emotion of love*: a complex set of feelings always, at the same time, self-centered and other-directed.

A contemporary of Klein (1988) and another British psychoanalyst, Donald Winnicott (1955), characterizes this same phenomenon as a child's struggle between *"pre-ruth"* and *"ruth"* (p. 262–277; see also Winnicott 1988, p. 36–50). Over time, the child thinks of pre-ruth as *ruthlessness*, but at the time pre-ruth is simply the fully enveloping self-absorption of being satisfied and gratified. Ruth implies the baby's sense of absolute or total omnipotence: others can be conjured up simultaneously with one's need for them. Yet when the infant is able to see the mother as something "not-me" and nonetheless essential to his or her well-being, feelings of care and concern toward the mother develop, only retrospectively felt as ruthlessness. The infant's concern for the mother, as a result of her consistent presence despite the rage she is sometimes subjected to, develops as she demonstrates again and again her capacity to survive his or her ruthlessness.

For Winnicott (1955), this process—pre-ruth, guilt, ruth—is essential in the infant's developing capacity to distinguish between an inner world—feelings, desires, needs, and fantasies, subjectivity—and an outside world of others not entirely subject to one's control, the objective environment. For Winnicott (1975), as for Klein (1988), love is the result of a reparative impulse, the psychic urge to repair the damage felt to have been done to the loved person—"to give and to construct and to mend" (Winnicott 1975, p. 204–218). Winnicott (1975) insists that the capacity to distinguish between what is produced subjectively with what is an objective impingement, while initiated in infancy, is a life-long challenge and defines the human condition.

As both analysts insist, reparation is an essential feature of individual development. With its appearance, the human being, in its concern for another, enters an interpersonal social world. The child now appreciates the necessity to preserve elements of certain intimate others for survival. The mother, in turn, empathically attuned to her child, must possess the capacity *to forgive*. Reparation operates unconsciously and is essential *both* to the aggressor, as apology, *and* to the recipient of this aggression, as forgiveness. When it does not occur, whatever the reason, the natural bond between individuals becomes severely strained if not broken. *Unconscious guilt* for one's own demanding self-centeredness and the danger it imaginatively presents to the other, in contrast, establishes an intimate, loving attachment between the two.

This unconscious guilt is a complex emotion that develops only slowly in the newborn infant and creates in him or her growing capacity for clear distinction between one's inner world and the limits of a providing outer world. Guilt is a set of affectively charged feelings to be respected, to be processed unconsciously and not to be dismissed.[2] In this form, this binding guilt is *necessary* to achieve a social world based on caring and reciprocation, replete with loving energy-generating connectedness. Not something to overcome, guilt unconsciously serves as an essential component to ensure affectively charged human relatedness.[3]

3 The Reparative Impulse Denied, Racism Empowered

Following the American Civil War, Southern Whites were in a position to initiate repair with those formerly enslaved. However, they failed to do so; the opportunity was squandered. The possibility for deepening the bond between fellow Americans went deeply awry. Initial efforts were repelled and, instead, dominion over African Americans continued through various forms of legal enactments: "slavery by another name" (Blackmon 2009). The failure by Whites to respond to reparative impulses, despite a period of unmitigated exploitation of those enslaved, indeed illuminates this critical feature of American racism: throughout post-Civil War history, except for a brief period of Reconstruction, a reciprocal unconscious cooperation between an African American and a White population has been vigorously *thwarted* (Du Bois 1994; Foner 2002; Kendi 2016). To this day, Blacks continue to occupy a subordinate place in a White supremacist racial hierarchy. Despite the end of slavery, Whites retain almost complete freedom to expect of African Americans their complicity in the hierarchical racial order. Nonetheless, the former continue to possess an emotionally immature relationship to the latter. In failing to acknowledge or act upon any reparative impulse, Whites refuse to concede their omnipotent and self-centered conception of themselves, or to accept an external reality where they do not occupy its voracious center. Notably, they have collectively refused to apologize for the harms committed to their fellow Americans.

Racism, in fact, thrives on this psychological space between Whites and Blacks, first established in the minds of the slave society and, since then, never effectively challenged. The failure to acknowledge past national wrongs has produced instead a collective psychology frozen in time when domination by race was a formal feature of America, and when bifurcation of Blacks and Whites, as slave and free, was codified as law of the land. The racial *binary,* refashioned because of a new post-slavery social order in which Blacks were formally free, nonetheless still continues to be cast as a natural, inevitable, and a permanent feature of American life. The slave society legislated against White care and concern for those enslaved and, therefore, the social arrangements likely posed less of a moral or psychological challenge to those in control. In post-slavery America, the suppression of a reparative impulse toward African Americans, in contrast, necessitated not only new laws of racial domination but also a greatly invigorated racism, with an amplified and elaborated set of justifications preserving racial domination. A more persuasive racism became articulated incorporating the new "race" science spreading throughout the Western world. This racism emphasized as its essential feature the *reality* of racial difference. In the name of White supremacy and the preservation of a bifurcated nation, racism, implemented within various institutional settings, was energetically deployed; efforts toward racial reconciliation concomitantly were repelled.

American racism has obscured from view the reality that psychologically Whites continue to preserve the fiction of themselves as self-sufficient and independent, reliant on no one but themselves. Blacks continue to be seen as "a social problem," not as equal claimants to the American nation (Du Bois 1994, p. 1). White refusal to *access* its own reparative sentiments preserves that fiction. To do otherwise is tantamount to psychologically abandoning their position as dominant, to perceive themselves as cohabiting the American nation, along with Blacks (and Indians). Whites, in short, psychologically remain *developmentally arrested*. They hold stubbornly to their position as omnipotent and demanding like children. Concurrently, they undercut any Black capacity, however patient they remain, to forgive.

D.W. Griffith's *The Birth of a Nation*, produced in 1915, helped consolidate for a very receptive White audience their refusal to access healthy reparative instincts. The film powerfully resonated with America's decision, forged over the 50 years prior, to choose a brutally racist alternative to the expression of humane concern for those formerly enslaved. It communicated their sense of themselves as occupying America's moral center, relegating all others to the periphery. Credited with being instrumental in creating the "second era" of the Ku Klux Klan following the Civil War, it invokes in its imagery the post-Civil War forms of racism establishing the biological differences between Whites and Blacks. Depicting African Americans as unruly and licentious *by nature*, *The Birth of a Nation* projected on to Blacks elements of Whites' own repressed primitive mind. It shifted blame and responsibility to those whom Whites had harmed, allowing Whites to defensively ward off their own responsibility. The film celebrated an *unnatural* post-Civil War birth, portraying the American nation as burdened by its childlike and immoral African American population. Stern parental intervention was required to secure a moral, democratic nation. *Birth of a Nation* offered a powerful visual representation that racial division itself—one White world and one Black one—remained as foundational to America as democracy itself.

American racism flourishes *concurrently with*, as a function of, White failure to acknowledge injuries inflicted on African Americans. Indeed, it is handmaiden to any denial of collective responsibility. Though true during the slave period, racism has been no less virulent—only different—following the end of slavery. As a result, there has been scant attention paid to assess the long-standing psychological consequences and material effects of the national failure *to apologize* to African Americans. Guilt for harms committed, rather than being acknowledged and felt, instead have been denied and repressed. African Americans, in turn, have never been allowed collectively to forgive those who subordinated them. *Psychological reconciliation* between American Whites and American Blacks has never occurred.

Yet the *thwarting* of the drive to achieve redress or reconciliation has produced devastating effects on the national collective psyche. *White* refusal to accept responsibility for its dominion over African American bodies and labor power has yielded a disfigured body politic infected by racist beliefs and practices. The American social fabric expressed through law, politics, legislation, economy family, religion, education, culture, customs, traditions, procedures, mores, and fantasies all have been contaminated and implicated. In place of reparation, White supremacy, in the end and despite some impressive efforts to dismantle it, has successfully disallowed the politics of social redress and reconciliation from finding voice.

4 Racial Reparations as Financial Transaction, Racism Empowered

In the context of American socio-political debate and discussion, the concept of racial reparations, holds a very different meaning than the psychoanalytic formulation of reparation discussed above. The dissimilarity reflects the powerful ways in which racism, among its many effects, has also served to frame political discussion. The objective reality of racial difference is a taken-for-granted presumption, never subject to interrogation on its own terms.[4] This is no surprise because racism has served precisely to distort the reparative impulse so as to be unrecognizable. Until recently, reparations were primarily cast as a form of *financial* compensation for social and personal harms committed in the past (see Brooks 2004a, p. 98–114). Especially in the case of African Americans, reparations as payment for losses suffered as a result of enslavement have never gained widespread public support, though it has been a claim consistently made *sub rosa* by engaged scholars and by members of the African American community (see Bittker 1973; Browne 1971; Feagin 2004; Kull 1995; Robinson 2001; Swinton 1990). The debate over restitution for African Americans, Japanese Americans, American Indians and other peoples of color has been so narrowly defined as to deplete it of psychological significance for either the recipients or the initiators.[5] In certain instances, efforts have been made to calculate in monetary terms the financial losses suffered by African Americans due to slavery and Jim Crow (Feagin 2004). When moral claims are elaborated for apology and restitution to African Americans, most often it is to provide justification for monetary compensation to the sufferers' descendants (see Brooks 2004). In the end, the discussion becomes organized over the technical problems reparations poses. It is largely summarily dismissed by raising certain practical questions: who, 250 years after slavery, are the rightful recipients of financial payment, why should this generation today be assessed for wrongs for which they were not responsible, and so forth. Reparations, it is argued, require the same kind of hardheaded realism as any other business transaction.

Psychologically, Americans have demonstrated especially a fulsome capacity to invert the discourse and view it through a powerful racist prism in which Blacks are viewed as making unreasonable demands on this generation of Whites. The seriousness of the issue becomes trivialized, the necessary initiators of reparations, as I argue, are inverted along with the rightful recipients of moral and psychological atonement. Those recipients who lay claim are experienced as the *initiators* of reparative claims—as hostile claimants—as grasping and as overly insistent. Whites have typically responded to reparation calls as if they expressed only revenge on behalf of the descendants of those who suffered.[6] The effected population, *objects* of White aggression and dependence, are felt instead to be reparations' aggressors, a perfect example, as Freud describes it, of *projection*. This constriction and distortion of the impulse has succeeded, thus far, not only in narrowing its rendering to a simple consideration of financial compensation but, over generations, succeeded through inaction to ensure racism's efficacy in preserving the *status quo* (Brooks 2004a).

This collective failure to address seriously the possibility for reparations has had profound ramifications for African Americans. White inability to acknowledge their own hostility means they act toward Blacks *as if* they know Black hostile intentions. Recent police shootings of unarmed Black men because of unwarranted fear for their own safety reveal the power of this displaced capacity to instinctively anticipate the antipathy directed toward them. This captures *projections'* deadly power. Similarly, for those who propose reparations as a vehicle of social redress, the White reaction is to claim instead this to be an unjustifiable attempt by the descendants of those enslaved to wrest back what is rightfully theirs. These calls have been rejected as a form of *ex post facto* theft, a ransom demand from individuals today for what had been done to their ancestors. Demand for reparations is typically scorned as yet another instance of Black refusal to move beyond the memory of slavery.

5 Racial Reparations Re-considered

Promising developments have recently pointed to new ways to think about White complicity in racial injustice. In a 2014 pathbreaking and award-winning article in *The Atlantic*, "The Case for Reparations," Ta-Nehisi Coates (2014) challenges the rendering of reparations as financial compensation for the wrongs committed during the slave period. Carefully documenting the continuing history of racial discrimination since the end of the Civil War, Coates demonstrates how African Americans remain the objects of unfair social and economic practices insuring their subjugation (see Blackmon 2009). Slavery first established a social abyss by race: free subjects, on the one side, and enslaved objects, on the other, absent any cohesiveness linking them together as equal members of American society. Little since then has changed, he argues, specifically to restore a sense of mutuality and interdependence between the African and European populations in America.

By focusing largely on housing discrimination, Coates' (2014) article demonstrates that Emancipation did not serve as a watershed moment in on-going practices of White supremacy. The methods to segregate and subordinate African Americans only changed; "a difference of kind, not degree," Coates' writes. Rather than undoing the separation of an enslaved population from those who were freed, post-Civil War America secured segregation between Blacks and Whites through newly conceived legal and extra-legal means. Both formal and informal mechanisms worked in remarkable synchrony to perpetuate Black subordination. With respect to housing, the implementation of Jim Crow legislation following Reconstruction, the Constitutionally defended imposition of restrictive covenants, redlining predominantly Black neighborhoods, and differential application of the GI bill for Blacks and Whites all served to maintain the American racial order (Coates 2014).

Evidence for this current racial disparity is ubiquitous. Average White household wealth in this country is $656,000, Black households $85,000 (Latinos $98,000). For the average Black household to reach parity with White households' wealth *today*, it would take 228 years (Collins and Asante-Muhammed 2016; Surowiecki 2016, October 3). Black unemployment rates have remained for decades on average *double* White unemployment rates, even *after* adjusting for demographic factors such as gender, age, and levels of education (United States Department Bureau of Labor Statistics 2011; Buffie 2015). Further, African Americans are paid less than Whites at every education level (Wilson 2016). Aggressive efforts to preserve the racial order and to secure White supremacy have rarely faltered. Coates (2014, p. 68) writes, "Black nationalists have always perceived something unmentionable about America that integrationists dare not acknowledge—that White supremacy is not merely the work of hotheaded demagogues, or a matter of false consciousness, but a force so fundamental to America that it is difficult to imagine the country without it."

The racial bifurcation in America, "one nation, two societies, one Black, one White," (United States National Advisory Commission on Civil Disorders 1988) has been a result of both continuing practices *preserving* differences in Black and White outcomes *and* a permanent acquiescence by all to a conviction in America's racial *brokenness* (see

Prager 2014, p. 284–316). The nation has demonstrated a remarkable equanimity or resignation in accepting the disparate quality of life and life chances for Blacks and Whites. There is, too, an extraordinary unanimity in accepting the reality of difference. Rather than being viewed as an artifact of racism and systemic White supremacy, all are viewed instead as a result of some combination of the specific features of Black Americans' 250 years of an enslaved past and the consequences that followed. Black subordination is approached as a *natural* feature of American history and society originating with the institution of slavery (see Buffie 2015).

American racial history might have been different. The psychological reality of an essential racialized difference and permanent incompatibility, both the linchpin of White supremacy and the hallmark of racism, has generated an external world that has molded itself in ways to conform to this psychic imaginary. Moreover, separate and unequal lives lived by Blacks and Whites, from slavery until now, recapitulate the collective whole's on-going unwillingness to fully acknowledge and address long-standing disparities. Its premise is based upon a refusal to apologize. Coates (2014) makes clear that the terms of debate for racial healing in the United States requires, in the first instance, an acknowledgment through reparative efforts of the continuing wrongs committed to a whole Black population. Cast in a psychological language, reparations imply the necessity to accept collectively the nation's unconscious guilt. Coates (2014) challenges the claim that the demand for reparations need simply be a response to a temporally finite period of time, i.e. the slave era, and linked to the issue of financial compensation. A discussion of reparations, instead, is necessarily a moral engagement with the history and on-going practices of White supremacy.

By documenting the unabated persistence of anti-Black sentiments and discriminatory practices, Coates (2014) characterizes the tenacity of the Black/White divide as an on-going tear in the social fabric of the country. The American community remains deeply split. A politics of repair, Coates (2014) suggests, might include financial or material compensation to African Americans to upend White supremacy. But also required are further ways to exhibit persistent *moral* or *ethical* failings of the nation by accepting American culpability, to apologize. "And so we must imagine a new country," Coates (2014) writes. "Reparations—by which I mean the full acceptance of our collective biography and its consequences—is the price we must pay to see ourselves squarely" ... "Reparations would mean a revolution of the American consciousness, a reconciling of our self-image as the great democratizer with the facts of our history" (Coates 2014).

6 The Politics of Anti-love and Love

With Coates' (2014) re-specification of reparation's broader meaning, the psychoanalytic and socio-political discussions converge. They now help inform one another. For Coates, opposition to reparations today is a *moral* failure of the American body politic. It is not a consequence of financial penury or insoluble technical questions about the rightful beneficiaries.

The inversion of the reparations question, as I described, has effectively prevented contemporary America from recognizing its own current need to promote social repair. It has refused to place itself in that position, much like a greedy baby who has had its way since the onset of slavery. What has not occurred in America is psychic capacity to move ahead: to acknowledge past wrongs or to implement affirmative policies explicitly to close or heal the divide of a racially divided *body politic*. As a result, there has been little inclination to challenge White racial privilege itself and/or to democratize social privilege across racial boundaries. Just as there has been an unwillingness by White Americans to accept the reality of their continuous history of hostility and aggression toward Black Americans, so too has there been a refusal to embrace specific compensatory efforts designed to undo racial privilege. The psychological consequences of this failure are profound. Most significantly, they inhibit the possibility of breaching the racial divide, a bifurcated *body politic*—White and Black—never to be contested. White denial has meant that the Black capacity to forgive their mistreatments, despite a remarkable history demonstrating their willingness to do so, has never really been possible. African Americans, too, accept this racial divide as essentially real.

Recent shootings of unarmed Black men as well as boys and women suggest that the collective racial consciousness in the United States has not moved beyond this psychologically primitive position. If love is understood as a thoroughly intersubjective achievement dependent upon each party accepting the needs and limitations of the other, it is clear that here love has been developmentally obstructed (Benjamin 2013). The effect has been that the singleness of all Americans continues to be denied, and African Americans continue to be psychically categorized, in relation to Whites, as subordinated humans. The capacity for Whites, under the umbrella of White racism, to develop with Blacks a sense of their common humanity, not demarcated by racial category, has remained dormant. When Michael Brown, an 18-year-old unarmed young Black man was murdered in Ferguson, Missouri, in the summer of 2014, the police allowed his dead body to lie out in the mid-afternoon sun, uncovered for more than three hours. His dead, uncared for body was in view of the entire community, including its children.

In another instance, in North Miami, Florida, a middle-aged Black behavioral therapist in July 2016 was attending to an adolescent autistic boy. When the boy ran out of the school onto the sidewalk, the therapist followed to ensure his safety, only to find police having drawn guns upon him. Lying on his back with his hands raised high, he yelled to the officers not to shoot him. To account for his behavior, he explained for all to hear his occupation and his professional responsibility to the boy. Nonetheless, he was shot in the leg. In disbelief, he asked the policeman why he fired at him. The policeman responded, seemingly as bewildered, "I dunno" (Alvarado et al. 2016). Indeed, the officer's instinctive reaction to shoot, as he himself acknowledges, overpowered any reflection or rational thinking that he might have been capable of. It is right to presume that the officer's response "I dunno," was an honest one: his unconscious and impulsive response to this Black individual, as dangerous, unsafe, and non-human, prevailed over any protocols of caution or restraint with which he may have been instructed.

These instances illustrate a much broader and deeper truth, implicating not only the police officers who precipitously fire arms but rather all Whites unconsciously susceptible to similar experiences. Black bodies, males especially, are experienced unconsciously as the site of potential danger, unpredictability, and aggression. For the officers, they are experienced as *unknown* and foreign, dimensions of their own psyche from which they are estranged. Unconsciously, African Americans are not *recognized* as human beings. In the minds of the police, they represent instead potential threats to their own personal safety and security.

Any inclination toward national restitution, what might be described as *a politics of love*, is not at hand. The contours of such reconciliation are not in view. White Americans still assume a defensive and denying stance toward Blacks. The "devouring population"—White Americans—has failed to forge an ethical response or the psychological insight to reconcile with those who have suffered its aggression. They do not acknowledge their own capacity for unbridled antagonisms. They make inaccessible to themselves recognition of their own guilt toward the Black population they regularly encounter. They deny their complicity in the many social practices and procedures that help to reproduce racial subordination. There is, in short, still no concession that Black otherness, now so real and *natural* as to be irrefutable, is a product of the White imagination (Hetey and Eberhardt 2014).

There is, however, certain ground for hope because of the attention these deaths in the Black community have received. Scientific evidence supports the existence of fantasies, fears, and preconceived ideas beneath the surface of conscious awareness. Recently, interest has focused more pointedly on research documenting "implicit bias" in human interaction. The subliminal correspondence has been demonstrated, for example, between images of Black men and impending danger (see Casey et al. 2012; Kang et al. 2012; Banks et al. 2006; Eberhardt et al. 2004).[7] Social science research on racial conflict also now finds itself more sympathetic to the view that systematic attention must be paid to "unobservable measures" beyond *intention* to discriminate and that contribute to different social and economic outcomes for African Americans when compared to Whites (Wilson and Rodgers 2016, p. 52).[8] Further, in 2015, the United States Supreme Court, as a result of a surprise ruling by Justice Kennedy, acknowledged that the law stipulates that racism in housing policy legally might be assessed when "disparate impact" on various racial communities is established. In this ruling, conscious intent to discriminate racially was determined as too narrow a standard by which to consider the effects of social policy (Texas Department of Housing and Community Affairs v. The Inclusive Communities, Inc. 2015). In another instance, President Obama, responding to the shootings of unarmed Blacks in various American cities, invoked the language of "unconscious bias," to better account for frequency with which police officers seemed "trigger happy" when encountering Black men (see Lawrence 1987).[9]

The uncovering of "unconscious racism," however, produces too sobering appreciation of the problem the nation confronts. American racism remains firmly lodged in the White mind. Its elimination cannot occur through any quick fix. We are left with an ever more profound and daunting appreciation of the nation's challenges as it seeks to undo a multi-generational, multi-century effort to secure the subordinated position of African Americans. Powerful defenses, not the least of which is racism itself, continue to be mobilized to protect against guilt and responsibility. They constitute an in-place and an on-going *politics of anti-love.* This politics describes Whites' *refusal* and incapacity to empathize with Black experiences. Whites are unconsciously incapable to feel Black suffering *as if* it is happening to them.

Klein (1988) describes this unhealthy response with regard to mother and baby as "an incapacity for identification" (p. 311). "We are only able to disregard or to some extent sacrifice our own feelings and desires, and thus for a time put the other person's interests and emotions first," Klein (1988) writes, "if we have the capacity to identify ourselves with the loved person." Identification implies the capacity to reverse roles. "This *making reparation*," Klein (1988) writes, "is in my view a fundamental element in love and in all human relationships" (p. 312–313; see also Gobodo-Madikizela 2016, 2016a).[10] Despite the interdependent demands on the situation that enable identification and love to develop, he or she seeks to modulate aggressive fantasies with *recognition* of the externality and necessity of the parent for survival (see Winnicott 1953).

When these conditions do not occur, love is thwarted. The incapacity for identification by Whites toward Blacks provides a more in-depth explanation for America's reluctance and unwillingness to move beyond its racism. In defending against the reality of African Americans' full humanity, Whites have preserved the psychic experience of Black as *undifferentiated* from them. In this imaginary, Blacks, by definition, do not exist separately. Identification is impossible because African Americans have never been provided their autonomy. Jim Crow laws, separate but equal statutes, and both formal and informal mechanisms that promote to this day on-going segregation help privilege White fantasy over reality. This is the paradox and conundrum of American racism: Whites, since the end of Reconstruction have insisted on wholesale *physical* estrangement from African Americans despite their proximity. Yet at the same time, Whites ensured that the two groups together would remain *psychically* enmeshed. As *appendages* of the White imaginary, Blacks remain indistinguishable and largely undifferentiated from White fantasy.[11]

The American hostility to a politics of reparations *by definition* denies collective interdependence or human relatedness between Whites and African Americans. Instead, only the former experience is defined as central and defining to *the* American nation. Blacks, in contrast, especially those who fit a certain physical profile, are presumed unsafe and dangerous, until, on a case-by-case basis, they can demonstrate through various measures their harmlessness. Because of psychic enmeshment, the Black body is invested with precisely those properties disallowed in the White body. The White body politic thus equates *Americanness* with Whiteness.

The nation collectively is unwilling to move beyond its paranoid anxiety and fear of the Black other, requiring Black individuals on their own, when so motivated, to attempt to traverse the racial divide. Anti-love, in rejecting even the consideration of reparations, describes the failure by the nation to achieve t*ruth*. It is a refusal to assume responsibility for the fate of both those who are the objects of aggression as well as admitting to oneself as being trapped in an ethos of denial. Whites refuse to recognize how they are implicated in the condition and fate of African Americans. Anti-love, consciously foreswearing either guilt or ruthlessness, operates to continually reproduce America's brokenness.

7 Is a Politics of Love Possible?

Black Lives Matter, a political organization established first in 2012 after the death of Trayvon Martin and of Michael Brown, has emerged as a national umbrella organization for all those wanting to protest these random killings. Its formation marked the first new organized national political challenge, mostly by African Americans themselves, in the last several decades. Its focus is a new one. By name alone, it expresses the kinds of concerns about the treatment of African Americans not articulated since the post-Slavery period and around which it is organized. As it says of itself, "when we say Black Lives Matter, we are talking about the ways in which Black people are deprived of our basic human rights and dignity" (Garza 2014).

The reality of African Americans greater physical vulnerability to arrest, to removal and incarceration, to their seemingly easier expendability due to unnecessary police shootings, and to their susceptibility to random acts of aggression and insult remain features of the contemporary American landscape. All serve to express a deep sense that they don't *matter*, that basic human rights and dignity can be easily disregarded. The precariousness and unpredictability of life itself for African Americans by virtue of their "special status" captures an important feature of slave society. Similarly, the commonplace of lynchings and vigilante justice describes the dangers faced especially in the nineteenth and early twentieth centuries. *Black Lives Matter*, for the first time, identifies an unbroken link from contemporary America to slavery: the omnipresent reality that, in an instant, by virtue of Blackness alone, life can be dramatically impinged upon, even stolen away.[12] The movement demands acknowledgment of the insecurity faced by African Americans for their physical safety and their corporeal integrity. Previous political struggles on behalf of African Americans have sought the guarantee of fundamental political and civil rights. But as is painfully evident in contemporary America, racism has not been eliminated. Nor have these political campaigns adequately identified the psychological mechanisms that keep White supremacy in place.

Black Lives Matter speaks to basic and fundamental psychological experiences of non-safety, insecurity and vulnerability. These concerns, ontologically prior to any politics of integration or civil rights, describe a deeper political and interpersonal reality for African Americans where bodily integrity is never felt to be entirely secure. The movement addresses an appreciation of these most elemental and primitive feature of American racism, entirely consonant with a psychoanalytic understanding of its unconscious roots. By *Black Lives Matter*'s name alone, it identifies in racism a failure to individuate African Americans as physically distinct human beings, not as emanations of White needs and desires, deserving the same basic respect and dignity bestowed to all individual citizens.

Reparations serves as a vehicle to help facilitate a politics of love. The proponents of *Black Lives Matters* insist that African Americans as founding members of the American community are to be recognized, equal respect and dignity accorded, and their current-day devaluation and mistreatment eliminated. Emancipation from the White imagination is the ultimate goal of reparations when African Americans each are guaranteed the same freedoms Whites bestow upon themselves. The German social philosopher, Axel Honneth (1996), describes a situation where one or the other member of a dyad is not accorded basic respect as a "relational disorder" (p. 106). America suffers from such a disorder. The price paid is what Honneth (1996) and the psychoanalyst Jessica Benjamin (2013) both describe as a failure to achieve "mutual recognition".

Reparations for the African American community is an appeal that America undertake *a politics of love*. Reparations require acknowledging America's shameful past and its continuing failure to recognize Black individuality. The politics of repair, of love, constitutes a rethinking of the American community shorn of its anti-human principle of White supremacy. Such a politics includes making available provisions for those who have, thus far, been denied capacity to live fully and freely in the nation. It is to extend the resources available in the United States according to principles that defy White supremacist thinking.

Yet a politics of love also requires repair work done to the aggressive child who has fought tooth and nail to avoid guilty feelings about assaults directed to the parent. Policies and practices insuring African American subordination serves as the vehicle through which the petulant White child refuses to grow up. This child has resisted love by refusing to know of its own interdependence with others. So love through reparations, though self-interested, also serves broad social interests and cements together a world characterized by human connectedness. A politics of reparation, seen in this way, shifts the focus of pathology away from, say, various features of the Black community, the family, or individual. Instead, should the language of pathology be invoked, it is to the White mind, a product of an American history steeped in determination to dominate African Americans.

James Baldwin (1962), the great American essayist, throughout his career embraced this politics of love. In *The Fire Next Time,* he writes:

> Love takes off the masks that we fear we cannot live without and know we cannot live within. I use the word 'love' here not merely in the personal sense but as a state of being, or a state of grace—not in the infantile American sense of being made happy but in the tough and universal sense of quest and daring and growth. And I submit, then, the racial tensions that menace Americans today have little to do with real antipathy—on the contrary, indeed—and are involved only symbolically with color. These tensions are rooted in the very same depths as those from which love springs, or murder. The white man's unadmitted—and apparently to him, unspeakable—private fears and longings are projected onto the Negro.... The price of the liberation of the white people is the liberation of the blacks—the total liberation, in the cities, in the towns, before the law and in the mind....In short, we, the black and the white, deeply need each other here if we are really to become a nation—if we are really, that is, to achieve our identity, our maturity, as men and women. (p. 95–97)

Acknowledgements I am deeply indebted to the encouragement and thoughtful responses to those who have read earlier versions: Nick Bartlett, Marcus Hunter, Arno Mayer, Maria Lymberis, Juliet Rogers, Debora Silverman and Alexander Stein. Thanks, too, to my Research Assistant, Markus Hicks.

Notes

1. There is a long and controversial history, beginning with Freud himself and extending to Critical Theorists as Erich Fromm, Theodore Adorno, Herbert Marcuse, and others who have linked an interpersonal psychoanalysis with social critique. In *Civilization and its Discontents,* Freud (1930), acknowledges the epistemological challenges posed by this gambit from the interpersonal to the collective. In this essay, he asserts the challenges faced by society when forced to powerfully repress both sexual and aggressive instincts inherent in the individuals who comprise it. Freud concludes it remains an unsettled question whether the forces of

love and *eros* might successfully counter the increasing dominance of *thanatal* forces of hatred and aggression. Freud (1930) does not shy away from social analysis based upon his original discoveries of individual psychology. Only by evaluating the usefulness and truthfulness of the analysis, he argues, can one assess psychodynamics' utility for sociology. In that spirit, my analysis proceeds. Does a careful application of psychodynamic evidence to these group processes yield insights and understandings that otherwise would be missed?

2. Freud (1961), in "The Economic Problem of Masochism," describes unconscious guilt as "moral masochism." He discusses the challenge to demonstrate to a patient the presence of "an unconscious sense of guilt." "We may," Freud (1961) writes, "give up the term 'unconscious sense of guilt', which is in any case psychologically incorrect, and speak instead of a 'need for punishment', which covers the observed state of affairs just as aptly." (p. 166).
3. In "The Economic Problem of Masochism," Freud (1961) makes clear that unconscious guilt or moral masochism, unlike conscious conscience, activates libidinal or Oedipal ties to parental figures. Unconscious guilt, when mobilized, represents a regression to sexualized ties and the evocation of loving feelings to those upon whom one needs (p.169–170).
4. Pierre Bourdieu in *Masculine Domination* (1991), makes a similar point in reference to his challenge of analyzing gender relations. He writes, "being included, as man or woman, in the object that we are trying to comprehend, we have embodied the historical structures of the masculine order in the form of unconscious schemes of perception and appreciation. When we try to understand masculine domination we are therefore likely to resort to modes of thought that are the product of domination (p.5)." This difficulty is no less the case when assessing American racial domination. Black and White, in America, do not exist as categories of analysis independently of the racist conviction in the separateness and difference between Blacks and Whites. In this regard, they are thoroughly relational terms describing a hierarchical social relationship of domination, nothing essential to the people themselves.
5. US federal law The Civil Liberties Act of 1988 granted reparations to Japanese Americans who had been interned by the United States government during World War II. Monetary payments were paid to each surviving internee. 82,000 individuals received redress checks. With respect to Indians, the Indian Claims Commission Act of 1946 was established

to adjudicate claims made by Indians to the US Government. Certain tribes succeeded in receiving large money judgments, the ICCA was a disappointment to most claimants. It defined its own mandate very narrowly, relied heavily on technical procedural rulings, and claimed monetary compensation as the only form of reparations. Only financial claims were considered while broadly defined moral claims for redress were nullified (see Newton 1993).

6. US Assemblyman John Conyers, in 1989 *and every year since* has introduced into a bill concerning reparations for African Americans. The Bill does not call for reparations but for a commission "to examine the impact of the nation's 250 years of slavery, and the discrimination that followed, on living Americans. The commission would suggest remedies" (Bogira 2019). The Bill has *never* gotten out of committee and brought to the full House.
7. "*Implicit bias* is the bias in judgment and/or behavior that results from subtle cognitive processes (e.g. implicit attitudes and implicit stereotypes) that often operate at a level below conscious awareness and without intentional control. The underlying implicit attitudes and stereotypes responsible for implicit bias are those beliefs or simple associations that a person makes between an object and its evaluation that 'are automatically activated by the mere presence (actual or symbolic) of the attitude object" (Dovidio et al. 2002, p. 62).
8. See the recommendations by the Economic Policy Institute report "Black-White Wage Gaps Expand with Rising Wage Inequality," September 20, 2016 (Wilson and Rogers) calling for the Bureau of Labor Statistics to work with organizations directly engaged in the education, workforce development, and employment of African Americans to identify the 'unobservable measures' that impact the Black-White wage gap.
9. In a speech to the nation on July 8, 2016, Obama declared "there are biases, some conscious and unconscious, that have to be rooted out." For a classic statement concerning unconscious racism in the law, see Charles R. Lawrence III, "The Id, the Ego and Equal Protection: Reckoning with Unconscious Racism," *Stanford Law Review* 39 (1987): 317–388.
10. Melanie Klein, "Love, Guilt and Reparations [1988]," *Love, Guilt and Reparations and Other Works 1921–1945,* Virago Press, 1988, pgs. 312–313. See also Pumla Gobodo-Madikizela, "Psychological Repair: The Intersubjective Dialogue of Remorse and Forgiveness in the Aftermath of Gross Human Rights Violations," *Journal of the American Psychoanalytic Association* 63:1085–1123.

11. The imposition of Jim Crow laws expressed the intent to separate the White body, perfect and free of imperfections, from the Black body, imperfect and soiled. Its aim was to ensure that White and Black bodies do not touch, nor that bodily fluids should intermingle. Toilets, drinking fountains, swimming pools, public seating, barber and beauty shops, and cemeteries all became legally segregated. The laws were enactments, expressing at its core the struggle by Whites to experience themselves as "civilized," shorn of their "savage nature.". All other features become channeled into the contaminated, dangerous and different—soiled—Black skin and body.
12. Complaints about *micro-aggressions* demonstrate the denial of respect and dignity as felt experiences by members of the Black community. There are many examples offered to expose the fact that for Whites the Black body is fair game for intrusion. African Americans are perceived as subjective extensions of the White mind. On college campuses, Black students report typical encounters of White students casually invading personal space by touching their hair without permission. Elsewhere, "Driving while Black" and "stop and frisk" police actions are instances too of the ease with which Whites feel entitled, perhaps even laced with sadistic pleasure, to invade personal privacy and autonomy. These examples serve as instances of the refusal of American Whites to have established Blacks as external and separate from the White imagination.

References

Alvarado, F., Miller, M. E., & Berman, M. (2016). North Miami Police Shoot Black Man Who Said His Hands Were Raised While He Tried to Help Autistic Group-Home Resident. Retrieved from https://www.washingtonpost.com/news/morning-mix/wp/2016/07/21/fla-police-shoot-black-man-with-his-hands-up-as-he-tries-to-help-autistic-patient/?noredirect=on

Balbus, I. D. (2004). The Psychodynamics of Racial Reparations. *Psychoanalysis, Culture & Society, 9*, 159–185.

Baldwin, J. (1962). *The Fire Next Time*. New York: Vintage International.

Banks, R., Eberhardt, J., & Ross, L. (2006). Discrimination and Implicit Bias in a Racially Unequal Society. *California Law Review, 94*, 1169–1190.

Benjamin, J. (2013). *The Bonds of Love: Psychoanalysis, Feminism, and the Problem of Domination*. New York: Pantheon Press.

Bittker, B. (1973). *The Case for Black Reparations*. New York: Random House.
Blackmon, D. A. (2009). *Slavery by Another Name: The Re-enslavement of Black Americans from the Civil War to World War II*. New York: Doubleday.
Bogira, S. (2019, September 21). It's Time, Finally, to Discuss Reparations for African-Americans. Retrieved from https://www.chicagoreader.com/Bleader/archives/2014/05/28/its-time-finally-to-discuss-reparations-for-african-americans
Bourdieu, P. (1991). *Masculine Domination*. Stanford, CA: Stanford University Press.
Brooks, R. (1999). *When Sorry Isn't Enough: The Controversy Over Apologies and Reparations for Human Injustice*. New York: New York University Press.
Brooks, R. (2004a). *Atonement and Forgiveness: A New Model for Black Reparations*. Berkeley: University of California Press.
Brooks, R. (2004b). Getting Reparations for Slavery Right—Response to Posner and Vermeule 80. *Notre Dame Law Review, 251*, 251–288.
Browne, R. S. (1971). The Economic Basis for Reparations to Black America. *The Review of Black Political Economy, 2*(2), 67–80.
Buffie, N. (2015). The Problem of Black Unemployment: Racial Inequalities Persist Even Amongst the Unemployed: CEPR Blog. Retrieved from http://cepr.net/blogs/cepr-blog/the-problem-of-black-unemployment-racial-inequalities-persist-even-amongst-the-unemployed
Casey, P. M., Warren, R. K., & Elek, J. K. (2012). *Helping Courts Address Implicit Bias: Resources for Education*. National Center for State Courts.
Coates, T. (2014, June). The Case for Reparations. *The Atlantic, 54*, 65.
Collins, C., & Asante-Muhammed, D. (2016, August 10). America's Racial Wealth Divide Is Nothing Short of Shocking. Retrieved from https://ips-dc.org/americas-racial-wealth-divide-nothing-short-shocking/
Dovidio, J. F., Kawakami, K., & Gaertner, S. L. (2002). Implicit and Explicit Prejudice and Interracial Interaction. *Journal of Personality and Social Psychology, 82*(1), 62–68. https://doi.org/10.1037/0022-3514.82.1.62.
Du Bois, W. E. B. (1994). *Souls of Black Folk*. New York: Routledge.
Eberhardt, J., Goff, P. A., Purdie, V. J., & Davies, P. G. (2004). Seeing Black: Race, Crime and Visual Processing. *Journal of Personality and Social Psychology, 87*, 876–893.
Fanon, F. (2008). *Black Skin, White Masks*. New York: Grove Books. (Original work published 1967).
Feagin, J. R. (2004). Documenting the Costs of Slavery, Segregation, and Contemporary Racism: Why Reparations are in Order for African Americans. *Harvard Black Letter Law Journal, 20*, 49–81.

Foner, E. (2002). *Reconstruction: America's Unfinished Revolution, 1883–1877*. New York: Harper Collins.

Freud, S. (1930). *Civilization and Its Discontents. S.E. Vol. XXI*. London: Hogarth Press.

Freud, S. (1961). *The Economic Problem of Masochism. S.E. Volume XIX, 169–170*. London, United Kingdom: Hogarth Press.

Garza, A. (2014). A Herstory of the #BlackLivesMatter Movement by Alicia Garza. Retrieved from https://thefeministwire.com/2014/10/blacklivesmatter-2/

Gobodo-Madikizela, P. (2016). *Psychoanalysis and Reconciliation. The Routledge Handbook of Psychoanalysis in the Social Sciences and Humanities*. London: Routledge.

Gobodo-Madikizela, P. (2016a). Psychological Repair: The Intersubjective Dialogue of Remorse and Forgiveness in the Aftermath of Gross Human Rights Violations. *Journal of the American Psychoanalytic Association, 63*(6), 1085–1123.

Hetey, R. C., & Eberhardt, J. L. (2014). Racial Disparities in Incarceration Increase Acceptance of Punitive Policies. *Psychological science, 25*(10), 1949–1954.

Honneth, A. (1996). Patterns of Intersubjective Recognition: Love, Rights, and Solidarity. In *The Struggle for Recognition: The Moral Grammar of Social Conflicts*, 92–130. Cambridge, MA: MIT Press.

Kang, J., Bennett, M., Carbado, D., Casey, P., Dasgupta, N., Faigman, D., et al. (2012). Implicit Bias in the Courtroom. *UCLA Law Review, 59*, 1124–1186.

Kendi, I. (2016). *Stamped from the Beginning: The Definitive History of Racist Ideas in America*. New York: Nation Books.

Klein, M. (1988). Love, Guilt and Reparations. In M. Klein (Ed.), *Love, Guilt and Reparations and Other Works 1921–1945* (pp. 306–343). London: Virago Press. (Originally published in 1937).

Kull, A. (1995). Rationalizing Restitution. *California Law Review, 83*, 1191–1242.

Lawrence, C. R. (1987). The Id, the Ego, and Equal Protection: Reckoning with Unconscious Racism. *Stanford Law Review, 39*, 317–388.

Newton, N. J. (1993). Compensation, Reparations, & (and) Restitution: Indian Property Claims in the United States. *Georgia Law Review, 28*, 453.

Prager, J. (2008). Healing from History: Psychoanalytic Considerations on Traumatic Pasts and Social Repair. *European Journal of Social Theory, 11*(3), 405–419.

Prager, J. (2014). Melancholia and the Racial Order: A Psychosocial Analysis of America's Enduring Racism. In *The Unhappy Divorce of Sociology and Psychoanalysis* (pp. 284–316). London: Palgrave Macmillan.

Robinson, R. (2001). *The Debt: What America Owes to Blacks*. New York: Penguin.

Surowiecki, J. (2016, October 3). The Widening Racial Wealth Divide. *The New Yorker*. Retrieved from https://www.newyorker.com/magazine/2016/10/10/the-widening-racial-wealth-divide

Swinton, D. H. (1990). Racial Inequality and Reparations. *America, The Wealth of Races, 157*, 40–55.

Texas Department of Housing and Community Affairs v. The Inclusive Communities, Inc., 135 S. Ct. 2507 (U.S., 2015).

United States Department Bureau of Labor Statistics. (2011). *Unemployment Rates by Race and Ethnicity*. Retrieved from https://www.bls.gov/opub/ted/2011/ted_20111005_data.htm

United States National Advisory Commission on Civil Disorders. (1988). *The Kerner Report: The 1968 Report of the National Advisory Commission on Civil Disorders* (1st Pantheon ed.). New York: Pantheon Books

Volkan, V. D. (2014). Enemies on the Couch: A Psychopolitical Journey Through War and Peace. Durham, NC: Pitchstone.

Wilson, V. (2016). African Americans are Paid Less Than Whites at Every Education Level. Retrieved from https://www.epi.org/publication/african-americans-are-paid-less-than-whites-at-every-education-level/

Wilson, V., & Rodgers, W. M., III. (2016). Black-White Wage Gaps Expand with Rising Wage Inequality. *Economic Policy Institute*. Retrieved from http://www.epi.org/publication/black-white-wagegaps-expand-with-rising-wage-inequality/

Winnicott, D. W. (1953). Transitional Objects and Transitional Phenomena—A Study of the First Not-Me Possession. *International Journal of Psycho-Analysis, 34*, 89–97.

Winnicott, D. W. (1955). The Depressive Position in Normal Emotional Development. In *Pediatrics to Psychoanalysis* (pp. 262–277). Collected Papers. New York: Int.

Winnicott, D. W. (1975). Aggression in Relation to Emotional Development. In *Pediatrics to Psycho-Analysis* (pp. 204–218). London: Karnac Books.

Winnicott, D. W. (1988). Interpersonal Relationships. In *Human Nature* (pp. 36–50). Taylor & Francis. New York: Schocken Books.

6

Aesthetics of Memory, Witness to Violence and a Call to Repair

Pumla Gobodo-Madikizela

In the Afterword to the twentieth anniversary of her book, *Unclaimed Experience,* Cathy Caruth suggests that our encounter with survivors' testimonies and with the theory developed from these testimonies evokes questions about how we listen to the "address" of a language that depicts pain and suffering—a language of mourning—and how we respond to "the challenge of traumatic realities that come to us through the wounds of intersecting histories". Answers to these questions, she argues, cannot be identified "with a single voice, nor articulated in a single language" (Caruth 2016, p. 139). Remaining open to this task, however, and enduring the uncertainties of the process is one of the most urgent challenges in the field of humanities, and from this uncertainty, she argues,

P. Gobodo-Madikizela (✉)
Stellenbosch University, Stellenbosch, South Africa

K. Wale et al. (eds.), *Post-Conflict Hauntings*, Palgrave Studies in Compromise after Conflict, https://doi.org/10.1007/978-3-030-39077-8_6

> the theory of trauma addresses us ultimately … with the possibility of life, but in a voice we cannot always identify, and in a language, enigmatic and resonant, that we must still learn to hear. (p. 139)

This final statement of Caruth's Afterword follows a stunning interpretation of the voice/s that depict trauma in her (and Freud's) signature literary story of trauma's re-enactment in Torquato Tasso's *Jerusalem Liberated*. The interpretation seems clearly to convey the "new mode of reading and of listening", which—she suggests in the introduction to her book—is what the trauma testimonies of the pain and suffering of victims demand. In this chapter, I respond to Caruth's address to her readers as an invitation to take a multi-layered, innovative approach to the interpretation of testimony. I explore ways in which the dramatic narrative and bodily dimensions of testimony can be used as a productive site for the exploration of the narrative and symbolic aspects of testimony, and consider the response to trauma testimony from a range of perspectives.

The discussion in this chapter returns to the archive of the Truth and Reconciliation Commission (TRC) of South Africa, and in the tradition followed by some of the scholars whose work has been foundational in the field of literary trauma theory (Caruth 1995, 1996; Tal 1996; Felman and Laub 1992), I shall engage with a select few of the testimonies presented at the TRC's public hearings in order to illuminate unique aspects of the TRC public hearings process and engage an interpretation of the testimonies that can contribute to the ever-growing field of trauma testimony. Exploring new avenues of inquiry from the TRC archive—the appreciation of TRC testimonies and of the unique moments of the TRC process—does not require the presentation of a large number of cases in order to advance theory about trauma testimonies and about other responses to historical trauma (Gobodo-Madikizela 2017). When Dori Laub and his colleagues at Yale University started the Holocaust Survivors Film Project, later known as the Fortunoff Video Archive for Holocaust Testimonies, his original data set was based on *four* interviews. This original set of testimonies has inspired scholarly debates and many theoretical insights have been advanced on trauma testimonies across a range of disciplines.

The discussion in the first part of the chapter looks at unique aspects of trauma's "address" in the context of public testimonies of the TRC process. In this regard, I am interested in how the body becomes a profound form of the language of testimony in the aftermath of gross human rights violations, and I explore new interpretive domains opened up by unique moments of communal responses to trauma testimony that emerged at TRC public hearings. This section of the chapter also considers the question of the "legitimacy" of the voice of the witness and reflects on the argument, advanced by some Holocaust scholars, that only victims who have died can speak authoritatively about the past.

The second part of the chapter examines a different kind of response to gross human rights violations and to testimonies about these traumatic pasts: the problem of denial of responsibility for the past. I explore some of the strategies that have been deployed to avoid accountability for the legacies of historical trauma and suggest the concept "reformative narratives" to describe the discursive strategies that sustain denial among perpetrators and among those who benefitted from apartheid. In my discussion here I point out that the language of forgiveness and reconciliation is too focused on a "goal"—to forgive and/or to reconcile—and I suggest that this does not leave room for engaging with the past and people's role in it more creatively, and instead leaves the door open for denial to thrive. The final section of the chapter explores an alternative way of framing dialogue about the past as "empathic repair". The chapter concludes with a discussion of an example of an artistic response to trauma testimony and a general reflection on the arts as a more promising approach to trauma and violence that can promote acknowledgement and accountability for the past.

1 Trauma Testimony and the Aesthetics of Memory

The problem of traumatic memory in the aftermath of historical traumas such as political violence, genocide and other violations of human rights has increasingly become a focus of scholarship and public attention in recent decades. There is also an emerging global perspective and consciousness around identifying the various manifestations of traumatic memory, not only among the generation of survivors who experienced these traumas directly, but also in subsequent generations, among the descendants of survivors. It is now clear that past traumatic experiences are often re-experienced *as if* the past is happening in the present.

With the publication of the relatively new journal *Psychoanalysis, Culture and Society*, which aims to address the role of psychoanalysis in the social world and in bringing about social justice, it is worth asking why psychoanalysis, a profession known for its individualistic focus, is concerned with shifting its focus to include social and political analysis. The publication of books on trauma as it interacts with history and politics in the late twentieth century (see Caruth 1996; Felman and Laub 1992; LaCapra 2004, 2009), and in the twenty-first (see Davoine et al. 2004) reflects an increasing trend towards recognition of the enduring effects of mass trauma and political violence in society. It is surprising—and perhaps refreshing—that this interest in the social and political after-effect of trauma has spread to include scholars in the psychoanalytic field. They have asked the question whether psychoanalysis might be used as a domain of inquiry that covers the entire scope of experiences of historical trauma (see, for example, Sverre Varvin and Vamik Volkan 2003; Sklar 2011; Oliner 2012; Frosh 2013). Recent analyses by scholars such as Galatzer-Levy (2007), Alford (2008), Murer (2009) and Frosh (2018) highlight this trend towards a socially conscious and socially responsive psychoanalysis in their work that seeks to deepen understanding of the brutal violence of political conflict that often leaves a trail of mass trauma in its aftermath. In this regard, Atkinson (2002), although not using a psychoanalytic lens, is an important voice that draws attention to the transmission of the trauma of colonisation and oppression of Aboriginal Australians across generations. Atkinson links contemporary violence in Australian Aboriginal communities to traumatic past of the parents' generation. Her book is also relevant to the second part of this chapter because she demonstrates how the notion of "healing the past" can be productively extended to identify ways of breaking the vicious cycles of transmission of the past.

An area of inquiry that scholars in the field of trauma have explored is the role of narrative in "working through" and healing trauma. "Testimony" and the importance of the process of narrating trauma in the aftermath of mass trauma and political violence have taken centre stage in the scholarship around trauma in social context. In considering the relationship between testimony and trauma, Felman and Laub (1992) have argued that testimony is one of the most vital responses to historical trauma. Prager (2008; 2011), in a move intended to link these insights directly to the work of the TRC advances a theory of memory that "places the rememberer *squarely in the middle of a world of people and things*, engaged in a continuing effort—sometimes conscious, often unconscious—to reconcile the inner world with a perceived external reality" (p. 83).

There is no doubt that the TRC played a crucial role in the transition stage from apartheid to a democratic South Africa. Victims' stories were pivotal in this process, and witnesses and their families often testified about the important role that the TRC played in their healing journeys. Yet despite the TRC giving victims a public voice, the TRC may have put victims in an "ambiguous position" because, according to Weine (2006), it made victims a vehicle for national reconciliation, which necessitated that victims hold back their pain for the sake of the country's agenda to "move on" and to embrace a reconciliatory ethos. At the same time, however, Weine argues, the voice of the victim is the voice of history: "Seeing the image of the survivor spontaneously giving his or her testimony sends the message that history belongs to survivors themselves" (p. 43). In their testimonies, survivors who suffered under apartheid want acknowledgment of their pain not in order to forget, but rather to reclaim the dignity of the living and the dignity and respect of loved ones who suffered dehumanisation in life and in death. In this sense, then, the testimonies are not only to get the listeners' "affirmation and validation". In several foundational texts on Holocaust testimonies, scholars such as Shoshana Felman and Dori Laub have argued that testimonies are deployed "essentially in order to address another, to impress upon a listener, to appeal to a community". This formulation of the purpose of trauma testimonies gives power to the listener as the one to bestow recognition on survivors and their suffering. If, however, we think of trauma testimonies as victims' assertion of agency and of the dignity of the communities to which they belong, trauma testimonies can be viewed as an important starting point seeking—perhaps even demanding—an ethical response from listeners. The purpose is in order to rid oneself and the collective memory of one's community of the subject position of the dehumanised other, and to wrest away from perpetrators and from the dominant culture the fiat power to destroy one's human spirit. Understood in this way, testimonies seek accountability. Archbishop Tutu aptly called the TRC public hearings process "the third way". It lifted the veil of lies perpetuated under apartheid, offering victims, perpetrators and "implicated others"—to borrow Rothberg's (2019) term—a language to speak about the horrific past.

In this chapter, I am interested not only in the question of how the way we listen to trauma testimonies in our role of witness might illuminate a violent history's impact and the conditions and consequences of the suffering endured by victims and survivors. My interest is also on how listening to trauma testimonies might obscure and conceal a different message conveyed by trauma testimony, one that may allow us to see and hear the testimony as a performative event that enters the prophetic realm, a foretelling of the future.

Anguished testimonies from the TRC hearings may be interpreted as representing a boundary crossing between testimony and performance, and therefore, may be "read" retrospectively as a foretelling of the scenes of violence that have played out repeatedly in contemporary South Africa. The significance of the performative aspects of these testimonies, I will argue, is not only in showing how the body explodes and breaks open a different kind of voice, precisely because of the symbolism it carries, but also how the performative, embodied aspects of testimony can be seen as a reflection of how memory is haunted by repetition. This argument about the prophetic dimension of trauma testimonies is my attempt to think through the current moment of horrific violence witnessed in South Africa, while at the same time contributing new modes of knowledge production in the field of historical trauma. At the same time, I am interested in exploring ways in which a sense of solidarity and responsible citizenship after mass political violence might be restored.

2 Aesthetics of Memory

2.1 Remembering Through the Body

East London, South Africa, April 1996. The Truth and Reconciliation Commission's (TRC) long awaited opening of its public hearings for victims of gross human rights violations begins. The large city hall is capacity-full—all black with the white TRC commissioners and some reporters the only visible white people in the audience. When the audience rose to sing a song that was at once a poem and an anthem of black pain, sung throughout the years of apartheid repression by black people at mass funerals, political rallies and peaceful protests, the song "*Lizalis'idinga lakho Nkosi*" (Fulfil your promise Lord), reverberated into the large hall, carrying the hope that the moment promised. The four widows of "The Cradock Four"[1] are among the witnesses to testify about the murder of their husbands by the apartheid security police. Nomonde Calata, the widow of Fort Calata is given the microphone to tell her story. Her husband was stabbed in the heart four times—as the post-mortem revealed—his body burnt by the apartheid security police in an effort to conceal the hand of the apartheid state in the crime. There is a moment during her testimony when she lets out a scream, wailing her pain, giving voice to it to be heard beyond the walls within which the public hearings are taking place. Imagine that, a piercing scream that seems to shatter the magnificent walls of the East London City Hall, a structure built in colonial times to celebrate Queen Victoria's Diamond Jubilee. When the TRC opens its public hearings, the memorial plaques for some of the fallen British soldiers when the British and the Afrikaners fought to take over South Africa are still displayed on the walls of the City Hall.

The scene of Nomonde Calata's testimony, surrounded by walls that hearken back to an earlier generational time, is a crying out to a past that goes back several generations. The violent movement of her body thrown back as she let out her scream seemed to carry the haunting weight of this past, seemingly expunging it into the TRC's public space of communal remembering. Using her voice and body in this way can be interpreted as a moment that represents at once an expression of anger and pain, a talking back to the past to confront this history that violently took the life of her husband and to expose those responsible for her irreparable loss. Objectified in so many ways as the racial and sexual "other" in order to legitimate the colonial and apartheid order, her testimony shifts the gaze from the object of oppression to shine the light on the depravity of the perpetrators.

When trauma is made visible in this manner, identification with the experiences recounted by trauma witnesses often occurs among those in the audience who have endured similar atrocities. The multiple layers of traumatic violations recounted by Calata—she was in an advanced stage of pregnancy with her youngest daughter when she had to identify the charred remains of her husband—were shared by other women in the audience. The atrocities of apartheid were denied by the former South African government, and thus their social representation was erased through a series of connecting strategies of political repression and manipulation of the news media. Calata's scream gave public voice to that silenced pain.

South African musician Philip Miller (2007) then resurrects this wailing voice from the archives of TRC narratives, producing a music/cry that is picked up by the iconic voice of South African soloist Sibongile Khumalo, who *re-presents* it through her magnificent and electrifying mezzosoprano. Later in the song, several other voices emerge, and merge into a choir, producing a chorus of collective voices, intermingled with the voices of other victims and survivors. Sometimes the victims' voices are dominated by those of perpetrators and their commanders, by their confessions, and their denials. The effect that Philip Miller produces is a seamless repetition that reverberates like a re-enactment of a wound that refuses to be silenced. Calata's reverberating music-cry seems to be telling the audience: This is not yet past—history playing itself out.

I want to argue however, that the language of this trauma goes beyond the repetition compulsion and re-enactment phenomenon. The "address" of this cry can be interpreted as an address that speaks *back* to the past while at the same time telescoping into the future. In its future-oriented voice of address, it is a foretelling of what is as yet to come, a lament about an anguished future. For this formulation I draw from Caruth's work (2016): her argument that trauma is a story of the way in which a person's trauma "is tied up" with the trauma of others, the living and those who may no longer be living and those who come after—the future generations.

It is possible then that Philip Miller's transformation of the cry into a stirring music performance may be his own voice of grief inscribed into Calata's cry. Similarly, the soloist's own performance of the music is another layer of address emanating from Calata's cry, which we may find points to a story of trauma as yet untold. It is a tale of folded-togetherness in which traumatic memories are entangled and shared at a deeper level—by virtue of a history that goes beyond the boundaries of one individual's story of suffering (see Sanders 2002; Steyn 2004; Nuttall 2009) and understanding memory as organised around the past in a way that "binds [people's] most intimate remembrances to each other" (Halbwachs 1992, p. 53), which calls to mind—to invoke Caruth (2016) again—the interpretation of victims' traumatic address as testimonies that convey "wounds of intersecting histories". In this sense then, while it is Calata's individual testimony of her history, however, collective histories come together and intermingle in her cry that now stands as a symbol of both the past and a foretelling of the anguish to come.

Archbishop Desmond Tutu (1999) referred to Calata's scream as "the defining sound that characterised" the TRC as a place where people could open up and cry out what had "remained locked up for so long, unacknowledged, ignored and denied" (p. 114). Tutu opens up the possibility of interesting interpretation of this moment of Calata's scream, given his own breakdown in tears when a male witness described in detail how he was tortured by apartheid security police. Testifying from a wheelchair with visible scars of what was done to him, the man seemed to be reliving the memory of his torture *through* his body as he recounted the torture he suffered. Archbishop Tutu broke down at the precise moment of impossible words, when the witness was struggling to find language to describe what he went through. Tutu's response to Calata's scream, however, was different. After an adjournment following Calata's dramatic scream, and as silence hovered over and covered the hall and the resonance of her piercing cry still reverberating in the collective memory of the audience, Archbishop Tutu sang the question that has been sung by black people throughout the decades of apartheid oppression: *Senzeni na*? (What have we done?). There was something enigmatic about this moment. Archbishop Tutu's singing, with the audience spontaneously following in unison, a reminder of the strong intergenerational connection between Tutu's own relentless struggle against violence, and the stories of pain and suffering recounted in the hall. His singing of the song was itself a witness testimony, a wailing cry of black pain whose resonance was a force that should have woken us up to another truth, that the wordlessness of a scream and the mournful sound of a song connected three generations of struggle—*will it ever end?*—and symbolised an abiding framework not only of a shared memory of the past, but also the telescoping of this past (Faimberg 2005) back to the past and across generations into the future. It symbolised a *presencing* of the future at the moment of testimony, presenting us with the possibility of looking at trauma not as a repetition of the past, but its continuity. Something that is repeated, that is re-enacted suggests a return after a break, say the break between generations. But what is conveyed by this notion of continuity is an enduring trauma that continues ceaselessly. There is no break, no "post".

2.2 The Voices of Living Witnesses: Communal and Reparative Responses

The language of music here is also a form of response inspired by the aesthetics of trauma's address, and as a voice of a "secondary witness"—as LaCapra (1999) refers to others' responses to traumatic testimony—it is incomplete in its representation of the trauma. Agamben (1999), too, has suggested that all testimony always falls short of fully capturing what the experience was like, because it is bearing witness to something that is impossible to bear witness to. But Agamben's argument goes further than simply pointing out the limitations of language in trauma testimony. According to him, the very act of bearing witness to the unspeakable atrocity of the Holocaust—speaking on behalf of the "true" witnesses who can no longer speak—reflects at its core bearing witness to "the impossibility" of witnessing because one is bearing witness "to something that cannot be borne witness to" (p. 34). This metaphor of the impossibility of witnessing appears also in works of other Holocaust scholars, and the idea that the Holocaust is "an event without a witness" (Felman and Laub 1992) has come to be associated with Holocaust studies of testimony and witnessing. Some have interpreted this perspective literally, advancing a perspective that suggests that only victims who have died can speak authoritatively about historical trauma. Yet Elie Wiesel (2008), survivor of Auschwitz in his highly internationally acclaimed memoir, *Night*, recognised the important role of survivor testimonies precisely because they bear witness on behalf of the dead and for the living. Rebuilding societies in the wake of gross human rights violations requires voices of witnesses from all sides of historical trauma to participate in facing the past in order to find ways of breaking the cycles of the violence of denials that aim to silence those who can no longer speak, those who, in Primo Levi's (1988) most dramatically visual metaphor, exist as "the drowned".

There are also different traditions of responding to catastrophe, and these go beyond notions of "secondary" witness and what has been suggested by Laub (1992) that secondary witnesses to trauma testimonies represent a "blank screen" (p. 57). These ideas seem more focused on individualistic responses to trauma testimonies rather than ritualistic responses by groups that subscribe to a more communal and relational ethos. LaCapra (2004) for example, advances an approach to listening and responding to trauma testimony that seems prescriptive. He suggests that an acceptable way of responding to historical trauma is through a "virtual" experience of trauma in which the secondary witness puts themselves in the victim's shoes "while respecting the difference between self and other" (p. 125). This response of "empathic unsettlement", he argues further, is necessary because the "secondary witness" cannot take the victim's place.

The invitation rendered by the aesthetics of memory in the trauma testimonies discussed in this chapter, however, evokes a different kind of response that is premised precisely on the idea that witness*es take the place of the victim* in their individual and collective response to the trauma testimony. This opens up the possibility of others' "encounter" with the original victims' experience and the telling of the story of what victims endured, which makes possible what I have called empathic repair (Gobodo-Madikizela 2008, 2018). Such a response is possible, because firstly, in a context such as the TRC public hearings, the audience of witnesses was comprised mainly of black and white South Africans who had lived through apartheid and either experienced trauma directly and/or were affected by these experiences, or were eye witnesses to traumatic abuses against victims.

Secondly, the social-relational ethos of *Ubuntu* (one's subjectivity being bound up with a community of others—which I will return to and elaborate later in the chapter), is built upon a foundation of interconnected "multi-subjective" relationships that call for accountability for and responsibility towards others in a way that transcends being empathically "unsettled". This interconnected-with-others subject position enables listeners to respond *as if* they were the other, as if they were feeling the same pain felt by the victim. The empathic response then seeks to connect to the victim's emotional state about their experience of the trauma rather than a stance that seeks to maintain a sense of distance from the victim. The possibility of repair—the third point I want to make—occurs in the context of the communal-ritualistic way in which the listeners render their response. When Archbishop Tutu invites a communal response to Nomonde Calata's scream at the TRC with the song *Senzeni Na?*, he is invoking a language that is culturally understood in this context. The communal ritual of spontaneous singing of a mournful song is a time-honoured response in the African cultural context in South Africa and an invitation to share in the suffering of others. This way of understanding the role of listeners in trauma testimony, and hence the possibility of drawing from this knowledge, is in danger of being lost because the dominant canons in the field of trauma testimony continue to inform both theory and practice and have overshadowed other forms of experience.

Philip Miller's engagement with the voices of victims from the TRC archive in his *Rewind: A Cantata for Voice and Testimony* can also be understood as an example of a communal response to historical trauma. Miller creatively illustrates this coming-together-in song around victims' testimonies. The power of the arts is that it goes beyond what is possible in the world of reality, and as Miller's work shows, he creates a chorus of voices in mournful song *as if* the pain belongs to the singers themselves, and at the same time, takes the ritual he has creatively composed to wider audiences where the same call-and-response form of address will unfold through the performance and post-performance dialogues with different audiences where the music has been performed transnationally.

Take, for instance, the testimony at the TRC of John Freeth, a priest of the Anglican Church and one of the clergy who were involved in calling attention to the evils of apartheid. Based on the meticulous recording of events on a particular day of the deployment of the South African Defence Force in one of the black residential areas of Cape Town known as Crossroads, Reverend Freeth's testimony was a detailed account of the collusion of apartheid's army with the 1970s violence that was reported in the media as "black-on-black" violence. Holding the notebook in which he documented the horrific events that unfolded, he read out the details that identified the army trucks with their official registration numbers, the pace at which the trucks were moving through the streets of Crossroads, the number of soldiers in the trucks, specific times at significant moments of the day, and described the murderous rampage of the black vigilante group that was known as the "witdoeke" (because of the white head-scarfs they wore). At one point in his testimony, Freeth described being haunted by the scream of a baby and its mother trapped in their burning home:

> One horrific experience was cries from a shack that was burning. It became clear that in fact there was a baby in there trapped and a desperate mother, and I regret that we were unable to save that baby. The memory of that haunts me still and has come back to me in my dreams in the last few days. (Rev. John Freeth, Cape Town TRC Hearings, 10 June 1997)

Freeth may not have experienced the trauma directly as its victim; however, he stands as a direct witness of what happened, with the authority of his ten-year-old archive of a notebook to back up his witness testimony. He was not only giving the facts. More importantly, he was attesting to the evils of the apartheid government through its army, and the destructive and sinister agenda in perpetuating the "black-on-black" violence narrative. The groups of "witdoeke", who seemingly were supported by the army, were carrying sticks, knives, panga's, axes, metal bars and similar weapons of destruction. His testimony was full of visual imagery, giving his narrative an aesthetic frame, which had an enduring quality in its impact on us as listeners. Consider this description of a man he found dying in the streets of Crossroads and the place where he found him:

> There is an entrance to the soccer stadium there, and there is also some sort of bus shelter, I think. He was lying on his back, naked from his waist up. There was no way of identifying him, but as I knelt beside him, I took my anorak off and put it over him and tried to render assistance. (Rev. John Freeth, TRC testimony, June 1997)

Trauma testimony is not supposed to be this clearly detailed and following a chronological order of events. We are getting the full story here—no filling of the "missing pieces" that Codde (2010) has written about in relation to the mediated accounts that the third generation descendants of survivors of the Holocaust get. Clearly, Rev. Freeth's narrative was not based on traumatic memory where witnesses' testimonies involve an attempt to transform the memory that exists only in visual images and visceral sensations into narrative form, but rather on an archival document that he created at the time of the tragic events he was recounting. Yet even so, one wonders whether giving testimony may not have been a kind of "working through" of this past for him in a similar way that narrating traumatic experience sometimes serves the purpose of working through trauma for direct victims. There is also the possibility that he may have been facing, or confronted with the trauma "belatedly"—in Caruth's (2016)—parlance. It is one thing to document traumatic events as they unfold moment-by-moment and to produce a written archive that is stored away. It is quite another to give oral testimony of these events many years later. Already, we know that Rev. Freeth experienced nightmares about the cries of the mother and child he was powerless and unable to save when he had to reconnect with his notebook archive in preparation for his TRC testimony. Here again, he alludes to the traumatic impact of his encounter with the dying man on the streets of Crossroads, again recounting the moment with imagery, and this time evoking both visceral sensations and visual imagery:

> I *remember* the warm blood on my hands. I put my hand on his head and prayed for him. And then I saw that he had a deep slash in the neck and in fact his head moved slightly to one side without his body moving and opened up this deep gash. (Rev. John Freeth, my italics)

The visceral sensation of the memory of the warm blood on his hands is evocative. The past is an embodied psychic reality for many people whose lives are marked by histories of violence. For Freeth, reading his own archive re-evokes the mental landscapes of the scenes of the violence he meticulously recorded, and the past is a felt, embodied memory. Something happens when one reads the text of a traumatic account that one has written. The written narrative has been put away with no opportunity for it to be heard by a listening audience. The validation of a testimony by others is what gives the testimony an edge, but it may also re-awaken and give form to what may have been hidden or pushed below the surface of consciousness. I have found resonance with this idea in insights from Lawrence Langer (1989), who has worked extensively with both written and oral testimonies of the Holocaust. Written texts of trauma testimony are "meaningless" without readers to hear it and to respond to it, Langer has argued. Giving oral testimony

> is the only chance [victims] have to move from invisible silence to visible expression …. [O]ral testimony gains validity from viewer response, from the search for a principle of organization concealed in the narrative that even the witness may not be conscious of. (Langer 1989, p. 311)

The voices of living witnesses are crucial, because the future belongs to the living. The truth about the past cannot be known without these witnesses' accounts. Their role is not only to remind us about how victims suffered, but also, perhaps crucially, to tell us about the depravity of the perpetrators. This, for me, is the essence of Rev. Freeth's testimony, providing a detailed eye witness account of the perverse nature of the cruelty of the system of apartheid in the name of "maintaining law and order". And on this point, and finally on the illustration of the critical significance of the voices of the living, Rev. Freeth's testimony showed that there are faces of human beings behind "the system" of apartheid. He tried several times to get help from the soldiers, waving at an army vehicle to stop, which he said was moving slowly past where he stood next to the badly injured man. At one point, he had eye contact with the driver. "[I]t was quite clear that he had seen me and seen the man and he just drove on. I couldn't believe it because here was a man dying." Freeth then ran to the clinic and returned with medical staff, but nothing could be done. "[T]hat man died in my arms", he said. He was later arrested and taken to prison. There he addressed a police officer, asking him why they had arrested him: these hands have held a dying man today, he told the police officer. "I have simply witnessed events and not committed a crime." Freeth wanted him to see the absurdity of his arrest, which was an appeal not just to his rational sense, but also to whatever moral sensibilities he might have. The police officer's response opens a small window into understanding how notions of "the enemy" are constructed, and shows the possibility of a shift from this perspective. Concluding his testimony, Freeth told the commission the response of the police officer he had confronted with the absurdity of arresting him, "his eyes fell, and after a few moments of silence he said you are free to go. That really concludes my evidence about the 9th of June [1986]."

2.3 The Problem of Denial of the Past

Confronting perpetrators at TRC hearings created horizon moments that oriented the country towards a future in which, it was hoped, there would no longer be denial or justification of the past. This was the public value of Rev. John Freeth's testimony, to expose the apartheid state's hand in the destruction that wreaked murderous havoc in black residential areas. The public exposure of perpetrators at the TRC, according to human rights scholar Michael Ignatieff (1996), reduced the number of lies that can be perpetuated about apartheid and go unchallenged.

We found out, too, that not all perpetrators rose to the challenge of truth telling. For example, the apartheid-era politician Clive Derby-Lewis, who was responsible for the assassination of the much-loved Chris Hani, the former head of the ANC military wing, invoked his Christian faith at his TRC public hearing as justification for the killing: "we as

Christians are told that it is our duty to fight the anti-Christ in whichever way we can". In this narrative strategy, expressions of accountability are inverted by simultaneously shifting blame away from the self in order to project it externally, often onto the victim or survivor. Remorse is unlikely to emerge under these conditions. This kind of splitting—a common psychological defence mechanism that "hides" unwanted parts of the self from awareness—has been observed frequently among white South Africans. Acknowledgment of complicity with apartheid is rare. Even when a window opens to acknowledge complicity, another may close, shutting out the rising tide of shame and guilt that threatens to engulf the subject. Constant confrontation with one's complicity—through the daily exposure to the legacies of apartheid in the lives of black South Africans and the reality of inherited privilege—exerts an intolerable toll at a deep psychological level. To deal with the force of these uncomfortable emotions, a more subtle form of denial emerges. Speech acts like those performed by Derby-Lewis's "we Christians" statement are deployed to "efface" the feeling of personal responsibility. This is dramatically illustrated in the statement heard repeatedly from some white South Africans: "The ANC government's policies of affirmative action are more racist than apartheid was." This perversion of the term *racist* is encountered frequently in post-apartheid South Africa. I have referred to this rhetorical strategy as "reformative narratives", narratives that are used to hide from the reality of one's past and to soften the intrapsychic blow occasioned by feelings of shame and guilt (Safier and Gobodo-Madikizela 2014). Overwhelmed by shame because of their association with apartheid oppression as beneficiaries of apartheid privilege, some whites find facing the past too much to bear. This leaves little room for acknowledging the pain of others and empathic concern for the continuities of apartheid oppression in the contemporary life of its victims and survivors. "White denial" of apartheid hinders the necessary process of redress and repairing the past.

3 Acknowledgement and Reparative Work in Humanism

The dialogic space of the TRC would often engender affective attunement with the victims' pain and suffering. Instead of denial and a foreboding feeling of fear, guilt and shame about the past, a feeling of containment sometimes engenders deeper awareness of the legacies of historical violence and enables acknowledgement and a sense of accountability that opens up the possibility of connecting with the plight of victims of historical trauma. A key factor in the emergence of this awareness on the part of beneficiaries of apartheid privilege and of perpetrators is the willingness of victims to maintain an invitational stance of openness, reaching out to the perpetrator with a gesture of promise that the process of facing the past is about building community. Thus, the victim holds the space of promise, inviting the perpetrator not as the "monster" marked by his evil, but rather as a human being who has the capacity for expressing acknowledgment for the pain he has caused, based on a clear sense of appreciation and understanding of what the victim has gone through. It is the only way out of the denial of history's violence. This enables perpetrators genuinely to confront their guilt. For, while we are separated by our pasts, our pasts also connect us, opening up a space for the potential emergence of unexpected human moments.

In restorative dialogue encounters in Rwanda and South Africa in the aftermath of genocide and apartheid-era crimes against humanity, victims have sometimes been moved to express forgiveness for perpetrators. As I have pointed out in the earlier section of the chapter, when victims and perpetrators live together in the same country—and sometimes as neighbours as they do in Rwanda—the transformative possibilities that play out in victim-perpetrator dialogue processes emerge in part because of victims' openness to a conciliatory stance for the sake of a transformed moral community. This means that the "responsibility" for the possibility of perpetrators' remorse may lie with victims themselves. Inspired by a sense of moral imagination—a reparative vision to engage in dialogue with one's former enemies in order to (re)build a moral community—sometimes victims provide a "holding" environment (Winnicott 1960) that allows the perpetrator to face their shame and to experience a sense of remorse. The dialogic context that is established thus becomes a facilitative environment in which a perpetrator feels less threatened, inspiring in them an ethical impulse that may obviate the need to hide from their shame and guilt. This is the "paradox of remorse", because while the perpetrator's actions create a chasm between them and the world of victims, their expression of remorse changes the intersubjective context, bringing closeness between victim and perpetrator by virtue of their readiness for re-admission to a shared moral community.

In this context, forgiving develops as a transformative lament that goes beyond the expression of words of forgiveness as a response to an apology in an interpersonal encounter. What lies "beyond" the forgiveness is a certain level of care for the perpetrator, an investment in the hope that the perpetrator may become a better human being. I encountered this wish to care for the perpetrator beyond forgiveness in my earlier research on forgiveness with women who had expressed forgiveness for perpetrators following their confessions at the TRC. The empathic response of the victim is imbued with a quality of wishing to "rescue" the remorseful perpetrator, as if to affirm their identity as a member of the human community (instead of a "monster" or "evil one"). This desire to rescue the perpetrator, I argue, constitutes the fundamental moment, a pivotal point in the intersubjective context in which forgiving feelings emerge.

The word forgiveness, I argue further, is the wrong word for describing what unfolds in these victim-perpetrator encounters. Forgiveness seems to suggest a fixed position, or a coming to an end—"I offer you forgiveness so that I can have closure and move on." There is a subtext here that seems to signify an act of leaving something behind, moving on without looking back. But I think that the act of forgiving in these post-conflict contexts is the opening of a new chapter, rather than closure as such. It involves a complex matrix of emotional and reflective dynamics that interact in a relational process that engages reciprocal recognition of the other's humanity, acknowledging the reality of the other's emotional condition in a way that creates pathways to caring for the other as a fellow human being. The quite obvious observation I am making here is that engaging in dialogue about the past is a multi-faceted terrain. In considering encounters between victims/survivors and perpetrators of gross human rights violations, what is perhaps necessary is shifting the lens from a focus on forgiveness and reconciliation (concepts that imply a goal) to "experience" (complicated, enigmatic, muddy, elusive and unpredictable), because I think that much of what happens in these encounters remains implicit, and the word "forgiveness" falls short of adequately capturing this complexity.

I have suggested that "empathic repair" captures more effectively the complexity of this dialogic process. The significance of the notion of "the reparative" lies in the fact that the work of healing after historical trauma must necessarily be an on-going process. "Reparative" suggests movement, an engagement in a constant search for the emergence of human moments that can create a sense of solidarity and transcend old dividing lines that promote othering. The quest for reparative humanism gestures towards transformative moments and new relational experiences. The goal is to recognise the humanity of victims and perpetrators alike for the sake of a transformed conception of society in order to help heal historical ruptures. This way of thinking about "the Other", even an other responsible for one's pain, arises out of concern for the broader societal goals of national healing, which advocate care and what Emanuel Levinas terms "responsibility for the Other". I want to suggest that the legacy of Nelson Mandela, and the work of the TRC that his leadership inspired, made it possible to imagine these moments of empathic repair. Nelson Mandela embodied the reparative ethical consciousness. It was a principled commitment to an ethic of care for the Other based on values founded in the relational framework of *Ubuntu*. Such a framework requires commitment to a stance of moral imagination, and to a certain intentional openness that reaches out beyond the self and towards others. Mandela's name became a symbol of this ethical vision of the self-transcendent position—a metaphor pointing to a more general horizon of an ethics of care, responsibility and accountability for building solidarity.

It is worth noting that *Ubuntu* was foundational in the legal framework that provided guidelines for the establishment of the TRC. The granting of amnesty was outlined in the post-amble of the Interim of the South African Constitution of 1993 in the section "National Unity and Reconciliation": past violations of human rights should be "addressed on the basis that there is a need for understanding but not for vengeance, a need for reparation but not for retaliation, a need for *Ubuntu* but not for victimisation. In order to advance such reconciliation and reconstruction, amnesty shall be granted in respect of acts, omissions and offenses associated with political objectives and committed in the course of the conflicts of the past."

The concept of *Ubuntu* is an ethic based on the understanding that one's subjectivity is inextricably intertwined with that of others in one's community. From the perspective of *Ubuntu*, all people are valued as part of the human community and worthy of being so recognised. This entails not blind acceptance of others, no matter what they do, but rather an orientation of openness to others and a reciprocal caring that fosters a sense of solidarity with others—the individual always in relation to others—rather than individual autonomy. The meaning of *Ubuntu* is best captured in the Xhosa expression *Umntu ngumntu ngabanye abantu*. Loosely translated, this means "a person is a person through other people". In other words, a person is a person through being witnessed by, and engaging in reciprocal witnessing of other persons. Alternatively, human subjectivity is defined by the multiplicity of relationships with others and through reciprocal mutual recognition of the others' human dignity.

The meaning conveyed by the expression is twofold. First, human subjectivity depends on being witnessed; the richness of subjectivity flows from interconnectedness with the wider community, and from the reciprocal caring and complementarity of human relationships. Second, the phrase conveys the kind of reciprocity that calls on people to be ethical subjects. Mutual recognition inspired by *Ubuntu* is fundamental to being a fellow human being, a relational subject in the context of community. A person with *Ubuntu* "is open and available to others, is affirming to others … My humanity caught up, is inextricably bound up, in yours" (Tutu 1999, p. 31).

Ubuntu allows entry into the other's life in a way that makes it possible to reconstitute the other's experience within the self. In this sense then, recognition is not simply recognition of the physical face of the other—it may not even be about the other's physical presence. Rather, it is about something more subtle, less visible than any of the physical elements of the encounter. In contrast to the Cartesian philosophy of "I think therefore I am", which positions the self at a distance from the Other, this is a stance that allows the self to feel the Other, and to stand within the Other's historical circumstances in order to connect with the Other through a shared humanity across time and space. While forgiveness may operate from a distance—it is "given to"—reparative humanism engages with an Other. Reparative humanism is grounded in mutual recognition and shared experience of humanity with the other. Reparative humanism allows for points of identification, entryways into the experience of others, which enable comparison across critical registers of difference. Animosity, hatred and anger at perpetrators for the destruction and pain they have caused arise out of love for one's loved ones against whom gross human rights violations were committed. The same factors that can ignite and perpetuate animosity and vengeance—the love for those killed or maimed by the perpetrator—might also suspend those negative sentiments by refusing to give in to destructive feelings in their name. By providing a way into the experience of the "enemy", reparative humanism provides a way out of violence. Ultimately, the reciprocal mutuality of reparative humanism enables restoration of social bonds in a way that constantly opens up new relational possibilities in the aftermath of violence. In the final section of this chapter, I turn to the arts to show how visual arts, as a response to historical trauma and as an ethical act of witness can become a platform for dialogues of social repair.

4 The Role of the Arts: *An Illustration*

"The Blue Dress" by Judith Mason depicts the story of the anti-apartheid activist Phila Ndwandwe, who was abducted by the security police, stripped naked and tortured before she was killed and her lifeless body thrown in an unmarked grave on the Elandskop Dairy Farm near Pietermaritzburg in the Kwa-Zulu Natal province of South Africa, a secret farm run by the apartheid government's covert operations unit. According to the testimony of her killers, Phila Ndwandwe was held naked in a concrete chamber and tortured for ten days. At the TRC hearings, her torturers recounted her defiant refusal to turn against her comrades, and described how they blindfolded her and made her walk from the torture chamber to the site where they shot her. When Ndwandwe's remains were exhumed, she was found lying in a foetal position with a single bullet wound to the top of her head. Her pelvis was covered with scraps from a blue supermarket plastic bag that had been fashioned in the shape of a pair of underwear. Ndwandwe may have found the scraps of plastic in the room in which she was interrogated, and used them to cover her "private parts". The artist, Judith Mason, wept as she listened on her radio to Ndwandwe's story as told by her killers on the live broadcast of the public hearings of the Truth and Reconciliation Commission in November 1996. This is the story that captured Mason's imagination, and she was inspired to tell Phila Ndwandwe's story creatively through her artwork, "The Blue Dress". Judith Mason's "Blue Dress" features in the central panel a sculpture of a long flowing dress stitched from pieces of blue plastic and ornamented with several lines of text painted on its hemline (Fig. 6.1).

Fig. 6.1 Judith Mason's *Blue dress* (1998), Centre Piece. Collection: Art of the Constitutional Court, South Africa. A triptych

Fig. 6.2a *Blue dress,* Panel I

The exterior panels are oil paintings of a blue dress in perfect (dis) embodied pose. To the right and behind each of the (dis)embodied dress-images is an animal caged by what looks like a fence in a honeycomb pattern. In the first panel (Fig. 6.2a), the animal appears to have torn off a piece of the blue dress, which it is dragging on one of its front feet. In the third panel (Fig. 6.2b), the animal appears to be lunging forward in attack mode with open mouth bearing its teeth, but it is trapped behind the fence. In the foreground of the third panel are three glowing braziers towards which the dress, without a physical body, appears to be moving, and a glowing mug positioned in front of the animal but out of its reach.

Fig. 6.2b *Blue dress,* Panel III

The image of the blue dress in the first exterior panel (Fig. 6.2a) is poised and in motion, suggesting elegant defiance in face of the threat posed by the predator. In the second exterior panel (Fig. 6.2b), Mason portrays the same flair of confidence, accentuated again by the graceful movement forward, leaving the predator behind, its face of evil visible, but trapped behind the fence and disempowered. The central sculpture of "The Blue Dress" (Fig. 6.1) is made of discarded blue plastic bags that Mason collected and sewed into a dress. It stands as a statement, both metaphorically and literally, of the triumph of Ndwandwe's dignity over the depravity of her captors. In a letter painted on the skirt's hem, Mason wrote:

> Sister, a plastic bag may not be the whole armour of God, but you were wrestling with flesh and blood. And against powers, against the rulers of darkness, against spiritual wickedness in sordid places. Your weapons were your silence and a piece of rubbish. Finding that bag and wearing it until you were disinterred is such an ordinary act. … Memorials to your courage are everywhere; they blow about in the streets, drift on the tide, and cling to thorn-bushes. This dress is made from some of them.

Mason's letter, a voice that resonates from the basement of her art studio to connect with the "voice" of a woman from a world separated from hers by the laws of apartheid, emerges as a symbol of solidarity, or at least the *possibility* of solidarity. She takes Ndwandwe's story out of the private realm into the public and political sphere, evoking gendered, racial, sexual and collective identifications. Discarded supermarket plastic bags that drift into all corners of the war-ravaged cities of "post"-conflict countries on the African continent, and in squatter homes that have mushroomed in and around the cities—or what's left of these cities—after wars and violent conflict, are a common sight. Mason imbues these discarded pieces of rubbish with symbolic meaning, redefining them as memorial fragments dotting the landscape of the war-ravaged African continent. Their ubiquitous presence symbolises the pervasive violence enacted on women's bodies, humiliated bodies, bodies that succumb to violence and those that withstand it, bodies targeted during wars and bodies targeted in peacetime, bodies shaped by history and politically inscribed. The shape and movement of "The Blue Dress" evoke the presence of a living female body, a present absence that couples the living and the dead in a significant way that resonates in the post-conflict context of women in other parts of the African continent—in the Liberian city of Monrovia, in Freetown, Sierra Leone, Kinshasa in the Democratic Republic of Congo, in Rwanda, Namibia and in the innumerable "informal settlements" that have emerged in post-apartheid South Africa.

Mason's *Blue Dress,* although an art form, recounts the experiences of thousands of South Africans who were tortured and suffered severely and their lives destroyed under apartheid. According to the report of the Truth and Reconciliation Commission (the TRC), which studied South Africa's violent years from 1960 to the fall of apartheid in the start of the 1990s, thousands of TRC testimonies described the scale of the destruction, breakdown of family bonds through loss of family and loved ones, extreme personal suffering and the magnitude of the rupture of dreams and fracturing of futures was sometimes staggering.

Art—such as Judith Mason's *Blue Dress*—offers a powerful means for recounting the past and *re*-presenting the voices of victims heard at TRC hearings—presenting them again for a deeper appreciation of the stories and the anguish experienced by the people who told these stories. Art's imagination brings to life and confronts the living with the haunting presence of the dead. Theodor Adorno's (1983) famous aphorism that "to write poetry after Auschwitz is barbaric" (p. 34) was not intended to be a dictum that negates the importance of representation after historical trauma. Representational images of violence that have been created to help societies come to terms with their pasts, are commonplace—from memorials, to visual art, fiction, film and theatre in Latin America, Kosovo, Northern Ireland, and many other countries that have suffered civil wars. Art is a visual conscience of society and art has played an important role in helping societies to find language to face their violent histories. Adorno (1974) would later clarify his position on the critical role of the arts as a medium through which victims can express their suffering: "Perennial suffering has as much right to expression as a tortured man has to scream; hence it may have been wrong to say that after Auschwitz you could no longer write poems" (Adorno 1974, p. 362).

5 Conclusion

The question of how to respond to historical trauma and to its victims' testimonies leads to another question: what does it mean to live together after so much violence, tragedy and loss? How do perpetrators live with the memory of their murderous deeds, and what does it mean for victims to continue living with the memory of what they have lost? These are questions that Adorno was wrestling with in the aftermath of WWII and the horrors of the Holocaust. In considering this question in the context of post-apartheid South Africa, and perhaps places like Rwanda where victims and perpetrators have to live in the same country, it seems clear that once people, even those who are adversaries, are faced with each other, innumerable possibilities—both destructive and restorative and all that cannot be reduced to these oversimplified categories—arise, both "within" and "between" people living together and trying to rebuild their society. The potential for the unexpected, unforeseen and thoroughly creative response, endemic to the human condition is always present. These are precisely the ideas that were embodied in the TRC, which was nothing less than an effort to imbue the realms of law, justice and politics with a relational cultural ethics of *Ubuntu* that recognised the possibility of a sense of shared humanity among victims, perpetrators and beneficiaries of privilege for the sake of a transformed conception of society.

Note

1. Four anti-apartheid activists from Cradock in the Eastern Cape of South Africa ("the Cradock Four"). They were murdered by apartheid security police and their charred bodies found in the outskirts of Cradock.

References

Adorno, T. W. (1974). *Negative Dialectics*. London: Routledge.

Adorno, T. W. (1983). Cultural Criticism and Society. In *Prisms*, 17–34. Cambridge, MA: MIT Press.

Agamben, G. (1999).*Remnants of Auschwitz: The Witness and the Archive*, trans. Daniel Heller-Roazen, New York: Zone Books.

Alford, F. (2008). Why Holocaust Testimony Is Important, and How Psychoanalytic Interpretation Can Help…But Only to a Point. *Psychoanalysis, Culture, and Society, 13*(3), 221–239.

Atkinson, J. (2002). *Trauma Trails, Recreating Song Lines: The Transgenerational Effects of Trauma in Indigenous Australia*. Melbourne: Spinifex Press.

Caruth, C. (Ed.). (1995). *Trauma: Explorations in Memory*. Baltimore: Johns Hopkins University Press.

Caruth, C. (1996). *Unclaimed Experience: Trauma, Narrative, and History*. Baltimore: Johns Hopkins University Press.
Caruth, C. (2016). *Unclaimed Experience: Trauma, Narrative, and History*. Baltimore, MD: John Hopkins University Press.
Codde, P. (2010). Postmemory, Afterimages, Transferred Loss: First and Third Generation Holocaust Trauma in American Literature and Film. In S. Rohr & S. Komor (Eds.), *The Holocaust, Art, and Taboo: Transatlantic Exchanges on the Ethics and Aesthetics of Representation* (Vol. 189, pp. 63–74). Heidelberg, Germany: Universitätsverlag Winter.
Davoine, F., Gaudillière, J., & Fairfield, S. (2004). *History Beyond Trauma*. New York: Other press.
Faimberg, H. (2005). *The Telescoping of Generations: Listening to the Narcissistic Links Between Generations*. London: Routledge.
Felman, S., & Laub, D. (1992). *Testimony: Crises of Witnessing in Literature, Psychoanalysis, and History*. New York: Routledge.
Frosh, S. (2013). *Hauntings: Psychoanalysis and Ghostly Transmissions*. London: Palgrave Macmillan.
Frosh, S. (2018). Rethinking Psychoanalysis in the Psychosocial. *Psychoanalysis, Culture & Society, 23*(1), 5–14.
Galatzer-Levy, B. (2007). Reparation and Reparations: Towards a Social Psychoanalysis. *Psychoanalysis, Culture & Society, 12*(3), 226–241.
Gobodo-Madikizela, P. (2008). Trauma, Forgiveness and the Witnessing Dance: Making Public Spaces Intimate. *Journal of Analytical Psychology, 53*, 169–188.
Gobodo-Madikizela, P. (2017). Response to Commentaries. *Journal of the American Psychoanalytic Association, 65*(2), 251–263.
Halbwachs, M. (1992). *On Collective Memory* (Lewis Coser, Trans.). Chicago: University of Chicago.
Ignatieff, M. (1996). Articles of Faith. *Index on Censorship, 25*(5), 110–122.
La Capra, D. (1999). Trauma, Absence, Loss. *Critical Inquiry 25*(4), 696–727.
LaCapra, D. (2001). *Writing History, Writing Trauma*. Baltimore: Johns Hopkins University Press.
LaCapra, D. (2004). *Representing History Representing Trauma*. Ithaca: Cornell University Press.
La Capra, D. (2009). *History and its Limits: Human, Animal, Violence*. Ithaca: Cornell University Press.
Langer, L. (1989). Interpreting Oral and Written Holocaust Texts. In M. Johnson & M. Stern Strom (Eds.), *Facing History and Ourselves: Elements of Time* (pp. 310–316). Boston: Facing History and Ourselves National Foundation.

Laub, D. (1992). Bearing Witness or the Vicissitudes of Listening. In S. Felman & D. Laub (Ed.), *Testimony: Crises of Witnessing in Literature, Psychoanalysis, and History* (pp. 57–74). New York, NY: Routledge.

Levi, P. (1988). *The Drowned and the Saved.* (trans: Rosenthal, R.). London: Abacus.

Miller, P. (2007). *Rewind: A Cantata for Voice, Tape and Testimony*. Cape Town: P. Miller.

Murer, J. S. (2009). Constructing the Enemy-Other: Anxiety, Trauma and Mourning in the Narratives of Political Conflict. *Psychoanalysis, Culture & Society, 14*, 109–130.

Nuttall, S. (2009). *Entanglement: Literary and Cultural Reflections on Post-apartheid.* Johannesburg: Wits University Press.

Oliner, M. (2012). *Psychic Reality in Context: Perspectives on Psychoanalysis, Personal History, and Trauma*. London: Karnac Books.

Prager, J. (2008). Healing from History: Psychoanalytic Considerations on Traumatic Pasts and Social Repair. *European Journal of Social Theory, 11*, 405–419.

Prager, J. (2011). Danger and Deformation: A Social Theory of Trauma. *American Imago, 68*(3), 425–448.

Rothberg, M. (2019). *The Implicated Subject: Beyond Victims and Perpetrators.* Stanford University Press.

Safier, R., & Gobodo-Madikizela, P. (2014). Conversation Between Ruth Safier and Pumla Gobodo-Madikizela on "Remembering the Past: Nostalgia, Traumatic Memory, and the Legacy of Apartheid". *Peace and Conflict: Journal of Peace Psychology, 20*(1), 95–99.

Sanders, M. (2002). *Complicities: The Intellectual and Apartheid.* Durban: University of Kwa-Zulu Natal Press.

Sarkin, J. (2004). *Carrots and Sticks: The TRC and the South African Amnesty Process*. Antwerp: Intersentia. Shea, 2000.

Sklar, J. (2011). *Landscapes of the Dark: History, Trauma, Psychoanalysis.* London: Karnac.

Steyn, M. (2004). Rehabilitating a Whiteness Disgraced: Afrikaner White Talk in Post-Apartheid South Africa. *Communication Quarterly, 52*(2), 143–169.

Tal, K. (1996). *Worlds of Hurt: Reading the Literatures of Trauma*. New York: Cambridge University Press.

Tutu, D. (1999). *No Future without Forgiveness*. London: Image.

Varvin, S., & Volkan, V. (2003). *Violence or Dialogue: Psychoanalytic Insights on Terrorism*. London: The International Psychoanalytical Association.

Wiesel, E. (2008). *Night*. London: Penguin.
Winnicott, D. (1960). The Theory of the Parent-Child Relationship. *International Journal of Psychoanalysis, 41*, 585-595.
Weine, S. (2006). *Testimony After Catastrophe: Narrating the Traumas of Political Violence*. Evanston, IL: Northwestern University Press.

Part II

Local Expressions of Collective Haunting and Healing

7

Haunting and Transitional Justice: On Lives, Landscapes and Unresolved Pasts in Northern Ireland

Cheryl Lawther

1 Introduction

Building on approaches to ghosts and haunting by Avery Gordon and Jacques Derrida, this chapter is concerned with practices of haunting and ghosting after conflict-related loss. This is not to suggest a focus on the occult or the paranormal, but to use these phenomena as a prism through which to understand the intersection between unresolved pasts and the transmission of trauma post-conflict. At first blush, the field of transitional justice—the overarching term for recognising and addressing a legacy of large-scale past human rights violations—may appear to have little in common with notions of ghosting or haunting. I would, however, argue that the opposite is true: ghosts can be key to understanding how the

The fieldwork on which this chapter is based was made possible by the award of an Arts and Humanities Research Council Early Career grant—AH/N001451/1—"Voice, Agency and Blame: Victimhood and the Imagined Community in Northern Ireland".

C. Lawther (✉)
School of Law, Queen's University Belfast, Belfast, UK
e-mail: c.lawther@qub.ac.uk

K. Wale et al. (eds.), *Post-Conflict Hauntings*, Palgrave Studies in Compromise after Conflict, https://doi.org/10.1007/978-3-030-39077-8_7

effects of mass murder, genocide, slavery or colonial oppression extend far beyond the moment of atrocity to engender trauma that echoes for generations (Schwab 2010; Schindel 2014). Likewise, the work of truth, justice, accountability and memory is precisely about responding to the unsettled ghosts of the past and their presence amongst the living. Indeed, Archbishop Desmond Tutu was a powerful advocate of the South African Truth and Reconciliation Commission because of his hope that it would tackle the problem of the past's "uncanny habit of returning to haunt one" and its refusal to "lie down quietly" (TRC Report vol 1, 7). Conversely, writing about the cultural memory of Soviet terror, Alexander Etkind (2009) argues that Russian civil society is haunted by the "unquiet ghosts" of the unburied Soviet past.

The ghost, according to Avery Gordon (1997, 63), "is the principle form by which something lost or invisible or seemingly not there makes itself known or apparent to us". She proposes that we do not think of ghosts as representations of missing or dead persons, but as "inarticulate experiences" and "haunting reminders" of the violence and complex social relations in which we live (Gordon 1997, 25). They offer a glimpse of "the fundamental difference between the world we have now and the world we could have had instead" (Gordon 1997, 127). For Derrida (1994), the spectre is the conveyor of legacies and demands from the dead. To live with, talk to and about ghosts, Derrida (1994, xviii) proposes, is all done "in the name of justice". This engagement with ghosts involves a politics of mourning, of memory and of inheritances that allows for a diversity of relations to the past (Wilke 2010). Reckoning with ghosts—through processes of truth recovery or reparations, for example—therefore does not negate the past but remains focused on what transitional justice can offer in the present "[b]ecause ultimately haunting is about how to transform a shadow of a life into an undiminished life whose shadows touch softly in the spirit of a peaceful reconciliation" (Gordon 1997, 208; Wilke 2010).

In this chapter, I argue for three conceptualisations of haunting when past traumas remain unaddressed—the haunting of lost lives, the haunting of landscapes and the haunting of the unresolved past. This conceptualisation demands that we, for example, see haunting as an animated state in which repressed or unresolved social violence is making itself known and see place-memory as capable of embodying ghosts and haunting reminders of the past (Robinson 2017). As Gordon (1997) argues, haunting and the appearance of spectres or ghosts is one way in which we are notified that what has been concealed, repressed or remains unanswered is very much alive and present with the potential for personal, social and political disruption. Ghosts thus prohibit the separation of the past, the present and the future. The chapter focuses on Northern Ireland, a post-conflict society described as being haunted by a "conflict calendar in which every day is an anniversary" (Rowan 2012). There, the dead remain a potent and emotive means of legitimising and perpetuating the ethnonational and sectarian characteristics of political debate (Graham and Whelan 2007). The dead have, for example, been used to perform the relevance of violence, demarcate borders, enact social martyrdom and perpetuate polarised conceptions of victimhood (Robinson 2017). The failure to "deal with" the legacy of the conflict by way of formal truth recovery means that for many victims and survivors, the spectres of the past remain in the present, precluding healing, closure or restitution and permitting space for the transmission of trauma into lives, spaces and the social and political fabric of everyday life.

The structure of this chapter is as follows. For those who are less familiar with the Northern Ireland context, the chapter opens with a brief background to the conflict, the nature and scale of victimisation and efforts to deal with the legacy of the past. It then deals with the first conceptual theme—"Haunting and Lost Lives". In this part of the chapter, I explore the existence and impact of "dead body politics", whereby victims and survivors of the conflict and legacy issues have frequently been appropriated for political gain. Yet, it is not only individual lives that have been scarred by the conflict. As Bell and Di Paolantonio (2009) argue, landscape and physical structures "hold" memories, conjuring up and housing spectres of the past. These dynamics are explored under the heading of the "Haunting of Landscape". The final conceptual theme is "Haunting and the Effect of the Unresolved Past"—how the failure to comprehensively deal with the legacy of the conflict has contributed to high levels of conflict-related mental health problems and transgenerational trauma. Through these three occasionally overlapping themes, this chapter makes two substantive contributions. First, in respect to the concept of haunting, the chapter demonstrates the relevance of the concept to the post-conflict landscape, expanding and nuancing our understanding of haunting and its different manifestations. Second, the prism of haunting adds a further conceptual and practical layer to the field of transitional justice. As this chapter demonstrates, in post-conflict or transitional contexts, increased scholarly and practitioner awareness of the continuing physical and psychological impact of a traumatic past that transcends discussions of, for example, the utility of truth commissions or the "victim centredness" of transitional justice mechanisms, is required. Rather, a greater appreciation of practices of ghosting and the haunting impact of the past in the present presses home the importance of "dealing with" the past in all its complexity. The chapter concludes by arguing that the presence of ghosts and the experience of haunting represent a "call to action" in the quest to deal with a legacy of violent conflict and human rights abuses.

2 Northern Ireland and the Past in the Present

For those who are less familiar with the Northern Ireland context, some brief details on the nature of the conflict and efforts to deal with the past are instructive at this stage. The Northern Ireland conflict began in 1969 and lasted over 30 years. In broad terms, it was fought between Loyalist and Republican paramilitary organisations and British state forces, including the British Army, Ulster Defence Regiment (an infantry regiment of the British Army) and the police force, the Royal Ulster Constabulary. During this period, approximately 3739 individuals were killed, giving an overall death rate of 2.2 per thousand of the population. It is estimated that a further 40,000–50,000 people were injured, while tens of thousands were displaced due to intimidation and political violence (McKittrick and McVea 2012). Research by the Commission for Victims and Survivors Northern Ireland (CVSNI 2011) reports that over one-third of Northern Ireland's population could be legally classified as a victim or survivor of the conflict.

The civilian population were the greatest casualties of the conflict. According to the Sutton Index of Deaths, 1842 civilians were killed; 1114 members of the security forces; 395 members of Republican paramilitary organisations; 168 members of Loyalist paramilitary organisations; and 10 members of the Irish security forces.[1] Republican paramilitary organisations—the Irish Republican Army (IRA) and Irish National Liberation Army (INLA)—were responsible for approximately 60% of all deaths, 1712 of which are attributable to the IRA. Loyalist paramilitary organisations—the Ulster Volunteer Force (UVF), Ulster Defence Association (UDA) and the Loyalist Volunteer Force (LVF)—were responsible for over 1000 deaths (approximately 30%), while state security forces were responsible for directly killing 363 people (10% of all deaths).[2]

Following the signing of the Belfast Agreement in 1998, Northern Ireland has been an active site of transitional justice, with the reform of the criminal justice system and security forces, the release and reintegration of political prisoners, the decommissioning of paramilitary weapons and the development of the Northern Ireland Human Rights Commission (NIHRC) all forming part of the peace process (Northern Ireland Office 1998; McEvoy 2001; Campbell and Ni Aolain 2003; Independent Commission on Policing 1999; NIHRC 2003). Lacking is a single comprehensive approach to dealing with the past. In this vacuum, an array of truth-finding efforts have emerged, including public inquiries such as the Saville Inquiry into the events of Bloody Sunday on 30 January 1972, when British army paratroopers unlawfully killed 13 unarmed civilians; "right to life" challenges under Article 2 of the European Convention on Human Rights; police-led truth recovery by the Office of the Police Ombudsman for Northern Ireland, which investigates historical allegations of police malpractice, and the Legacy Investigation Branch based within the Police Service of Northern Ireland (PSNI), responsible for a cold-case review of all outstanding conflict-related deaths; and victim-led and civil society-sponsored initiatives around, for example, local storytelling and community-based commemoration. Largely a "criminal justice" response to a transitional context, this approach to the past has been uneven, incomplete and compromised by the weaknesses of the individual mechanisms (Lawther 2015). In response, there have been consistent calls for a full examination of the past.

The latest iteration of this debate can be found in the Stormont House Agreement (SHA), signed in December 2014 by a majority of Northern Ireland's main political parties and the British and Irish governments. Aimed at resolving the outstanding issues of the peace process, its recommendations on the past are fourfold: a Historical Investigations Unit, "an independent body to take forward investigations into outstanding Troubles-related deaths"; an Independent Commission on Information Retrieval "to enable victims and survivors to seek and privately receive information about the deaths of their next of kin"; an Oral History Archive "to provide a central place for people from all backgrounds to share experiences and narratives related to the Troubles"; and an Implementation and Reconciliation Group "to oversee themes, archives and information recovery" (Stormont House Agreement 2014). These bodies effectively amount to a "truth commission" designed to unpack, discharge and begin to heal the wounds of Northern Ireland's past. At the time of writing, the results of a government-led public consultation on the detail of the proposed legacy bodies are under review. If agreement can be reached, particularly around the British state's unwillingness to disclose sensitive "national security"-related information to families affected by the conflict and discussions over an amnesty for British soldiers who served in Northern Ireland, the government has indicated that the relevant bill will be introduced in Westminster in the Spring of 2019, with the mechanisms "going live" in autumn 2019.

3 Haunting and Lost Lives

Reflecting on the use of the dead for political purposes in Eastern Europe, Katherine Verdery (2000, 29) presents a powerful examination of the utility of the dead:

> Dead people come with a curriculum vitae or resume – several possible resumes, depending on which aspect of their life is being considered… Their complexity makes it fairly easy to discern different sets of emphasis,

> extract different stories, and thus rewrite history.... Words can be put in their mouths – often quite ambiguous words – or their actual words can be ambiguated by quoting them out of context.

Verdery's work can be readily applied to a range of post-conflict and transitional jurisdictions including Israel/Palestine, Colombia and South Africa, where the dead and their contested victimhood have become sites and sources of political and ideological conflicts. Writing in respect to the Israel-Palestine conflict, Hillel Cohen (2015, 258) describes competition over victimhood as "the greatest Jewish-Arab rivalry of all: the competition over who is the aggressor and who the victim, who the overlord and who the underdog". As Bouris (2007) points out, images of the dead and victimised are powerful, gripping and integral to helping us make sense of conflict, particularly in making moral calculations and determining who is "good" and who is "evil". Claiming ownership of the dead and the victimhood of the living therefore constitutes a powerful political resource.

In Northern Ireland, the dead and victims and survivors of the conflict have frequently been appropriated for political gain. The sharpest manifestation of this debate concerns the definition of "who" is a victim of the conflict. The Victims and Survivors (Northern Ireland) Order 2006 provides the statutory definition of a victim or survivor. According to Article 3, Paragraph 1 of the Order, this is

> (a) someone who is or has been physically or psychologically injured as a result of or in consequence of a conflict-related incident;
> (b) someone who provides a substantial amount of care on a regular basis for an individual mentioned in paragraph (a); or
> (c) someone who has been bereaved as a result of or in consequence of a conflict-related event.[3]

As an inclusive definition of victimhood, the Order includes all those affected by the conflict—civilians, members of the security forces, former members of paramilitary organisations and their families.

While the Order passed into law in 2006 with little political opposition, it has since become a focal point for debates over so-called innocent and guilty victims and the existence of a "hierarchy of victimhood"

(Brewer 2010, 2011; Lawther 2014a, b). One of the most obvious manifestations of this debate concerns the publicity associated with the launch of the Report of the Consultative Group on the Past (CGP) in 2009. Established in June 2007 by the then Secretary of State for Northern Ireland Peter Hain, the CGP was mandated to

> consult across the community how Northern Ireland society can best approach the legacy of the events of the past 40 years; to make recommendations, as appropriate, on any steps that might be taken to support Northern Ireland society in building a shared future that is not overshadowed by the events of the past. (CGP 2009, 44)

Following a period of extensive public consultation, the Group published its report and recommendations in January 2009.[4] A total of 31 recommendations were made on how Northern Ireland should deal with its past. These included the establishment of a "Legacy Commission"—essentially a bespoke truth commission-like body covering the areas of "Review and Investigation", "Information Recovery" and "Thematic Examination" and, most controversially, an ex-gratia "Recognition Payment" of £12,000[5] to all victims and survivors of the conflict.[6]

The political spectacle that followed appeared to suggest, in Walter Benjamin's (cited in Edelman 1988) words that "even the dead will not be safe from the enemy if he wins". Having previously briefed the media about the contents of the report, including the proposed payment to all of those defined as victims, the launch of the report in Belfast city centre, attended by the author, was marred by angry protests from different victims' groups directed against the Consultative Group themselves, prominent Republicans present such as Gerry Adams and other victims—almost all of it directed against the £12,000 payment. The recommendation provoked a very negative reaction amongst Unionist politicians in particular. For example, the then Democratic Unionist Party (DUP) leader Peter Robinson criticised the Report's failure to distinguish between "innocent victims and terrorists", while a former unionist politician critiqued the failure to respect *"our honoured dead"* (DUP 2009, 4; Lawther 2014a, 35). The dead were similarly invoked in the accompanying press coverage. One of the most lurid examples of the appropriation of victimhood came in the Irish News, the main nationalist newspaper. The weekend prior to the launch, the front page carried the headline *"Butchers, Bombers, Victims – They Are All the Same"*. The photographs below juxtaposed Lenny Murphy (leader of the UVF Shankill Butchers), Thomas Begley (the IRA member killed in the Shankill bomb) and nine-year-old Patrick Rooney, the first child killed in the conflict.

Integral to these debates over victimhood and the meaning of conflict is the appropriation of the dead to fulfil contemporary political and social objectives. As the above example of the framing of Lenny Murphy, Thomas Begley and Patrick Rooney illustrates, those dead who speak to key themes of competing political ideologies become the "exemplary dead" (Brown and Grant 2016). In this respect, the dead offer the living "a usable past" whereby violent histories are accommodated and used to bolster partial political perspectives (Moeller 1996). Both the dead and the living are therefore haunted by the attempt to *fix* historical meaning and to *master* a contentious past (Osiel 1997).

Equally concerning is that within the politics of the dead, certain victims' voices and their calls for truth may be prioritised because of the heavily politicised message that they carry, while leaving others at the margins. There are, as journalist Susan McKay (2018) argues, "…those who use the dead to fight old battles". For example, within republicanism, calls for truth recovery into high profile cases of suspected collusion have dominated the Republican narrative on the past. Brown (2011) argues this is part of an implicit perspective on victimhood within republicanism that privileges paramilitary deaths, particularly where they relate to the purported "oppression" of the British state, over civilians in commemorative space and narrative. There is also little consideration or calls for truth into the cases of approximately 227 Catholic civilians killed by members of Republican paramilitary organisations (Lawther 2014a). As regards unionist political elites, the claim has been made that members of the security forces who died during the conflict occupy a higher position in the hierarchy of victimhood than civilians (Lawther 2013). A concurrent critique, made to the author during a period of fieldwork with victims and survivors organisations, is that individual victims, whose deaths lack "political currency", have been forgotten in the call for truth and justice into collective tragedies for the unionist community.

Conversely, those members of the unionist or loyalist community who are the victims of state collusion are missing from the unionist narrative on the past by virtue of the complex nature of their deaths (Dawson 2007). In the absence of a formal process of truth recovery, this contest over the rightful "status" of the dead has led to hierarchal conceptions of truth, a politically polarised privileging of the truth of "my dead" and a reluctance, if not refusal, to acknowledge the truth of "your dead".

4 The Haunting of Landscape

In 1998, the then President of Argentina, Carlos Menem, issued a decree to demolish the Escuela de Mechanica de la Armada (ESMA), used as a clandestine detention centre during the dictatorship of 1976–1983, in the name of "reconciliation".[7] The building was not only a reminder of the past, but also triggered a demand in the present—*how will you live* with this unsettling presence in your midst? (Bell and Di Paolantonio 2009). Linking arguments in favour of the preservation of commemorative sites with the work of human rights, Menem's proposal was contested by a number of human rights groups, who protested that the past cannot be simply obliterated. Rather, and reflecting Derrida's call to justice, they argued that the way to live with ghosts is not to destroy their haunts, but to give ghosts their proper place in the future, in order that they might inform, abstractly, the post-conflict landscape (Bell and Di Paolantonio 2009).

This example demonstrates the capacity of conflict-affected places and spaces to "hold" memories and conjure up and house the spectres of the past. Transcending space and time, violent events frequently mark the real and imagined landscape, irrespective of what remains of the physical fallout of the event (Trigg 2012). As the increasing attention paid to the "transformative" capacity of atrocity sites attests, the ghosts of the past can be housed and their experiences put to future use. Yet, where the past remains contested, such sites are

> ...ghost-places, haunted places, places that blur the temporal lines between life and not-life. When places of memory are made, they are not made simply to put the ghosts to rest (a gravestone, a cairn, a shrine...),

> they are *performing their haunting in public*, and the performance is designed to instruct an audience in *how* to remember the life that was lost. (Robinson 2017, 26)

As much as lives can be haunted by the past, this part of the chapter will make the case for the haunting of landscape. One of the primary ways in which landscape can be haunted is through the "freezing" of geographical space and suspension of the time-space-memory continuum. As Feldman (1991, 67) argues, "Ghost tales map the history of death in local space, disrupting the linearity of time". For Feldman, ghosts are spectral traces, whose reason for existing (or persisting) is to call attention to what happened in a particular place and to demand that that place does not pass from memory. The concept of social haunting, which Till (2005, 23) adapts from Derrida therefore demonstrates both how "The process of selectively calling forth the dead and the past through place is one way individuals and groups try to fill absence and represent loss in the present", but also how claims to geographical haunting are part of the politics of place making, memory and social identity.

Across Northern Ireland, a number of "political/conflict tours" are offered by a diverse range of victim, ex-combatant, community and campaign/advocacy groups.[8] As part of the broader practice of "dark tourism" or "conflict heritage", the tours are designed to be of interest to visitors, students and researchers (see for example: McDowell 2008; Skinner 2016). They typically involve exploring a specific geographical area (urban and rural), with the tour guide providing an insight into the local experience of violence. Stops are frequently made at local memorials, wall murals and other unmarked sites of violence. As part of a broader project exploring the intersection between victimhood and dealing with the past in Northern Ireland,[9] I undertook eight of these tours during 2016–2017. One tour, led by a local victims' group in rural County Fermanagh, in the West of Northern Ireland, well illustrates the haunting of place. Described as a "educational tour given by local guides providing the stories from each region and showing the real effects of Terrorism on local families and individuals", this tour involved driving around the local area and stopping at different locations where the tour guide, a life-long resident of the area, explained particular aspects of local history and the experience victimhood and loss.[10] Some of the stops were clearly marked with formal or informal memorials, while others bore no identifying marks.

Individually and collectively, the stops demonstrated how time can be circumscribed and memory fixed in the physical landscape. For this tour guide, as with others encountered by the author, there was a clear sense that on recounting the details of specific atrocities, both time and geography were frozen in that particular moment. Thus, a bus stop used by local school children was not just "a bus stop", but *the bus stop* at which a bomb exploded; hills and ditches in the surrounding fields were not mere aspects of topography, but part of the arsenal of paramilitary organisations who used the natural landscape to their advantage when planning operations; likewise, an empty farm building was deemed emblematic of the attempted destruction of local life and the need for constant vigilance. While this freezing of place and time may be a function of trauma, as Till (2005, 13) argues,

> Returning to places that haunt our imaginations fold and warps imagined times and selves (past, present, future), yet the ritual practice of returning creates a sense of temporal continuity and coherence. When someone goes back home (and each of us have many homes), he or she may experience such vivid memories that it may appear (even momentarily) as though the place and the person returning are exactly the same as they once were.

Equally, the specific locations chosen to be shared with visitors spoke to a particular experience of victimhood that not only fed into claims of, for this Protestant community, "innocent victimhood" and the unjustifiability of "Terrorist" violence, but the experience of violence in a rural setting and its impact upon families, farms and the close-knit nature of rural life. In this respect, the landscape was haunted physically and cognitively, acting as "the story of a wound that cries out, that addresses us in the attempt to tell us of a reality or truth that is not otherwise available" (Caruth 1996, 6).

These dynamics of haunting are also replicated in respect to local forms of memorialisation. By way of example, best known for the sectarian segregation of its residential space into the two opposing neighbourhoods of the Loyalist Shankill Road and the Republican Falls Road, West Belfast sustained a high incidence of conflict-related deaths (440 out of a total of approximately 3700) throughout the conflict, and the past is visually omnipresent in the cultural landscape (Graham and Whelan 2007). Since the paramilitary ceasefires of 1994, West Belfast, like many other areas in Northern Ireland, has been actively marked by the construction of what many local people regard as tangible sites of suffering, hurt and loss. These symbolise the locations where lives were lost and actualise many other deaths which occurred outside the area. Permanent monuments, statues, plaques and memorial gardens are all located prominently in public space (Graham and Shirlow 2002).

While acting as homes or repositories for the ghosts of the dead, local sites of memorialisation also demonstrate the disruption of the time-space-continuum and the freezing of geographical memory (Hamber and Wilson 2002). For example, as Robinson (2017) argues, if the death(s) were violent or unjust, the ghost-place may confront the audience with a violent unsettled past, and the ghosts who haunt the place may cry from within for truth and justice. Conversely, deaths that do not "fit" the dominant narrative are concealed. In Republican areas of West Belfast, for example, sites where security forces, informers and civilians were killed by Republicans are elided from the memorial landscape. Such dead remain a haunting presence by virtue of their "complex victim" status. Moreover, in her anatomy of memory, politics and place in the new Berlin, Till (2005, 9 and 195) writes of "ghosts" of places of memory being "created … to give a shape to felt absences, fears and desires that haunt contemporary society" and through which "contemporary dreams of national futures are imagined". As Till (2005) suggests, local forms of memorialisation can be used to inscribe political meaning on space. Thus, the "duty-to-tell" function of commemorative sites in Northern Ireland has been used for partial political claims making, perpetuating polarised and hierarchal conceptions of victimhood and haunting the present with competing narratives of the past.

5 Haunting and the Effect of the Unresolved Past

That Northern Ireland has one of the highest rates of male suicide in Western Europe, a prescription rate for anti-depressants that is one of the highest in the world and increasing evidence of transgenerational trauma suggests that it is a society that is far from managing the traumatic legacy of conflict (Tomlinson 2012). This, according to Brewer et al. (2018, 15), is the legacy of how "violence brutalizes everyday life". The brutalisation of everyday life is evidenced in three ways: the brutalisation of mundane, common sense language, ideas and beliefs; the brutalisation of everyday social practices and behaviours; and the brutalisation of everyday cultural and cognitive maps and frames through which sense is made of the world (Brewer et al. 2018). The final part of this chapter focuses on the in-ward manifestation of the brutalisation of everyday life—the relationship between trauma, haunting and unresolved pasts. It focuses on two areas arising from the failure to comprehensively deal with the legacy of the conflict in Northern Ireland and the failure to adequately respond to the psychological legacy of conflict—the prevalence of conflict-related mental health problems and transgenerational trauma.

The intensity and intimacy of the Northern Ireland conflict appears to have had a defining impact on its emotional and traumatic legacy. Given the small geographical size of Northern Ireland and the fact that the conflict was at its most concentrated in a small number of communities (particularly in North and West Belfast), the daily experience of violence and victimhood was personal and intimate. Research by Bunting et al. (2013) estimates that in Northern Ireland, 39.9% of the population have experienced a conflict-related traumatic event (for example, bombings, shootings and mutilations), while 16.9% have witnessed a death or serious injury. Likewise, research by Shirlow, Mesev and Downs (2009) indicates that in the most conflict-affected areas, at least 80% of the local population knew someone who had been killed or injured as a result of the conflict. The impact on mental health has been stark. At the time of writing, it is believed that around 15% of the adult population have experienced conflict-related mental health difficulties (CVSNI 2015). This equates to around 213,000 adults out of a population of 1.8 million (CVSNI 2015). Arguably, the starkest indicator of the continued legacy of the conflict has been the increase in suicide deaths since the conflict ended. The number of suicides has doubled from approximately 150 deaths per year in the mid-1990s to more than 300 deaths by the year 2010 (O'Connor and O'Neill 2015). Men, and in particular young men, are at risk. As of November 2018, the Northern Ireland rate of suicide deaths is 16 per 100,000—the highest in the United Kingdom and for males, double that of England (O'Neill and Hamber 2018).

Particular mental health challenges have been identified for former members of paramilitary organisations. Influential factors include long-term unemployment, poverty, relationship breakdowns, alcohol and substance abuse and, at times, the existential anxiety of the "terrible futility of the things" they were involved in (Gallagher et al. 2012, 66). Recent research by the author of this chapter with loyalist ex-combatants revealed a further layer of interlinked negative emotions, including the mourning of lost friends and family members, guilt, fear, regret and humiliation experienced during interrogation and imprisonment (Lawther 2017). This assessment is further evidenced by research with former politically motivated prisoners which found that among loyalist ex-combatants, 38.4% reported feelings of despair and not wanting to go on living, 53.3% experienced intrusive memories and 65.8% used avoidance techniques as a coping mechanism (Jamieson et al. 2010). Across loyalist and republican ex-combatants, the same survey revealed that 68.8% of respondents engaged in hazardous levels of alcohol abuse, while 32.6% had received prescription medication for depression in the previous year—a prevalence rate that is five times higher than the Northern Ireland average for men. The following statement by an ex-combatant well illustrates the haunting influence of the past:

> ...personally a lot of them struggle to live with the effects of what they have done, never mind speak about it...You are taking tablets, you are taking drink and a brave lot of them are committing suicide. Other ones just want to talk to people. I have people coming to me regularly, sitting to 2 or 3 in the morning and they offload quite a lot. ... Then I am sitting there at 4 o'clock going 'where do I go with that', but I wouldn't turn anybody away.

Given that at least 15,000 people were incarcerated during the conflict, the effect of the unresolved past on individuals and the knock-on effect onto extended families cannot be underestimated.

The second element of the haunting influence of the unresolved past is transgenerational trauma. Perhaps most prominently associated with the Holocaust and explored in the field of psychoanalysis, transgenerational trauma is the unconscious transference of emotional, physical or social pain from one person to their descendants. This unconscious transmission is what Abraham and Torok (1994) define as the dynamic of transgenerational haunting. It is understood in a number of ways. Adonis (2016) for example points to the transgenerational haunting of colonialism, slavery, exploitation and discrimination among African Americans and the intergenerational effects associated with the traumatic history of the First Nations peoples in Canada. Others have used the term transgenerational haunting to refer to the way trauma is secreted in families and passed across generations (Luhmann 2009). Thus, while victims of trauma live with its physical and psychological scars, the recipients of transgenerational trauma live with a second-hand "post memory" (Schwab 2010). Such "post memories" are received through the actual stories of parents or guardians, but also through unexplained silences and the expression of grief, rage and despair (Hirsch 2008). Trans-generational haunting thus speaks to the capacity of atrocity memories to develop a "durational time" that disrupts chronological time, but also, in its physical and psychological manifestations, how the ghosts of past traumas—"that which appears to be not there" are in fact a "seething presence" (Langer 1995; Gordon 1997).

The existence and impact of transgenerational trauma in Northern Ireland has been the focus of recent attention. A number of contextual and background factors have been put forward—coping with the death or imprisonment of a parent(s); growing up with a parent(s) who has Post Traumatic Stress Disorder (PTSD); living in the shadow of a brother or sister killed during the Troubles; suffering from domestic violence and various forms of physical and sexual abuse; and being forced to relocate as a result of political intimidation (Gallagher et al. 2012). The effects are multiple. The impact of violence, traumatic experiences and social segregation can impact upon parenting practices which affect early attachment and the capacity of the child to self-regulate, thereby increasing the risk of mental health disorders, behavioural problems and as discussed above, suicide (CVSNI 2011). Alternatively, the experience of trauma and/or victimhood may result in a parenting style that is characterised by over-protectiveness and over-identification with assumed "dangers"—resulting in a "cocoonement of over-protection", as described by one victim interviewed by the author:

> When we were at home at 19 and we were out past 10 o'clock my mother would never sleep to all of us were back in the house and the door locked. She walked the floors. So, we didn't go out, it was awful and the rows. It was all about my mother's fear of losing another child.

In children, this urge to "protect" can, as suggested above, lead to resentment and frustration, but can also translate into a hypervigilance and pervasive mistrust of others, compromising the child's "own sense of security" (Danieli 1985; Rowland-Klein and Dunlop 1998, 367). Children of ex-combatants and serving and ex-security force members may be at particular risk. Speaking to these themes in Northern Ireland, Black has reported that children of serving policing officers were impacted by fear, social isolation and their parents' mental ill health (Black 2004). Similarly, the impact of arrest, prison visits and stigmatisation and the fear of recrimination are believed to affect the children of ex-combatants (Rolston 2011).

In other cases, and as is well documented in respect to the Holocaust, many parents who have survived trauma have employed silence on the past as a way to cope with their own experience and as a way to protect their children. Yet, the unspoken can be omnipresent as this victim support group worker in Northern Ireland explained:

> There would be a picture on a wall of a man who they have never met, who is an uncle, who is dead before they are born and they go at Christmas, birthdays and Easter to the graveyard, speeches are made and stuff is done. They don't directly ask their parents or their grandparents about that person because when they do so they are upset. But it has such an effect on their lives, transgenerationally, that why does their mummy cry at night, why if the TV is on at particular times it offends them and they get angry.

Euphemisms, or in Cohen's (2001) terms, techniques of interpretive denial, have similarly been employed:

> One person's grandchildren referred to it as the accident – Granda's accident – the IRA put a bomb under his car and he lost his leg and other parts of his body. Another man who was shot by loyalists and left crippled said exactly the same.

These techniques of denial and silence have been found to result in a number of maladaptive behavioural problems amongst children (McNally 2014). In their research with families affected by the Northern Ireland conflict, Downes et al. (2013, 590–595) found evidence that children "invented [their] own explanations"; the existence of a physical and cognitive space where "the truth [was] dangerous"; where facts were "hidden but not hidden"; where children attempted to "block out their feeling for fear of the consequences"; and a case in which one child developed the "propensity to be the 'good girl' [in] a conscious attempt to avoid causing her own mother any more stress". These experiences are not of course unique to Northern Ireland. They do however illustrate that ghosts or practices of haunting are not some invisible or ineffable excess (Gordon 1997). Rather, they speak to the capacity of unquiet ghosts to permeate the present, transmitting a "memory of offence" that can remain painful or disturbing generations after the original violation (Levi 1989, 47).

6 Conclusion

This chapter has argued that notions of ghosts and haunting can act as a prism through which to understand the intersection between unresolved pasts and the transmission of trauma post-conflict. Focusing on the case study of Northern Ireland, three conceptualisations of haunting were identified—the haunting of lost lives, the haunting of landscapes and the haunting of the unresolved past. Each theme demonstrates the enduring and unsettling impact of an unaddressed legacy of violent conflict and human rights abuses—on individuals, communities and societies. Haunting and ghosting then is not about "horrorism" or the paranormal, but as Harris et al. (2018) suggest, haunting can be thought of as an "ethical orientation" that requires us to seek out and embrace ghosts in the spirit of justice. To engage with ghosts as Derrida (cited in Wilke 2010) proposes involves a politics of mourning, of memory, and of inheritances that allows for a diversity of relations to the past. To inherit involves making a "critical choice"—"one must filter, sift, criticise, one must sort out several different possibilities that inhabit the same injunction" (Derrida 1994, 18). In more familiar phrasing, Derrida is speaking to the key tenets of transitional justice—to "narrow the range of permissible lies", to counter denial and to flatten hierarchies of victimhood (Ignatieff 1996, 113). Expanding the transitional justice gaze to practices of ghosting and haunting can therefore contribute to the realisation of truth, justice and acknowledgement and the ultimate hope of transforming "a shadow life into an undiminished life" (Gordon 1997, 208).

Notes

1. Sutton Index of Deaths: http://cain.ulst.ac.uk/sutton/ (accessed on 10 October 2018).
2. This final figure leaves out the matter of state collusion. It is now clear that the security forces and intelligence services had infiltrated both Republican and Loyalist paramilitary organisations and were complicit in multiple murders.
3. The Victims and Survivors (Northern Ireland) Order 2006. Available at: https://www.legislation.gov.uk/nisi/2006/2953/contents (accessed on 4 December 2018).
4. The group received 290 written submissions, 2086 standardised letters and met privately with 141 individuals and groups.
5. The figure of £12,000 was derived from the Irish Government's "Remembrance Fund" and "Acknowledgement Payment" of €15,000 to the surviving spouse, their children or the parents of an individual who was either fatally injured in Ireland or who was resident in Ireland at that time.
6. The controversy surrounding the "Recognition Payment" closed down debate and discussion on the Report of the CGP. The Group's legacy proposals concerning "Review and Investigation", "Information Recovery" and "Thematic Examination" have however closely informed subsequent efforts to deal with the past, including the past facing mechanisms proposed in the Stormont House Agreement.
7. Approximately 30,000 people disappeared during the Argentine "dirty war".
8. See, for example, https://deadcentretours.com/; http://coiste.ie/tours/; https://www.rucgcfoundation.org/ruc-gc-memorial-garden/.
9. Victims and Dealing with the Past, available at: https://victimsandthepast.org/ (accessed on 16 December 2018).
10. https://seff.org.uk/research-and-publications/ (accessed on 17 December 2018).

References

Abraham, N. & Torok, M. (1994). *The Shell and the Kernel: Renewals of Psychoanalysis* (Vol. 1, N. Rand, Trans.). Chicago: University of Chicago Press.

Adonis, C. (2016). Exploring the Salience of Intergenerational Trauma among Children and Grandchildren of Victims of Apartheid-Era Gross Human Rights Violations. *Indo-Pacific Journal of Phenomenology, 16*(1+2), 1–17.

Bell, V., & Di Paolantonio, M. (2009). The Haunted *Nomos*: Activist-Artists and the (Im)Possible Politics of Memory in Transitional Argentina. *Cultural Politics, 5*(2), 149–178.

Black, A. (2004). The Treatment of Psychological Problems Experienced by the Children of Police Officers in Northern Ireland. *Child Care in Practice, 10*(2), 99–106.

Bouris, E. (2007). *Complex Political Victims*. Bloomfield: Kumarian.

Brewer, J. (2010). *Peace Processes: A Sociological Approach*. Cambridge: Polity Press.

Brewer, J., Hayes, B., Teeney, F., Dudgeon, K., Mueller-Hirth, N., & Lal Wijesinghe, S. (2018). *The Sociology of Everyday Life Peacebuilding*. Basingstoke: Palgrave Macmillan.

Brown, K. (2011). Rights and Victims, Martyrs and Memories: The European Court of Human Rights and Political Transition in Northern Ireland. In M. Hamilton & A. Buyse (Eds.), *Transitional Jurisprudence and the ECHR. Justice, Politics and Rights* (pp. 52–80). Cambridge: Cambridge University Press.

Brown, K., & Grant, A. (2016). A Lens Over Conflicted Memory: Surveying 'Troubles' Commemoration in Northern Ireland. *Irish Political Studies, 31*(1), 139–162.

Bunting, B., Ferry, F., Murphy, S., O'Neill, S., & Bolton, D. (2013). Trauma Associated with Civil Conflict and Posttraumatic Stress Disorder: Evidence from the Northern Ireland Study of Health and Stress. *Journal of Trauma Stress, 26*(1), 134–141.

Campbell, C., & Ni Aolain, F. (2003). Local Meets Global – Transitional Justice in Northern Ireland. *Fordham International Law Journal, 26*(4), 871–892.

Caruth, C. (1996). *Unclaimed Experience: Trauma, Narrative and History*. Baltimore: John Hopkins University Press.

Cohen, H. (2015). *1929: Year Zero of the Arab-Israeli Conflict*. Waltham: Brandies University Press.

Cohen, S. (2001). *States of Denial: Knowing about Atrocity and Suffering*. London: Polity Press.
Commission for Victims and Survivors Northern Ireland. (2011). *Troubled Consequences: A Report on the Mental Health Impact of the Civil Conflict in Northern Ireland*. Belfast: Commission for Victims and Survivors Northern Ireland.
Commission for Victims and Survivors Northern Ireland. (2015). *Towards a Better Future: The Trans-generational Impact of the Troubles on Mental Health*. Belfast: Commission for Victims and Survivors Northern Ireland.
Consultative Group on the Past. (2009). *Report of the Consultative Group on the Past*. London: Northern Ireland Office.
Danieli, Y. (1985). The Treatment and Prevention of Long-Term Effects and Intergenerational Transmission of Victimization: A Lesson from Holocaust Survivors and Their Children. In C. R. Figley (Ed.), *Trauma and Its Wake* (The Study and Treatment of Post-Traumatic Stress Disorder) (Vol. 1, pp. 295–313). New York: Brunner/Mazel.
Dawson, G. (2007). *Making Peace with the Past? Memory, Trauma and the Irish Troubles*. Manchester: Manchester University Press.
Democratic Unionist Party. (2009). *Dealing with the Past in Northern Ireland*. Belfast: Democratic Unionist Party.
Derrida, J. (1994). *Specters of Marx: The State of Debt, the Work of Mourning and the New International* (P. Kamof, Trans.). New York: Routledge.
Downes, C., Harrison, E., Curran, D., & Kavanagh, M. (2013). The Trauma Still Goes On...: The Multigenerational Legacy of Northern Ireland's Conflict. *Clinical Child Psychology and Psychiatry, 18*(4), 583–603.
Edelman, M. (1988). *Constructing the Political Spectacle*. Chicago: The University of Chicago Press.
Etkind, A. (2009). Post-Soviet Hauntology: Cultural Memory of the Soviet Terror. *Constellations, 16*(1), 182–200.
Feldman, A. (1991). *Formations of Violence: The Narrative of the Body and Political Terror in Northern Ireland*. Chicago: University of Chicago Press.
Gallagher, E., Hamber, B., & Joy, E. (2012). Perspectives and Possibilities: Mental Health in Post-Agreement Northern Ireland. *Shared Space: A Research Journal on Peace, Conflict and Community Relations in Northern Ireland, 13*(March), 63–78.
Gordon, A. (1997). *Ghostly Matters: Haunting and the Sociological Imagination*. Minneapolis: University of Minnesota Press.
Graham, B., & Shirlow, P. (2002). The Battle of the Somme in Ulster Memory and Identity. *Political Geography, 21*, 881–904.

Graham, B., & Whelan, Y. (2007). The Legacies of the Dead: Commemorating the Troubles in Northern Ireland. *Environment and Planning D: Society and Space, 25*(3), 476–495.
Hamber, B., & Wilson, R. (2002). Symbolic Closure Through Memory, Reparation and Revenge in Post-Conflict Societies. *Journal of Human Rights, 1*(1), 35–53.
Harris, B., Eyles, J., Munyewende, P., & Goudge, J. (2018). Something Happened: Storytelling in a Violent Field. *International Journal of Transitional Justice, 12*(2), 356–367.
Hirsch, M. (2008). The Generation of PostMemory. *Poetics Today, 29*(1), 103–128.
Ignatieff, M. (1996). Articles of Faith. *Index on Censorship, 5*, 110–122.
Independent Commission on Policing. (1999). *A New Beginning: Policing in Northern Ireland. The Report of the Independent Commission on Policing in Northern Ireland.* Belfast: The Stationery Office.
Jamieson, R., Shirlow, P., & Grounds, A. (2010). *Ageing and Social Exclusion Among Former Politically Motivated Prisoners in Northern Ireland.* Belfast: Community Foundation of Northern Ireland.
Langer, L. (1995). *Admitting the Holocaust.* New York: Oxford University Press.
Lawther, C. (2013). Denial, Silence and the Politics of the Past: Unpicking the Opposition to Truth Recovery in Northern Ireland. *International Journal of Transitional Justice, 7*(1), 157–177.
Lawther, C. (2014a). *Truth, Denial and Transition: Northern Ireland and the Contested Past.* Abingdon: Routledge.
Lawther, C. (2014b). The Construction and Politicisation of Victimhood. In O. Lynch & J. Argomaniz (Eds.), *Victims of Terrorism: A Comparative and Interdisciplinary Study* (pp. 10–30). Abingdon: Routledge.
Lawther, C. (2015). Criminal Justice, Truth Recovery and Dealing with the Past in Northern Ireland. In A.-M. McAlinden & C. Dwyer (Eds.), *Criminal Justice in Transition: The Northern Ireland Context* (pp. 27–46). London: Hart.
Lawther, C. (2017). The Truth about Loyalty: Emotions, Ex-combatants and Transitioning from the Past. *International Journal of Transitional Justice, 11*(3), 484–504.
Levi, P. (1989). *The Drowned and the Saved.* London: Abacus.
Luhmann, S. (2009). Gender and the Generations of Difficult Knowledge: Recent Responses to Familial Legacies of Nazi Perpetration. *Women in German Yearbook, 25*, 174–198.
McDowell, S. (2008). Selling Conflict Heritage Through Tourism in Peacetime Northern Ireland: Transforming Conflict Or Exacerbating Difference? *International Journal of Heritage Studies, 14*(5), 405–421.

McEvoy, K. (2001). *Paramilitary Imprisonment in Northern Ireland: Resistance, Management and Release*. Oxford: Oxford University Press.
McKay, S. (2018, March 25). How Old Ghosts Are Haunting Ireland. *The Guardian,* n.p.
McKittrick, D., & McVea, D. (2012). *Making Sense of the Troubles: A History of the Northern Ireland Conflict*. London: Penguin Books.
McNally, D. (2014). *Transgenerational Trauma: Dealing with the Past in Northern Ireland*. Belfast: WAVE Trauma Centre.
Moeller, R. (1996). War Stories: The Search for a Usable Past in the Federal Republic of Germany. *The American Historical Review, 101*(4), 1008–1048.
Northern Ireland Human Rights Commission. (2003). *Human Rights and Victims of Violence*. Belfast: Northern Ireland Human Rights Commission.
Northern Ireland Office. (1998). *The Belfast Agreement: An Agreement Reached at the Multi-Party Talks on Northern Ireland*. London: The Stationery Office.
O'Connor, R., & O'Neill, S. (2015). Mental Health and Suicide Risk in Northern Ireland: A Legacy of the Troubles? *The Lancet (Psychiatry), 2*(July), 582–584.
O'Neill, S., & Hamber, B. (2018). *Addressing the Legacy of Northern Ireland's Past: The Need for a Victim and Survivor Centred, Trauma-Informed Approach*. Stormont House Agreement Consultation Response. Available at: https://docs.wixstatic.com/ugd/198ed6_eab04aabfb044793b464a9ea6ac24d3e.pdf. Accessed 17 Nov 2018.
Osiel, M. (1997). *Mass Atrocity, Collective Memory and the Law*. London: Transaction.
Robinson, J. (2017). *Transitional Justice and the Politics of Inscription*. Abingdon: Routledge.
Rolston, B. (2011). 'Trying to Reach the Future Through the Past': Murals and Commemoration in Northern Ireland. *Crime, Media, Culture, 6*(3), 285–307.
Rowan, B. (2012, November 16). *Delay, Dithering and Deadlock on the Past*. Available at: http://eamonnmallie.com/2012/11/delay-dithering-and-deadlock-on-the-past/. Accessed 18 July 2018.
Rowland-Klein, D., & Dunlop, R. (1998). The Transmission of Trauma across Generations: Identification with Parental Trauma in Children of Holocaust Survivors. *Australian and New Zealand Journal of Psychiatry, 32*(3), 358–369.
Schindel, E. (2014). Ghosts and Companeros: Haunting Stories and the Quest for Justice Around Argentina's Former Terror Sites. *Rethinking History, 18*(2), 244–264.
Schwab, G. (2010). *Haunting Legacies: Violent Histories and Transgenerational Trauma*. New York: Columbia University Press.

Skinner, J. (2016). Walking the Falls: Dark Tourism and the Significance of Movement on the Political Tour of West Belfast. *Tourist Studies, 16*(1), 23–39.
Shirlow, P., Mesev, V., & Downes, J. (2009). The Geography of Conflict and Death in Belfast, Northern Ireland. *Annals of the Association of American Geographers, 99*(5), 893–903.
South African Truth and Reconciliation Commission Report, volume 1, p. 7.
Stormont House Agreement. (2014). https://www.gov.uk/government/uploads/system/uploads/attachment_data/file/390672/Stormont_House_Agreement.pdf. Accessed 24 July 2018.
Till, K. (2005). *The New Berlin: Memory, Politics, Place*. Minneapolis: University of Minnesota Press.
Tomlinson, M. (2012). War, Peace and Suicide: The Case of Northern Ireland. *International Sociology, 27*(4), 464–482.
Trigg, D. (2012). *The Memory of Place: A Phenomenology of the Uncanny*. Ohio: Ohio University Press.
Verdery, K. (2000). *The Political Lives of Dead Bodies: Reburial and Postsocialist Change*. New York: Columbia University Press.
Wilke, C. (2010). Enter Ghost: Haunted Courts and Haunting Judgments in Transitional Justice. *Law and Critique, 21*(1), 73–92.

8

Listening for the Quiet Violence in the Unspoken

Marietjie Oelofsen

When we come together to narrate our traumatic experiences, we invite others not only to listen to what we have to say, but journey with us as we 're-find' ourselves and re-find the language that has been lost.
—Van Der Merwe & Gobodo-Madikizela 2008, p. 27

1 Introduction

Talking with others about traumatic experiences has potential to create a public narrative that makes it possible to work through experiences of post-conflict or political trauma (Gobodo-Madikizela 2012; LaCapra

The A.W. Mellon Foundation provided financial support for the research that informs this chapter. The National Research Foundation (NRF) provides funding support to the South African Research Chair Initiative (SARChI) Chair in Violent Histories and Transgenerational Trauma at Stellenbosch University, which provided the space for writing this chapter.

M. Oelofsen (✉)
Studies in Historical Trauma and Transformation, Stellenbosch University, Stellenbosch, South Africa
e-mail: hmoelofsen@sun.ac.za

K. Wale et al. (eds.), *Post-Conflict Hauntings*, Palgrave Studies in Compromise after Conflict, https://doi.org/10.1007/978-3-030-39077-8_8

2014; McAfee 2008; Schaffer and Smith 2004). In the talking with others, personal experiences of trauma seem to take on new meaning in reflection to the experiences of one another. It is in the spaces of coming together where possibilities are generated for re-finding a new language of *us* and of who we are in relationship to one another.

But, how do we curate talking spaces where traumatic experiences of injustice are articulated in terms that seem dissonant, or hard to hear? What do talking spaces look like where dissonance and that which is uncomfortable to listen to find resonance and generate possibilities for transformative human *and* political relations?

In this chapter, I explore the possibility of political talking spaces as spaces where South Africans come together to narrate traumatic experiences of the past in order to re-find the language of a South African body politic. The political talking space is different from, but not less or more important, than spaces where narratives of past trauma serve a therapeutic, healing goal. The difference of the political talking space lies in its room for negotiating, contesting and representing the "different grammars" (Benhabib 1996, pp. 2–5) of a diverse, but cohesive body politic that recognises its common interest in dealing with the ghosts of apartheid injustices. These ghosts continue to bedevil possibilities for social cohesion in South Africa. I have argued elsewhere (Oelofsen 2017) that South Africa's "democratic moment" in 1994 raised questions about the prospects of democracy to contain diversity and difference. It also raised theoretical and practical questions about the formation of the "body" of a body politic, who and what it means to be a citizen, and the spaces that are available for expressing difference. The search, in dialogical engagement, for a new description of our political selves, requires more than an invitation. It requires consideration for *who* are invited to join these conversations, and *how* those who come together are prepared to tune in to listen to one another—even to voices that struggle to articulate, are hesitant, even incoherent, or speak in a tone that may be uncomfortable to listen to. Re-finding a new language in this instance, goes to the heart of what it means to be part of a South African body politic.

To imagine these political talking spaces, I draw on Arendt's notion of "speaking in the presence of others" as "appearance" in the political realm (1958, p. 26). The ability to talk about and navigate our different lived experiences in the presence of others, says Arendt, is crucial in a free society. We "appear" to others as we articulate our unique selves in the company of others who are different from ourselves. Put differently, we get access to the experiences of one another when we articulate who we are, and what our lived experiences are in the company of others. This company of others requires diversity—a plurality of voices articulating different experiences—to give meaning to the idea of political freedom (Arendt 1960). The articulation of a plurality of experiences creates a common public space out of which a "political realm" emerges where citizens can talk and act together as equals (1958, p. 198).

In South Africa, there is a contradiction between the assertion of the equality associated with political freedom and the persistence of subjugation in the lived experience of most of its citizens. The status of freedom, says Arendt, is not a given following the act of liberation. Political freedom is animated when free citizens gain access, through "word and deed" to the common public space of the "politically organized world" (1960, pp. 29–30). This politically organised world is what I have in mind when I refer to political talking spaces in this chapter.

To illustrate the dissonant, hard to hear, or inaudible voices that struggle for space in South Africa's political talking spaces, I introduce in this chapter the narrative of Daniella Jantjies,[1] whom I interviewed as part of a research project that examined the effect of apartheid trauma on intergenerational relationships in three communities in South Africa's Western Cape Province. Daniella's narrative embodies the struggle to articulate the contradiction between the promise of political freedom and the persistence of subjugation based on race, class and gender. Her narrative reveals a struggle to understand how and why she remains trapped in a life she did not imagine for herself. In this, her story accounts for a contradiction that many South Africans face, between a life imagined as a free agent in a post-apartheid society and a life that remains in a state of subjugation in the post-1994 reality. The contradictions emerging in the banality of Daniella's everyday existence haunt her. This haunting is evident in her struggle to find the words to describe the layers of injustice that constitute her lived experience. The loss for words leaves her, not voiceless, but floundering and entangled in what seems to present as a state of "quiet violence": It is violent in that it suppresses her agency and it is quiet in that it maintains her states of subjugation. Endured in silence, and unarticulated in meaningful terms, the haunting of the contradictions that mark her existence destroys possibilities for Daniella to imagine authority to participate in political talking spaces. In the absence of possibilities to hear her experience resonate with other experiences, the violence of her subjugation remains unnamed, quiet to the external world but violent and volatile in her inner world.

For Daniella to "appear" in the political talking space, requires a reconsideration of conditions that determine who and what can be heard in political talking spaces. These political talking spaces are inherently contentious, agonistic, and may not be easy to navigate. In these spaces, seeing things from multiple perspectives as Arendt suggests, or talking with a view to reach consensus as Habermas suggests, is not enough (Mouffe 2013, p. 10). To have a voice in this agonistic space is conditional and requires certain resources to give voice the kind of materiality that makes it matter.

> Having a voice requires resources: both practical resources (language) and (the seemingly purely symbolic) status necessary if one is to be recognized by others as having a voice. Both are part of the materiality of voice, the 'matter' without which voice is impossible; like most matter, they are unevenly distributed. (Couldry 2010, pp. 7–8)

To imagine political talking spaces with possibilities to account for Daniella's voice, and voices like hers, I draw on the relatively new field of political listening theory (Bassel 2017; Bickford 1996; Tanya Dreher 2009; Garman 2018a; Lacey 2013; Lipari 2014). By shifting the focus from having a voice on to how conventions and privilege shape who and what can be heard, political listening provides a language that examines the prospects for listening as a politically transformative act with possibilities for reconfiguring ways in which South Africans talk *and* listen to diverse experiences of apartheid. It is in the listening to the difficulties of articulating experiences that are unfamiliar, hard to hear, or indeed, what Garman (2018b, p. 96) terms, "unhearable", that political talking spaces emerge which galvanise understanding for where and how different experiences are embedded in South Africa's past, and how it might be possible to work through and beyond these experiences.

I will start this chapter with a brief conceptual description of "quiet violence" as I consider it here. I then introduce Daniella Jantjies. Her voice is a reminder throughout the chapter of the barriers that exclude some from appearing in, or being invited to join in the journey of "re-finding ourselves", and "re-finding"—or re-defining—the language that fully describes a South African body politic. With Daniella's voice in mind, I then take account of the nature of political talking spaces in South Africa, before exploring the notion of political listening as a theoretical and practical proposal for hosting dissonant, hard to hear experiences in political talking spaces.

2 Quiet Violence

I first came across the concept of "quiet violence" in K. Sello Duiker's novel, *The Quiet Violence of Dreams* (2001). In the novel, Duiker tells the story of Tshepo, a young, Black South African man[2] who struggles to find his place in a South Africa free from the constraints of apartheid. Set at the end of the 1990s, early 2000, Tshepo drifts through the pages of the book—and Cape Town—haunted by his mother's violent death and a broken relationship with his father. He seems at home in the Cape Town streets and suburbs and at the same time fiercely alienated, almost lost, as he drops in on friends, and out of friendships, and in and out of places to stay. The alienation drives him mad—literally. He is institutionalised, and it is here where he feels observed as a case rather than being seen as a person:

> They see a case, something that they must work out, decode, diagnose. My mind is merely a jigsaw puzzle to them. They are fascinated by its fragments. They marvel at the broken pieces and swap stories with each other about what they see and hear. They listen to what they want to hear and write down what they understand. Everything else, the gestures, the pauses, the looks of despair and desperation disappear in a vacuum called therapy. We are nothing but question marks and full-stops to them, that is why they will never understand us. (Duiker 2001, p. 141)

Forced to learn the quiet language of meekness to appease the nurses by day, Tshepo's ghosts manifest in his dreams where he is "shut away from the music of the living" and all he hears is "the music of the dying and the dead" (Duiker 2001, p. 139).

Penfold proposes a reading of Duiker's *Quiet Violence of Dreams* that accounts for the "liminal social formation" (2017, p. 1050) in which South Africans are forced to shape their citizen identity. Focusing on the theme of "madness" in Duiker's book, Penfold situates quiet violence as a condition that manifests in the lived experience of Black South Africans,[3] as they navigate the rules of a new inclusive democratic space but where they often find old rules of exclusion still apply.

While not referencing Duiker, McAfee (2008) proposes the concept of "the political unconscious" as a way of understanding the social and political effects of the forced silence brought on by repressive contexts. She argues that while it may take time for people to find their voice in settings of transformation, it is also possible that speechlessness or the failure of some to find a space for channelling their voice could be the result of the trauma of repression, oppression and "of what is deemed foreign, strange, and terrifying" (2008, p. 26).

> Sociosymbolic orders founded on silencing, sacrificing, even annihilating what is other breed the kind of terror they purport to oppose. They created a semiotic public sphere that forecloses the possibility for some to speak and belong and they reenact the trauma of repression and exclusion. (2008, p. 27)

The quiet violence embodied in Daniella's story raises questions about South Africa's semiotic public sphere and possibilities for the political talking spaces in this sphere to hold voices like Daniella's in order to find a way from "speechlessness to participation" (McAfee 2008, p. 13).

3 Listening to the "*Unhearable*"

I interviewed Daniella Jantjies in March 2016 on a farm in the Western Cape Province of South Africa. I met Daniella briefly the previous day when I arrived on the farm to interview Anton, the farm owner, and also Daniella's employer. Anton,[4] an unpretentious, jovial man with a large frame and a gregarious manner, pointed to her as we walked to the back-door to enter the house: "This is Daniella. She helps me with the dogs".

Daniella was feeding the dogs that form part of the farmer's breeding stock. She was dressed in blue overalls and yellow gumboots. When I extended my hand and introduced myself, she looked surprised. She shook my hand, looked into my eyes and said hallo with a soft, shy voice.

During our interview the next day, Daniella spoke softly in Afrikaans, her mother tongue. As we started off, she used words sparingly. I had to prompt her for information after every short response.

Me:	*Did you grow up here?*
Daniella:	*On the farm, yes.*
Me:	*So, do your parents work here on the farm?*
Daniella:	*Yes.*
Me:	*And did you go to school here [in town]?*
Daniella:	*I completed my primary school here at the school on the farm and high school in town. [That is where I] finished matric.*

Up to this point, Daniella's responses were almost monosyllabic. She seemed eager to "give up the floor" (Abell and Myers 2008, p. 148). She offered little information other than the questions suggested. This changed when I asked her what it was that she had planned to do after finishing school. She sighed a deep sigh:

> *My begeerte was om verder te gaan studeer. (It was my desire to further my studies.)*

The Afrikaans word Daniella used here—*begeerte*—is significant. A more colloquial response would be *Ek wou verder gaan studeer (I wanted to further my studies).* The word, *begeerte,* expressed more than a want—it expressed a deep desire; a deeply held aspiration. This moment presented a turn in the tone of the interview. Daniella leaned forward and her voice took on an urgency that had not been there before this question.

The question about her expectations for her future seemed to unlock a moment of loss. And, as she considered this loss in the course of the interview, she often seemed at a loss for words. The question, and the presence of someone to listen, seemed to have opened up a space for trying to find words to describe an unarticulated incomprehension deep inside of her of how she ended up where she was—working on a farm with few prospects of realising her dream of studying and becoming a teacher.

As I took on the task of "looking for the outside story that is part of the inside story" (Back 2007, p. 9), I became deeply aware of my place, not only as interviewer but also as listener.

> To hear women's perspectives accurately, we have to learn to listen in stereo, receiving both the dominant and the muted channels clearly and tuning into them carefully to understand the relationship between them. (Anderson and Jack 2006)

As I listened to Daniella talking in the interview, this is the story I heard in the muted channel:

Daniella comes from a poor, Coloured family of farm workers who were excluded from land ownership in a racially segregated South Africa. Daniella is part of the "born-free" generation. She did not experience apartheid in its legal form. She did well at school and applied for a place at a local college to study to become a teacher. The college accepted her application, but Daniella had to return forms, signed by the farm manager—the brother of Anton, her current employer—to ensure a place at the college. Daniella and her mother took the forms to the house of the farm manager to sign. He was not in at the time, so they left the forms at his house. The deadline for returning the forms to the college to confirm Daniella's registration passed. Daniella never heard from the farm manager, and she did not go back to enquire why he seemed to ignore her request for assistance. She says she does not know why the farm manager did not sign the forms. She "thinks" the forms were "about money". Without alternative options, Daniella remained on the farm where she is excluded from the higher paying jobs because she is a woman, and she is unlikely to get her own house. She stayed with her parents. When her parents' house got too small for her, the only way out was to get married. To earn more money, Daniella took on extra work as a cleaner on Saturdays. Undisrupted patriarchal values perpetuate her role as cleaner and cook in her own home. In between her morning and afternoon shifts on a Saturday, she travels into town to buy food for the week for her own household. On Sundays—her only "free" day—she does the laundry and cooks a Sunday lunch for her, and the extended family. She wants to get her driver's licence, but she does not know where to find the time to practice, or a car to practice with.

Through the dominant channel, Daniella's story sounds like this:

> *I always wanted to be someone that people look up to. My dream is to ... I want to be there for everyone who needs me. If anyone is in need, I want to be the one to help them. I want to be prepared to help them. I want to say, do not worry, I will make a plan or, ... Do you understand? I ... that is the kind of person I am. And my dream is ... I also wanted to be independent someday. To walk into a shop, to buy things that I want and ... Do you understand? And I also want to say in two, three years I can buy myself a car. I can go for my learner's [licence]. I told my boss I also want to ... I want to go this year. But it is like, ... I do not know. To me it feels that it will not happen because I work every day and on weekends there is no time because I must come [to work] in the mornings. Yes, on the weekends I must come in every morning and then I must come in [to work] again at 16:00. And in the day I must get to town because we need things to eat on Sunday or in the week. So, there is never ... there is no time. And that is my wish, ... I want to, ... I see myself, ... I should have had my own transport already. I should have been able to drive.*

In the dominant channel, Daniella talks in uncertain terms about the life she imagined for herself, and the life she lives instead. Her voice often trails off as if she cannot find the words to describe the disconnect between the life she imagined to be possible and the life which she lives.

I asked Daniella if she could think of a reason why she did not go back to the farmer's house to ask for the forms he had to sign. With this question, my aim was to get a sense of her perception of herself as an agent. Does she see herself as someone who deserves attention, or to be acknowledged? When she says she does not know why the farmer did not sign the forms, is she saying she does not know, or is she saying that she does not know how to describe the layers of experiences that came before, and subsequent to the incident of the unsigned forms?

> *Why do you think the farm manager did not come back to you or why did he not sign the forms?*

Daniella hesitates before she responds. It is as if she is considering the question for the first time.

> *Maybe he thought I am not good enough to study.*
> *I … There are some days that I tell myself that I could have made it [in college] … that I could have made it … But those kind of thoughts make me think I do not deserve it ….*

No matter how many times Daniella tells herself that she could have made it in college, the unsigned forms are like ghosts hovering over her head, telling her she is not good enough—that she has unrealistic expectations for a woman in her position.

The farmer never talked to her about his reasons for not signing the forms to get her into college.

> *All I can say is, he kept us dangling. Then my mother said I must leave everything.*

In Afrikaans, Daniella said: *My ma het gesê ek moet dit uitlos.*

Although *leave everything* is an idiomatically correct translation, I want to propose other possible interpretations for the word, *uitlos.* In Afrikaans, you will use the phrase, *jy moet dit uitlos,* or *los dit uit,* when you urge another person to stop thinking about an emotionally hurtful act—even if the act seems to be an unforgiveable transgression. What you are suggesting to the other person is to forget about this act; erase it from your memory.

In urging Daniella to erase the incident of the unsigned forms from her memory, Daniella's mother is urging her to leave the experience unexamined—to leave the experience as it is. Do not go back to it. But, as Van der Merwe and Gobodo-Madikizela remind us after Ricoeur, we tend *not* to leave our life experiences as they are; we "examine and interpret them, to link them to one another" (2008, p. 1).

Daniella has urged herself to *los dit uit [leave it alone],* but now, after almost a decade, she still does not understand what exactly happened.

> *It was only … he had to sign, or his wife had to sign and I think there was a fee involved. And we were not financially strong and my mother asked him to help but we did not receive an answer.*

She pauses. *Then I accepted it like that. We do not have money. So, I will leave it.*

Daniella says she has seen how her parents have lived on the farm and "how it goes". She has always promised herself she would never be a farm worker.

> *But with time, I think by myself, I think: There are many people who say they will never do it but you still do it. I always said I will never work for a farmer. And look where I am today.*

The silences, the unsaid, in Daniella's narrative become like a third frequency carrying a quiet violence that emerge in unsettled thoughts—a sense of bereavement for a self that she longs for but cannot describe.

> *Sometimes I ask myself, is it too late? To make a change in my life ... I must just accept it. It is like it is. I will not, I will not, obtain that which I am supposed to ...*

This quiet violence reveals itself in Daniella's description of a difficult relationship with her parents. She talks about angry and potentially violent exchanges between her parents and between her mother and herself:

> *And still, I have not spoken to anyone about it. [I have] told no-one. And it feels to me like there are many days I want to talk about it but it always feels to me like I cannot talk to my mother about it. My mother is very strict and speaks harshly and so, to me it feels like she is going to scold again. That is because I ... I long for that relationship, that relationship with my mother. And they say, give the flower while she lives and I do not want to cry and carry on the day she dies. The day she dies I want to know I shared everything with her. I was there for her and I made her proud and so.*

Her parents seem to have difficulty relating to her.

> *To me, it sometimes feels as if I disappointed my parents. Maybe it is about the studying.* Daniella pauses. *She (her mother) always makes jokes (about Daniella's love of books), and it actually hurts me when they do it. I love books a lot. And.* Daniella pauses and starts to cry. *When I sit at the table, reading*

> *my book, then she (my mother) or my dad will always say, you should have sat like that in an office. They make those kind of jokes and put me down. My mother would always then point out that this auntie's child is studying or that auntie's child is already working but I am at home.*

In the muted channel, Daniella's parents "teasing" sounds like a projection of their own confusion about the continued presence of apartheid rules and boundaries when they are supposed to be free of these rules and boundaries. Rather than being disappointed with Daniella, they may be disappointed in the unfulfilled promise of a "new" South Africa in their lives. The effects of race, class and gender subjugation on all their lives remain unspoken in the household. The violence of this lost vocabulary manifests in their making fun of her dream. They project their loss for words to name their confusion, regret and embarrassment on Daniella. And, she has no choice but to endure the projection.

In my own reading of Ricoeur, the incident of the unsigned forms is an "anchor-point" (1991, p. 433) in Daniella's story. It is the point that roots a seminal life experience of loss. It represents an imaginary of what she could have been. But because the experience is not fully examined—it seems easier to succumb to her mother's call to *leave it alone*—it distorts the logic of plotting and understanding her own story. It leaves her with an incoherent narrative without a clear articulation of the reference points that account for the lack of choices she now faces. She jumps from talking in the past tense and talking in the present tense. She lives with the questions, asks new questions every day, and every day the answers are more elusive.

> *I still think about it … And, I always said, I saw how my parents live on the farm and how it goes and I always said I want to study. I want to make my parents proud. I want them to say, my child studied … my child … Do you understand?* She takes on the voice of her parents: *My child took her school career further.* She slips back into her own voice: *That is what I always wanted.*

Disconnected from political talking spaces where Daniella can tell her story in the presence of others, where she can "appear" as a member of a collective and where she can find reference points in other experiences,

Daniella's pain remains mostly in her own head, unheard and unresolved. Like the distress or the shock emanating from the trauma of a lost limb, Daniella's dream of what could have been seems like that of a phantom limb—a haunting wound with no rational explanation.

4 The Political Talking Space in South Africa

Almost 25 years after the apartheid state ended, South African society seems, like Daniella, suspended in the contradiction of the post-apartheid dream and a post-1994 reality. South Africans talk freely about the dream in which they were liberated from apartheid to re-imagine a society that contains possibilities for all its citizens to be equal, emancipated participants in an inclusive political project. We are less vocal about the post-1994 reality in which race, class and gender subjugation remain tied to the ghostlike moorings of colonial and apartheid structures. When I say we are less vocal, I do not mean that we do not talk about the persistence of apartheid ghosts among us; I mean that we seem unsure how to talk about these ghosts, and how to listen and respond to their haunting expression in people's lives. To be precise, South Africans—those who were oppressed by apartheid and those who remain in privileged positions because they were privileged by apartheid—are unsure how to acknowledge the presence of these ghosts. We have, says Ramphele (2008), "difficulty acknowledging the depth of our trauma" and "our wounds fester partly as a result of our denial of their extent and their impact on attempts to transform society" (2008, p. 15).

Before 1994, the political talking spaces that marked the resistance to apartheid—protest marches, meetings, organised efforts to encourage encounters between different race groups—seemed to have been integrated and inclusive of a range of voices across race, class and gender divisions. The evolving resistance to apartheid up to the formation of the United Democratic Front (UDF) stemmed from an understanding of politics and political talking spaces as being rooted in the personal of the lived experience (see Neocosmos 1998 for the historical significance of the UDF and popular power; Suttner 2005, 2014). In these talking spaces, the effect of apartheid on the lives of Black South Africans found political meaning as these personal experiences were shared, where they resonated, and transformed into a force that sparked and sustained the dynamic of political change. In the act of talking together, stories of personal subjugation were translated into vocabularies with political meaning. In the language of Arendt, these talking spaces offered opportunities for a plurality of voices to negotiate differences and give birth to a new understanding of political justice and what it means to be human in the presence of political others.

After 1994, the Truth and Reconciliation Commission (TRC) was arguably one of the most important talking spaces for revealing diverse experiences of human rights violations effected by the apartheid regime. For two years, more than 20,000 people appeared before the Commission, creating a space for South Africans to talk about their experiences to others—not just the Commissioners—who were compelled to listen to them. Landman (1999, p. 415) argues that the TRC process introduced the possibility of storytelling as a means to healing. The potential of healing after appearing at a single public hearing is limited (Verwoerd 1999, p. 307), and should not be overestimated. But the TRC did create a platform where "the marginalised voice speaks to the public ear, the unspeakable is spoken – and translated – the personal story brought from the innermost of the individual bind us anew to the collective" (Krog 1998, p. 237 in; Verwoerd 1999, p. 308). More importantly, the TRC created an exchange that brought together those who took the testimony stand, those who witnessed the testimonies, and those who listened to the proceedings on the radio, or watched it on television, exemplifying a "relationship of systems" that opened up possibilities for destabilising identities and making way for renewal (McAfee 2008, p. 104).

The problem is the opportunities in South Africa, offered by political talking spaces such as the TRC seem to have been suspended as the TRC wrapped up its proceedings. Lacking spaces that offer room for people to come together with the intention to talk to one another about the effect of apartheid on people's current lived experience, South Africans now seem to be at a loss for a political language that could contain the contradictions of what it means to be part of the South African body politic. Lacking political talking spaces, like the TRC, where personal stories resonate, and find collective meaning in the stories of other similar or dissimilar lived experiences, or where stories disrupt or destabilise identities, South

Africans struggle to re-find a language to describe "new selves", and new ways of describing who we are and how we move forward. At a loss for words, South Africans seem to defer their voices to political commentators, talk show hosts and other experts. Now the political talking space belongs to politicians and elites who know how to talk "politics". Politics have become the consequence of elite conversations (Political commentator, Professor Piet Croucamp on "Praat Saam," 2019).

The problem is not that marginalised South Africans do not talk. Protest action is, as it has been historically, part of the repertoire of political expression in South Africa's vocal political landscape. Since at least 2005, demands for improved service delivery have become a hold-all interpretation for protest in mostly poor, and/or rural communities (see Brown 2015; Duncan 2016, for an analysis of recent protest action in South Africa). In 2015 and 2016, student protests under the banner of #feesmustfall disrupted universities across South Africa. In both cases, the frustration seems to be rooted in the contradiction of the post-apartheid dream and the post-1994 reality. There is a "quiet violence" intrinsic to the noise of these loud and disruptive voices. The register of their voices, despite its public tone, does not seem to resonate in mainstream political talking spaces. The voices of the service delivery protestors are rendered inaudible when, rather than the substance of protest action, government officials, the police, and researchers quibble over definitions of what constitute protest action. The lived experience behind the frustration is silenced by journalists who provide simplistic or superficial accounts of the protestors' demands, and choose to cover those incidents that are most likely to provide visual spectacle to media consumers (Davis 2018). Political commentators, university staff and others in positions of power often alleged that the students' demands were incoherent, unreasonable, or that they were negotiating in bad faith. Leaders of the student protests accused the university management of not acknowledging the "silent violence" intrinsic to the commodifying of education (McNulty 2016). Negotiations between the governing authorities, academic staff and students to address the students' demands proved problematic and often broke down. The problem, says Garman, was not just a lack of listening; rather the problem was that those in power in these environments were "being required to listen to *something in particular that is very hard to hear* and very possibly *unhearable*" (2018b, p. 96 italics in the original text).

5 Listening in Political Talking Spaces

In a television interview, academic, and former member of South Africa's Truth and Reconciliation Commission (TRC), Wilhelm Verwoerd—who is also the grandson of apartheid architect, Hendrik Verwoerd—talked about the ramifications of his decision to join the struggle against apartheid defying the political beliefs of his family and his grandfather particularly. Asked what question he would ask his grandfather if he were alive today, Verwoerd responded: "I would ask him why it was so difficult for him to hear how apartheid affected the lives of those who suffered under it" (2019). In Verwoerd's response, he places the responsibility for listening on his grandfather. It was not the responsibility of the repressed to have a voice; it was the responsibility of those with power to listen.

This response helps to situate the act of listening as it is under examination in this chapter: as an act of political consequence and as an act for which those with assumed power and authority over the "socio-cultural means of interpretation and communication" (Fraser 1986, p. 425) carry the burden of responsibility.

Dreher (2009) is unambiguous about who carries the weight of responsibility for a different kind of listening. In her work on the relationship between journalists and marginalised communities, Dreher proposes a shift in the "focus and responsibility for change from marginalized voices and on to the conventions, institutions, and privileges which shape who and what can be heard in the media" (Tanja Dreher 2010, p. 85). In this chapter, my construction of political talking spaces assumes that talking spaces are mediated spaces, and like other kinds of mediated spaces, governed by asymmetrical power relations.

Bassel's politics of listening (2017) emanates from an experience of spaces created for dialogue in the wake of the Tottenham "riots" in London during 2011. She illustrates the silencing effect on some participants in the talking space when neighbourhoods and those involved in the "riots" were depicted as "notorious and outside of the decent political community" (2017, p. 39). When those involved in the riots tried to explain their political position, their claims were dismissed as "excuses" for criminality. They had difficulty being heard because of an unwillingness on the part of those who regarded themselves as outside the riots to listen to the "rioters", except in terms of "us" and "them".

> In this binary space there is little recognition of other narratives as equal, or any attempt to consider the world as someone else constructs it for you, to make sense together in recognition of intersubjective equality. (Bassel 2017, pp. 38–39)

For Bassel, the politics of listening has a particular purpose: to transform audibility in political talking spaces and to break down binaries between the audible—"Us"—and the silent or stigmatised others—"Them" (2017, pp. 5–7). With this, Bassel identifies listening, together with speaking, "as a site of struggle and a source of transformation" (2017, p. 19), but also as a different way of doing politics (2017, p. 4).

Bickford (1996) conceives of politics, like Bassel (and after Arendt), as inherently conflictual and contentious, and of listening, or political listening, as a particular kind of attention we pay to one another in political talking spaces. It is this particular kind of listening attention that has potential to keep us from being "doomed to war, anarchy, or the relentless clash of unyielding wills" (Bickford 1996, p. 2). Bickford pushes against Habermasian conceptions of communicative action as means to reach consensus or agreement.

> Politics is not simply about shared interests or shared conceptions of the good; it is how we decide what to do in the face of conflict about all these things. Politics in this sense is constituted neither by consensus nor community, but by the practices through which citizens argue about interests and ends – in other words, by communication. It is through such communicative practices that we come to understand our interests and our identities in ways that inform our decisions about what to do. (1996, p. 11)

In this fractious and contentious atmosphere, listening cannot be seen as a therapeutic or as a "caring or amicable practice" (Bickford 1996, p. 2), but rather as an act of intention that enables the body politic to resolve conflict through speaking and listening. Bassel concurs with Bickford: Listening is a matter of politics. It is not an "art" in the way Back (2007) proposes. As politics, listening makes explicit the context of conflict and inequality. These are not "the conversations of friendly associates. Politics means naming the social forces that deflect from particular voices, and is necessarily adversarial as well as active and creative" (2017, p. 7).

McAfee (2008) combines the political world and the world of psychology and offers the concept of "the political unconscious" as a way of understanding the social and political effects of repression that is driven underground in post-conflict contexts. McAfee makes it clear that her aim is not to draw a parallel between the macro realm of the political public sphere and the micro realm of analyst and analysand. Rather, her aim is to show a connection in how "our particular and collective traumas *show up* in the sociosymbolic public sphere".

> That is where they *circulate.* It is from there that repression and oppression and potentially liberating media *operate.* Hence, … public talk may serve a psychoanalytic function for the public sphere. (2008, pp. 24, emphasis in the original text)

McAfee draws on the psychoanalytic notion of talking as a medium that enables the traumatised person to work through the trauma rather than continuously repeating, acting out or re-enacting the trauma. Different forms of "public talking", she argues, hold similar mediating possibilities for reconstituting a political community in which the members of the community work through, rather than repeat, act out, or re-enact the trauma.

McAfee proposes that public talking requires a certain "posture"—a posture "where members of a political community ought to lean to each other, rather than digging in their heels and leaning back" (2008, p. 84). In proposing this posture, listening seems implicit in McAfee's argument. If political listening could be conceived of as a way of witnessing another, then "bearing witness in a political community can transform the community itself" (McAfee 2008, p. 97).

While leaning on psychology, Lipari's notions of listening resonate with the political dimension of listening as a disruption of identity. Listening, she argues, "involves an encounter with radical alterity that disrupts our everyday understandings and habits of thought" (2010, p. 350). In that moment of *being* unsettled lies the possibility for reflection and transformation.

It is in McAfee (2008) and Lipari's (2010) work that I see a merging of a talking space, which not only is political and adversarial but also holds aspects of care and healing. The tentative voice of Daniella directs us to such a space: marginalised voices unaccustomed to talking among others, some or most of whom are unfamiliar to them, requires a space with room for a telos of caring or healing.

McAfee's vocabulary of the "political work of mourning", witnessing and "working through, through narrative" (2008, pp. 82–107) locates political talking as a vital act, not only for working through difficulties of political disagreement but also as providing therapeutic, or healing spaces in which unheard, or neglected voices can "appear" (McAfee 2008, p. 13).

Lipari's (2010, 2014) understanding of listening, *not* as a path to agreement, or seeing the world through the same lens, resonates with the political dimensions of listening proposed by Bassel and Bickford. For Lipari, listening positions the participants in a talking space in a particular form of being—a place from which to extend an offer of hospitality to an (other). This suggests a stance, or again a posture, of invitation and hosting that contains a space for disagreement and diversity while simultaneously offering potential for healing.

> Listening being is thus an invitation – a hosting. This hosting of other is as guest, as a not-me. I don't have to *understand,* although you may feel 'understood'. I don't have to translate your words into familiar categories or ideas. I don't have to 'feel' what you feel, or 'know' what it feels like to be you. What I do need to do is to stand in proximity to your pain. To stand with you, right next to you, and to belong to you, fully present to the ongoing expression of you. Letting go of my ideas about who you are, who I am, and what 'should' be. I let all that go, and stay present, attending, aware. (2010, pp. 350–351 all italics in the original)

In another chapter in this book, Keynan refers to Lapari's notion of *being,* as well as—after LaCapra and Volken—the collective work of "working through" the violence of past trauma as proposed by McAfee. Keynan proposes that face-to-face encounters provide a relational space that "frees the self from a subjugating self-centralism" and that facing another creates "an openness to the other's vulnerability" (Keynan 2020).

Garman's examination earlier in this chapter, of political talking spaces in South Africa, shows that the face-to-face encounter, while a critical starting point, may not in itself be enough to create conditions for freedom from "self-centralism"; another's face may not necessarily signify "an openness to the other's vulnerability". In these face-to-face encounters, it may also be necessary to pay particular attention to the act of listening to the "unhearable" as Garman suggests earlier. Creating political talking spaces where Daniella's experience can be heard as a shared experience may be contingent on a shift in emphasis from "giving voice to the voiceless" to pay more attention to how habits of discursive privilege impact on willingness and capacity to listen—to receive and recognise marginalised voices in the encounter. This shift requires an adjustment in the way in which those who have assumed participatory authority in political talking spaces consider others who share the talking space:

> Listening here is, first and foremost, the act of recognizing what others *have to say*, recognizing *that* they have something to say or, better, that they, like all human beings, have the capacity to give an account of their lives that is reflexive and continuous, an ongoing, embodied process of reflection. (Couldry 2009, pp. 580, emphasis from the original text)

It further requires a consideration of listening as being present in a talking space cognisant of the political, relational and ethical implications of this presence:

> Thus listening becomes a prior ethical act; we belong to the matter addressed when the ethical call enters us and become part of us, when we have made a space for it, a home for it, inside us where we are not. This is the self-transcendence, the gift, of listening. It is where I make a space where I am not – where I have, however, temporarily renounced my projects, goals, and understandings in order to *listen be* with the other. (Lipari 2010, p. 350)

The more pertinent question, as Spivak points out, is not whether the subaltern can speak, but who will listen (Gunew 1990, p. 59).

6 Conclusion

What would spaces look like where Daniella's story and stories like hers can take on a different meaning in a context of political transformation? What kind of talking space would transmute Daniella's inaudible story into a *hearable* experience that may be transformative for Daniella herself, *and* for those who listen to what she has to say?

Daniella's story points to at least two conditions to consider in curating political talking spaces that would enable Daniella to find an "anchor-point" in her story with which to examine, plot and understand her own story in the context of a political community.

First, there is a spatial dimension to her exclusion from political talking spaces. She lives on a farm, outside of rural town. The socio-economic conditions she describes limit her ability to access existing political talking spaces. Political talking spaces are still largely "inviting" of people with economic and social resources to access these spaces. For researchers, the starting point in settings like these is to understand the physical places where Daniella is already in conversations with others. Here, the potential lies in smaller, more intimate political talking spaces as a starting point that include Daniella's immediate circle of friends, family and co-workers. What are the possibilities to insert some questions, and attention to modes of listening between the participants that may build confidence to access, and even initiate other spaces for political talking?

The second consideration that emanates from Daniella's story is to pay attention to the dynamic of "leave it alone", and "move on". This dynamic is a feature of the wider conversation in South Africa's political talking spaces. Daniella's description of her relationship with her parents reflects the dilemma, not only between different generations of South Africans, who were disadvantaged through apartheid, but also between Black South Africans and their white counterparts. Through her parents, Daniella's only reference point remains the conditions that shaped her voice as a third-generation farm labourer. In this setting, her voice is audible, but in her head, the more audible voice seems to be that of her mother who is a persisting presence in her narrative. Daniella's mother first appears as she escorts Daniella to the farm manager's house to ask for his signature on Daniella's college registration forms. As it becomes clear that the farm manager is not paying attention to the request to sign the forms, her mother tells Daniella to forget about her dream to study—to "leave it alone", to erase the dream of being a teacher from her memory. Daniella's mother also appears in the story as someone who makes fun of Daniella's love of reading. These intergenerational exchanges between Daniella and her mother may be indicative of a form of double bind: The mother looks at herself through the eyes of her daughter, and, bounded by the conditions that limited her own voice, she seems reluctant to insist on transforming the conditions for her daughter. The voice of the older generation, shaped by habits of subjugation, drowns out Daniella's younger voice and submits it to the same subjugation.

The same double bind seems to govern political talking spaces where those who suffered the trauma of apartheid meet with those who benefited from apartheid. Still living with the authority and privilege bestowed on them by apartheid but embarrassed by their complicity, or unwilling to acknowledge their part in the effects of the system they maintained, white South Africans urge Black South Africans to "leave it alone"—*los dit uit*—and move on.

In this context, it is easy to recognise the problem with proposing communicative modes where the act of listening is more prominent than the act of having a voice. Victims of apartheid trauma need to draw on the weight that voice carries to assert their power in political talking spaces. And those who have assumed participatory authority in political talking spaces through habits of having the voice will not easily submit to calls for them to listen—an act that is seen as passive and belonging in the private sphere (Lacey 2013, p. 3).

Political talking spaces that bring together victims of apartheid, and those who were at the very least complicit in maintaining it, requires a reconsideration of the listener, the voice and the talking place itself. In order to shift or destabilise identities of those who come to political talking spaces with participatory authority assumed through historical privilege, the emphasis cannot continue to be on voice. The responsibility must shift from having voice to listening in—to tune into—and to listen for that which may be "very hard to hear", or indeed, inaudible. Daniella's "appearance" in a political talking space is dependent on those with the assumption of participative authority to surrender their voice and to embrace the position of *being* listening.

The epigraph of Van der Merwe and Gobodo-Madikizela (2008) that frames this chapter implies a journey with ethical implications. A journey, as Lipari reminds us, that requires those with participatory authority to "belong to the matter addressed", to be prepared to renounce their own projects, goals and understandings in order to *"listen to be"* with the other (2010, p. 350).

To continue the process started by the TRC to forge a new nation, a South African body politic that accounts for diverse experiences of being South African, it is essential to create political talking spaces where participants come together with the intention to tune in to several layers of frequencies in the vocabularies of marginalised voices. Such spaces will enable Daniella Jantjies and others who sound like her to "appear", and to embark with others on a journey to "re-find" and indeed *re-define* the lost language of a South African body politic.

Notes

1. Not her real name.
2. References to race in this chapter conform to protocols used by Statistics South Africa. Racial classification is problematic but necessary to understand the enduring legacy of apartheid classification in South Africa's political, social and economic narrative.
3. I use "Black" here as an encompassing category including Coloured and Indian people in South Africa.
4. Not his real name.

References

Abell, J., & Myers, G. (2008). Analyzing Research Interviews. In R. Wodak & M. Krzyżanowski (Eds.), *Qualitative Discourse Analysis in the Social Sciences* (pp. 145–161). New York: Palgrave Macmillan.

Anderson, K., & Jack, D. C. (2006). Learning to Listen – Interview Techniques and Analyses. In R. Perks & A. Thomson (Eds.), *The Oral History Reader* (2nd ed., pp. 129–142). London/New York: Routledge.

Arendt, H. (1958). *The Human Condition*. Chicago/London: The University of Chicago Press.

Arendt, H. (1960). Freedom and Politics: A Lecture. *Chicago Review, 14*(1), 28–46.

Back, L. (2007). *The Art of Listening*. Oxford/New York: Berg.

Bassel, L. (2017). *The Politics of Listening – Possibilities and Challenges for Democratic Life*. London: Palgrave Pivot.

Benhabib, S. (1996). The Democratic Moment and the Problem of Difference. In S. Benhabib (Ed.), *Democracy and Difference – Contesting the Boundaries of the Political* (pp. 2–18). Princeton: Princeton University Press.

Bickford, S. (1996). *The Dissonance of Democracy – Listening, Conflict, and Citizenship*. Ithaca/London: Cornell University Press.

Brown, J. (2015). *South Africa's Insurgent Citizens*. London: Zed Books.

Couldry, N. (2009). Rethinking the Politics of Voice. *Continuum, 23*(4), 579–582.

Couldry, N. (2010). *Why Voice Matters: Culture and Politics after Neoliberalism*. London: Sage.

Davis, R. (2018, 13 July). Why Counting Service Delivery Protests is More Complicated Than it Seems. *Daily Maverick*, https://www.dailymaverick.co.za/article/2018-2007-2013-why-counting-service-delivery-protests-is-more-complicated-than-it-seems/

Dreher, T. (2009). Listening Across Difference: Media and Multiculturalism Beyond the Politics of Voice. *Continuum, 23*(4), 445–458. https://doi.org/10.1080/10304310903015712.

Dreher, T. (2010). Speaking Up or Being Heard? Community Media Interventions and the Politics of Listening. *Media, Culture & Society, 32*(1), 85–103. https://doi.org/10.1177/0163443709350099.

Duiker, K. S. (2001). *The Quiet Violence of Dreams*. Cape Town: Kwela Books.

Duncan, J. (2016). *Protest Nation – The Right to Protest in South Africa*. Pietermaritzburg: University of KwaZulu-Natal Press.

Fraser, N. (1986). Toward a Discourse Ethic of Solidarity. *Praxis International, 5*(4), 425–429.

Garman, A. (2018a). *Hosting as Listening: Creating Spaces for Attunement in South Africa*. Paper presented at the Politics of Listening, University of New South Wales

Garman, A. (2018b). When the Students are Revolting: The (Im)Possibilities of Listening in Academic Contexts in South Africa. In T. Dreher & A. A. Mondal (Eds.), *Ethical Responsiveness and the Politics of Difference* (pp. 93–115). Cham: Palgrave Macmillan.

Gobodo-Madikizela, P. (2012). Remembering the Past: Nostalgia, Traumatic Memory, and the Legacy of Apartheid. *Peace and Conflict: Journal of Peace Psychology, 18*(3), 252–267.
Gunew, S. (1990). Questions of Multi-culturalism. In S. Harasym (Ed.), *Gayatri Chakravorty Spivak* (pp. 59–66). New York/London: Routledge.
Keynan, I. (2020). Ethics of Memory, Trauma and Reconciliation. In K. Wale, J. Prager & P. Gobodo-Madikizela (Eds.), *Post-Conflict Hauntings: Transforming Memories of Historical Trauma*. Basingstoke: Palgrave Macmillan.
Krog, A. (1998). *Country of My Skull.* Johannesburg: Random House.
LaCapra, D. (2014). *Writing History, Writing Trauma*. Baltimore: Johns Hopkins University Press.
Lacey, K. (2013). *Listening Publics – The Politics and Experience of Listening in the Media Age*. Cambridge: Polity.
Landman, C. (1999). Telling Sacred Stories – Eersterust and the Forced Removals of the 1960s. *Religion & Theology, 6*(3), 416–427.
Lipari, L. (2010). Listening, Thinking, Being. *Communication Theory, 20*(3), 348–362. https://doi.org/10.1111/j.1468-2885.2010.01366.x.
Lipari, L. (2014). *Listening, Thinking, Being – Towards an Ethics of Attunement.* University Park: The Pennsylvania State University Press.
McAfee, N. (2008). *Democracy and the Political Unconscious.* New York: Columbia University Press.
McNulty, K. (2016). Student Protests in Democratic South Africa. *South Africa History Online* https://www.sahistory.org.za/archive/interview-shaeera-kalla-former-src-president-wits-university-interviewed-kyla-mc-nulty
Mouffe, C. (2013). *Agonistics – Thinking the World Politically*. London/New York: Verso.
Neocosmos, M. (1998). From People's Politics to State Politics: Aspects of National Liberation in South Africa. In O. O. Adebayo (Ed.), *The Politics of Opposition in Contemporary Africa* (pp. 195–240). Stockholm: Nordiska Afrikainstitutet.
Oelofsen, M. (2017). *Hearing the Citizens: Inequality, Access to Journalists and the Prospects for Inclusively Mediated Spaces of Political Deliberation in South Africa.* (Doctor of Philosophy), Rhodes University.
Penfold, T. (2017). A Specific Kind of Violence: Insanity and Identity in Contemporary Brazilian and South African Literature. *Journal of Southern African Studies, 43*(5), 1049–1067.
Praat Saam. (2019). Radio Sonder Grense (RSG) South African Broadcasting Corporation (http://www.rsg.co.za/potgooi-soek.asp?ProgramID=75).

Ramphele, M. (2008). *Laying Ghosts to Rest – Dilemmas of the Transformation in South Africa*. Cape Town: Tafelberg.
Ricoeur, P. (1991). Life: A Story in Search of a Narrator. In M. J. Valdés (Ed.), *A Ricoeur Reader: Reflection and Imagination* (pp. 425–437). Toronto/Buffalo: University of Toronto Press.
Schaffer, K., & Smith, S. (2004). *Human Rights and Narrated Lives – The Ethics of Recognition*. New York: Palgrave Macmillan.
Suttner, R. (2005). Legacies and Meanings of the United Democratic Front (UDF) Period for Contemporary South Africa. In C. Hendricks & L. Lushabe (Eds.), *From National Liberation to Democratic Renaissance in Southern Africa* (pp. 59–81). Dakar: Codesria.
Suttner, R. (2014). Popular Power, Constitutional Democracy and Crisis: South Africa 1994–2014. *Strategic Review for Southern Africa, 36*(2), 7–30.
Van Der Merwe, C. N., & Gobodo-Madikizela, P. (2008). *Narrating Our Healing – Perspectives on Working Through Trauma*. Newcastle: Cambridge Scholars Publishing.
Verwoerd, W. J. (1999). Toward the Truth About the TRC: A Response to Key Moral Criticisms of the South African Truth and Reconciliation Commission. *Religion & Theology, 6*(3), 303–324.
Verwoerd, W. J. (2019, 19 January). *Wilhelm Verwoerd/Interviewer: H. Van Wyk*. Kwêla, DSTV, Channel 144, https://kyknet.dstv.com/program/kwela

9

Intergenerational Nostalgic Haunting and Critical Hope: Memories of Loss and Longing in Bonteheuwel

Kim Wale

> *[They] miss those days, you can hear it in their voices… as my mom and them, they were all running around the streets freely, they could play.*
> —Group One, Bonteheuwel 2017

> *Those days the people… were free… you could just go to work without being robbed or being stabbed or whatever. But nowadays… it's got worse.*
> —Group Two, Bonteheuwel 2017

These two quotes come from focus group interviews with South African youth in a township called Bonteheuwel, formerly designated for people classified as "coloured" under the apartheid regime. The parents and grandparents of the young South Africans interviewed were forcibly removed under

The A.W. Mellon Foundation provided financial support for the research that informs this chapter. The writing of this chapter was made possible through the support of the South African Research Chair Initiative (SARChI) Chair in Violent Histories and Transgenerational Trauma at Stellenbosch University funded by South Africa National Research Foundation (NRF).

K. Wale (✉)
Stellenbosch University, Stellenbosch, South Africa
e-mail: kwale@sun.ac.za

K. Wale et al. (eds.), *Post-Conflict Hauntings*, Palgrave Studies in Compromise after Conflict, https://doi.org/10.1007/978-3-030-39077-8_9

the oppressive Group Areas Act from communities across Cape Town to the space of Bonteheuwel, losing their homes and livelihoods in the process. These quotes are indicative of a common sentiment expressed by youth in the three focus groups conducted that their parents "miss" the past which is constructed as a time of greater freedom and safety in relation to the present.

The year 1994 marked the transition of South Africa to a non-racial democracy after many years of racist oppression, dehumanisation, violence and resistance. The term "born-free" came to denote the generation of young South Africans who were born into democracy and therefore imagined as free from the burdens of this painful history (the second generation). Yet, as indicated in the quotes above, these born-free from Bonteheuwel speak about the past that was experienced by their parents with a nostalgic sense that it was better back then, and it is worse now. What is striking and disconcerting about this construction of "those days" is that although they are speaking about the period of violent apartheid oppression, the second generation (re-)remember this period as a time of greater freedom and safety in relation to their personal experiences of "nowadays" which are felt as a time of great fear and insecurity.

The aim of this focus group research in Bonteheuwel was to explore how the generation born after apartheid, to the parents and grandparents who suffered this oppressive system, remember this violent time that preceded their birth. It sought to understand the intergenerational transfer of memories of apartheid trauma and how the second generation makes sense of these memories in relation to their everyday lived realities of post-apartheid South Africa. The intergenerational transmission of traumatic memory has been described as a haunting that spans generations (Abraham and Torok 1994). In the post-Holocaust context, theorists demonstrate how this intergenerational haunting occurs partly through a tendency to "cocoon" such memory in silence creating a "conspiracy of silence" and a related sense of shame that is passed down to the next generation (Danieli 1984; Hoffman 2004).

Eva Hoffman has called the second generation of survivors of the Holocaust the "hinge generation" and described how they inherit a sense of responsibility to keep this memory alive (Hoffman 2004: xv). Similarly Marion Hirsch coins the term "post-memory" to describe the powerful relationship that the second generation has to the traumatic memories of the first generation that they seem to "constitute memories in their own right" (Hirsch 2008: 103). While not overtly spoken, these memories become a powerful "living presence" that is communicated through embodied scars and everyday material objects (such as photographs) that as "testimonial objects…carry memory traces from the past and embody the process of its transmission" (Hirsch and Spitzer 2006: 353; Kidron 2009). Parents may not overtly tell their children about their traumatic memories, yet their children experience these haunting memories through non-verbal and embodied forms of communication.

In the chapter by Kagoyire, Vysma and Richters (2020) in this volume on the "pathways of intergenerational transmission" from mother to child following the Genocide in Rwanda, these authors demonstrate how it is not only trauma but also healing that is passed down through the intergenerational bond. In South Africa, Frankish and Bradbury (2012) have demonstrated how grandmothers do not share their traumatic memories of apartheid with their "born-free" grandchildren; rather they pass on nostalgic stories as potential resources of strength and hope for the younger generations.

The literature on the transfer of intergenerational trauma has focused on the haunting of silenced, painful and shameful memory across generations. Yet the focus group interviews analysed in this chapter indicate that intergenerational hauntings may be expressed through the ghosts of nostalgic longing for a time before one's birth. This chapter seeks to draw on this research to theorise the complex role played by intergenerational nostalgic memory in relation to both a traumatic past and a traumatic present in the South African context. It seeks to demonstrate the role that intergenerational nostalgia plays in relation to trauma in two ways. On the one hand, it will show how the second generation shares their experiences of moments when they witness their parents being haunted by nostalgic memory from the past. These moments can be described as "intergenerational memory encounters" and they open up a channel from the past to the present through which the second generation connects both to what is longed for and also to the less overt, darker twin of nostalgic memory—traumatic memory.

The second relationship between trauma and nostalgia explored in this chapter is in relation to the present day violence and suffering experienced by these young South Africans. The trauma of the present is narrated through a nostalgic yearning for a past imagined as a time of safety and connection. It is argued that this nostalgic haunting from a past that came before their birth provides young South Africans with an imagination through which they express their critique of the present and their hopes for change in the future. In doing so, this chapter seeks to excavate the seeds of critical hope that lie within the haunting power of intergenerational nostalgia for the youth within communities that suffered apartheid violence and continue to suffer post-apartheid violence.

1 The Many Faces of Nostalgia: A Conceptual History

Nostalgia is generally understood to be a longing and desire for a lost place (home) or a lost time (the past). The concept of nostalgia was first coined in 1688 by a Swiss doctor, Johannes Hofer, to diagnose a medical condition of homesickness. He brought together two Greek words, *Nostos* (return to home) and *Algia* (painful longing), to capture the essence of the condition he was treating (Hofer 1934[1688]). Nostalgia remained a diagnostic category throughout the eighteenth and nineteenth centuries.

Gradually over the course of the twentieth century, nostalgia transformed from an individual medical condition of a potentially fatal longing for place (home) to a collective, sentimental mode of remembering an earlier time. Some attempts to theorise this new mode of collective nostalgia were more sympathetic, viewing it as serving a soothing function in times of change and uncertainty (Davis 1979). On the whole, however, evaluations of nostalgia were critical and dismissive, characterising it as excessively sentimental weakness, resulting in an inauthentic or partial remembering of history, which was prone to ideological manipulation by reactionary and conservative forces (Jameson 1991; Lasch 1991; Doane and Hodges 1987; Stewart 1984). In response to the "hostile and dismissive" critique of nostalgia, Stuart Tannock, argued that nostalgia can be a valuable way of remembering the past (Tannock 1995: 453). He suggested that nostalgia is a "structure of feeling" and is not inherently ideological. Rather he proposed that we think of "multiple nostalgias", and in each case ask who is nostalgic for what, and in the name of which community?

This line of thinking was further developed in Svetlana Boym's (2001) seminal work on nostalgia where she distinguishes between "restorative" and "reflective" nostalgia. Restorative nostalgia focuses on the restoration of a prefabricated notion of "home" and "the past". This is an uncritical and backward looking form of nostalgia, which presents itself as truth and tradition and is dangerous in its vulnerability to divisive, ideological manipulation.

In psychological language, restorative nostalgia may be understood as a form of melancholia, or the inability to mourn the past. Following Freud, melancholia involves a process of idealisation of the lost object through nostalgia while at the same time splitting off and repressing the unwanted aspects of this memory (Duncan et al. 2012). Letting go of the idealised lost object is avoided because it would imply the integration of the repressed, uncomfortable, unwanted aspects of past memory (Duncan et al. 2012). Derek Hook further demonstrates how nostalgia can work like a "sweet" screen memory which draws attention away from a more painful, traumatic memory. Defending against the unwanted memory, nostalgia acts like a static snapshot and often contains particularly exaggerated and vivid details (Hook 2012). As screen memory, the heightened and static nature of nostalgic memory serves to lock out the painful repressed memory and to overcompensate for what is denied.

Politically, nostalgia can similarly function to create a defensive collective identity based on an idealised view of the past in the face of present experiences of insecurity and social change (Davis 1979). This collective melancholia can be seen, for example, in the nostalgic memories of many white South Africans who draw on idealised versions of the apartheid past to defend against their experiences of political uncertainty following the transition to democracy as well as to defend against the integration of shameful knowledge about the apartheid past (Gobodo-Madikizela 2012).

In contrast, reflective nostalgia represents the shared existential human experience of longing that resists the urge to return home even as it longs for it. It welcomes the creative possibilities for the future which emerge from this space of ambiguity (Boym 2001). Jacob Dlamini's (2009) work on black South African nostalgia for township spaces under apartheid is an example of reflective nostalgia. Rather than a desire to return or recreate this past, nostalgia is being used in the mode of reflective critique of the dominant ways in which township spaces under apartheid are remembered only as sites of human degradation or resistance to apartheid.

Instead, he seeks to remember forgotten memories of the past in order to critique both the hegemony of memory and the betrayal of promises of liberation in the present context.

Building on the recognition of the positive potential contained within nostalgic memory, more recent social-psychological literature emphasises nostalgia's function as a psychological resource which increases self-esteem, fosters social connectedness, enhances meaning and eliminates existential pangs (Sedikides et al. 2008; Routledge 2016). Nostalgia can also hold hopeful, progressive and even utopian potential when it is directed toward creating better futures (Pickering and Keightley 2006; Bradbury 2012). A 2010 special issue on nostalgia in the *Journal of Memory Studies* edited by Atia and Davies (2010) presents a positive appraisal of nostalgia through focusing on how it is functioning in particular circumstances. In general this approach demonstrates that nostalgia can be "more mobile, more active and more self-aware" than the literature has generally allowed for (Atia and Davis 2010: 182).

Another development within the work on nostalgia which points toward its therapeutic and transformative potential is in relation to its embodied connection to the senses (Seremetakis 1994; Kitson and McHugh 2015). There is a sensory depth that can be evoked by nostalgia, because it reminds us of other possible selves and other times and places that exist alongside the present moment (Atia and Davis 2010). In the words of Svetlana Boym, reflective nostalgia "explores ways of inhabiting many places at once and imagining different time zones" (xviii). It "takes sensual delight in the texture of time not measurable by clocks and calendars" (2001: 49). It is this capacity for nostalgia to hold past, present and future together in a moment, that gives it its therapeutic and ethical capacity to connect to, reflect on and transform memories of the past that threaten our present and future.

Susan Radstone (2010) proposes that we view nostalgic memory as transitional memory, which is a dense site of connection between inner and outer worlds, collective and individual memories, and past and present time. As a site of congealment of time and space, as well as restorative and reflective impulses, nostalgic memory can provide an entry point into dialogue, critical reflection and therapeutic engagement with memories of the past in relation to the present.

This chapter seeks to contribute to the evolving line of inquiry into the progressive potential that lies within nostalgic memory. Specifically it seeks to contribute to the theorising of nostalgia in relation to trauma for the generation born after apartheid. In doing so, it demonstrates the therapeutic, critical and hopeful possibilities that emerge from this connection between nostalgia and trauma (past and present) as it emerges for the "born-free" generation in South Africa through their retelling of their parents' memories of apartheid in relation to their present inheritance of continued structural violence.

2 The Case of Bonteheuwel: Multiple Layers of Historical Violence

The Western Cape former-township of Bonteheuwel was chosen as a case study to conduct research on memories of violence and their intergenerational repercussion because it is a site of both traumatic memories of violence under apartheid, as well as the continuation of violence in the present democratic era. This section seeks to briefly contextualise the nature of violence experienced by the first generation under apartheid, because it is the memories of this period of life under apartheid that the research asked the second generation to reflect on.

Bonteheuwel is historically a "coloured township" situated in the Cape Flats, an area previously known as "apartheid's dumping ground" in Cape Town. From the 1950s, under the group Areas Act, the urban centres were designated as "white only" spaces and black South Africans were moved to the Cape Flats at the outskirts of the city. Bonteheuwel was declared a Group Area in 1965 and accommodated people who were designated as "coloured" and removed from areas such as District Six, Claremont and Diep River (Tapscott 1977: 143). Forced removals had a devastating impact on the fabric of community and people's sense of home, family, safety and belonging. This is indicated in the quote below from a life history interview that was conducted with a man from Bonteheuwel who experienced the forced removals as a young boy. He highlights the impact that this historical trauma had on the fabric of community, family connection and people's livelihoods:

> *It [forced removal] was a very painful experience ...All the families were scattered so there wasn't that close bond that the family had. The real family bond was broken and people were scattered...People were very scared of each other because they didn't know what kind of people they were... That is how gangsterism also started, because of the poverty [because] their belongings were taken away from them [during forced removal]. They lost their belongings because they were forced to move out. So some people took to crime.* (Life History Interview, Bonteheuwel, 2016)

This shared history of forced removal to Bonteheuwel described above represents a tragic example of what Kai Erikson (1994) describes as "collective trauma", the "blow to the basic tissues of social life that damages the bonds attaching people together and impairs the prevailing sense of community" (Erikson 1994: 233). In the life history quote above, the collective trauma of forced removal in Bonteheuwel is demonstrated through the way in which it broke bonds of community trust and stripped people of their belongings and livelihoods. This is then further connected to the crime and gangsterism that presently plagues the Bonteheuwel community.

The people who settled in Bonteheuwel suffered another wave of traumatic violence during the anti-apartheid youth struggle which followed the Soweto student uprising against apartheid in 1976. Bonteheuwel became a key site of anti-apartheid resistance and, in 1984, a group of school children between 14 and 18 years old formed the paramilitary defence unit called the Bonteheuwel Military Wing (BMW) to protect themselves and their families from police and render Bonteheuwel ungovernable (Marks and Mckenzie 1998; TRC 1999). The fights that ensued between the defence unit and the police meant that township spaces became similar to war-zones and a number of these youths were arrested, tortured and assassinated by the apartheid police.

In the context of the present, Bonteheuwel is considered one of the most dangerous areas in Cape Town. The community suffers ongoing instances of gang violence, as well as pervasive drug and alcohol abuse (Staniland 2011). Following the transition to democracy, many of the former youth activists who were involved in anti-apartheid struggle became jobless and without education. Many turned to alcohol, drugs and gang networks to cope with their traumatic memories and survive their socio-economic hardship (Marks and Mckenzie 1998; TRC 1999). The history of violence in Bonteheheuwel, as in many other communities that were oppressed under apartheid, can be described as layered and continuous in nature. Certain key periods of violence, such as forced removal and struggle violence, set these continuous strands of violence into motion. Through breaking "the basic tissues of social life", these collective traumas generate further forms of insecurity, poverty and violence, which in turn layer into present conditions of violence in Bonteheuwel.

3 Methods of Data Collection: Second-Generation Focus Groups

The focus group data analysed in this chapter are drawn from a broader research project entitled Memory, Trauma and Representations of the Past.[1] While there were three different communities that were included in this research, this chapter focuses on the data from Bonteheuwel as a case study. There were two stages involved in this research. The first was the collection of life history interviews with the first generation that lived through the violence of apartheid. The quote cited in the section above came from one of these life history interviews. The second stage of research was with the second generation. It is this second stage of data collection in Bonteheuwel with the "born-free" generation that this chapter focuses on. Three focus group interviews were conducted in Bonteheuwel in early 2017. Research participants were recruited through snowball sampling and self-selecting methods including word of mouth, personal referrals, social media posts and organisational networks of the Institute for Justice and Reconciliation (IJR), who assisted with the research co-ordination of the project. The focus groups contained a mixture of male and female participants between the ages of 18 and 35 years, but with an average age of 22 years. The groups were limited to 12 participants each.

While the focus of these discussions was for youth to speak about what they knew about apartheid, what their families shared with them about their memories of apartheid, and what these stories meant to them, the discussions also covered broader topics such as their experiences of life in Bonteheuwel. The section below focuses on the analysis of the second generation's retelling (re-remembering) of their parents' and grandparents' memories of apartheid and what these mean for them in the present context. In particular, it analyses the way in which the youth retell their parents' nostalgic memories of the apartheid past. It demonstrates the central role of nostalgia as a means through which traumatic memories of the past are communicated to the second generation and how the second generation draws on these memories to critique the present context.

4 Intergenerational Memory Encounters: Transferring the Nostalgia-Trauma Complex

The central place of trauma within the story of nostalgic memory is demonstrated in Tannock's (1995) description of the rhetoric of nostalgia as containing three ideas. First there is the idea of a "prelapsarian era" (the golden Era), this is followed by "lapse" (the cut, the catastrophe, the separation), and third there is the post-lapsarian world (the present world felt to be lacking or oppressive) (Tannock 1995: 456–457). Nostalgia and trauma are intimately connected to one another. If the longing emotion of nostalgia appears, it is likely that its traumatic counterpart of tragic loss or overwhelming shame is close by. Through psychoanalytic theory, nostalgia has been theorised in relation to trauma as a melancholic defence through which split-off, painful or shameful memory is denied (Gobodo-Madikizela 2012; Hook 2012). It is useful to think therefore of a nostalgia-trauma complex. This section seeks to demonstrate the way in which traumatic memories held by the first generation are transmitted to the second generation through the haunted channel of embodied and sensory nostalgic memory. Through the embodied senses of sight and hearing, entire memory worlds are brought into being for these participants in their nostalgic intergenerational memory encounters with their parents that are then re-communicated in the focus groups. The two sec-tions below will demonstrate this process of intergenerational nostalgic haunting, firstly in relation to the painful memories of forced removal and secondly in relation to the painful memories of struggle violence.

4.1 When Dad Stares at the Houses in Cape Town

Bonteheuwel is a township that holds many different memories of violence during apartheid times. Yet when we asked the youth about what the older generations told them about these times, there was a notable sense that the first generation did not want to verbally share these memories with them. One youth explained that she did not want to bother her parents by asking them about the past because it is "too hurtful for them to speak about". As a result it is "like you're living in a country, but you don't know the history" (Group One, Bonteheuwel, 2017). While these young South Africans have a sense that their parents are carrying pain around the past, many express that their parents do not like to speak about this traumatic memory. Instead, they told stories about witnessing their parents' nostalgic embodied remembering of the past. This was not told as a story, but rather as embodied memory encounters—moments when they have witnessed their parents' whole bodies become possessed by their longing for the past.

It is this rich sense of embodied longing, or nostalgia for a past that preceded their birth that is transferred between generations. In the quote below, a young woman retells her experience of witnessing her father's face when he stares at the houses in Cape Town that represent the community that he was forcibly removed from during apartheid:

> *Whenever we go to Cape Town, my mom and dad and I, then I can see how my dad stares at the houses and the longing is there … the sadness…you can see it written over his face, he is sad about … this is my place, but it's not my place anymore because this is where I want to be, but I can't be here, it's like taking a bone away from a dog.* (Group Two, Bonteheuwel, 2017)

The quote presented above demonstrates how a sense of "missing" and "longing" for this time and place before forced removals is communicated to the second generation in the mode of embodied memory. This is a memory that is witnessed and felt through the way in which her father "stares" at the houses and the longing that is "written over his face". She tells a story about how nostalgic memories are evoked for her father when his physical body returns to the place which holds them.

Michael Bell (1997) shows us that ghosts or "the sense of a presence of those who are not physically there" are a pervasive aspect of the lived experience of space. In other words, spaces are haunted by people and events that are no longer present. This is demonstrated in this young South African's retelling of what happens to her father when he passes through the spaces where he once lived before the removal. His entire body relives the loss that occurred there at another time as if it was happening all over again.

This young woman also demonstrates her sense of the traumatic side of her father's embodied nostalgic remembering. It makes its appearance through his interpretation of the longing she witnesses on her father's face "this is my place, but not my place anymore". The trauma within this longing is captured in the metaphoric phrase of "taking a bone away from a dog". This metaphor is particularly painful because it connects the sense of nostalgic longing to the trauma of the dehumanisation that people experienced through apartheid processes of forced removal. Van der Merwe and Gobodo-Madikizela (2008) highlight the impact of trauma on identity as it "shatter[s] people's ordinary sense of themselves". The young woman is painfully aware of this shattering of her father's sense of self in relation to the past that he longs for, because of the dehumanising way in which this past was lost to him.

A similar memory encounter is retold in the quote from another young woman reflecting on her mother's memories of the community in which she lived before being forcibly removed to Bonteheuwel:

> *They miss those days, you can hear it in their voices. I can see it on her facial expression, all the memories they have there, as my mom and them were all running around the streets freely, they could play. Again, like one of them said, you can trust your neighbours, you can leave your door open and go to wherever you want to, sleep with an open window, you can't sleep with an open window today. And they were hurt for the fact that they just had to pack up, they had no say over their house, and just leave.* (Group One, Bonteheuwel, 2017)

The sensuous power of nostalgic memory is demonstrated through this young woman's retelling of her mother's nostalgic memories in a way that evokes not simply the meaning but also the feeling of this memory. These memories, which are not her own, are told as if she were there and in a way that invites us to listen with our senses to the sounds of children playing, or the feeling of a warm breeze at night while sleeping with a window left open.

The sensuous power of nostalgia has been similarly demonstrated by Nadia Seremetakis in her work on Greece. As an embodied memory of the senses, nostalgia is often triggered by a familiar smell, taste, sound or sight which transports one into a memory of the past (Seremetakis 1994). Kitson and McHugh (2015) build on a sensuous understanding of nostalgia to demonstrate how it generates an experience of "sensual attunement" to what is near. They define nostalgia as "an enchantment with distance that cannot be bridged…engendering attentiveness to what is near, to sensing closely" (492). The experience of "sensual attunement" evoked in the nostalgic which brings them to the mode of "sensing closely" to the present, through their longing for the past, is further demonstrated in the quotes above as something that also occurs between generations. We see the role of the senses and the process of sensual attunement that occurs in transferring nostalgic memories. Through re-communicating her mother's sense memory, this young woman also invites us, to engage our own sense organs to remember with her a time that she did not in fact experience, but has been communicated to her in a similar embodied nostalgic memory encounter.

Again the traumatic twin of nostalgia trails along with this nostalgic memory captured in the phrase "they were hurt" because "they just had to pack up and leave". Trauma is often caused by a sense of powerlessness in the face of adversity which overwhelms an individual's capacity to cope (Herman 1992; Hamber and Lewis 1997). The sense of pain and powerlessness that accompanied the loss of freedom and safety is indicated in this phrase which connects this young South African to the unspoken traumatic memory connected to forced removals. Yet there is another phrase, which indicates toward the trauma of the present in relation to this nostalgic memory, "you can't sleep with an open window today". In their retelling of these nostalgic memory encounters, these young South

Africans are not simply connecting to a trauma experienced by their parents in the loss of what is longed for. They are also commenting on their own traumatic present in juxtaposition to the sense of freedom and safety imagined in the past.

4.2 When Grandmother Remembers the Milkman

While the section above focused on the embodied transfer of the nostalgia-trauma complex in relation to memories of forced removal, this section speaks to the memories of township life under apartheid during the violent struggle years of youth resistance and police retaliation. The collectively inherited memory of the milkman emerged across different focus groups to indicate a sense of nostalgia for township life in Bonteheuwel under apartheid. When mentioned this memory symbol acted as a shared "testimonial object" (Hirsch and Spitzer 2006) carrying a well-known sense of the past, which resulted in ripples of delighted recognition and laughter within the focus groups. Stephen Frosh argues that haunting can be both vertical—where something unseen moves across generations over time (such as intergenerational trauma), but it can also be horizontal—where something unseen moves across bodies in space at the same time (Frosh 2013). This horizontal dimension of nostalgic haunting evoked through the symbol of the milkman is highlighted in the ripples of delight and laughter as the young South Africans in the group responded with an embodied knowing to the power of this nostalgic memory that seemed to tickle the group from a hidden place.

During the first focus group interview, a participant posed a question to the group: "Do you think the thought of apartheid will ever go away? Do you think it will? Because I would like an answer. I would like to know. Would it ever just like go away?" (Group One, February 2017). Another participant answered the question by recounting the story of when her grandmother remembers the milkman of the past that represents a nostalgic memory encounter between three generations of women. As the mother, she witnesses and retells the interaction between grandmother and grandchild:

> *No, I don't think so, because there would always be that somebody, even if it's now an older generation...there would always be somebody or something that would remind ... say, for instance, something happened now, I asked my daughter to go buy a litre of milk, then my grandmother would come up with a story of "kan jy onthou (can you remember) when you were a child, toe ry die milky nog op die bicycle?" (the milkman was still riding on a bicycle) to deliver the milk in a glass bottle almost something similar to this en dan gaan die klokkie af (and then a bell rings). So there will always be that somebody that will remember something about back then, so I don't think you will ever forget, because you will always hear a story from way back then.* (Group One, February 2017)

This story given in response to the question of whether or not the memory of apartheid will ever go away indicates that it will not, because symbolic memory objects such as milk are imbued with meaning about the past. The embodied nature of memory is again demonstrated through an interaction with the testimonial object of milk (that holds within it the nostalgic memory for the milkman and his bicycle) as well as through the metaphor of the bell ringing. It is as if the sound of a bell indicates that the world of the past has arrived into the present moment. This arrival is not simply felt by her grandmother, but also by herself and her daughter. The metaphor of the bell ringing for the memory of the milkman appears to indicate an invitation for all three generations to "sensually attune" into the memory of the milkman and in doing so to empathetically "be... together in concerted time", even if that time belongs to a past that only one of them was present for (Sharon 1982).

At the same time, there are other memories that haunt this seemingly benign entry point into a shared memory encounter with the past in the present. The same young woman talks about her young daughter and how she is riveted by these stories of the milkman. At the same time, her daughter witnesses the scars of violence on her grandmother's head and the burn on her back—which indicate a more traumatic history etched both into the physical and psychic scars of the grandmother:

> *My five year old daughter, she has some wisdom already, and she would sit there and listen to all these that I have heard now a thousand times over and over... the milky (milkman) that came around on a bicycle because that time, there*

> *weren't house shops. You would have to put your bottle outside and he would take your bottle and give you milk again and whatever. So it's already been passed on to her. And she's … how can I say? She's very inquisitive; she would want to ask questions like "What did they do, Mamma?" And my mommy was also part of the struggle and she went to school one day and a riot broke out, I don't know, and it was just chaotic and they threw her with a stone, there was a hole in her head and because she wears her hair short, you can still see the mark here. She was burnt on her back, so the mark is … the scar is still there, so that is also already the story that has been told to her, so it's already been passed on.* (Group One, February 2017)

The scars are not overtly spoken about in the nostalgic memory of the past, yet they are visibly carried on the body and invisibly on the psyche of the grandmother who was wounded in the struggle violence of the late 1970s and 1980s. These scars are also forms of embodied memory, and they belong to the same world evoked by the memory of the milkman. This is why the granddaughter is able to connect the scars to the milkman story. She appears to have the awareness that the participant describes as "wisdom" or "curiosity" to connect the meaning of the milkman with the meaning of the scars and a knowing sense that these two memories belong together in the same time.

The close connection between memory objects that invoke nostalgia and those that invoke trauma is highlighted by Nicolas Argenti in his discussion of Marcel Proust's use of the term "souvenir". While the inherited intergenerational *souvenir* has the "uncanny power…to evoke vanished worlds" throwing us "effortlessly back into the voluptuousness of a lost Edenic world, *reminiscence* – equally unbidden and involuntary – marks the return of memories of banishment from that world" (Argenti 2019: 17). Through the milkman as souvenir, the three generations enter into the nostalgic memory of a lost Edenic world when the milkman delivered milk to the community. In her retelling of the grandmother's nostalgic memory, the memory evoked by the souvenir is closely followed by the memory of banishment from this world in the reminiscence of the struggle violence symbolised by the scars carried on the grandmother's body. In the case of these young South Africans, it is not simply their (re-)remembering of their parents' memories of past banishment from an imagined world of safety, connection and freedom which constitute their engagement with traumatic histories. Rather the traumatic memory that rises up with the nostalgic memory is connected to the past but also to the present—as a present in which these young South Africans continue to experience post-apartheid forms of violence. In the section that follows, the way in which this memory from the past in the present is also very much about the present and toward the future is demonstrated.

5 Nostalgia for the Future: Seeds of Critical Hope

In the case of South Africa, violence and oppression are not simply part of apartheid history, they remain a painful and confusing part of life under democracy for these young people. It is in relation to the present that this nostalgic memory for the past takes on further meaning and purpose. In a sense, the "hinge generation" (Hoffman 2004) also unhinges these nostalgic memories of the apartheid period from their place in the past to give them new purpose and meaning in relation to the present in ways that move beyond an inherited responsibility to mourn their parents unworked through trauma. This section demonstrates how the second generation's nostalgic memories do further work to critique the forms of violence that young people experience in the present and to imagine new possibilities for the future in the mode of critical hope.

On the one hand, these nostalgic memories are shared as a form of critique of the present. Part of this critique is directed toward the dire socio-economic conditions that the youth are presently struggling with. One participant described how even though her mother had been "forced to leave school at a very young age", she still "had more opportunity then, she lived a life that was much better in a way" and "there were more job opportunities than there are now" (Group 3, Bonteheuwel, 2017). This critique is also powerfully leveled at a sense of loss of past relationships of ethical care that are constructed as having existed within the Bonteheuwel community during apartheid. This is seen in the retelling of another common nostalgic memory symbol shared in the focus groups, of the sugar-sharing neighbour. In the quote below, this symbol is nostalgically remembered in relation to the conditions of the present. It allows the younger generation to draw on the past to critique the present by comparison.

> *The neighbours looked out for each other. You wouldn't go and ask someone for sugar and the next minute they gossip about you. They shared with each other during apartheid, because everyone had it rough. During those years, no-one had money and you couldn't go everywhere because of apartheid. But they were like one big family, not separated like now, people acting whiter than you. Everyone stood together. And the gangsters during those years, they didn't just shoot to kill. They protected the elderly before doing their thing. And they had a lot of respect for each other's parents. If someone cursed someone's mother, they wouldn't leave it at that. You had to go apologise. And you would probably receive a couple of slaps. But no senseless killing.* (Group Two, Bonteheuwel, February 2017)

In this nostalgic recollection of apartheid, sugar represents that "neighbours looked out for each other". There is a sense that things were rough back then, but the destructive force came from outside rather than inside the community. The past is constructed as "one big family", a caring collective and juxtaposed with a sense of "separation" and competition with "people acting whiter than you". Where the past is remembered as one in which the community banded together to fight against the destructive force of white superiority, today it is felt that that same force, and the oppressive disconnection that it represents, now structures community relationships.

In a similar vein, the memory of the milkman makes another appearance in order to juxtapose past conditions of freedom and safety with present conditions of fear and confusion.

> *Bonteheuwel used to be a nice place to stay in. Like those who couldn't even wait for the person dropping the milk. That guy with the bicycle (laughter), he used to come and sell his milk and his juice and you were all excited, you want to go outside and wait for the guy. But nowadays we can't even go to the shop to buy milk. Because, it's like you're … you're scared. Even if you have children or so … uhm … you don't want to send them outside or let them play outside. What I can say about Bonteheuwel, it used to be nice. But not anymore. I mean, we were so proud to say "I stay in Bonteheuwel". I mean, if I walk*

> *around the corner or maybe at work I say I stay in Bonteheuwel then people say "What?! Daai plek wat vol gangsters is. Daai's dan deurmekaar." ("What?! That place that is full of gangsters. That place is crazy / upside down / confused"). I mean, but then those days when you might have said you live here in Bonteheuwel, they were like, proud, man, yoh.* (Group Two, Bonteheuwel, February 2017)

The content of the memory further demonstrates a powerful critique of the present, as well as a hope for a different social world than the one that the second generation has inherited. The younger generation is not simply connecting to the nostalgia of their parents; it is powerful for them because it encapsulates their own sense of loss and longing even for that which they never had. This is a loss experienced in the present, a loss of a sense of socio-economic opportunity, ethical care, safety and pride.

In contrast to past memories of community care and solidarity, present day Bonteheuwel has come to represent a space that is described as "crazy", "turned upside down" and "full of gangsters" that no longer serve a protective role. In both of these quotes, there is a sentiment expressed that today the enemy is inside the community. The force of destruction, oppression and hate is now represented by the gangsters and their violence against the community as well as the general sentiments of competition and disconnection that seem to have infiltrated the "community" in the new era of "freedom".

The use of nostalgia as critique is similarly demonstrated by Jacob Dlamini when he argues that the longing expressed in nostalgia for the apartheid past is not for the despicable system of apartheid oppression. Rather it represents a critique of "the present" as "not the land of milk and honey" that was promised by the liberation movements in the past (2009: 12). In the present, people continue to suffer violence and oppression, which indicates for them that this past promise has been betrayed and the nostalgia for the past represents this sense of betrayal of past promises in the present.

At the same time, this nostalgia for apartheid focuses specifically on the ethics governing human relationships. In his discussion on the ethics of memory, Avishai Margalit argues that at the centre of ethical relations is caring: "At its best caring enhances a sense of belonging. It gives the other a feeling of being secure in having our attention and concern, irrespective of their achievements" (2002: 34–35). It is this breakdown in ethics which structured community relationships in townships during apartheid that is being remembered nostalgically and, through this inherited memory, these young South Africans are lodging a powerful critique of the present. They do not wish to return to a time when their communities were oppressed. However, in this democratic era, this nostalgia critiques the lack of community care, connection and security that has come to structure their sense of post-apartheid "community".

The symbol of milk and sugar, often invoked in the nostalgic (re-) remembering of apartheid times, are both powerful metaphoric images that carry memory, emotion, critique and hope. At an archetypal level, milk calls to mind images of the mother and mother's milk as symbols of nurturing and care. It also calls to mind biblical images of the Promised Land as a "land flowing with milk and honey". While participants do not mention honey, they do talk about sugar and remembering the past through the nostalgic lens of a time when neighbours shared their sugar. The metaphors of milk and sugar which re-emerge through these repetitions of nostalgia speak to the content of the nostalgic memory, which is an important source of imaginative content through which these young South Africans comment on the present.

On the one hand, these metaphors operate in the mode of social critique. While the land of milk and honey was promised to the future (of the past), for these young South Africans this future has been betrayed in the present. This is demonstrated through the comparative nostalgia that indicates that the past was better than the present. At the same time, there is hope for the present and future contained in the imaginative content of these second-hand memories because they capture a desire for a re-creation of ethical modes of relating and building community spaces based on an ethics of safety and caring. As Bradbury suggests, nostalgia may act as a resource for imagining "new possible horizons and hopeful futures" (2012: 341). In the case presented here, it seems that there is indeed a critical hope to be found in these memories of memories. For the ethical work of remembering, the content of the intergenerational nostalgia emphasises the desire for repairing relationships of community care in the present and future that have been broken by generations of oppression and violence.

6 Conclusion: Nostalgia and Memory Work

In his work on post-colonial nostalgia, Dennis Walder argues that it is important to maintain a reflexive relationship to nostalgic memory in order to allow it to open up a nuanced dialogue between past and present as well as between self and the other (Walder 2010). In this chapter, I have demonstrated how intergenerational nostalgia in the South African context of Bonteheuwel facilitates the unfolding of this dialogue between past, present and future. Through intergenerational embodied encounters with nostalgic memory, a doorway to the past opens up in the present. The second and third generations are able to connect to and question that which remains verbally silent (the memories of violence) in the stories of the first generation. This is important for intergenerational post-conflict memory work as it provides a gentler doorway into the pain of the past. In contexts, such as Bonteheuwel, where the present remains plagued by violence, nostalgic memory also provides the doorway out of the past and into the present and the future. The content of their nostalgic memory for the past provides the seeds of critical hope that feed their imaginative capacity to imagine and hope for a different kind of world than the one they have inherited.

There is an important difference between on the one hand allowing nostalgia to guide us back into the longing for the past and a sense of hopelessness in the future (melancholy), and on the other hand allowing nostalgia to disrupt our structures of the known and guide us into the unknown space between what we desire and our current reality. In the case of intergenerational nostalgia in Bonteheuwel, it appears that the nostalgia for milkmen and sugar-sharing neighbours is not about living in the past (melancholia), but rather about connecting to the past in order to (re-)remember something that feels lost in the present and give imaginative content to what may be hoped for and created in the future.

This chapter theorises the connecting, critical and hopeful potential alive within the intergenerational nostalgic memories of young people in Bonteheuwel. This reflection leads to a conclusion that nostalgia is a powerful and potentially useful entry point into doing intergenerational memory work. At the same time, a word of warning arises. This research has focused on the nostalgic memories of descendants of an oppressed group for the period of oppression. When the descendants of those who benefitted from the oppressive system of apartheid remember this time nostalgically this represents a more problematic form of ideological and melancholic memory (Gobodo-Madikizela 2012). It is therefore important to handle nostalgia with care. Just as it can be a useful tool toward working with the past and creating new futures, it can also encourage a melancholic tendency to remain stuck in the past or be used as an ideological tool in service of power.

To ascertain how nostalgia is working and how it may be harnessed in a more reflective, imaginative, critical and therapeutic mode, it is important to interrogate what experiences the nostalgic memory highlights and denies, and to what purposes? Further research could explore under what conditions, if at all, ideological and melancholic forms of nostalgia may be turned toward reflective, critical or hopeful ends. How can what is denied be brought into creative dialogue with what is remembered though the doorway of nostalgic memory? How does this creative tension alert us to present struggles and future possibilities, contained within the imaginative and symbolic power of nostalgic memory? Exploring these questions can help us to further unlock the power of intergenerational nostalgia to transform haunting memories from the past into the seeds of hope and imagination for the future.

Note

1. The Trauma, Memory and Representations of the Past project is a five-year project funded by the A.W. Mellon Foundation. It is led by Professor Pumla Gobodo-Madikizela at the Historical Trauma and Transformation Research Initiative. The research was conducted in collaboration with the Institute for Justice and Reconciliation (IJR) in 2016. Some of the stories collected in the Life History phase of this research have been published in the recent book *These Are the Things That Sit with Us* (Gobodo-Madikizela et al. 2019).

References

Abraham, N., & Torok, M. (1994). *The Wolf Man's Magic Word: A Cryptonomy*. (Nicholas Rand, Trans.). Foreword: Jacques Derrida. Minneapolis: University of Minnesota Press

Argenti, N. (2019). *Remembering Absence: The Sense of Life in Island Greece*. Indiana: Indiana University Press.

Atia, N., & Davies, J. (2010). Nostalgia and the Shapes of History. *Memory Studies, 3*(3), 181–186.

Bell, M. (1997). The Ghosts of Place. *Theory and Society, 26*, 813–836.

Boym, S. (2001). *The Future of Nostalgia*. New York: Basic Books.

Bradbury, J. (2012). Narrative Possibilities of the Past for the Future: Nostalgia and Hope. *Peace and Conflict, 18*(3), 341–350.

Danieli, Y. (1984). Psychotherapist's participation in the conspiracy of silence about the Holocaust. *Psychoanalytic Psychology, 1*(1), 23–42.

Davis, F. (1979). *Yearning for Yesterday: A Sociology of Nostalgia*. New York: Free Press.

Dlamini, J. (2009). *Native Nostalgia*. Auckland Park: Jacana.

Doane, J., & Hodges, D. (1987). *Nostalgia and Sexual Difference: The Resistance to Contemporary Feminism*. New York: Methuen.

Duncan, N., Stevens, G., & Sonn, C. C. (Eds.). (2012). Introduction to *Of Narrative and Nostalgia. Peace and Conflict: Journal of Peace Psychology, 18*(3), 205–213.

Erickson, K. (1994). *A New Species of Trouble: The Human Experience of Modern Disasters*. New York: Norton.

Frankish, T., & Bradbury, J. (2012). Telling Stories for the Next Generation. *Peace & Conflict, 18*, 294–306.

Frosh, S. (2013). *Hauntings: Psychoanalysis and Ghostly Transmissions*. Basingstoke: Palgrave Macmillan.

Gobodo-Madikizela, P. (2012). Re-membering the Past: Nostalgia, Traumatic Memory and the Legacy of Apartheid. *Peace and Conflict, 18*, 252–267.

Gobodo-Madikizela, P., Bubenzer, F., & Oelofsen, M. (2019). *These are the Things that Sit with Us*. Johannesburg: Fanele, Jakana.

Hamber, B., & Lewis, S. (1997). *An Overview of the Consequences of Violence and Trauma in South Africa*. Research report written for the Centre for the Study of Violence and Reconciliation. https://www.csvr.org.za/publications/1778-an-overview-of-the-consequences-of-violence-and-trauma-in-south-africa

Herman, J. L. (1992). *Trauma and Recovery: Domestic Abuse to Political Terror*. London: Pandora.
Hirsch, M. (2008). The Generation of Post-Memory. *Poetics Today, 29*(1), 103–128.
Hirsch, M., & Spitzer, L. (2006). Testimonial Objects: Memory, Gender, and Transmission. *Poetics Today, 27*(2), 353–383.
Hofer, J. (1934[1638]). Medical Dissertation on Nostalgia. Trans. Carolyn Kiser Anspach, *Bulletin of the Institute of the History of Medicine* 2: 376–91
Hoffman, E. (2004). *After Such Knowledge: Memory, History and the Legacy of the Holocaust*. New York: Public Affairs.
Hook, D. (2012). Political Nostalgia and Psychoanalysis: Screened History, Fantasmatic Memory and Retroactive Time. *Peace & Conflict, 18*, 225–239.
Jameson, F. (1991). *Postmodernism, or, The Cultural Logic of Late Capitalism*. London: Verso.
Kagoyire, G., Vysma, M., & Richters, A. (2020). The Ghosts of Collective Violence: Pathways of Transmission between Genocide-Survivor Mothers and Their Young Adult Children in Rwanda. In K. Wale, P. Gobodo-Madikizela & J. Prager (eds.), *Post-Conflict Hauntings: Transforming Memories of Historical Trauma*. Basingstoke: Palgrave Macmillan.
Kidron, C. A. (2009). Toward an Ethnography of Silence: The Lived Presence of the Past in Everyday the Life of Holocaust Trauma Survivors and Their Descendants in Israël. *Current Anthropology, 50*(1), 5–27.
Kitson, J., & McHugh, K. (2015). Historic Enchantments – Materializing Nostalgia. *Cultural Nostalgia, 22*(3), 487–508.
Lasch, C. (1991). *The True and Only Heaven: Progress and its Critics*. New York: Norton.
Margalit, A. (2002). *The Ethics of Memory*. Cambridge: Harvard University Press.
Marks, M., & Mckenzie, P. (1998). Militarized Youth: Politicized Pawns or Social Agents? In J. Cock & P. Mckenzie (Eds.), *From Defense to Development: Redirecting Military Resources in South Africa* (pp. 208–221). David Philip: Cape Town.
Pickering, M., & Keightley, E. (2006). The Modalities of Nostalgia. *Current Sociology, 54*, 919–941.
Radstone, S. (2010). Nostalgia: Home-Comings and Departures. *Memory Studies, 3*, 187–191.
Routledge, C. (2016). *Nostalgia: A Psychological Resource*. New York: Routledge.
Sedikides, C., Wildschut, T., Arndt, J., & Routledge, C. (2008). Nostalgia: Past, Present, and Future. *Current Directions in Psychological Science, 17*, 304–307.

Seremetakis, C. N. (1994). The Memory of the Senses, Part 1: Marks of the Transitory. In C. N. Seremetakis (Ed.), *The Senses Still: Perception and Memory as Material Culture in Modernity*. Boulder: Western Press.
Sharon, A. (1982). Dimensions ofTime. *Studies in Symbolic Interaction, 4*, 63–89.
Stewart, S. (1984). *On Longing: Narratives of the Miniature, the Gigantic, the Souvenir, the Collection*. Baltimore: John Hopkins University Press.
Staniland, L. (2011). *A Tale of Two Townships: Race, Class and the Changing Contours of Collective Action in the Cape Town Townships of Guguletu and Bonteheuwel, 1976–2006*. Unpublished PhD Thesis, University of Edinburgh.
Tannock, S. (1995). Nostalgia Critique. *Cultural Studies, 9*(3), 453–454.
Tapscott, C. (1977). *The Effects of the Structure of Local Government on Crime*. Unpublished Masters Dissertation, Department of Public Administration, University of Cape Town, South Africa.
Truth and Reconciliation Commission (TRC). (1999). *TRC Final Report. Vol 4 Ch 9*, p. 43.
Van der Merwe, C., & Godobo–Madikizela, P. (2008). *Narrating Our Healing: Perspectives on Working Through Trauma*. Newcastle: Cambridge Scholars Publishing.
Walder, D. (2010). *Postcolonial Nostalgias: Writing, Representation, and Memory*. New York: Routledge.

10

The Ghosts of Collective Violence: Pathways of Transmission Between Genocide-Survivor Mothers and Their Young Adult Children in Rwanda

Grace Kagoyire, Marianne Vysma, and Annemiek Richters

1 Introduction

After cessation of collective violence in the social world, the reverberations of that violence turn inward, trapped, sometimes for generations, in the bodies and psyches of those who lived through it. The violence is trapped because there is no language to express the suffering, and survivors can only act-out the anguish and anger in family interactions. This chapter reports on a study that explores, from the point of view of young adults, how they experience their mothers—both in the past and in the present—who survived the 1994 genocide against the Tutsi in Rwanda.

G. Kagoyire
Stellenbosch University, Stellenbosch, South Africa

M. Vysma (✉)
Webster University, Leiden, The Netherlands

A. Richters
Amsterdam Institute for Social Science Research, Amsterdam, The Netherlands

K. Wale et al. (eds.), *Post-Conflict Hauntings*, Palgrave Studies in Compromise after Conflict, https://doi.org/10.1007/978-3-030-39077-8_10

In other words, in what follows, what interests us is the intergenerational dyad, the parent-child relationship consisting of a survivor mother and a child born shortly before, during, or just after the genocide. Beginning in 2011, the mothers participated in a psychosocial support group, which opened up new ways of being-in-the-world for them. Afterwards, the mothers' violent emotional storms acted out in the home which could only be *endured by* both mothers and children, gradually transformed into stories of experience *between* mothers and children. We present, in their own words, how the now young adult children both actively influenced, but also encountered and understood that transformation. We argue that the path from being *haunted* by the ghosts of the past collective violence, to *getting to know* the ghosts, to being *accompanied by* these ghosts not only enhances the quality of life of mothers and children but also raises new challenges, particularly in the self-other relationships of the young adult children.

We will show that before the psychosocial intervention of sociotherapy, the children experienced their mothers mostly as an "absent presence" (Kogan 2012), in that she was there as a person wracked by emotional storms in which she alternatively lashed out at family members or needed care herself, but rarely as a full and caring mother. Nonetheless, even during that long period, in the relatively calm intervals between the emotional outbursts, the children persisted in questioning their mothers about their past, seeking information about experiences during the genocide.

In order to provide a context for understanding what these young adult children speak about, we begin with some background information about the 1994 genocide in Rwanda, its aftermath, and the particular experiences of their mothers.

During the genocide in Rwanda, an estimate of between 800,000 and 1,000,000 people were killed (MINALOC 2004). Many women experienced rape as one of the many genocide atrocities (African Rights 2004). This left inedible marks on the lives of those women who survived the genocide violence, as happened to the mothers of the young adults who feature in this chapter. The traumatic events experienced by these women included hiding to avoid being killed; witnessing of the violent killing of children, spouses, and other family members; rape, often repeated, and often by multiple men, at times resulting in pregnancies; and loss of home and property (Richters and Kagoyire 2014). An individual's systemic and autonomous response to these overwhelmingly terrifying or agonizing experiences is to depersonalize during the events, and to use all available psychic energy to wall off (or dissociate) the overpowering and devastating effects after the events. As a result, first-generation survivors do not talk easily about their experiences. They do not talk because they *cannot* talk: the violent (or traumatic) experiences have been registered in a fragmented way that they are unable to catch into a narrative sequence (see, for instance, van der Kolk 2014). But the inability to speak is not always silence. For the survivors' children (the second generation), this "silence is not silent": it is alive with acted-out emotions and violent expressions of anger and anguish. So the children see their mother's suffering and may suspect its provenance, but are in the dark about the actual and specific stories.

This is in stark contrast to their social world, where public knowledge of the genocide abounds. Some time after the genocide ended, the Rwandan government instituted a new version of a traditional grassroots justice system, called Gacaca (Ingelaere 2016). Gacaca was designed to find the truth about genocide crimes on which judgement of people accused of genocide crimes could be based, and healing and reconciliation could be set in process. The newly installed Gacaca courts, in full operation at the local level throughout the country from 2005 to 2012, provided a space for genocide survivors, perpetrators, and witnesses to give their accounts of what happened during the genocide. Even though the truth generated by Gacaca was mixed with deceit and evasions (Ingelaere, ibid.), it contributed to raising awareness of the violent history of Rwanda among the generation that did not consciously live through the genocide or was born after it. The annual commemoration of the genocide provides another space for sharing the genocide history publicly. Like the genocide, the commemoration lasts a hundred days, starting each year on the seventh of April. During the first week, commonly called the mourning week, government representatives give speeches about this history and survivors testify about their personal genocide experiences as part of a range of events organized at the national and local level. While many people participate in these events, the memories provoked by these events can be so re-traumatizing that survivors may choose to isolate themselves inside the family home. In this way, they endure the floods of raw unbearable emotions of re-experiencing what happened to them during the genocide.

This chapter focuses on not only how traumatic experiences that cannot be easily shared fractures the capacity for relationship between the mothers and children, but also how a healing experience of the mother can likewise be intergenerationally transmitted, through reviving the parent-child relationship. We trace this process using the concept of the "ghosts", which we hold are the non-narrativized, unrepresented experiences of collective violence.

A few words about the context of those "healing experiences" of the mothers. While in this chapter, the now young adult children refer to the change in relationship between them and their mothers using the shorthand of "before and after" sociotherapy, the process included other aspects. The mothers began sharing their traumatic memories in 2011, in interaction with other women with similar experiences while participating in a psychosocial support group called community-based sociotherapy.[1] At roughly the same time, the women began constructing their life histories in long conversations over a two-year period with the first and third author, this became known as the story-telling project. The stories of the mothers were compiled in a booklet published in Kinyarwanda in 2013 (Kagoyire et al. 2013) and distributed widely.[2] Subsequently, the two authors had regular informal meetings with the mothers, culminating in the current study of the intergenerational transmission of genocide ghosts from the perspective of their children. Because of this long process, it proved impossible to write the chapter without referring to sociotherapy. However, the focus of our exploration here is not the effects of sociotherapy, but rather how a healing experience in the survivor generation can, through a recovery of the capacity for relationship, have important intergenerational consequences.

2 Methodology

The study that informs this article was conducted in the Eastern Province of Rwanda, Bugesera District. This district is recognized as having been an epicentre of the 1994 genocide. The respondents comprise 12 young adults just on the cusp of entering adulthood, each with a mother who had participated in sociotherapy and the story telling project. Data were collected between August and December 2017.

The data collection methods included individual semi-structured interviews with each of the twelve respondents preceded by two focus-group discussions in which respectively three and seven of them participated. The interviews lasted between 60–90 minutes; the focus-group discussions lasted approximately two hours. The study sample consisted of five young men and seven young women. One respondent was born shortly before the genocide, one during the genocide, and ten just after the genocide. At the time of data collection, the age range was 18–25.

Five out of twelve respondents completed secondary school, three of them were still in school at the time of study, three had dropped out of school, and one attends university. Six youngsters live with their widowed mothers, three live with both their parents, one lives with her mother and step-father who is also a survivor, another one lives with her mother who had separated from her husband long ago, while number 12 lives with her grandmother after her mother found a new partner to cohabitate with. Two children lost their father during the genocide and two lost their father due to a natural death. Five respondents have unknown rapist fathers, while another three still have their father.

The data were collected in Kinyarwanda and subsequently transcribed and translated from Kinyarwanda into English. After the transcription of the interviews, we analysed the data guided by the phenomenological method (Giorgi 2012), which aims to "gain a rich, nuanced understanding of the essential elements of the participant's narratives, rather than to assess the degree to which those findings may be generalizable to the population from which the sample is drawn" (Matz 2015, 189). The method allows the researchers to enter into the phenomenal world of the respondents to see how they situate themselves in their world.[3]

During our analysis, we read and re-read the transcribed interviews; then (manually) identified common/similar emerging themes, which were then regrouped into a codebook. This left us with still too many topics; therefore, we extracted the most prevalent themes and summarized them in a simple table of important points which could address our research questions. Because the interviews were collected in Kinyarwanda and transcribed verbatim, some words or terms that were difficult to translate accurately, or those words that needed an expert view in the domain of the mental and psychosocial field, were shared with two Rwandan colleagues (each received a list of the Kinyarwanda words that needed translation, and was requested to assist with the descriptive translation into English). Where words had quite different meanings, the list was shared with a third Rwandan colleague. Finally, the remaining words with heterogeneous meaning were discussed among a team of Rwandan colleagues before being used in this chapter.

3 Presentation of the Findings

What we show in the findings below is that before the mothers experienced healing in the context of sociotherapy and the conversations of the story-telling project, there was a very fractured relationship between the mothers and children. The mothers were haunted by the ghosts of their experiences, and the children sensed the same ghosts because when they appeared, they disturbed the parent-child relationship. The children's reaction to the ghosts was to question the mother when there was an opportunity, in a search for information. But that search for information was perhaps not only "a search for information" but also "a search for the mother", that in the hope of understanding her experiences, they would be able to have a better relationship with her. When, because of the healing experiences of the mothers, the parent-child relationship was also gradually transformed, the mothers could respond to the children's questioning, with bits and pieces of their story. This contributed to strengthening the relationship between parents and children, but it also was a burden to the children. Because of the empathic bond between mothers and children, the story was in the first instance almost like a re-experiencing of the violent events. The importance of the "information" is not "facts" but emotional experiences that overwhelm understanding. For the second generation, learning the truth may in one perspective be the end of a search, but in another perspective also the beginning of struggle to give meaning to what they learned. This struggle tests the newly transformed parent-child relationship (i.e. the children's first reaction is to hide their pain and confusion from their mothers) and also presents new challenges to the young adult: how to relate to others in the social world who carried out the violence that caused such suffering?

We therefore organize our findings along three units of meaning. In the first, we show that the children actively try to break through the silence of their mothers. In the second, we demonstrate that the children can, in simple and compelling detail, vividly articulate the changes in the parent-child relationship. And finally, we present how descendants indicate that the effects of finding what they so avidly searched for, the stories of their mothers' experiences, were deeply ambivalent.

3.1 Searching for Information in a World of Silence

The majority of respondents said they yearned to be told about the experiences of their parents. They were especially interested in understanding the strategies their mothers used to survive during the genocide, as untold others were killed. In addition, they spoke of a preoccupation of knowing about the "unseen" relatives (those who were killed or missing: older siblings, aunts and uncles, grandparents, and, of course, absent fathers). Families are a source of support and confronted by ill health and poverty of their mothers, the descendants said they needed to know to whom they could turn, contributing to a sense of social safety. While these youth have access to the public discourse about the genocide, there is a longing to know the personal stories, to fill in the gaps and voids in their family constellation, allowing them to begin "the process of identity reconstruction" (Hogwood et al. 2017; Kagoyire and Richters 2018).

Although it is not expressly said by the respondents and the temporal tense they use (as if it happens in the present) makes it a bit confusing, a contextual reading of the responses as a whole seems to indicate that the resistive, averting reactions by the mothers are more indicative of the period before sociotherapy than after.

Solange (21-year-old): *Most of the time, children of our age have many and different questions to ask in search of tangible information. There is some part of information we get from school and some other parts we should be told by our parents. As children, we have specific questions we ask or we wish to ask in order to know further our families. The most asked questions by children to their parents have to do with the history of our country and the way of sorrow, the path of torment and agony, of our parents during the genocide.*

By comparing the genocide history about which descendants hear from other sources with the way their parents tell it, most respondents suspect their mothers have secrets or hold back information. Madeleine (23-year-old, born during the genocide) said: *There is something they never tell me. Tutsi were many. The marshland is small compared to the number of Tutsi here in Bugesera. So I wonder how they managed to survive from there. I do not understand how they hid. In particular, people who had children, or who were pregnant and gave birth when they were in the swamps. I wonder how it is possible that a child is born in those conditions and manages to survive, without being damaged. My mother will not tell me that. Mothers had no breast milk. For those who gave birth during that period or when they were running, full of fear, I wonder how a child born there can survive without eating or being breastfed. When I think about that I find it as something that is beyond my level of understanding.*

In a sort of empathic imaginative pondering, the children struggle to understand the specific story of their mothers in terms of the more general knowledge they have, as for instance Patel (22-year-old): *My mother told me that in order to survive, she hid in the house of someone who was committing genocide. She had a small child. She said she had nowhere else to go, she was ready to accept as it must be. I wish to know more, but I avoid deepening my questions. That killer, who hid my mother and my brother, left them in his home and went to kill others. Did he tell them the names of people he killed? But I do not want to awaken the wound my mother faced while she was there. Perhaps when she left that house she had to face even more than what she experienced in that killer's house.*

This young man is very aware of his mother's trauma and is caught in a dilemma between wanting to know more and understanding that pursuing that knowledge may hurt his mother. Children are extremely aware of the outline of blank spots in the parental story, yet reluctant to trespass lest they touch painful emotions that may trigger the return of traumatic emotions. Julia (20-year-old, whose mother used to change behaviours during the week of genocide mourning in April) narrated this: *There is a question I always ask my mother especially during the commemoration period. When this period starts, I see my mother isolating herself without any will of going to the memorial sites like others. So I ask her why she does not want to join others. She tells me that she avoids going there because she may get madness if she reaches that place. She explains some of the elements I ask her, but she also avoids talking about some other elements. I ask her how they hid during the genocide.*

Because there are so many missing men, the subject of fathers is of great interest. Asia (22-year-old born from genocide rape) explained that she was motivated to know who her father is because she never saw any man in the house: *I wanted to ask that question because when I grew up, I found myself living with my mother alone; there was no father at home.* Estonia (22-year-old) narrated it in this way: *I asked her who my father is and stressed that it is time to disclose it to me. My mother said that I should not ask her such a thing. She said 'I gave birth to you, I am here, I raised you and you are growing up in a good way. Why should you ask that question?' She told me that my father is a worthless person, that she lost her children during the genocide and then that man raped her after the genocide, but she told me that in a superficial way.* "Superficial" is the nearest literal translation of the Kinyarwandan word that means "cool, unemotional, hiding truer or deeper feelings"; the way of speaking communicates to the listener to stop asking any further questions because of the emotional suffering it causes in the speaker; or because it may cause suffering for the listener; or because the speaker does not trust the listener. In any case, the tone has the effect of closing the subject of conversation.

This dynamic between the search of the second generation for stories of their survivor parents and finding only walls of silence has been commented on by others. Danieli (1984), for instance, refers to it as a "conspiracy of silence" that serves to protect surviving elders from the traumatic memories while also protecting their progeny from the horrors of their experience. When the second generation understands that the implicit message of the silence is "please do not ask" and obeys it, there arises the phenomenon of a "double wall of silence" (Bar-On 2006). But what we found is that many of our respondents showed a perseverance in their search; with stealthy compassion they waited for moments when their mothers were able to share, and then asked again.

3.2 Transformation of Parent-Child Relationship as Part of the Healing Experiences of the Mother

> *My mother started to go to sociotherapy a long time ago, when I was still in primary school. Before that, she was like a person who did not like to speak, she could answer using [only] one word. We thought she hated us. She insulted us, saying I was just like my father, even though I do not know him. When I committed a mistake, she could beat me up to near death. She gave us school materials but did not give affection as a parent; she could not talk to us. She was always angry. She was often sick and said she was dying. One day she brought us juice. She offered it to us. The next day I asked her what happened to her and she said she had kept things in her heart because she had no one to share them with, but now she had found a friend who can listen to her, she found a place where she meets other ladies to discuss these things. If before my communication with her was like five percent, it became like 80 percent. My mother stopped seeing me as a person who is nasty like my father* [rapist of the mother]. *She now feels I belong to her.* (Diana, 19-year-old)

This quote contains most of the elements we find in more or less detail in all the recollections of the descendants of family life before sociotherapy: a silent, scowling, defensive parent, with a continual air of anger around her that could erupt at any time into an outburst, or dissolve into anguish; and a general sense of ill health. As Madeleine, who often saw her mother faint when suffering through a trauma crisis describes: *At that time* [before sociotherapy], *I was saddened by the way my mother was. I was afraid that my mother will get madness. I used to feel distress when she gets angry and cries. I was always anxious, wondering on what I will do if my mother becomes a mad person. Since she got healed, I feel safer. When she was crying, I felt helpless; I ran away or called my siblings so that they come to rescue me.* The "madness" was a re-experiencing of some of the horrific periods of the genocide, as related by John (18-year-old): *She was always desperate, always sat with her head in her hands, far in her thoughts. Sometimes she could make noises, calling for people to rescue her, showing me people who are coming to kill her. For me, I could not see those people she showed me. In some instances we had to call neighbours to calm her down. Afterwards: no more re-experiences; she started to laugh and the wrinkles on her face began to disappear. She can meet others.* In other words, the mother became a social being again, and developing relationships with others, able to show her child how to be a social being as well.

The children mark that there was a decided change after participating in sociotherapy: from moody, volatile and reclusive people, their mothers become concerned and involved, interested in the lives of their children. *Before she joined sociotherapy my mother was not open to us. I could spend the day in the bed, but she could not ask me why. After sociotherapy, maybe due to having conversations with people who have various problems themselves, our mother became open to us. She can for instance ask you what happened if she finds you sleeping during the day. This is different from before. From the discussion she had with other women, she learned how to talk to us and how to advise us, probably as it is done when they are in their group* (Solange, 21-year-old).

In addition, the children report that the mothers leave the house and become socially connected to others in the community. Patel (22-year-old) said, *Before she spent her time thinking about the past only and did little else. She looked unhappy all the time and was always angry. Now she helps and cares for (advises) others who still suffer from anger and sadness, who are the way she used to be, she encourages them. Because she has integrated her own experiences* [via sociotherapy] *she can contribute to something good.*

Gerard (18-year-old): *Before joining sociotherapy my mother was not happy. Now her sorrow has decreased. We can converse with each other. She now greets me in the morning when she wakes up.* It is the quality of the relationship that changed. After sociotherapy, mothers became mothers again, being interested in and interacting with their children, and this allowed the children to take their own place in the family constellation. Julia (20-year-old): *And for me, I was unhappy, depressed and angry. Someone could talk to me, but I wouldn't be able to answer, I was mute. After sociotherapy, she [the mother] started to have love towards us. She started socializing with others, helping others. She approached us* [instead of keeping to herself and telling us to stay away], *offering advice. She became open, and I could ask her anything that I wanted to. We interact properly as a family, she gives us time and treats us with affection.* And yet, the mother-child relationship before sociotherapy was at times so destructive and the mothers' suffering so deep, that in an effort to make sense of this, some children turn to guilt, or self-blame. Asia (22-year-old, born from rape; her mother told her after sociotherapy): *She is a quiet person. Due to the life she has experienced I do not know what can make her happy. I have never seen my mother being joyful. I always asked her about my father. Before sociotherapy I was angry at her because I thought she was an immoral person, and that is why she was hiding things from me. After sociotherapy I learned my mother was raped. My mother had not planned to have me, I was not in her plan. Her suffering started with my birth.* Emmaus (25-year-old): *I think I am the source of her sadness. Because I do not do what she tells me. There are no changes after sociotherapy. The only thing that can change me is if I learn what I want to know about my father's family. Nothing else can change me.*

3.3 Reactions to a Mother's Story

As their mothers regained their capacity for relationship through the sharing and support beginning with sociotherapy and continuing with group and individual conversations, the descendants slowly and gradually were told more details about their mothers' experiences. One seeming paradox is that while they had avidly sought the more personal information, once they received it, it was very difficult to process. Our respondents said that the particulars of their mothers' experiences were deeply troubling to them, and they reported compulsive thinking, intrusive feelings, disturbances in sleeping, headaches, and stomach aches. In addition, they talked of grappling with feelings of bitterness and abhorrence for those who had committed the violence against their mothers, and difficulties in finding a way to relate to all members of the group who are held responsible for genocidal violence. *The victims of trauma are not only those who survived the genocide. Most of the youth, who were born after the genocide, suffer from trauma crises. When my mother tells me how she struggled to find dry herbs to cover her sister's wounds when they were hiding, I automatically imagine how it was, capturing/zooming in on the whole picture of how it was raining on them, without having any cloth to cover the small children, the new-borns. They were together and remember how they threw small children against the walls and I feel as if the genocide is happening now. I suddenly feel as if it is happening now.* (Solange, 21-year-old).

How to understand the paradox articulated by this respondent, that of re-experiencing something that was never experienced in the first place, because it took place before she was born? We can use the idea of secondary traumatic stress: the emotional duress that results when someone hears about the first-hand trauma experiences of another. But the experience as described seems more visceral and immediate than that, a sort of radical empathy (Caswell and Cifor 2016) or doubling of consciousness. And so we fall back on the language of haunting and the metaphor of the ghost: it is as if the ghost of the mother's experience, because it isn't fully embedded yet in a "shared story", returns to haunt Solange during those moments.

Because elements of the story are so extreme, so emotionally affecting, the descendants struggle to make sense of what they have heard. *The first consequence is to keep on thinking about that bad story your mother has shared with you. I wonder why my mother survived alone. Sometimes, I ask God (in my heart), why he did leave my mother alone, a woman who is already vulnerable? Why did God let this happen to my mother? I spend much time asking myself such questions. The unfortunate result of thinking about this is that at the end I feel pain in my head (headaches), and sometimes I cannot sleep. This mostly happens to me when I am at home, after my mother told me her past experiences* (John, 18-year-old, with a mother widowed and disabled due to beatings during the genocide).

"Making sense" of shocking, overwhelming things is something that can only be done, if at all, in relationship, in dialogue with others, which is what descendants feel they do not have. Under stable cultural circumstances, one's parent is the first source of mediating between the inner world and the social world, between what you feel and how you should act. But in post-conflict societies such as Rwanda, that parent has suffered unimaginably at the hands of others in the social world, making such mediation immeasurably more difficult. Here perhaps the "double wall of silence" could reappear, in that the young adults of the second generation minimize and hide their own struggles from their mothers so as not to re-open the wound. Here there is a need for a meta-narrative that is still missing in the social world, one that would contribute to understanding how genocidal violence can take place at all, a narrative that attempts to go, in Jessica Benjamin's memorable phrase "beyond the doer and the done to" (Benjamin 2018).

Madeleine, born when her mother was hiding and had no milk, was fed by sweet potatoes chewed and mixed with saliva by her sister. When she sees a well-fed baby of the group associated with genocidal acts, she feels bitterness, because the baby has what she didn't have. Hours later upon reflection she will think: *That child is innocent....* She said, upon learning that her mother was raped during the genocide; *I felt my brain changing .... I wonder all the time why people did such bad acts. You cannot forget it. The thoughts keep coming back into your mind. We young people may feel dissatisfied with our lives because of the wounds our parents have, children do not forget easily.*

As these quotes show, the consequences of learning about parental genocide experiences in general creates intense turbulence in the inner worlds of the second generation. They struggle with shock, vicarious pain and suffering, as well as deep bitterness. Eventually, learning their mothers' stories may also provide motivation to work towards a better future life, for themselves and for their mothers, something that is known in Rwanda as "positive anger", an emotion that can be used to overcome one's difficulties. This is illustrated by what Diana shared. Her mother had been raped during the genocide and was raped again in its aftermath and was subsequently forced to marry the rapist. Diana was born from the rape after the genocide. She said, *I have a heart that can forgive, but* [this] *I cannot forgive.* And yet, she struggles to transform these feelings into a vision of her future self in which she can contribute to healing her mother. *I am among the top students in our class. I wish to make the difference; I wish to reach far* [in life] *so that I cover that emptiness caused by my father's family which has caused my mother to suffer.*

4 Analysis of the Findings

In analysing our findings, we distinguish four pathways of intergenerational transmission of experience after collective violence. Three of these present in detail the emotional pain and suffering that is the traumatic and traumatizing legacy of such collective violence in general and the genocidal violence in particular. In the fourth, we analyse in more detail what the mothers' breaking through the silence implied for their capacity for relationship, especially the crucial attachment relationship with their children, suggesting that not only wounding but also healing may be transmitted between generations. And finally, in this section, we also take a first look at the new challenges children face in their emotional life and their self-other relationships as a result of knowing the particular story of their mothers.

The frame for our analysis comprises the well-known sequelae of trauma, which we briefly summarize here. In the aftermath of the genocide, the lives of mothers were marked by depersonalization and dissociation. Both are psychiatric terms for psychological and emotional defence (or coping) mechanisms aimed at supporting the survivor self who has to go about the day-to-day business of continuing to live, and helping children and other family members to live. Findings from neuroscience research confirm what has long been known clinically.

> At this point the emotional brain, which is not under conscious control and cannot communicate in words, takes over. ... The emotional brain (the limbic area and the brain stem) expresses its altered activation through changes in emotional arousal, body physiology, and muscular action. ... As a result, the imprints of traumatic experiences are organized not as coherent logical narratives but in fragmented sensory and emotional traces, images, sounds, and physical sensations. (van der Kolk 2014, 176)

When this occurs, the traumatic events are prevented from occupying their proper position in the individual's history and continue to invade the present (Rothschild 2000, 9). It is this fragmentary nature of how these experiences are stored, and their emotional intensity, that, when they are activated, overwhelms the person and are then re-experienced, instead of narratively communicated and shared.

Papadopoulos (2007) argues that a focus on trauma as "event-related" and symptom-producing systematically overlooks not only the individual who is suffering, as well as the culture-based responses that could emerge, but could miss altogether compensating new growth. He suggests a spectrum—which might also be seen as a sequence—of an individual's response to traumatic events in which post-traumatic stress disorder (PTSD) and its penumbra of pathologies is the most severe outcome, resiliency is more positive, and "adversity-activated development" is the most encouraging outcome. Resiliency in this conception is defined as a restoration of adequate physical/emotional functioning in the service of everyday life. But this functioning, while crucial for life going on, depends on the active and continual avoiding of memory triggers of the violence experienced. Such avoidance serves to repress the overwhelming pain of re-experiencing raw, unbearable affect—what both the mothers and their children refer to as *Ihahamuka* (panic attacks)[4] and "madness"—in an attempt to keep it out of relational interactions. But such avoidance is experienced as silence or non-communication or withdrawal from the parent-child relationship by the descendants in our study.

The growth and development that represent healing after psychosocial interventions and encounters, can be seen as a gradual return of a measure of epistemic trust (Fonagy and Allison 2014) allowing for a renewed capacity for relationship.

4.1 First Pathway: The Ghost as a Haunting Presence

The violence experienced during the genocide was by its very definition interpersonal: there was a victim and a perpetrator, a doer and a done to (Benjamin 2018). And it was a violence during which the "third" (Gerson 2009; Benjamin 2018) was entirely absent: there was no witness to stop it, or even register this violence, neither on the intersubjective or cultural level nor even on the international level. It is important to understand that, because of an absence of an intervening or meaning-making third, the survivor has incorporated as it were (embodied, taken in), both the doer and the done to experience.[5] Many survivors feel both victim, the "done to", but *at the same time* also a sense of culpability, of "doer", as if they must have been responsible for what happened to them. Gerson (2009) quotes a witness who as part of the liberating allied forces was one of the first persons to enter the concentration camp of Bergen-Belsen and reports that the survivors, barely alive, felt as if they were contaminated and therefore contaminating. Because there *was* no external witness ("a third") to stop the violence, there *is* no "inner witness" to take a moral position that differentiates the doer from the done to.

After the violence stops and a period of collective (social/cultural) "normalcy" is slowly and painstakingly being rebuilt, the emotions of the experience of violence, both of the survivors and of the perpetrators, need to be walled-off in the service of life going on.

The mothers' silence regarding their experiences during the period of collective violence—such as the rapes and other sexual violence, the killing of relatives (children, spouses, siblings, parents), and the period of being hunted and hiding in the marshes or latrines—is not a neutral silence. This silence is filled with the tumultuous and chaotic emotions of the survivors: the feelings of anguish—pain, fear, hopelessness; but also anger and hate—of the mothers. That is, these emotions are seen and felt by the descendants, though unexplained and unrepresented by the mothers. It is this dynamic that has been theorized as having the characteristics and behaviour of a "phantom" (Abraham and Torok 1994; Gerson 2009). A phantom or ghost is something that is both there and not there at the same time. Psychoanalyst Nicolas Abraham suggests that if a parent carries a deep secret (and for the purposes of the current article "secret" is defined as: something experienced but not expressed), this is sensed and absorbed by the child in a myriad of emotional interactions with the parent, producing in the child a recurrent anguished and anxious inner feeling state that can be recognized, but feels alien, empty of meaning.

> It is a [meta-psychological] fact that the 'phantom', whatever its form, is ... the gap that the concealment of some part of a loved one's life [has] produced in us. ... Consequently, what haunts are not the dead, but the gaps left within us by the secrets of others. (Abraham and Rand 1987)

The Israeli psychoanalyst, Ilany Kogan, who works with adult children of Holocaust survivors, writes something similar. Such patients, she writes, seem to have

> a psychic hole … which represents a part of their parents' history that has disappeared [and which they experience] as a persistent wound in their psyche or a gap in their emotional understanding … [T]his psychic hole … is different from a denial or repression of one's own traumatic experience … but is formed through the denial or repression of the trauma by their parents. (Kogan 1995)

This "psychic hole" is always a distinct "body"—she uses the metaphor of a "black hole" in the world of physics—the encapsulation of the unconscious fantasy of the traumatic past of the parent, which has an impact on the whole life of the patient (Kogan, ibid.). It is this body, which is experienced as fear, that functions phenomenologically like a ghost, which comes and goes.

Julia (20-year-old) explains that her mother's inability to answer her questions has the effect of rendering her silent, as if it robs her of her own expressive capacity. *Some questions I address to my mother seem to be difficult for her. When I insist, she refers me to my big sisters. After knowing my mother was cut during the genocide, I felt so disheartened, that I could not talk to other people. When I think about that* [her experiences] *I feel angry and stop talking. You could be there talking to me, and I would not be able to answer, I would only keep quiet, like a mute person.* Similar to her mother, she would like to talk but cannot. It is as if the inability of the mother to capture her experiences in language is directly passed to her child, invades her child.

So here we have one version of the intergenerational transmission of trauma: the descendants did not experience the actual historical period of violence, but that violence is inscribed on the bodies and in the psyches of the survivors, and anyone coming into intimate contact with those bodies and psyches can see the scars on the body and feel the emotional violence that still continues to radiate within them, as it were. It is precisely that which is felt but not seen that behaves like a ghost, some entity that haunts the house, and sometimes even the parent herself: it is real, but not acknowledged or explained. A ghost is also a temporal entity, one that belongs to the past but invades the present. So the emotion that is trapped between the parents and children belongs to the experiences during collective violence and not to the current parent-child relationship. In that sense, it is a foreign body.

4.2 Second Pathway: Family Violence Leading to Insecure Attachment

Post-collective violence is experienced and re-experienced in parent-child relationships (or: attachment relationships) that are characterized by periods of oppressive silence and unpredictable and frightening emotional outbursts of anger or despair.

Because the intrapersonal defensive structures (coping mechanisms) of the survivors are not only *porous*—that is, the emotions seep or slip through from the unconscious of the parent to the unconscious of the child (Gerson 2009)—but also *imperfect*, there are many times when these pent-up emotions by the parents are explosively released by small day-to-day family interactions. A normal intra-familial frustration, such as a demanding child or intimate partner dynamics, can set off a chain of intrapersonal associative reactions—memories of other children or family members who were killed; or of the helplessness during the genocide just to name a few of the endless possibilities. As a result, the highly charged affect—either volatile anger or deep anguish—that had been so carefully walled-off is explosively abreacted/acted out towards their partners and also their children (Asen and Fonagy 2017a, b).

In such family dynamics, the parent-as-survivor becomes the helpless and unwilling perpetrator of interpersonal violence towards her children, who say: "*She used to beat me. She insulted me all the time.*" When a child who has been born of rape, as some of our respondents were, asks about her father, the mother lashes out, "*You think he's so much better? Go to him then!*" The children, however, because they realize that their actions are in some way the triggers of that interpersonal violence, feel themselves to be the perpetrators of the pain and suffering they see (and empathically sense) in their parents. "*Her life was ruined because she got me.*" "*I see that my questions change her mood.*" "*I feel like I am the source of her sadness.*"

Because the emotional exchange is acted out and not "mentalized"—that is: the ability to understand one's own and others' behaviour in terms of mental states (Bateman and Fonagy 2010)—children can only make sense out of such exchanges *as if* they themselves are the cause. And so, on a micro level the repetition compulsion (Freud 1920/2003) of the victim-perpetrator dynamic is re-enacted: the mother (as suffering victim) hurts her child; and the child, because s/he feels that it is his/her persistent questioning that has caused the anger of the mother, identifies as perpetrator. It is this unpredictable, inconsistent relational dynamic that is the matrix in which the whole range of insecure attachment schemes of the young adult descendants may be formed. Some children withdraw, avoiding relationships outside of the family; others attempt to give their mother the care they seek in vain from her, in an attempt to turn the mother into a reliable parent; and still others are diffident and wary in forming any relationships outside the family.

In the context of this framework, we argue that it is the pain and suffering belonging to the previous collectively violent situation that emerges—like a ghost—in the family context and suggest that the range of resultant insecure attachment patterns between mothers and children is a second pathway of the transmission of intergenerational effects of collective violence.

4.3 Third Pathway: Vicarious Trauma Through Empathic Identification

The sharing of personal details of the stories between parent and child, when it does take place, can set up a third pathway of transmission of intergenerational trauma. As the parents may eventually tell their own horrific experiences bit by bit, this communication is received by the descendants less as a "story" (i.e. with some emotional distance), but through empathic identification that is present between loved ones, especially parents and children, almost as an "experience" in itself. When the children learned of the violent particulars of their mothers' stories, they ruminated on and imagined these experiences as if it were happening to themselves, in a way that is akin to encountering the emotional intensity of the actual violence. As one of the respondents said, *"I felt what she felt!"*

And so, for a period afterwards, they report many symptoms that can be grouped under the concept of suffering from vicarious trauma: intrusive thoughts about what happened to their parents "*I can't stop thinking about it*"; an increase in anxiety; and somatization. "*I started to suffer from stomach aches, I could not concentrate on my studies because I was always thinking about what happened to my mother. I became afraid it will happen to me, because I am not a tree. I suffer from persistent headaches.*"

The danger of the latter could be that, in an effort to protect their parents from their own inner pain, the descendants may begin to employ the same destructive coping mechanisms as their parents before them—silence punctuated by emotional outbursts when avoidance is no longer possible. This may eventually affect the relations with their own children, and so the violence may, on an interpersonal level, invade (like a ghost) and affect the third generation. In a recent internet-meme, Wagner (May 2018) expresses it well: "Pain travels through families until someone is ready to feel it." We would add: until someone is able to share it, for which you need not only words, but a listening other as well. The hope is that, now that the ghosts are known to the children, the children feel the pain, and if they are able to give words to it and to start sharing the pain with others, the intergenerational transmission of trauma to the third and following generations may well be modified.

4.4 Fourth Pathway: Intergenerational Reparative Effects of Moving Beyond Silence

In this last section of our analysis, we try to conceptualize and understand how the healing effects experienced by the mothers were carried over into a more constructive and supportive mother-child attachment, which in turn translated into a positive change in the children's inner and outer lives.

Immediately after collective violence, a period of "madness" sets in, as the mothers expressed it: feeling "not like a human being" (only experiencing raw pain; inability to care for self and others: hardly washed, ate, or slept); then a long period of day-to-day survival self follows: caring for self and children on a barely minimal level; only nominal and superficial interaction with others in the social world; silence punctuated by emotional outbursts in the home and parent-child relationships. The mothers describe themselves as neither alive nor dead. Their emotional outbursts, whether of anger or sadness, are experienced and feared by both the mothers and the children as the momentary return of the immediate post-violence madness. Because the violence had been communal, the social space was completely devoid of trust and the women experienced this period as "social death"; as such, the most recurring symbolic expression of the change wrought by their participation in sociotherapy was "as if being born again": rebirth (see Richters and Kagoyire 2014).

How can we understand this change that amounts to a transformation? In the opening of this chapter, we said that the reverberations of collective violence move from the social space (where it took place) to the family and inner world. Certainly, the annual commemorations and gacaca courts provided social spaces for processing the repercussions of the genocide, very important as such, but both remain in the "doer" and the "done to" narrative. Sociotherapy is a *new* kind of social space, a "third space", beyond doer and done to (Benjamin 2018), a space for people to explore and share their day-to-day concerns, especially those of family life, and so a space for remaking meaning in what it is to be a member of a community. This remaking of meaning is facilitated by guiding the participants of a sociotherapy support group through phases of discussing the meaning of safety, trust, care, and respect for themselves and others.

Sociotherapy, as such, is a space to understand not only one's own behaviour in terms of emotional states but also that of others ("being mentalized"), to witness the pain and struggle of others, and also to be witnessed in one's own. It is a space within which to explore and practise basic human interactions, the building blocks of social relationships. In short, it is a space to experience what it feels like to be a human being again.

What the mothers repeatedly mentioned is the importance of giving and receiving of advice as happened in the sociotherapy group they participated in. Let us digress into a small exposition about "giving and receiving advice". In Rwanda, exchanging advice is an integral aspect of caring for someone's life today and in the future. It is related to active empathy, in that one takes an interest in someone's life and problems in order to help with finding solutions. While in a Western cultural context giving and receiving advice can be experienced as criticism, intrusive and meddlesome, in Rwanda it is an aspect of feeling connected to each other, as illustrated by the Rwandan proverb: "God joins those who advise each other." The Kinyarwanda phrase for "giving advice" (*kugira umuntu inama*) is related to the concept of *ubuntu*. Ubuntu is a philosophical concept in sub-Saharan Africa, there is a version in all Bantu languages, and is most often translated as "I am because we are". Following Gobodo-Madikizela (2015), we understand it to mean that one's subjectivity, one's humanity, is inextricably intertwined with others in one's community, as when she wrote, "A person becomes a human being through the many relationships with others" (p. 1089). Or as another Rwandan proverb has it: "One pillar does not make a house."

The idea of "becoming a human being again" is also how we may understand at least one motivation (there are undoubtedly others) behind the ongoing questioning by the children of their mothers. Although our respondents themselves often referred to it as a search for information, a closer reading of what they said can be interpreted as looking for answers to two overriding questions: How did you survive? And: Tell me about our relatives—yours and mine—the relatives who died. It may be understood as a search for the human being in the mother: Who are you? Who are we together? So that we may better care for (or advise) each other. But also, and more painfully, perhaps a search for the human being in the rapist-father and his relatives, for the child to understand: So that I may know who I am. As one respondent said, "*So that I may know what to tell my own children at some point.*"

The questioning by the descendants reveals that they are not merely passive recipients of the parent-child relationship fractured by the historical collective violence, but that there is active engagement with parents and the familial history. This is in part a search for stories of the emotional violence they have already "experienced" in the relationship with their traumatized mothers, so that they can make "sense" of these observations and feelings. "*Before I was angry at her, but now I understand her better.*" And in part, it is a preparation for incipient parenthood of themselves.

After their mothers participated in sociotherapy and the story-telling project, descendants described the relationship with their mothers as more open, as being interested in the inner and outer lives of their children, in other words, supportive interactive human relating beyond the minimal caring for the physical raising of their children, such as food and school-fees. The children also used the terminology of "she gives me advice" to characterize this betterment in their relationship. This post-traumatic growth (Grayson 2017, 2018), we emphasize, is not only *inside* the traumatized individual, but it expresses itself as a renewed capacity for care and relationships.[6] This allowed the children to enter into their own lives with more confidence. Several children said explicitly: "*Without the changes in my mother and in our relationship, I would not be where I am today, especially in my schooling.*"

5 Conclusion

In this chapter, we show that decades after the genocide in Rwanda, the ghosts of the past linger on and haunt the family, contributing to insecure parent-child relationships, which can negatively impact subsequent relationship patterns as those children grow and start their own families. But our research also shows that if the ghosts are recognized, through the witnessing and being witnessed effects of psychosocial support, not only do the participants themselves benefit, but these reparative effects are carried into the relationship with their children, the next generation. Nonetheless, the insights gained by those children into the suffering of their parents that are made possible by those reparative effects continue to be a very heavy burden for the second generation, and it is not clear how carrying this burden will shape their lives. This chapter is based on the first foray of qualitative research, individually and as part of two focus groups, with the next generation. While the descendants do indeed describe a strengthened, more open, interactive, and secure relationship with their mothers, they also talk of the emotionally dis-regulating effects—sleep-disturbances, feelings of helplessness, sadness, bitterness—of learning the particulars of the violence experienced by their mothers. This finding may add a note of caution and a shade of nuance to the growing body of evidence that silence and sharing of truth are both phases in a much longer journey of healing that does not end with truth-telling (see, for instance, Brounéus 2010 or Gates-Madsen 2016).

It is too early to know what the longer-term experiences of these descendants will be. Will they find ways of continuing to move beyond the doer/done to dynamic or will there be a repetition of it? While focus-group discussions are not at all the same thing as a psychosocial support group such as sociotherapy, nonetheless they too can be seen as a social space in which descendants discover that they are not alone in their experiences, that they form part of broader patterns. As one participant said, *I learned a lot today from our discussions, and that empowered me*. In subsequent research of this long-term project, we hope to continue to understand the ghosts so that they may go from haunting to accompanying, so that individual traumatic suffering may be transformed into shared social experience, in order to contribute to post-traumatic growth.

Acknowledgement We thank our respondents and their mothers for having entrusted their stories of pain and suffering to us and letting us accompany them in their courageous struggles to overcome this pain and suffering in a constructive way. We also appreciated the moments of laughter and joy we all shared together, which made us believe that your open minds will be a mainspring in the reconstruction process to a more peaceful country. Our hope is that your voices will light the way for other youth growing up in post-conflict societies.

Notes

1. A full discussion of the sociotherapy approach is beyond the scope of this chapter. Briefly, community members, whose combined social history comprise a range of genocide-related experiences, are invited to participate in a group of 10–15 people meeting once a week for a period of 15 weeks. The meeting-places are in the local community: underneath a tree, at a church or school, or at the house of a group member. People always sit in a circle, signifying equality (no one is at the head or front or back), and no one can hide. The groups are led by two sociotherapists or facilitators, who are themselves members of the same local community. The discussion is about daily problems and worries. Sociotherapy applies

a group dynamic approach; it is not a trauma therapy. For more information, see, for example, Richters et al. (2010) and Ingabire et al. (2017).
2. This booklet contains 19 stories. Shortened versions of 10 of those 19 stories were published in English translation in Richters and Kagoyire (2014).
3. This method, based on the work of Husserl and Merleau-Ponty, is aimed at studying the whole person and not isolated psychological processes. For a full discussion of the method, see Apprey and Stein (1993, p. 119).
4. Mental health professionals in Rwanda label the distress of *ihahamuka* as a symptom of post-traumatic stress disorder, while Hagengima et al. (2003) categorize *ihahamuka* as somatic panic attacks.
5. Such a paradox is true of both the victim *and* the perpetrator, the latter also often feels "done to"; his or her acts are so horrifying and ego-alien that they can only have been committed because s/he was forced to, by others or by circumstances.
6. Grayson (2017, 2018) builds on Tedeschi and Calhoun (2004)—who coined the term "post-traumatic growth" (PTG) in 1995—and other work of these same authors in taking up the challenge to contextualise and adapt its related tools for use in specific socio-cultural contexts. She identified "personal strength" and "relating to others" as particularly helpful in accounting for positive change in post-genocide Rwanda. While Staub and Vollhardt (2008) see overlap between PTG and what they coin as "altruism born of suffering" (ABS), they regard the latter as a domain of theory and research in its own right. They identify finding healing in social support and significant human relationships as conditions for ABS, which the children in our sample experience as being cared for as a result of sociotherapy. Even though relevant for a more detailed analysis of our findings, it is beyond the scope of this chapter to delve into differences and overlaps between the concepts healing, resilience, PTG, ABS, and related concepts. See for an in-depth study of post-traumatic growth in the testimonies of male and female genocide survivors in Rwanda: Williamson Sinalo (2018).

References

Abraham, N., & Rand, N. (1987). Notes on the Phantom: A Complement to Freud's Metapsychology. *Critical Inquiry, 13*(2), 287–292.

Abraham, N., & Torok, M. (1994). Secrets and Posterity: The Theory of the Transgenerational Phantom. In N. Abraham and M. Torok (Ed.), *The Shell and the Kernel* (pp. 165–190). The University of Chicago Press. (First publication 1975).

African Rights. (2004). *Broken Bodies, Torn Spirits: Living with Genocide, Rape and HIV/AIDS*. Kigali: African Rights.

Apprey, M., & Stein, H. (1993). *Intersubjectivity, Projective Identification, and Otherness*. Pittsburg: Duquesne University Press.

Asen, E., & Fonagy, P. (2017a). Mentalizing Family Violence, Part 1: Conceptual Framework. *Family Process, 56*(1), 2–21.

Asen, E., & Fonagy, P. (2017b). Mentalizing Family Violence, Part 2: Techniques and Interventions. *Family Process, 56*(1), 22–44.

Bar-On, D. (2006). *Tell Your Life Story: Creating Dialogue Between Jews and Germans, Israelis and Palestinians*. Budapest: Central European University Press.

Bateman, A., & Fonagy, P. (2010). Mentalization-Based Treatment for Borderline Personality Disorder. *World Psychiatry, 9*(1), 11–15.

Benjamin, J. (2018). *Beyond the Doer and Done to: Recognition Theory, Intersubjectivity, and the Third*. New York: Routledge.

Brounéus, K. (2010). The Trauma of Truth Telling: Effects of Witnessing in the Rwandan Gacaca Courts on Psychological Health. *Journal of Conflict Resolution, 54*(3), 408–437.

Caswell, M., & Cifor, M. (2016). From Human Rights to Feminist Ethics: Radical Empathy in the Archives. *Archivaria, 81*, 23–43.

Danieli, Y. (1984). Psychotherapists' Participation in the Conspiracy of Silence About the Holocaust. *Psychoanalytic Psychology, 1*(1), 2342.

Fonagy, P., & Allison, E. (2014). The Role of Mentalizing and Epistemic Trust in the Therapeutic Relationship. *Psychotherapy, 53*(3), 372–380.

Freud, S. (2003). *Beyond the Pleasure Principle*. London: Penguin Classics. (First publication 1920).

Gates-Madsen, N. J. (2016). *Trauma, Taboo, and Truth-Telling: Listening to Silences in Postdictatorship Argentina*. Madison: University of Wisconsin Press.

Gerson, S. (2009). When the Third is Dead: Memory, Mourning, and Witnessing in the Aftermath of the Holocaust. *International Journal of Psychoanalysis, 90*(6), 1341–1357.

Giorgi, A. (2012). The Descriptive Phenomenological Psychological Method. *Journal of Phenomenological Psychology, 43*(1), 3–12.

Gobodo-Madikizela, P. (2015). Psychological Repair: The Intersubjective Dialogue of Remorse and Forgiveness in the Aftermath of Gross Human

Rights Violations. *Journal of the American Psychoanalytic Association, 63*(6), 1058–1123.

Grayson, H. (2017). A Place for Individuals: Positive Growth in Rwanda. *Eastern African Literature and Cultural Studies, 3*(2–4), 107–130.

Grayson, H. (2018). Articulating Growth in Rwandan Terms: Adapting the Post-traumatic Growth Inventory. *Studies in Testimony, 1*(1), 4–30.

Hagengimana, A., Hinton, D., Bird, B., Pollack, M., & Pitman, R. K. (2003). Somatic Panic-Attack Equivalents in a Community Sample of Rwandan Widows Who Survived the 1994 Genocide. *Psychiatry Research, 117*(1), 1–9.

Hogwood, J., Mushashi, C., Jones, S., & Auerbach, C. (2017). "I Learned Who I Am": Young People Born from Genocide Rape in Rwanda and Their Experiences of Disclosure. *Journal of Adolescent Research I-22*. https://doi.org/10.1177/0743558417713302.

Ingabire, M. C., Kagoyire, M. G., Karangwa, D., Ingabire, N., Habarugira, N., Jansen, A., & Richters, A. (2017). Trauma Informed Restorative Justice Through Community Based Sociotherapy in Rwanda. *Intervention, 15*(3), 241–253.

Ingelaere, B. (2016). *Inside Rwanda's Gacaca Courts: Seeking Justice After Genocide*. Chicago: University of Wisconsin Press.

Kagoyire, G., Rutayisire, T., & Richters, A. (Eds.). (2013). *Narapfuye ndazuka: Ubuzima bw'abagore barokotse jenoside yakorewe Abatutsi mu Rwanda mu 1994*. Bugesera Sociotherapy Program.

Kagoyire, A., & Richters, A. (2018). "We are the Memory Representation of Our Parents": Intergenerational Legacies of Genocide Among Descendants of Rape Survivors in Rwanda. *Torture, 28*(3), 30–45.

Kogan, I. (1995). *The Cry of Mute Children: A Psychoanalytic Perspective of the Second Generation of the Holocaust*. London/New York: Free Association Books.

Kogan, I. (2012). The Second Generation in the Shadow of Terror. In M. G. Fromm (Ed.), *Lost in Transmission: Studies of Trauma Across Generations*. London: Karnac Books.

van der Kolk, B. (2014). *The Body Keeps the Score: Brain, Mind, and Body in the Healing of Trauma*. New York: Penguin Books.

Matz, D. (2015). Interrupting Intergenerational Trauma: Children of Holocaust Survivors and the Third Reich. *Journal of Phenomenological Psychology, 46*(2), 185–205.

MINALOC (Ministry of Local Administration, Community Development and Social Affairs). (2004). *Dénombrement des victimes du génocide. Final report, Kigali, Rwanda*. Retrieved from: http://cnlg.gov.rw/fileadmin/templates/

Publications/denombrement_des_victimes_du_genocide_perpetre_contre_les_tutsi_avril_2004.pdf

Papadopoulos, R. (2007). Refugees, Trauma and Adversity-Activated Development. *European Journal of Psychotherapy & Counselling, 9*(3), 301–312.

Richters, A., Rutayisire, T., & Dekker, C. (2010). Care as a Turning Point in Sociotherapy: Remaking the Moral World in Post-Genocide Rwanda. *Medische Antropologie: Tijdschrift over Gezondheid en Cultuur, 22*(1), 93–108.

Richters, A., & Kagoyire, G. (Eds.). (2014). Of Death and Rebirth: Life Histories of Rwandan Female Genocide Survivors. Torture, *24*(Supplementum 1).

Rothschild, B. (2000). *The Body Remembers: The Psychophysiology of Trauma and Trauma Treatment*. New York/London: W.W. Norton & Co..

Staub, E., & Vollhardt, J. (2008). Altruism Born of Suffering: The Roots of Caring and Helping After Victimization and Other Trauma. *American Journal of Orthopsychiatry, 78*(3), 267–280.

Tedeschi, R. G., & Calhoun, L. G. (2004). Posttraumatic Growth: Conceptual Foundations and Empirical Evidence. *Psychological Inquiry, 15*(1), 1–18.

Williamson Sinalo, C. (2018). *Rwanda After Genocide: Gender, Identity and Post-Traumatic Growth*. Cambridge: Cambridge University Press.

11

How Shall We Talk of Bhalagwe? Remembering the *Gukurahundi* Era in Matabeleland, Zimbabwe

Shari Eppel

We are afraid of this place, what is the name of this place?
—"Siyayesaba lindawo, itiwa yini?" IsiNdebele and English translation of song sung at Bhalagwe Camp on 21 February 2018

On 21 February 2018, for the first time, mostly youthful members of Ndebele pressure groups in Matabeleland, Zimbabwe, were allowed by the state to undertake a memorial activity in the Bhalagwe valley. Bhalagwe is the topographical name of a long granite hill situated 120 km south from Bulawayo, the main city in Matabeleland. To reach Bhalagwe, one has to navigate a winding, disintegrated road, whose tar strip is only one car wide, meaning a dangerous game of sliding off the precipitous tar margins into potholed dirt, to avoid minibuses and dilapidated trucks careening towards one. Hungry cows and children walking far-too-far

IsiShona, meaning, "the first rain of spring that washes away the chaff from the last season."

S. Eppel (✉)
Ukuthula Trust, Bulawayo, Zimbabwe

K. Wale et al. (eds.), *Post-Conflict Hauntings*, Palgrave Studies in Compromise after Conflict, https://doi.org/10.1007/978-3-030-39077-8_11

home from school add to the hazards of travelling through the spectacular, mountainous poverty of rural Matobo district. Hills give way to a virtual desert of thorn bushes and the occasional goat, and then the road makes a single right turn through Maphisa village, to finally reach Bhalagwe. A winding dirt road traverses a few homesteads to arrive at a landscape devoid of human activity, seldom visited. It is a lonely, haunted place. Dust billows in gusts of wind, and trees with more elbows than leaves push out painfully bright flowers ahead of scarce rains.

It was a small, intense gathering at Bhalagwe. Most in attendance were not yet in their 40s and had been toddlers or not-yet-born when the post-independence *Gukurahundi* massacres took place, between 1983 and 1985. With one or two exceptions, all were there for the first time. Mostly, what they knew—or did not know—of Bhalagwe was what they had heard whispered, or imagined whispered in corners, by their parents and grandparents. Bhalagwe is synonymous with the worst violence in the history of this western region of Zimbabwe, home to the minority Ndebele ethnic group.[1] This violence took place in the post-colonial Zimbabwe of the 1980s, in what is referred to as the "*Gukurahundi* Era", or by the Mthwakazi and Ibhetshu LikaZulu[2] pressure groups, as the "*Gukurahundi* Genocide". Bhalagwe operated as a torture and death camp from January to April 1984. Thousands of civilians, mainly men and some women aged between 15 and 60 years, were transported here from all over Matabeleland. Detainees were beaten and interrogated by the notorious Fifth (5) Brigade, a North Korean trained, Shona-dominant unit outside of the usual line of army command, often following instructions from the Central Intelligence Organisation (CIO). People were accused of being Ndebele and therefore being "dissidents", or of feeding or hiding "dissidents". Sexual torture was common, as were other unusually cruel abuses (CCPJZ and LRF 1997). Many died and bodies were routinely thrown down nearby mineshafts. Human remains surfaced during the 1990s, when Antelope Mine, nearby Bhalagwe, was reopened: footage was shown on Zimbabwean television of human bones being passed out of the mineshaft in buckets (CCJPZ and LRF 1997).

Also present in 2018 were a few older people and one or two scholars of the region. Being materially there in the place of violence was a significant aspect of it being possible to talk of the violence and the damage it had done. This very first commemorative event at Bhalagwe became the lived, visible embodiment of intergenerational transfer of both trauma and memory.

1 Theories of Trauma

In recent years, there has been significant criticism of Caruth's (1996) western and psychoanalytic-centric theories of trauma, from a growing body of post-colonial trauma theorists. The emphasis for Caruth and others was on single traumatic events, that led to "crippling effects of trauma: memory is situated entirely under the sign of post-traumatic melancholia" (Luckhurst 2008, 210). Many have pointed to the fact that phenomena such as slavery or colonialism are not single traumatic events, but can last for generations, and that it is important to note not just the "pathological and negative" but the "creative and political" responses of individuals and communities to such prolonged experiences of oppression (Craps 2012, 127).

Rothberg (2008) has appealed for the critique of Caruth and others to move beyond a discussion of what trauma is *not* and to redirect the theory from its focus on "individual, temporal and linguistic" to "collective, spatial and material" (228). He claims that theories of trauma need to "assert the relevance of localized models of belief, ritual, and understanding, thereby undermining the centrality of Western knowledge and expertise" (27). Craps (2012) refers to the need to take social and historic relations into account and to acknowledge recuperation through social activism.

This chapter offers an account that speaks to the issues raised by Rothburg and Craps. It describes the importance of material and spatial realities for communities in Matabeleland, as they strive to understand and give voice to the still largely officially denied *Gukurahundi* era, by confronting and reclaiming not just the spaces of torture, but the very bones and narratives of the murdered dead. In the world of post-colonial violence in Matabeleland, narratives are embodied in physical landscapes, in mass graves, in the schoolyards where rapes and beatings occurred, of this still mainly un-worded history. *None of these spaces has been formally monumentalised*. In June 2019, there remains no single state-endorsed memorial to the estimated 10,000–20,000 massacre victims of the 1980s (CCJP and LRF 1997).

It is now almost four decades since the violent events, meaning that many of those directly affected by beatings, burnings and as eyewitnesses to massacres, are old or already dead. But the anger of their children and grandchildren has gained strength and visibility since the removal from power of Robert Mugabe, via a coup in November 2017, after 38 years of oppressive rule. Many of the leading perpetrators of *Gukurahundi* have remained in powerful state positions, including the "new" President, 78-year-old Emmerson Mnangagwa, who was deeply involved in the CIO in the 1980s. Nonetheless, there has been a partial opening of space that has allowed for transgenerational memories of violence to make themselves loudly heard and seen. This chapter will recount this phenomenon and the contestation of memory that at times has taken the form of persons physically destroying one another's monuments at Bhalagwe, in an angry quest to place—or prevent the placing of—the post-colonial violence of Bhalagwe into the legitimate and material space of recorded memory. The telling of violence and how it is being transferred as collective memory is in itself a story of time and places that will be partially unravelled here. Zelizer has indicated that "Collective memory has texture, existing in the world rather than in a person's head" (1998, 4). Landscapes can provide a bridge between private memories of violence and loss, and public narratives and commemorations (Filippucci 2012). The group gathered at Bhalagwe in 2018 was looking to the landscape to provide such a bridge, as they sought to build a "collective memory", which has been recognised as "the language by which individuals and groups struggle over their own identity and make demands in the public sphere" (Rubin 2013, 1). The desolate landscape of Bhalagwe was the "geography of pain" for those present (Mueggler 2001, 199).

The chapter aims to add to the existing literature on trauma and intergenerational transfer of memory by exploring the ways in which physical spaces, material objects and political activism have contributed to making memories of violence tangible in Matabeleland. More so, the chapter will illustrate that Zimbabweans have found culturally appropriate ways of addressing the needs of the tortured dead, through witnessed exhumations and reburials that have facilitated the recovery and intergenerational transfer of historical memory. The chapter will also illustrate the fascinating tensions between imaginaries of the past, empirical "facts" and common, more embellished versions of histories. The chapter questions "historical truth" and what representations of the past may tell us about what marginalised groups hope for in the future.

2 Methodology

I will draw on events personally observed by myself since the coup of November 2017 and also on hundreds of interviews conducted by Amani Trust since 1998: known since 2014 as Ukuthula Trust, Amani was a non-governmental organisation directed by me and dedicated to working with victims of torture and organised violence. These are mainly from the *Gukurahundi* era, but also encompassing colonial violence and violence since the so-called Zimbabwe crisis, which began in 2000 and continues to date. The NGO consists of staff who began as conventional health professionals—myself as a psychologist, others as counsellors and physical therapists. Our intention has always been to be *results and evidence based* in terms of our interventions, and we have diligently documented all our interactions with rural community members and key informants. We have hundreds of transcriptions of individual and community interviews, some of which remain confidential, as part of clinical and therapeutic records, and many of which we have permission to use in the formal research domain. They constitute a rich record of community interpretations and priorities with regard to a long history of state-organised violence. They also illustrate how community demands shifted our focus away from a conventional, western definition of trauma with a focus on post-traumatic stress disorder (PTSD), anxiety and depression, to acknowledge that the worst problem left by the violence, as defined by communities themselves, was that of the "angry dead" (Eppel 2006).

Our team has now fully retrained in the skills of forensic archaeology and anthropology, to exhume and rebury the murdered dead: to heal the living, we recognised a need to "heal the dead". In doing this since we first exhumed in 1999, we preceded Rothberg's call (2008) to recognise local traditions and beliefs when conceptualising how violence is experienced. Interacting with communities has transformed not just our theoretical position but our skill base, so that we can practically engage in the material landscape of violence, by literally (as opposed to theoretically) unearthing the dead, to give a voice to bones. Exhumations can vindicate and restore historical memory, while at the same time righting cultural wrongs and bringing some closure. As Zimbabwe remains a deeply oppressive place, exhumations are not being presented as a perfect solution, but in our observation, resolving "ambiguous loss" (Boss 2000) has empowered many individuals and families to process their histories of violence usefully. Each exhumation is a catalyst to scores of family and community members, who observe the uncovering of the bones. Some talk, some are silent: some remember what happened, others are learning for the first time what happened. Others slowly recover memories, often hidden away for years as too terrifying to explore. Personal effects and photos are hesitantly retrieved from hiding places. This process begins months before an exhumation, during the act of documenting pre-, peri- and post-mortem information about the deceased: how tall they were, how old at death, injuries and illnesses that might have affected bones over their lifetime: who saw the murder, who witnessed the burial. After exhumation, family members are included in analysis of remains, to establish peri-mortem trauma, or what happened during the hours leading to death. This allows the dead to speak to their final experiences of torture. The reburial, invariably at the family homestead, leads to new acts of witnessing as family and community members, in the physical presence of the murdered person, recount to many hundreds in attendance yet more memories of what happened right there in that landscape.

3 Background to *Gukurahundi*

During the course of a long civil war for independence that lasted from the 1960s until 1979, antagonism grew between the two guerrilla armies that fought the war—the Zimbabwe African National Liberation Army (ZANLA), armed wing of the Zimbabwe African National Union (ZANU), and the Zimbabwe People's Revolutionary Army (ZIPRA), armed wing of the Zimbabwe African People's Union (ZAPU). Mugabe's own political party, ZANU-Patriotic Front (ZANU-PF), swept most of the seats in the first democratic election of 1980—except in Matabeleland and parts of the Midlands, areas where the Ndebele minority reside. Here, ZAPU, headed by longstanding nationalist Joshua Nkomo, won all the seats.

In 1980, integrating three armies into one—ZANLA, ZIPRA and the Rhodesian National Army—proved difficult. Almost immediately, ZIPRAs reported ostracism, beatings and disappearances from their ranks (Alexander et al. 2000). This led to defections and small bands of "dissidents" in rural Matabeleland. The same phenomenon occurred in other parts of the country, where ZANLAs also defected, but the rhetoric was simply against ZAPU and its "dissidents" (CCJPZ and LRF 1997). The government itself acknowledged that the dissidents never numbered more than 400 at their peak, which made the level of state violence that ensued hard to explain (CCJPZ and LRF 1997, 167).[3]

Fifth Brigade was deployed in rural Matabeleland North in January 1983 and there was immediately epidemic violence (CCJPZ and LRF 1997). Ndebele civilians were accused of supporting ZAPU and therefore of being dissidents. Men and sometimes women were massacred throughout the province, in well-witnessed community-based murders, including villagers burnt to death in huts. In spite of a massive information clampdown, stories of horror began surfacing, via remote, rural missions. By April 1983, the outcry caused 5 Brigade to be withdrawn.

The 5 Brigade was redeployed in Matabeleland South in 1984: civilians were now moved to various bases, of which the largest was Bhalagwe Camp. Here they were tortured, often to death. Burials were now often clandestine and anonymous. After further outcries, 5 Brigade was again withdrawn: in early 1985, it was deployed once more. They then moved to the sinister policy of enforced disappearances: wanted individuals were taken in the dead of night, never to be seen again. The disappearances targeted ZAPU rural leadership prior to national elections in June 1985—yet Matabeleland once more voted overwhelmingly for ZAPU. This led to a new tactic of negotiating a Unity Accord, which ended both the violence and the existence of ZAPU, in 1987: Zimbabwe became de facto a one-party state. The damage done by the *Gukurahundi* era remains immeasurable: scarcely a family in Matabeleland and parts of the Midlands were not directly affected by the killings, beatings, property loss and disappearances of the 1980s.

4 The Aftermath: Silence and Whispering Bones

While working in remote, rural villages in Matabeleland South, it became apparent to me in the late 1990s that wounds were still raw and fear blanketed these villages. Beneath the fear was terrible grief over the fate of those who had been killed or disappeared. In terms of local belief systems, the angry spirits of the dishonoured dead were the most serious legacy of the massacres (Eppel 2002, 2014). Ancestral spirits play a daily role in the lives of the living and if you have not buried your loved one in the right place, with traditional rituals, in front of the right people, then they have been dishonoured and will punish you, with droughts, failed marriages, failed development projects, infertility and illnesses (Werbner 1991; Daneel 1995). According to traditional leaders, we were told that "Culturally it is not right for someone's bones to be exposed. It brings bad luck which denies people rain." A chief commented to me, "Human bones are in the bush and some are exposed – I don't think God is happy with that" (Eppel 2014, 7).

The bones of the murdered were key and active players in the well-being of their communities and Amani Trust began to "heal the dead". While the government position was that the past must be forgotten, families found themselves unable to forget their aggrieved loved ones. The Argentine Forensic Anthropology Team (EAAF) agreed to come to Matabeleland at the request of Amani Trust, to conduct exhumations and develop capacity to exhume in Zimbabwe. For four years, Amani Trust exhumed together with the EAAF, developing a skill base in forensic anthropology and archaeology. When a new political crisis led to a wave of state-led violence in the wake of the 2000 elections and the rise of a new political opposition (Raftopoulos and Savage 2004), exhumations stopped for some years. However, the process of skill building of the Ukuthula Forensic Anthropology Team (UFAT) continued and, in 2014, exhumations resumed on an ad hoc basis.

"Healing" is not a simple event, but allowing the living and the dead to speak to each other and to allow the dead to be acknowledged, witnessed, listened to and reburied in the right place with the appropriate rituals, unlocked events and began to give words to memories. It was apparent that some families, driven by intense fear which led to an inability to talk about the past, had effectively "disappeared" relatives and all evidence of them from their family tree and lexicon. They might know where their relative was buried, but felt unsafe to remember this publicly.

4.1 Cultural Trauma and Bone-Memory

It is possible to reject a theory that focuses on trauma simply as an individual, internal process, while nonetheless accepting that for some at least, "Caruth's notion of the ultimately unknowable and inexpressible nature of trauma wounding" remains authentic (Visser 2015, 251). The difficulty of finding one's linguistic bearings in the past was painfully obvious at the Bhalagwe memorial ceremony in 2018, even at the same moment that collective or cultural trauma was being lived by those present. Individuals and communities often have gaps in their narratives, particularly in their first attempts to recount events. At the same time, some individuals can be very forthright and complete in their ability to recall traumatic events, pointing to the unevenness of the impact of violence. Kirmayer's theory of traumatic silence (1996) claims that the trauma of extreme violence by its very nature can preclude the possibility of giving it meaning, as it is beyond comprehension.[4] Langer (1991, 23) reports an Auschwitz survivor stating, "I don't live with it, it lives with me." Memory is the "history that cannot be written" (Lambek 2006, 211)—and that at times cannot be spoken. Memories may be obliquely conveyed, by silences, perceived fear or stubborn avoidance. They are considered to be transmissible intergenerationally, including where such memories could be referred to as "cultural trauma".

> Cultural trauma refers to a dramatic loss of identity and meaning, a tear in the social fabric, affecting a group of people that has achieved some degree of cohesion. In this sense, the trauma need not necessarily be felt by everyone in a community or experienced directly by any or all. (Eyerman 2001, 2)

People in Matabeleland perceive themselves to have been collectively targeted as Ndebeles and/or as ZAPU-supporters, meaning that *Gukurahundi* is understood as an experience that all Ndebeles can claim, and not just those who directly experienced the violence.

It is my contention that as those most affected by *Gukurahundi* continue to live in its landscape of terror, the very rocks and bones that surround them can facilitate the breaking of the silences and can provide victims and their children and grandchildren with the catalysts to spoken memory. Exhumations can be powerful provokers of repressed memory. The slow exposure of remains in front of family and community allows the bones to speak on behalf of everyone. Exhumations do in actuality what psychotherapy tries to do metaphorically: they dig up the past, reveal aspects of long-hidden truths, facilitate their discussion, and then allow for the bones (the past) to be once more laid to rest in a way that will no longer cast a troubled shadow into the future.

The bones are the literal embodiment of memory of violence. Forensic expertise can help to fulfil the humanitarian objective of the "right to know" what happened to family members, which is linked to the "right to truth", both recognised rights in terms of the United Nations Commission for Human Rights (E/CN.4/2006/91, A/HRC/5/7). Importantly, exhumations may reveal the eyewitnesses as truthful, when the evidence of the bones confirms their accounts. Bones can restore historical memory, as bone trauma may explain forensically what happened to the murdered individual in the hours leading to death: blunt, sharp, burnt and ballistic peri-mortem trauma can be discriminated (White and Folkens 2012). The ways in which the dead were buried are part of the recovery of truth. Bones huddled in animal holes, shoved into crevices or deliberately burnt have, in Matabeleland, spoken to a systematic pattern of clandestine and disrespectful burials. For one example of how bones reclaim truth, two witnesses reported to us that after excessive torture in a 5 Brigade base in 1984:

> Daniel could not walk, he had blood coming out of his ears – we were forced to push him on the wheelbarrow for a long distance, then the soldiers took him into the hills. We heard gunshots, and never saw him alive again. (Interview with eyewitness, 2014)

In 2014, UFAT exhumed Daniel from a crevice in the forest and his cranium was in 64 pieces. After reconstruction, a minimum of two bullet-paths through the skull was apparent. This vindicated the memories of the witnesses and gave credibility to all they had said, in the face of a government that was still resistant to such truths. His white patent leather belt and other clothing, also recovered, were a poignant reminder of Daniel, a renowned singer and drummer.

In almost every case, as an exhumation looms, the "missing" unmentioned family member gradually eases back into conversation among family members. A long-hidden, almost forgotten photographic image of the person might one day be produced, once it is finally safer to refer to that person. Daniel's brother unexpectedly produced two beautiful portraits of him, a few days before his reburial. A relative reported:

> Yesterday, when one of his daughters saw the photos for the first time, she said that she had never seen her father before – although she used to dream about her father a lot, he had no face in her dreams. (Comment during reburial, 2014)

The exhumations thus become catalysts for a broader reclaiming of the dead. Exhumations restore personhood to the dead. This same uncle reported that "I could not talk to Daniel's sons then, because it was painful. But now we have got proof of how it ended and so I feel free to fill in the gaps of their father's history and the type of man he was." It is our observation that it is often only at the reburials that the next generation of the family begins to hear not just about the death but also about the *life* of their murdered relative.

4.2 Bones and Bhalagwe

In 2000, human bones exposed by rains at Bhalagwe Camp were reported to Amani Trust. It was not surprising that human remains had surfaced in these stony soils, considering the murders there in 1984. The EAAF and Amani analysed the assorted collection of bones and concluded that they represented a minimum number of three, incomplete, individuals.

These remains were reburied at a site identified by the Governor of Matabeleland South, Steven Nkomo, on the periphery of Bhalagwe Camp.[5] By 2000, the camp, once a vast expanse of more than a hundred semi-circular corrugated asbestos shelters, was well advanced down its pathway to oblivion. An aerial photograph in the CCJPZ and LRF (1997) report shows what the camp looked like in 1982, when it was still an intact military base. By 1992, another photograph shows that most of the asbestos shelters had been smashed by winds. In 2000, eight years on, the camp was no longer visible to a casual pedestrian wandering through the valley. However, if one walked observantly through the thorn scrub into remote parts of the valley, giant curved shards of asbestos could be found in the shadows, as well as open pits, alleged to be empty mass graves, whose occupants had been dug up and thrown down mines (personal observation).

4.3 The Spoken and the Unspoken

The reburial of these three unknown Bhalagwe victims was attended by various nervous government officials, pastors, local leadership and the exhumers. The burial speeches were remarkable for what they avoided stating: the officials, all senior ex-ZAPU, but now representing ZANU-PF in the post-Unity Accord era, were well aware of the history of Bhalagwe Camp. That these officials attended at all was tacit recognition of the importance of these bones. So it seemed anomalous that none of these senior (once) ZAPU officials would admit that ZAPU cadres were tortured and died at Bhalagwe.[6] However, their behaviour was understandable in terms of Eyerman's observation: "If a family or community agrees that a trauma did not happen, then it vanishes from collective memory and the possibility for individual memory is severely strained" (2001, 2). This is also the case where a nation has decreed that a certain moment in history did not happen: the capacity for individuals of once-targeted groups to recall publicly their memories of this officially non-existent history becomes such an act of dangerous political subversion as to be almost impossible. The intention of Zimbabwe's state at that time was to totally repress the *Gukurahundi* past: even very senior ZAPU (now ZANU-PF) officials felt obliged, partly to protect their own precarious political positions, to obfuscate what this reburial was about. This was strongly indicative of how deeply Matabeleland (officially) had internalised the need for silence around *Gukurahundi*.

The bones were buried in a single coffin and locals later inscribed the words "Mass Grave" in the cement surrounding the grave. Years later, further human remains were exposed at Bhalagwe and were buried in another coffin adjacent to the first burial, once more with "Mass Grave" inscribed on the rim (personal communication). For 18 years, these two mass graves would remain the only material evidence that anything untoward had ever happened in that isolated valley.

5 The Rise of New Activism

The years in Zimbabwe after 2000 were stormy. Political violence once more became a cruel reality, with the rise of the Movement for Democratic Change (MDC). The MDC almost dislodged ZANU-PF in 2000 elections and won the national election outright in 2008 (Raftopoulos 2013). However, in spite of its popular support, MDC was unable to formally dislodge the military power of the ZANU-PF state (Raftopoulos and Eppel 2008).[7] Zimbabwe was plunged into abject poverty and the once-industrialised, agro-based economy collapsed (Sachikonye et al. 2018). Massive diasporisation took place (Solidarity Peace Trust 2009). Young people from Matabeleland in particular headed *en masse* to South Africa.[8]

At the national level, *Gukurahundi*'s history continued to be repressed. For 35 years it remained effectively impossible to honour the dead of that era, with no official national day or memorials. However, there were a few brave attempts to place the atrocities into the public domain. In 2010, a young artist, Owen Maseko, dedicated an art exhibition to *Gukurahundi* and was arrested and charged with "undermining the authority of the President" and "offending an ethnic group", simply for portraying the atrocities (Duval Smith 2010, April 4). Significantly, Maseko, a man too young to have been directly affected by the massacres, was the one who undertook these risks. It became clear that it was the children and grandchildren of those who suffered and died who would take up the struggle to voice this history. Their actions have demonstrated that "remembering is oriented not to the past, but to coming to terms with the past in a present that is continuously troubled by it" (Argenti and Schramm 2012, 17). The complex mechanisms of transgenerational trauma are not fully understood, even while there is acknowledgement that "some memories, particularly the traumatic ones, are highly transmissible" (Berliner 2013, 3). Berliner contends that "beyond historical events and continuous change, the past does not evaporate, but rather persists, creatively, in multiple ways".

What made Matabeleland intriguing in 2018 was that the reality of transgenerational memory began to make itself visible in multiple public fora, 35 years after the massacres, in the context of a broader shift in the national dynamic. Mnangagwa, who replaced Mugabe after the November 2017 coup, was almost as implicated as Mugabe in the massacres. However, he was eager to portray a more democratic leadership and spaces began to open up, uncertainly. The new constitution, adopted in 2013, made a National Peace and Reconciliation Commission (NPRC) a legal necessity. The Commission, with seven Shona commissioners and only one from Matabeleland, rolled out in February 2018.[9] The first NPRC meeting ever was held in Gwanda, a small town in Matabeleland South: it was telling indeed. It was attended mostly by second-generation survivors. One after another, they stood up and confronted the Commission in ways that made it apparent that they had picked up the burden of the past in ways that their parents could not and were carrying it into the future. The layout of the room, formally set up with the mainly Shona commissioners in front, provided the context in which they could be conflated with the Shona-speaking perpetrators of *Gukurahundi* and accused of all the crimes of the state. "There is only one Ndebele (commissioner) here today. This commission is the face of marginalization. How can someone go to address murders committed by his siblings?"[10] (Speaker (sp.)1). There were repeated demands for the truth. "How can you say let bygones be bygones if we have not had the truth? How can I forgive you?" (Sp. 2). The Commission was a "commission of perpetrators" (Sp. 3).

Gukurahundi was represented as having never ended. The speakers told of ongoing structural violence, of cultural and economic oppression. A young father asked the Commission why his six-year-old child was being taught in IsiShona, the "language of the oppressor", instead of in IsiNdebele, when it is every child's constitutional right in Zimbabwe to be taught in their native tongue (Sp. 4). A young woman asked why all senior government officials in Gwanda are Shona-speaking: "is the entire of Matabeleland not capable of producing one person who can be a District Commissioner, so that s/he can address residents in IsiNdebele, the only language understood by most?" (Sp. 5). Practical examples of current ethnically driven hardships were mixed with family memories of *Gukurahundi*:

> We have been denied permission to bury our loved ones decently. We have our parents that disappeared during that genocide. How do they get death certificates? Our sisters who were raped and left pregnant during *Gukurahundi* – whose burden was it to make sure those children went to school? If you need rituals for the dead, how do you facilitate this? (Sp. 6)

Profound ethnic tensions were repeatedly expressed: "We know one reason people were killed is they failed to speak Shona. Deep in our hearts we hate one another to the core" (Sp. 7). And most ominously—"We have come from genocide and are heading to another one" (Sp. 8).

In Bulawayo the following day, the NPRC meeting was entirely disrupted by activists from Mthwakazi and Ibhetshu LikaZulu. These young men and women toyi-toyi'd and prevented the commissioners from speaking: a few victims were chosen by the activists to tell their stories of horror (personal observations). Among their angry demands were calls for a separate Ndebele nation. However, on discussions with the activists, it was clear this was more of an angry position than a real demand for a separate Mthwakazi nation (interview MF, October 2018). This was an appeal from a strident generation wanting to draw national attention to the suffering in their region and who justifiably held little faith in the government. The alienation of this generation from the body politic has left them with a regional, rather than a national, identity. These first meetings by the NPRC illustrated how historical violence can negatively "force open pre-existing fault lines, while also possibly affirming a sense of belonging, kinship and mutual trust" (Erikson 1994, 237). It is largely political violence, and transferred memories of this violence, that has propelled the growth of Ndebele separatist groups.

6 How Shall We Talk of Bhalagwe?

For several years, these pressure groups have attempted to hold commemorations at Bhalagwe Camp. As previously described, there is only one route to this remote valley, meaning it is easy to prevent access: one police road block can effectively do this. In Zimbabwe, it is required by law to inform the police of any public gathering days in advance, meaning that the police always have the power to intervene. Year after year, every time Ibhetshu and Mthwakazi attempted to get to Bhalagwe, they were stopped by police. This is what made the unimpeded commemoration there on 21 February 2018 so surprising. What was perhaps less surprising was the air of bewilderment shown by the small crowd that assembled in what was now an overgrown valley, most of them for the first time.[11] Where was the physical materiality of this much-heard-about torture base? Simply proceeding to Bhalagwe had entailed acts of personal and collective bravery, but now the reality of this valley of inherited myths presented new challenges. The infrastructure had fallen into disarray over nearly four decades. The crowd was without landmarks: Bhalagwe as a long-imagined landscape of torture was different to its actuality in 2018: "It was not what we expected – we expected to see buildings, structures" (interview MF, October 2018).

One of the UFAT teams guided the group to the site of the two mass graves, which nobody else present was aware existed, and the commemoration was held there. Unease and deep fear were reflected in the songs and prayers. The words of the opening song were, literally, "The Bhalagwe issue - we are afraid to speak it out, speak it out - let it out, let it out."[12] Bearing in mind the reality that "translations always leave a residue, an unexplored layer of history that cannot be captured in the move between languages" (Vaisman 2013, 1), I asked someone familiar with the era to explain to me what the words of this song conveyed to him (interview PTN, November 2018). He confirmed the gist as follows: "What happened at Bhalagwe is too overwhelming for words: emotions choke our throats so that it is impossible to speak out, but we must try." The Bhalagwe group then sang the song subtitling this chapter, which conveyed a similar sense of fear, misgiving and dread, that even defied naming Bhalagwe.

The first prayer was deeply moving, referring to Ezekiel and the valley of dry bones: "Remember our tears, our cries, our pain - we are not a people - we now live as nobodies, we have lost our sense of humanity ... pour out your spirit in us: like dry bones, may we live again." The first speaker, of Ibhetshu LikaZulu, referred to the strangeness of being there:

> We are here to mourn: as we came here, we could not find our way to this place, as we have never before been granted permission to come here. This place should be familiar and known to all .... There must be clear pointers and signs that lead us to this place, as here lie our relatives who were not buried properly.

Recalling trauma has been referred to as "listening to something absent": extreme violence can be so devastating that the mind literally cannot register its force (Agamben 1999, 13). Memories of violence may remain, "a record that has yet to be made" (Laub 1991, 12), and it can be the task of the next generation to hear and feel that impact. This process of groping towards the reality of the traumatic past seemed to be actively occurring at Bhalagwe on 21 February 2018. Argenti and Schamm (2012) believe that the next generation can incorporate into themselves bodily memories which become social, memorial practices: "Phantoms or ghosts may thus take the form of bodily practices handed down as transgenerational traumatic memories, or transgenerational haunting" (13). This may be hard to empirically prove, in the same way that the forming of collective memory is a "slippery phenomenon" (Kansteiner 2002, 180). "Collective memory is not history, although it is sometimes made of the same material .... It can take hold of historically and socially remote events but it often privileges the interests of the contemporary" (ibid.). The speeches at Bhalagwe highlighted the current alienation and marginalisation of *Gukurahundi*-affected regions, speaking of collective suffering in the present, linked back to past events.

Furthermore, the way the Bhalagwe valley presented itself as a blank landscape that failed to live up to its imaginary is symbolic of the broader history around *Gukurahundi*. It is difficult now, with so many eyewitnesses gone, to reconstruct the precise events for every village and valley, although the broader political context is known and recorded (Alexander et al. 2000; CCJPZ and LRF 1997; Doran 2017). Written accounts remain few and far between, and are either out of print or available only internationally, in the form of expensive and often academically dense texts (ibid.).

Almost four decades of state suppression have had an impact. It suited the state to allow Bhalagwe to vanish into the wilderness. But blanking out this history nationally has created a space in which multiple versions of events, some exaggerated and based on raw emotion, now coexist with more empirical accounts: the state must perhaps simply reap what its oppression has sown. In any event, history is formed not just by empirical events driven by precise numbers and dates but also by memory and collective memory, which is "not a simple, unmediated reproduction of the past, but rather a selective re-creation that is dependent for its meaning on the remembering individual or community's contemporary social context, beliefs and aspirations" (Huyssen 1995). The shifting, unstable process by which these activist groups are attempting to create their own multiple understandings of their pasts, relies in part on the silences and gaps left by those primarily affected, their parents and grandparents, who may still be living through what has been referred to as "traumatic amnesia" (Argenti and Schramm 2012, 12). Even where they have words for memories, those immediately affected may be reluctant to talk to their descendants about what happened, which was almost inevitably humiliating and degrading. Where events have been talked about, it has been in hushed tones, in confusion as to why these atrocities happened at all.[13]

> It is precisely because memory cannot be trusted as history that it needs to be explored, not as a record of the past, but of the present of those whose interests, views, experiences and life-worlds are somehow inimical to or have fallen outside of the historical project. (Argenti and Schramm 2012, 3)

The current generation in Matabeleland, which has indeed "fallen outside of the historical project" of the Zimbabwean state, commonly perceives the events as genocidal, and this is how it is therefore being re-presented. *Gukurahundi* has been, and will continue to be, a contested history. While at an international summit in January 2018, President Mnangagwa was challenged on dealing with *Gukurahundi* (Mananavire

2018, January 27). His response was revealing: he simultaneously acknowledged that the past needed to be dealt with and challenged the journalist's figure of 20,000 dead as exaggerated. In September 2018, Zenzele Ndebele, who was a child during *Gukurahundi*, released a film titled *Gukurahundi Genocide*. This moving documentary claimed that 40,000 had died, double the number popularly associated with the massacres. But who should contradict his figure? Ndebele's response when I challenged him was to say, "Let the state come forward with evidence of how many died, let them say how many they killed" (Interview ZN, October 2018). Predictably, Ndebele was hounded by the CIO prior to his launch in Bulawayo, and it was only the attendance of the NPRC that ensured it went ahead (personal observation).

The lack of agreement around how many died in Matabeleland is illustrative of the "continuous struggle between dominant and marginal voices in the production of history/memory". To what extent do "facts" shed light on, or alternatively deny, the lived experience of ordinary people, which, at some level, "is ultimately the only historical fact there is"? (Argenti and Schramm 2012, 7). *Gukurahundi* is the epitome of a past continually in the process of being produced from "partial, unstable, often contested" memories, that are and will remain "sites of struggle" (Matsuda 1996, 6).

6.1 Contested Memorial Rights at Bhalagwe

The acre around the two mass graves at Bhalagwe was designated a "District Heroes Acre" at some unclear point. This was a strange development, as in Zimbabwe, Heroes' Acres are exclusively the sites in which heroes of the 1970s War of Liberation are buried.[14] Declaring the land around these *Gukurahundi* mass graves a Heroes' Acre seemed an attempt to obfuscate the circumstances in which the Bhalagwe remains had come to be there: they were neither victims nor heroes of the liberation war. Over the years, this Heroes' Acre became the site of the burials of three ex-ZIPRAs who died nearby. These newer graves were laid in a direct line with the two pre-existing mass graves.

During 2018, Bhalagwe became an increasingly contested memorial site. Mbuso Fuzwayo, one of the Ibhetshu leadership, returned in June to the Bhalagwe mass graves with the intention of erecting a plaque nearby to commemorate those who died during *Gukurahundi* (Nkala 2018, June 12). He had a clear intention that what happened at Bhalagwe should not be forgotten and that the "pointers" sign-posting the history, as asked for at February's ceremony, should be provided. However, Fuzwayo was bullied by the CIO, who knocked down his plinth (interview MF, October 2018).

In August 2018, there was an aggressive response to the February and June attempts to claim *Gukurahundi* memorial rights at Bhalagwe, which ZANU-PF considered to be "their" Heroes' Acre. Senior war veterans approached the Ministry of Works to build a "Tomb of the Unknown Soldier", barely metres away from the *Gukurahundi* mass graves. This was completed in August 2018. It was perceived by many as provocative, to reify soldiers in the valley where Zimbabwe's soldiers murdered and tortured so many (Muvundisi 2018, September 12). To add insult to injury, the Ministry of Works smeared cement over the words "Mass Grave", on one of the mass graves, in a puerile act of denying its material reality. I was interested in this blunt attempt by the state to obliterate evidence of victims of *Gukurahundi* and drove to the site a few weeks later—only to discover that the tomb of the unknown soldier had already been smashed to pieces! It became clear that the war veterans had erected the tomb unilaterally, without consulting the broader community near Bhalagwe (interviews, October 2018). Considering the intensity of emotions and personal memories that Bhalagwe evokes, it was hardly surprising that before the cement on the tomb was dry, it was destroyed, apparently by some local person/s. This wilful vandalisation of a tomb commemorating those who died in the War of Liberation sent an unprecedented message to the state of the deep feelings that Bhalagwe evokes.

Currently it seems it is impossible for simple, mutually accommodative conversations to take place in Bhalagwe village. It is not yet clear which attempts to claim memorial space have won the day at Bhalagwe. The plinth to commemorate the 1980s victims was openly knocked down by the CIO; the tomb to the soldiers of the 1970s was backed by the

Ministry of Public Works, which did not prevent the midnight sabotage of the state's preferred memorial.

The battle of who has the right to commemorate whom at Bhalagwe continued into 2019. Ibhetshu returned in the dead of night on 21 February 2019 and erected a plinth to ensconce the plaque they had failed to erect in June 2018. The plaque read, "In loving memory of our innocent and defenceless children, mothers and fathers who perished during the Matebeleland Genocide 1983–1987. Siyalikhumbula" (meaning, we remember you). Triumphant photographs of the plaque were posted on social media, some showing activists wearing T-shirts provocatively emblazoned, "I am the Dissident that the Fifth Brigade was looking for." Predictably, both the plaque and plinth were destroyed before the week was out, presumably by state agents.

Whose heroes count, whose victims count, and who has a right to decide? This debate is being carried out largely through the activism of second-generation *Gukurahundi* survivors, in increasingly open confrontation with various representatives of the state. They will continue to condemn what happened. "Genocide has no culture, even God above hears us, even our ancestors are watching our efforts" (speech SH, 21 February 2018). Whether pressure groups in Matabeleland are able to successfully articulate what may become firstly a collective memory, and eventually a national memory, will depend largely on the prevailing politics of the future. Ultimately, such groups will have a chance to shape national memory only if it suits Zimbabwe's political elite. "Collective memory continually negotiates between available historical records and current social and political agendas" (Zerubavel 1995, 5).

It has been made apparent through these events in the material spaces of violence, which include Bhalagwe and the sites of exhumations, that current generations are actively engaged with the tragedy of the past. The challenge for Matabeleland and for the nation is how to take the dialogue into the future constructively. "How do the claims made in the name of memory enable and constrain the emergence of new kinds of politics, publics, and feelings of national belonging?" (Rubin 2013, 1). Pressure groups in Matabeleland have sent a strong message of anger and alienation, and it could be asked how representative they are. Discussions with leaders, including chiefs and church leadership both rural and urban, show that many of the older generation in Matabeleland feel indebted to this younger, braver generation. Far from feeling that their rage at government should be curbed, they are relieved that this generation has picked up the baton. Key informants in Bulawayo openly expressed gratitude to these pressure groups for raising so powerfully the pain and anger in the region, in a way that they, as elders, would be too afraid or respectful of authority to do. These groups are seen as a to-be-expected outcome after 35 years of suppression. An Anglican priest explained that "the trouble with we Ndebeles is we remain silent and in pain for a long time, and then explode in anger. These youths offer us all catharsis" (interview MD, May 2018).

The past cannot be separated from the future. The current generations of Matabeleland have raised cogent issues in every public forum that was made available to them since 2018 and this should be interrogated: what future is Matabeleland, ravaged by violence, trying to envision? What is the forward-looking subtext in the current outrage about the past? Remembering can be a way of pointing to new futures: "it can be transformative, sometimes politically subversive, 'a weapon'" (Berliner 2013, 1). The danger is that if ways for meaningful conversations about *Gukurahundi* are not forged at the national level, and if the state's current tendency to either downplay or suppress memory is maintained, then subsequent generations in Matabeleland, far from forgetting, will increasingly build an identity in which pain and anger at the past remain unassuaged. This could become explosive in decades ahead.

Notes

1. There are a dozen ethnic groups in Zimbabwe, often grouped into "Shona" and "Ndebele", based on the dominant language spoken in any area. Approximately 80% of Zimbabweans are considered "Shona", the balance being predominantly "Ndebele".
2. "Mthwakazi" indicates the separate Ndebele nation these activists aspire to, encompassing the land once governed by the first king of the Ndebele polity/state. "Ibhetshu LikaZulu" is the animal-skin loin cloth worn by Ndebele warriors: the group promotes Ndebele traditions.

3. Emmerson Mnangagwa, current president of Zimbabwe, gave this figure to the Boston Lawyers for Human Rights in 1985, cited in CCJP and LRF.
4. Some survivors are able to articulate what happened, but this may be an uneven reality. For example, many women talk of being beaten, and few of rape. There are different opinions on whether it is beneficial to talk of past trauma: and certainly not all exposed to state violence should be labelled "victims". The point is that trauma may be passed on unintentionally, subliminally within families and communities.
5. Personal recall.
6. My observation.
7. The horrific violence of 2008, between the initial harmonised elections and the presidential run-off, led to the MDC withdrawing and a power-sharing deal brokered by South Africa (Raftopoulos 2013).
8. Many Ndebele of Matabeleland consider themselves descendants of the Zulus of KwaZulu Natal, and IsiNdebele is closely derived from Zulu.
9. In May 2018, a second Ndebele was appointed Chairperson of the NPRC, Retired Justice Selo Nare.
10. From author's notes/audio recordings from this first NPRC meeting, names of speakers not known, for these quotes and all those following.
11. Impressions of this event from my observations, digital recordings and transcriptions by a work colleague, Nicholas Ndlovu, who was interviewed about the event: other impressions from interviews with Mbuso Fuzwayo, who organised the event.
12. *Indaba ye Bhalagwe, siyasaba ukuyikhuluma, ukuyikhuluma – yiyekele, yiyekele.*
13. Personal observations based on two decades of interactions with communities.
14. The biggest Heroes' Acre is in Harare and commemorations take place here every year.

References

Agamben, G. (1999). *Remnants of Auschwitz: The Witness and the Archive*. Cambridge: Zone Books.

Alexander, J., McGregor, J., & Ranger, T. (2000). *Violence and Memory: One Hundred Years in the Dark Forests of Matabeleland*. London: Heineman.

Argenti, N. and Schramm, K. (2012). (Eds.). Introduction. In *Remembering Violence: Anthropological Perspectives on Intergenerational Transmission* (pp. 1–40). New York: Berghahn Books.

Berliner, D. (2013, September 25). Integration: Memory and Transformative Durability. Correspondences, *Cultural Anthropology.* https://culanth.org/fieldsights/383-integration-memory-and-transformative-durability. Accessed 12 Nov 2018.

Boss, P. (2000). *Ambiguous Loss: Learning to Live with Unresolved Grief.* Cambridge: Harvard University Press.

Caruth, C. (1996). *Unclaimed Experience: Trauma, Narrative, and History.* Baltimore: Johns Hopkins University Press.

Catholic Commission for Justice and Peace in Zimbabwe (CCJPZ) and the Legal Resources Foundation (LRF). (1997). *Breaking the Silence, Building True Peace: A Report on the Disturbances in Matabeleland and the Midlands 1982–1988*. Harare: CCJPZ and LRF.

Craps, S. (2012). *Postcolonial Witnessing: Trauma Out of Bounds*. Basingstoke: Palgrave Macmillan.

Daneel, M. (1995). *Guerrilla Snuff.* Harare: Baobab Books.

Doran, S. (2017). *Kingdom, Power, Glory: Mugabe, Zanu and the Quest for Supremacy, 1960–1987*. Gauteng: Sithatha Media.

Duval Smith, A. (2010, April 4). Zimbabwe Artist Defies Robert Mugabe. *The Observer.* https://www.theguardian.com/world/2010/apr/04/zimbabwe-artist-arrest-mugabe-censorship. Accessed 12 Nov 2018.

Eppel, S. (2006). Healing the Dead: Exhumation and Reburial as a Route to Truth Telling and Reclaiming the Past in Rural Zimbabwe. In T. A. Borer (Ed.), *Telling the Truths: Truth Telling and Peace-Building in Post Conflict Societies* (pp. 259–288). Notre Dame: University of Notre Dame Press.

Eppel, S. (2002). Reburial Ceremonies for Health and Healing After State Terror. *The Lancet, 360*, 9336.

Eppel, S. (2014). 'Bones in the Forest' in Matabeleland, Zimbabwe: Exhumations as a Tool for Transformation. *International Journal for Transitional Justice*, 1–22. https://doi.org/10.1093/ijtj/iju016.

Erikson, K. (1994). *A New Species of Trouble: Explorations in Disaster, Trauma, and Community*. New York: Norton.

Eyerman, R. (2001). *Cultural Trauma: Slavery and the Formation of the African American Identity*. Cambridge: Cambridge University Press.

Filippucci, P. (2012). In a Ruined Country: Place and the Memory of War Destruction in Argonne (France). In Argenti, N. and Schramm, K. (Eds.),

Remembering Violence: Anthropological Perspectives on Intergenerational Transmission. Chapter 7. New York: Berghahn Books.

Huyssen, A. (1995). *Twilight Memories: Marking Time in a Culture of Amnesia*. New York: Rutledge.

Kansteiner, W. (2002). Finding Meaning in Memory: A Methodological Critique of Collective Memory Studies. *History and Theory, 41*, 179–197.

Lambek, M. (2006). Memory in a Maussian Universe. In S. Radstone & K. Hodgkin (Eds.), *Memory Cultures: Memory, Subjectivity and Recognition* (pp. 202–216). New Brunswick/London: Transaction.

Langer, L. (1991). *Holocaust Testimonies: The Ruins of Memory*. New Haven: Yale University Press.

Laub, D. (1991). Truth and Testimony: The Process and the Struggle. *American Imago, 48*(1), 75–91.

Luckhurst, R. (2008). *The Trauma Question*. London: Routledge.

Mananvire, B. (2018, January 27). ED Refuses to Apologise for Gukurahundi. *Daily News Live*. https://www.dailynews.co.zw/articles/2018/01/27/ed-refuses-to-apologise-for-gukurahundi. Accessed 12 Nov 2018.

Matsuda, M. (1996). *The Memory of the Modern*. New York: Oxford University Press.

Mueggler, E. (2001). *The Age of Wild Ghosts: Memory, Violence and Place in Southwest China*. Oakland: University of California Press.

Muvundisi, J. (2018, September 12). Govt Tampers with Gukurahundi Mass Graves. *Daily News Live*. https://www.dailynews.co.zw/articles/2018/09/12/southern-news-govt-tampers-with-gukurahundi-mass-graves. Accessed 12 Nov 2018.

Nkala, S. (2018, June 12). CIO Operative Reported for Cellphone Theft. *Newsday*. https://www.newsday.co.zw/2018/06/cio-operative-reported-for-cellphone-theft/. Accessed 12 Nov 2018.

Raftopoulos, B. (Ed.). (2013). *The Hard Road to Reform: The Politics of Zimbabwe's Global Political Agreement*. Harare: Weaver Press.

Raftopoulos, B., & Eppel, S. (2008). Desperately Seeking Sanity: What Prospects for a New Beginning in Zimbabwe? *Journal of Eastern African Studies, 2*(3), 369–400.

Raftopoulos, B., & Savage, T. (Eds.). (2004). *Injustice and Political Reconciliation*. Cape Town: Institute for Justice and Reconciliation.

Rothberg, M. (2008). Decolonizing Trauma Studies: A Response. *Studies in the Novel, 40*(2008), 224–234.

Rubin, J. S. (2013, September 4). Field Notes: The Politics of Memory. Correspondences, *Cultural Anthropology.* https://culanth.org/fieldsights/375-field-notes-the-politics-of-memory. Accessed 12 Nov 2018.

Sachikonye, L., Raftopoulos, B., & Kanyenze, G. (2018). *Building from the Rubble*. Harare: Weaver Press.

Solidarity Peace Trust. (2009). *Gone to Egoli*. Johannesburg: Solidarity Peace Trust.

Vaisman, N. (2013, September 11). Translation: Temporality and Memory. Correspondences. *Cultural Anthropology.* https://culanth.org/fieldsights/378-translation-temporality-and-memory. Accessed 12 Nov 2018.

Visser, I. (2015). Decolonising Trauma Theory: Retrospects and Prospects. *Humanities, 4*, 250–265.

Werbner, R. (1991). *Tears of the Dead: The Social Biography of an African Family.* Harare: Baobab Books.

White, T. D., & Folkens, P. A. (2012). *Human Osteology*. Oxford: Academic Press.

Zelizer, B. (1998). *Remembering to Forget: Holocaust Memory Through the Camera's Eye*. Chicago: University of Chicago Press.

Zerubavel, Y. (1995). *Recovered Roots: Collective Memory and the Making of Israeli Tradition*. Chicago: University of Chicago Press.

Part III

Transforming Haunted Memory Through Artistic Interventions

12

Symptom as History, Culture as Healing: Incarcerated Aboriginal Women's Journeys Through Historic Trauma and Recovery Processes

Judy Atkinson

We live storied lives. We organise experience into stories as we share life interactively with others. The plot, characters, and morals of the stories we hear influence our synaptic connections, they change our brains. Stories also live through us. We are born into stories, those of our families, nations, religions and cultures.
—Lewis Mehl-Madrona in Healing the Mind through the Power of Story 2010, p. 180

1 Introduction

When we look back over our lives we see where we have been through a different lens. That also applies to history. The long lens allows us to look back into history while also examining our own intergenerational

J. Atkinson (✉)
Southern Cross University, Lismore, NSW, Australia

We Al-li, Goolmangar, NSW, Australia
e-mail: judyatkinson1@me.com

K. Wale et al. (eds.), *Post-Conflict Hauntings*, Palgrave Studies in Compromise after Conflict, https://doi.org/10.1007/978-3-030-39077-8_12

individual and collective stories, seeing where sometimes these journeys intersect. More often, however, we don't see those intersections, nor how we have been formed by the historical consequences that make us who we are. That is, until we retrace our steps looking through that different lens, into understanding, the knowing. Once I took my first steps into the unknown I could not go back to unknowing. My journey into the unknown began as a doctoral researcher with my study designed as an attempt to understand violence within Aboriginal communities in the Australian post-colonial context. *Dadirri (da-did-ee)* the quality of "inner deep listening and quiet still awareness" (Ungunmerr-Baumann 1993) was used as a research methodology. This included listening in contemplative relationships, mapping stories of generational pain and trauma within individuals and families, and using genograms. Within six months I was reading trauma theory, as I worked with small groups who issued the challenge to contextualise and explicate not only their violence trauma stories, but how they could heal!

This involved group work in a three-year process of mapping the active steps of healing or recovery from violence-related trauma. These included (1) creating safety, (2) supporting people to share their stories, (3) assisting them to make sense of those stories, (4) allowing feelings to be expressed in safety to self and others, (5) providing structure for people to move through their layers of loss, grief and trauma to a belief that (6) they can claim their cultural and spiritual identities (Atkinson 2002, 215, 263). Over those years the stages of healing from historical trauma were mapped as we worked together. There was no reliance on therapy or therapists. Education was named as the most critical factor for change and healing. We called our educational approach Indigenous Critical Pedagogy, in its theory and application, *educaring* using life stories, story mapping and cultural tools for recovery action (Atkinson 2014). These cultural tools for healing trauma involved Indigenous healing practice: story, art, dance, music, theatre, ceremony in communal activities.

Knowing also requires responsibility to act. The responsibility I took to act is presented in this chapter through describing and reflecting on a case study of adapting and applying the educaring approach developed through my doctoral work and in response to historic trauma in the Australian context. In 2015, the Kunga Stopping Violence Program

(KSVP) engaged me to develop an intensive trauma-specific violence prevention program through We Al-li (www.wealli.com.au/) to be run twice a year in Alice Springs Correctional Centre (ASCC). The chapter contextualises the practices that contribute to historic trauma, and in understanding that collective intergenerational journey, focuses on the lives of Aboriginal women, incarcerated in ASCC, undertaking a four-week pre-release educaring program 'The Circle of Wellbeing - Loss Grief Trauma - Anger Violence Boundaries Safety'. An outline of the program and a conceptualisation of their lives will be told through their stories, art in pictorial images and an 'I am poem', which is part of the course of study.

2 Context of Enquiry

In 1987, the Aboriginal Coordinating Council (ACC), which comprised the chair and deputy chair of the 14 Aboriginal communities originally established by the Queensland (Australian) government under the Aborigines Protection Act 1897 and later the Community Services Act of 1984, was holding a meeting in a small community in Cape York, Queensland, Australia. I was their co-ordinator/research officer. An elder woman approached me, telling me a five-year-old child had been raped the previous week. She asked for help. Could we 'do something'? Doing something meant first approaching the 27 men and one woman who comprised the chair and deputy chair of the ACC. They said: "do what you can". Approaching those government departments responsible for this small community, seeking a response to the needs of the child for safe physical and psychological services in response to her distress and, more particularly, a legislated responsibility to charge the offender with his crime, I was told this behaviour was 'cultural' and there was not much they could do, hence disregarding the voice of a senior law woman and custodian (Atkinson 2014, 42–3). Nonetheless, some weeks later, when a 'white' nurse working within the community was raped, a police plane flew in the next day, the nurse was flown out for medical attention and the perpetrator arrested. Australian/Queensland law then was applied differently to the Aboriginal child, and to the white adult female. The lesson, implicit in these two distinct responses, to the [black] child and the [white] adult, is embedded in a colonial history of who has value and considered of worth, and who has a right to justice in the colonised space.

I argued then, as I do now, that much of the behaviour resulting in high physical and sexual violence rates is a distressed response to the culture of violence which was enacted and applied through colonial state policies and practices. This involves the structural and systemic violence of subjugation of Indigenous groups, including enforced domination, discrimination, economic and social exclusion, in the application of racist legislation and laws (Atkinson 2002; Baker 1983; Evans 1992).

Colonisation is violence. From the late fifteenth to the early twentieth centuries, large-scale manmade disasters occurred worldwide to Indigenous societies as European countries enacted colonialism (Giddens 1989, 52). These activities have reshaped the environmental, social, spiritual and cultural face of the globe (Giddens 1989, 54–5), with outcomes that were unforeseeable at the time. European colonialism was a "brutal age; an age in which swarms of savage invading males slew, raped, plundered and enslaved … or decimated with exotic diseases, after which they replaced them in some instances by hardier and more complacent slaves" (Price 1963, 51–2).

Australia has a history of invasion, introduced diseases, physical violence and incarceration as capitalist industry. Physical violence is one of the quickest ways to enforce subordination, whether it is on whole populations such as in colonisation, control of people who have been enslaved, or subordination of women, or slaves.

In May 1770 Lieutenant James Cook ventured up the coast of the lands that are now called Australia, sailing past the eastern most tip, which he named Point Danger. From his vantage on the *Endeavour*, he saw and then named a mountain peak, Mount Warning.

What Cook did not know was that from the eastern tip of Australia (Point Danger), to the top of Mount Warning (known by Bundjalung peoples as Wollumbin) there were over 100 ceremonial sites where Bundjalung peoples came together in ceremony, building and maintaining relationship—wellbeing of country and wellbeing of people. Both words he used could be considered a *warning* to the future *danger* that would come to these lands and the peoples of the lands, 18 years later.

The American Revolutionary War (1775–1783) required another country to relocate English, Irish and Scottish prisoners. In May 1787 a fleet of 11 ships sailed from England with its cargo of convicts, prison-warders and marines, with instructions to establish a penal colony. The ships dropped anchor to establish the first convict station at what is now called Sydney Cove on 26 January 1788, on the waterways and lands of the Gadigal clan of the Eora Nation. A penal colony was established.

Memmott describes the initial impact of colonial violence as involving "dispossession of land, population decimation, sanctioned and non sanctioned murder, massacres, maltreatment, fatal diseases, opium and alcohol addiction, slave labour, exploitation, all resulting in chronic anxiety" (1990, 2). The story from an Aboriginal point of view is more personal: "We were hunted from our ground, shot, poisoned, and had our daughters, sisters, wives taken from us … they stole our ground where we used to get food, and when we got hungry and took a bit of flour or killed a bullock to eat, they shot us or poisoned us. All they give us now for our land is a blanket once a year" (Dalaipi quoted in Petrie 1904, 182–3).

Historian Lyndall Ryan at the University of Newcastle has mapped over 250 massacre sites from 1788 to 1930. Professor Ryan said: "massacres don't seem to stop, they continue well into the 20th century" (Australia Broadcasting Corporation 27 July 2018).

Colonial governments voiced disapproval of the violence of the frontier; however, in the way of government, they turned a blind eye or, when forced to respond, established commissions of enquiry. In every instance, as a result of these commissions of enquiry, police power over Aboriginal people expanded. In Queensland the Home Secretary commissioned a report which Kidd (1997, 22) says "makes appalling reading", because it detailed physical violence on Aboriginal lives of "shocking dimensions". William Parry Okeden, the Police Commissioner, became responsible for the Aboriginal Protection and Prevention of the Sale of Opium Act 1897, which by 1939, through a series of amendments, became a total Police Act, with full power over Aboriginal lives vested in the Director of Native Affairs with state police acting as enforcers (Atkinson 2002, 65–69).

The structural violence of specific legislation was designed to control Aboriginal people with forced removals to missions and reserves. Kidd

(1997, 121) again highlights the brutal circumstances under which the 'protectors' operated.

> Two women and two men were forced at gunpoint, chained together for 240 miles (380 kilometres) and forced marched across the peninsula to Laura for transportation to Palm Island. A previous group were beaten by the police, flogged on route several times, including one woman who was six months pregnant, and sexually assaulted.

Aged 13, young Aboriginal girl Dolly was transported to Yarrabah Aboriginal Mission in 1903. She had been housed at Normanton for ten years in the kitchen of a station property run by white men, since she was two years of age. She never received wages for the work she performed as a 'kitchen hand'. At removal the only possessions she owned were two articles of clothing, two hessian bags used as maternity smocks. She was seven months pregnant (Robinson 2002). Clearly she was a young Aboriginal girl who had been sexually misused and abused. However in his reports to the Home Secretary's office of the Queensland Government, 1901–1908, Dr Walter Roth, government protector and medical doctor, wrote that he could find no instance of what now would be called child abuse, within any of the tribal groups he was responsible for at that time in colonial history (Roth W reports: 1901–1908). This violence against children came with the colonisers.

The Royal Commission into Aboriginal Deaths in Custody 1987 to 1991 highlighted the reality of this total control system; documenting individual lives of those who were psychologically crushed, in government files, sometimes fatally; murdered, committing suicide in police or prison cells (Atkinson 2002, 68).

> All had files - hundreds of pages of observation, and moral and social judgements on them and their families –officials recorded all, judged all and yet knew nothing about the people whose lives they controlled. … Aboriginal people were removed at the whim of others, crowded into settlements and missions and in impoverished camps on cattle stations. Always there were non-Aboriginal people giving orders, making decisions … Aboriginal families separated, children removed if judged too light

> skinned, placed in homes or boarded out as servants to non-Aboriginals. (RCiADC 1991, vol 2, pp. 502–503)

Baker (1983, 35) calls this psycho-social dominance "cultural and spiritual genocide". Professor Helen Milroy, after serving on the Royal Commission into Institutional Responses to Child Sexual Abuse as commissioner (2013–2018), named what the commission found 'cultural genocide' on Aboriginal peoples. Cultural and spiritual genocide occurs when oppressors believe that those they are oppressing are non-persons (Harr'e 1993, 106). By defining Aboriginal people as non-persons and continuing to do so across colonising histories, the oppressors justify their behaviours and in turn the oppressed may come to believe this about themselves (Atkinson 2002, 69).

Salzman and Halloran (2004, 233), in naming cultural trauma, outlines the destruction of cultural worldviews which have sustained Indigenous peoples for millennia; a collective experience across diverse cultures and peoples: the Yup'ik of Alaska; Navajos and Athabaskan Indians; Hawaiian Natives; Maori in New Zealand and Aboriginal Australians, all having experienced similar physical, social, behavioural and psychological symptoms (e.g. high rates of suicide, alcoholism, accidental deaths and intentional deaths, incarceration and layers of loss, grief, trauma). Such trauma fractures our cultural identities. Muid calls this historic trauma "the collective emotional and psychological injury, in the life of an individual or of a community, both over the life span and across generations" (Muid 2006, 36). Trauma is both individual and collective at multiple levels, a soul wounding (Duran et al. 1998).

Bessel van der Kolk (1987, 2–3) says the essence of psychological trauma is the loss of faith that there is order and continuity in life. Previously Aboriginal lives were ordered, with continuity across seasons and ceremonies, between people and country. Further van der Kolk points out that trauma occurs when the sense of having a safe place to retreat to within or outside oneself has been destroyed.

Cultural and spiritual genocide engenders in people a belief that they are of no value and their cultural practices and traditions are inferior and hence so are they. Consequently they may "build their own prison and become simultaneously prisoner and warden" (Baker 1983, 40), and even executioner. Prisons are places of violence. Our violence rates reflect our incarceration rates in institutions of the state, child removals, juvenile detention and adult prisons, from 1788 continuing today. The Australian Human Rights Commission, in its Social Justice Report of 2008, named the devastating trauma which is continuously acted out, re-created in contemporary Aboriginal culture, historic or generational trauma. Staff at the Kimberley Aboriginal Medical Service become aware of the interaction between generational trauma, family dysfunction, child sexual abuse and youth suicide (Ralph et al. 2006). Kreig (2009) outlines the signs and symptoms of trauma in Aboriginal Australian populations that must be considered in any health, education and legal responses to recovery: a deep mistrust of self and others, even within the family, self-directed violence, including suicide and risk-taking behaviour, substance misuse, unremitting grief, shame and humiliation, intergenerational conflict, violence against women, role diffusion, including sexual abuse and boundary violations, cultural genocide and loss of traditional values. Such symptoms can only be understood within the context of Aboriginal experiences of colonial history, 'symptom as history', deserving itself of enquiry.

3 Symptom as History

Today, the over-representation of Aboriginal and Torres Strait peoples in Australian prisons is at crisis level. The Human Rights Law Centre and the Change the Record Coalition (2017) point out that while Aboriginal and Torres Strait Islander peoples make up 3.3 per cent of the Australian population, Aboriginal women comprise 2 per cent of Australian adult female population and comprise 34 per cent of women in prison. The Australian jurisdictions with the highest percentage of incarcerated Aboriginal women are Western Australia followed by the Northern Territory (Leeson et al. 2016). The percentage of women being imprisoned in the Northern Territory increased from 2004 to 2014 at a rate exceeding 440 per cent (ABS 2015).

A recent Australian study of domestic and family violence in the Northern Territory (NT) reported that violence against Aboriginal women is the highest in the world with 75 per cent of Aboriginal women having been the victim of violence in relationships (Kerr 2016). Aboriginal women experience violence at the hands of both Aboriginal and non-Aboriginal men. The same study concluded that Aboriginal women in the Alice Springs region of Central Australia experienced a severity of physical harm and death higher than any other region in the NT. This situation can only be understood within the context of historical trauma resulting from the layered impacts of colonisation and the use of alcohol as enabler. In another town in the same region, missionary practice of corporal punishment in response to the perceived misbehaviours of Aboriginal men, women and children at the mission station provides important insight into the mission's patriarchal system of governance. It had a gendered practice which highlights the importance of sexuality, with conflicting effects of mission life on Aboriginal women and girls. They were specific targets for the missionaries' beatings. Aboriginal male subordination of women and girls was thus reinforced by mission attitudes and behaviours (Curtis-Wendlandt 2016). At one stage during the Kunga Stopping Violence prison program, there were three generations of women in prison from this community, at the same time: a grandmother 65 years old, her daughter aged 38 and her granddaughter aged 18. Further many of the women, and on the other side of the prison wall, the men, come from the Central Australian region of the last recorded state-sanctioned killing: the Coniston Massacre. Documentation of the Coniston Massacre shows how experiences of trauma across colonial history are layered and can be mapped in the history of a country. In the first generation, males are killed and imprisoned, and females are sexually abused; in the second generation, men and women turn to alcohol and other drugs as their cultural and spiritual identity is damaged, and their self-worth is eroded; in the third generation, social trauma results in increasing spousal assault as traditional laws and customs are fractured; in the fourth generation, abuse moves from spousal assault to neglect and child abuse, or both; in the fifth generation, the cycle repeats itself, as trauma begets violence begets historic trauma (Blanco, in Levine 2007).

There is clear racial profiling within the region. Racist oppression and discrimination are toxic. People are dislocated and many of the women are homeless. Poverty, ill-health created by processed foods and substance misuse, takes their toll. Most of the women have had their children removed by agents of the state. Their incarceration is a symptom of the history and the legal process that now defines them as violent offenders, even though they may only be on remand and have not been found guilty or sentenced. On the other side of the prison walls are Aboriginal men, a large percentage of whom are incarcerated because of their violence on their partners, or in their communities. 'Symptom as History' is both individual and collective. Recovery from historic trauma requires specific processes and approaches, outlined below in response to the invitation to work with Aboriginal women in prison.

4 Australia as a Penal Institution: Taking Healing into Prisons—A Case Study

4.1 Kunga Stopping Violence Program

This section outlines the theory, the methods and the tools used in the development and delivery of an intensive trauma informed violence prevention program (9 am to 3 pm each weekday for four weeks twice a year) in Alice Springs Correction Centre (ASCC).

Kunga, from the Pitjantjatjara language of Central Australia, means young woman. The Kunga Stopping Violence Program (KSVP) is endorsed by the North Australian Aboriginal Justice Agency (NAAJA) who provides legal aid to Aboriginal people throughout the Northern Territory. The KSVP, based in Alice Springs, Northern Territory, works with Aboriginal women who have been incarcerated for alleged violent offences. They may also be incarcerated for unpaid fines, or driving without a license. However all women incorporated into the KSVP program have a history of involvement in the 'justice system' for use of physical force. The Kunga program provides pre-release support to Aboriginal women in the prison including the four-week trauma informed course described below. When the women are released from prison the Kunga program continues to provide support to the women.

The packages were compiled with an assumption that if the way of life of a people has been attacked and infected by colonising impacts, rebuilding pride in self and culture was a vital requirement of the educational approach. Further, because Aboriginal cultures are communal, the group process would need to build on a communal, shared learning approach, and that the life stories of the women would provide the vital learning-teaching components. However, a curriculum was necessary for ASCC approval. The third assumption was a trauma recovery theory evolving out of Aboriginal healing processes of educaring—located within an Indigenous Critical Pedagogy which generates critical conversations, self-reflection and mindfulness—would have best results. Stories, art and poems in reflective discussion became tools for sharing deeper insight and learning together.

Three separate but interlinking modules for delivery were developed—the Circle of Wellbeing; Anger Violence Boundaries Safety and Loss and Grief—within an overall trauma informed approach, returning to the Circle of Wellbeing to finish. An assessment report for the prison compiled with each woman would complete the program. The course has now been delivered seven times in the ASCC to 60 women. The original intention to address 'violent offending' which is what enabled its approval by prison psychologists has now been amended. Important lessons have been learnt. The development of the packages was based on a knowledge of the history of the region with an assumption that the women would have been impacted by violence-trauma at various levels in their lives and across generations. However, the package still had to address the factor that the women were in prison for supposedly violent offences. An assumption was they needed to feel culturally safe, to consider their behaviour, so the Circle of Wellbeing was vital as an introduction and time for the women to settle as we built safety. Bonding and trust would be critical.

4.2 The Circle of Wellbeing

This was a vital first step in the first days of the program to create a felt sense of safety for the women, in the prison educational environment, while also grounding the work in deep cultural processes. The women were told that each morning as they left the general section of the prison, moving into the education space, we would create our own learning environment. To open the day, we used *Dadirri* by Miriam Rose Ungunmerr-Baumann as an opening reflective meditative practice.

> A special quality, a unique gift of the Aboriginal people is inner deep listening and quiet still awareness. Dadirri recognises the deep spring that is inside us. It is something like what you call contemplation. The contemplative way of dadirri spreads over our whole life. It renews us and brings us peace. It makes us feel whole again. In our Aboriginal way we learnt to listen from our earliest times. We could not live good and useful lives unless we listened. (Ungunmerr-Baumann 1993)

The intent was not just to create a sense of safety in individuals within the group, but to open an awareness of listening to others, and being listened to, as a ceremonial cultural healing. The women were asked to find their own language word or words for this practice. Each morning the women were invited to contribute with a word or sentence to reflect how they were feeling. In the beginning the standard word was: 'good', which was what they believed they were expected to say. Some of the women were so shy they could not lift their heads, speaking in whispers. They moved through the eight points of the Circle of Wellbeing: spirituality, environment (land-spirit), relationships, emotions, physical body, sexuality, stress (culture in family wellbeing), life-purpose (identity). While these were non-threatening conversations supported by scrapbooking, art and music, the women quietly reflected on deep inner hurt, for example on issues around relationships, sexuality and the loss of their children.

4.3 Anger Violence Boundaries Safety

By day four conversation around the issues of anger violence boundaries safety began. Specific learning modules in this section were:

- Anger violence boundaries safety (definitions)
- Feelings—how we communicate
- Anger triggers—the anger cycle—authentic anger—unauthentic anger
- Parenting > being parented > parenting our children
- Understanding the evolution of anger from childhood
- Changing the game—parenting our children—parents as teachers
- Hot violence—including rage—cold violence—assertiveness
- Managing anger > breaking the cycle > alcohol and other drugs>gambling>jealousy
- How violence affects children, families and communities
- Cultural rules for safe expression of anger
- Being assertive
- Body scan—relaxation—mindfulness practice
- Resilient behaviour, as a child living with distressed family behaviour, can become enabling adult behaviour, which deepens trauma.

The women cut coloured cardboard to create 'the violence non-violence tree' which was placed on the wall and added to during each session: the roots as causes of violence; the trunk as contributing factors and the branches as outcomes, the leaves as feelings. This tree stayed on the wall for the full four weeks of each program delivery and was added to by the women as they had insight. By delivery four the tree changed to the 'feeling-healing tree', with flowers as healing intentions. This was at the suggestion and design of the women. They had come to know and name feelings.

During this work we noticed that the women had insight exceeding many professional workers, in what had contributed to their entering prison, accompanied with a voiced sense of powerlessness, moving to feeling more empowered to change. The deeper teaching started when they felt safe enough to share their own stories with each other or enter into informed discussions. When Lewis Mehl-Madrona wrote, "Stories contain and convey the meanings and values of our lives … giving us our cultural identity … we are our stories" (2005, pp. 8–9), he was writing about simplicity and complexity. The women's stories were told with such simplicity; however, in discussion, they began to unpack the complexity. Their individual stories interlinked with their collective narratives. They were both. Working with stories is meaning making, transformative political healing action. There was an awareness of the injustice they faced, accompanied with a felt sense that it would be very hard to change their circumstances. However they wanted to try.

The term 'stopping violence' was used because many of those who come into the program have committed an act of violence under Australian law, generally on someone who had harmed them, often under the influence of alcohol. However "we circle into truth through stories" (Lederach 2005). Their stories, blended with discussion about the fact that domestic or family violence is a major risk factor for death or serious injury for Aboriginal women in Central Australia, gave them courage. Often however we found the reason for the women's incarceration was because they had been trying to get away from violence (driving without a licence), or fighting back (to protect themselves). Some of the women had symptoms of foetal alcohol spectrum disorder (FASD). Some had acquired brain injury from repeated blows to the head in beatings. Some of the women who had children have had their children removed from them, not just because they were in prison. Hence respectful conversation on specific topics meant some women would talk and others would listen, until they felt ready to contribute to the discussions. One of the most important lessons was how powerful group work, named as Yarning Circles, was for the women. A formal structure to Yarning Circles evolved: first round—how I am feeling today; second round—what I would like to talk about today; third round—unstructured supported discussion on those topics chosen for the day; fourth round—closing the circle. They began to support each other, in informal conversations while doing both individual and group art, inside and outside the formal course activities.

4.4 Loss Grief Trauma

The third part of the designed program focused on loss and grief, through loss history mapping. It was important not to assume that every woman had experienced trauma. This was one-on-one with a worker supporting each woman, in deep reflection as they mapped their own life stories and continuing as they painted after the session. The women worked on butchers paper, from birth to the day they constructed the map, naming on a time line, dominant memories of good experiences and not good experiences. Many of their experiences were clearly traumatic. After the first delivery loss history was redefined as loss trauma history. The supportive discussion (yarning) was informal, gentle, as the women chose to disclose and explore painful experiences. The women were able to return to this any time during the program; add further insights and memories and explore in more depth painful experiences. One woman came to the age of 13, and left a blank space up to the age of 16. When she came to that section she said: "I'm not talking about this". Some days later, again sitting together, I put my hand over the blank section, and said: "I respect your decision to not talk about this part of your life, but look when you started drinking and getting into trouble". She was silent, went away and painted for some days, and then came back ready to talk about that time in her life.

The major themes that came from the women were their experiences as children witnessing domestic, family and community violence, feeling unsafe; racist bullying at school; and as young women, sexual assault, moving into racist violence on streets and domestic violence in their early adult lives. Aboriginal women are unsafe in their homes, and on Australian streets. They named fractured mother-child, family-community relationships. They could see how such patterns continued into their adult lives, and into the lives of their own children. They named the cultural strengths of their grandparents' parenting, which was lost when their own parents started to drink. As example, in anger violence boundaries, defining forms of violence—one of the women said, "his words gave me a bad anger", and this was carried into deep ongoing discussions. Words hurt. What is a 'bad anger' when so many of them, in a disassociated state, have no memory of the rageful feelings or the actions that resulted? Hot violence—cold violence—assertiveness was supported by play-back theatre, the women giving words expressed through body movement. In the afternoon the women painted and listened to music. We always had one or two women with foetal alcohol spectrum disorder (FASD) or an acquired brain injury (ABI) and they became our disc jockeys, accessing music relevant to the discussions for the day. Music allowed feelings and deep inner reflection.

One afternoon as I was sitting beside a woman who was painting I became aware of music, and the words of a song being repeated over and over again. "Mistake Mistake we keep making the same mistake again and again; … running from the darkness. You can call it critical … but you keep making the same mistakes again and again" (B2M—used with permission). That morning she had said she would not be able to change—her life was 'too messy'. Now she had found a song that she played 20 times over an afternoon, telling her she could, even if she had to go home to a place where people were drinking and fighting. Later she said: "I will try (to change), but I will need help". As I sat with her, I reflected. We talk about decolonisation, and we see post-colonial powers and systems making the same mistakes again and again, as if they do not know how to break their own cycles of violence and power misuse.

The Kunga workers took this time to sit with the women, to learn about them, from them, to sit beside them as they painted, entering gentle conversations while they built relationship. In supporting the women to map their life stories from birth to the day they made the map, the Kunga workers saw clearly the need to talk about experiences the women may have had as children and the painful shameful experiences they have had as women, to bring understanding about violence-trauma into our discussions. These became rich deep educational discussions, which resulted in the women teaching each other in their conversations, exploring together new insights, wanting to know more and read more. They all received a workbook which covered all the educational materials. While the lessons were in English, all of the women had English as a fourth or fifth language. The women are discouraged by some guards at the prison to speak in their own language elsewhere in the prison. However in our 'classroom' the women were encouraged to talk with each other across their language proficiency, as they made sense of what they were coming to understand. They grappled with looking more deeply at the behaviours that contributed to their incarceration; painful and shameful, moving into resolve and courage.

One woman had no feeling words. She sat with her head down, unable to engage, unable to speak. She felt shame. But she painted. As she painted, sitting beside her, I heard a story of deep childhood trauma: a car accident at the age of two, years of hospitalisation with few family visits—multiple injuries, including a leg removed, for which she felt a profound wounding. Raped at nine. She could not run away. A marriage which was violent. Trying to reconnect with her parents, she hit her mother who was drunk. The conversation covered the feelings she must have felt as a little girl, in those hospital rooms, waiting for someone to come: sadness and anger—grief and rage. The day she was given the date of her release from prison, she busied herself with the cardboard, cutting out leaves and flowers for the feeling-healing tree, walked over and put them on the branches, five feeling words: *excited, frightened, ready, anxious, inspired.* She never spoke the words, but she named them.

In the first delivery of the program, in the practice of art as healing, a young woman would not or could not speak. But she painted. Her first painting was small and exquisite. Completing it, she painted over it, and started another image. Completed it and painted over it. I was mesmerised and frustrated. Seven images all destroyed by another layer of paint. Why destroy such beautiful images? Three years later she returned to prison, this time engaging at every level. Again she started to paint and again I sat beside her. The four images were like a window into her soul. This time I asked if she would tell me what they meant.

4.5 Story of Feelings (Fig. 12.1)

I asked about her previous paintings, the ones she had painted over three years previously. Why? She said she was so full of confusion she could not speak. She did not know what she was feeling. She could only paint, and each feeling moved quickly into another and another so she had to keep painting to capture the different feelings she was experiencing. However at that time she had no words for them. Now she had words illustrated by her artwork.

A further tool offered were poems as active "I am" (reclaiming the self). The women were given the opportunity to write words against a series of 24 questions: "If you were a season, an animal, a bird, something to eat, an activity ending in 'ing', what would you be?" We asked them to use the words to make sentences. Once they had done that, we asked them to put "I am" at the beginning of what they had written, with some

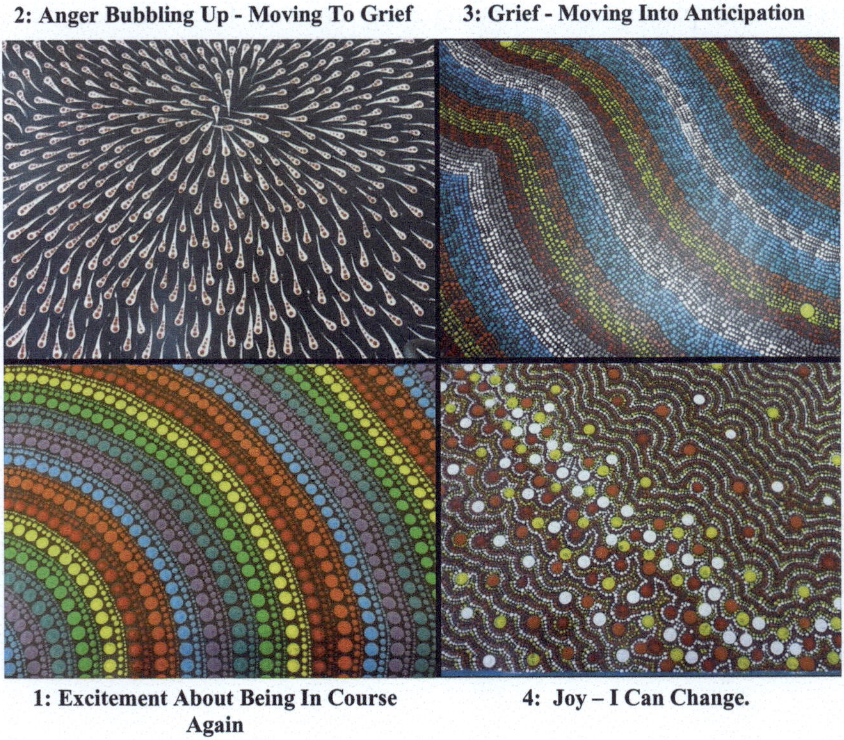

Fig. 12.1 Story of feelings paintings (Copyright 2018: Cecilia Wayne—used with permission)

small rewriting. These poems are often their first creative writing. Each woman was then invited to recite their poem, standing strong, lifting their head as they read their poem to the other women in the room. Their poems are also read by them at graduation, in front of invited guests and prison hierarchy. The poem is designed as strengths-based affirmation. No woman has ever written a negative first "I am" poem. In reading the poem below, be aware that Katrina was in prison on remand for 11 months, because she protected her young daughter from a sexual predator, before her case was heard in court. Leaving prison, returning to her community she attended the regional council meeting, where she told the counsellors what she had learnt in the course, how violence affects children, and the responsibility to protect children from violence. Note how while affirming land, home, bush, food, health, animals, birds, a land holding Dream Time stories, she also confirms responsibility to keep children safe.

I am
hot summer,
and winter, a cool breeze
over the mountains of the Flinders Ranges.
The hunting season for kangaroo, witchey grubs, honey ants
and kipara - wild turkey are calling me singing to the soft blue sky,
playing music to the purple mountains of home Pipalyatjara,
the special rock, holding our Dream Time stories.

Under the healthy green tree full of leaves,
I am dancing dancing to a sunflower morning,
while patilpa 26 parrot seeks bush medicine Irrmangka Irrmangka.

The children
play on the red sand,
while their mother digs for a goanna
that can be for supper, making sure they are safe
from the hurt that comes when we are not prepared to protect them.

5 Discussion

The "I am" poem has been placed at the close of this section to demonstrate that the women choose cultural images as they reflected on their lives, both in their poems and in their art. This is vital in the first stages of healing from historic trauma; a proclamation of agency in creating safety and revitalising positive metaphors of self in country and culture. However Katrina mapped a four-generational, historic trauma which included her grandmother's passed down terror of being chased by a 'white man on horseback' at the time of the early frontier in remote Australia. She creates powerful images of a cultural nurturing landscape, providing both spiritual and physical nourishment. She reclaims potency in her final two lines. She, as mother, provides food for her children, while protecting them from hurt or harm. This is a powerful affirmation. However in protecting her daughter from harm, she was punished, hence spends 11 months on remand in ASCC.

In mapping the women's lives, compiling their individual and collective stories it is clear that they have clear diagnosis of complex trauma. They are surrounded by complex trauma enablers: barriers to health, housing and basic social support services; a policing legal court corrections system that fails them. There is systemic failure across the whole service delivery, with incapacity to acknowledge, understand and respond to the women's trauma experiences and provide alternatives to prison (Bevis et al. 2020).

The women taught us that activities which could be called the making of art in healing—to allow memory and conversation to redefine experience, to enable insight in a nonthreatening manner, and to reclaim authority—work with traumatised populations. It shows, through story, how art in various forms can provide engagement with and balance between the doing-feeling brain functions which, during trauma exposure, might become locked into a trauma vortex. With intent, the design of the educational program locates agency in the feeling-thinking-reflective brain body recovery experiences, as both individual and collective.

Once the results of the first three deliveries were reviewed it was clear the major work and the major shifts in the women occurred in the loss grief trauma section; that the vital issues in the lives of the women were *loss grief victimisation and traumatisation,* demonstrated through their loss/trauma history maps. This affirms the need to take into consideration historic trauma in any recovery program. It was in this section, with the support of their art as mindfulness, where they made the most progress, and started to choose changes they would make in their lives.

Deakin University School of Law—Centre for Rural Regional Law and Justice conducted an evaluation of the program (Carnes 2015). In an assumption that the KSVP was designed to confront a legal system that was unjust to colonised disempowered Aboriginal women, they understood that we were using education, an Indigenous Critical Pedagogy, to contextualise the failure of law, health, social services across history. They said the course "exists at the nexus of education, health/wellbeing/ Indigenous pedagogy [with an approach drawing on] Indigenous and non-Indigenous teaching learning healing in a unique way". Further they said: "Not all trauma informed policy and practice is attuned to the nuances of intergeneration (historic) trauma".

6 Conclusion

The theory and practice of the model described in this chapter is built from a number of wisdoms and principles. The English word 'education' is derived from the Greek word *educere*: to draw out—lead—show the way, using the Socratic method of introspection and reflexion, in learning based on dialogue where insight and wisdom from experience are shared, and critical thinking is encouraged. This is innately Indigenous.

Paulo Freire (1973) says communication gives life meaning. The women learnt to trust themselves and each other as they came to deeply reflect on and learn from life experiences. They came to see these as valuable life lessons. Hence education can be an awakening into a critical consciousness. Sharing with others deepens and strengthens the capacity to challenge past prejudice and reclaim the self in relationship with others. "At the basis of Indigenous philosophies and educational strategies are the underlying principles of *relationships and balance* … the individual is required to develop to the full, those personal attributes that can enhance the life of the group" (Townsend-Cross 2004, p. 3).

At the re-constructive post-apartheid, post-colonial interface is tension. Sitting with the women in prison, presenting a curriculum that prison psychologists had passed while using concepts from what Paulo Freire called "Education for Critical Consciousness; Education for Freedom" (1973, 1998), the women's decisive understanding, and their possible liberation, came in the shared stories generating dialogue, and in their paintings where they felt safe enough to critically reflect. Their paintings, processes of deep meditative reflection, their poems a reclamation of self: "I have never painted before, and I have never felt this level of grief before". While education consists of acts of cognition, problem-posing education involves a constant unveiling of reality. This then allows the emergence of consciousness and critical intervention in reality. Hence we can follow Freire's call for education as the practice of freedom (1998), responding to Fanon's documentation of colonisation as dehumanisation on individuals and the collective (1963).

That however is not enough if we are to create post-colonial–post-apartheid worlds. The evidence and the theory of collective historic trauma also must acknowledge the "psychological blow to the basic tissues of social life that damage the bonds attaching people together and impair the prevailing sense of community" … "a gradual realization that the community no longer exists as a source of nurturance and that part of the self has disappeared" (Erikson 1976, 233).

Collective (historic) trauma applies in the lives of the women in the KSVP. They cannot repair the bonds within community—a source of nurturance—until they reclaim those parts of themselves that have disappeared and the power they need to exercise in recovery. Others cannot do this for them. Silove (2007) writes of the intentional necessities for recovery from the violence of war zones; Hobfoll et al. (2007) of the work required to rebuild after major disasters. Building on their work, the following six intentional steps for healing the violence of colonisation and worldwide human-made environmental disasters are prescribed:

1. **Safety and security:** To locate, develop and support safe places and safe caring people. Work together to help promote a sense of individual and collective safety and security, through programs of mutual care and trust. Build on these capacities and commitments while promoting the understanding that change and healing are possible.
2. **Calming—re-bonding after crisis:** Calming is important as traumatic events increase emotional turmoil. Hence sharing circles (which can move into learning circles and healing circles) can provide bonding through the structure of talking together to build community connections, communal attachment, community awareness of issues, with the desire to work together to support change and healing.

Activities could include "education and training of coping skills, including deep muscle relaxation, breathing control, assertiveness, role playing, covert modeling, thought stopping, positive thinking and self- talk" (Hobfoll 290). For the women, art worked.

3. **Attachment and belonging:** "Large-scale community outreach and psycho-education about post-disaster reactions should be included among public health interventions" (Hobfoll 292). Introducing an *educaring* program in communities, working with local people to deliver these packages, with educational modalities, that provide skills for community empowerment and a felt sense of efficacy, supporting communities of care. The educational model of reflective discussions and practice helps draw out what people already know, emphasising the central importance of social support and sustained attachment and belonging, building cultural and spiritual strengths, essential for ameliorating stress and trauma.
4. **Justice fairness dignity:** "Damaging effects of trauma events on people's sense of meaning, justice and order can have extremely stressful effects. [People will] struggle with a sense of meaning and justice in the face of shattered assumptions about prevailing justice in the world" (Hobfoll, 285). Providing support and resources for people to build their community recovery involves a commitment to justice reinvestment, for a sense of self and collective efficacy, fairness and dignity.
5. **Valuing self—valuing others in self and collective identity:** "Following trauma exposure people are at risk of losing their sense of competency to handle events they must face" (Hobfoll 293). All humans must have a sense of control over their life circumstances and that such control will result in positive outcomes, more particularly through self-regulation of thought, emotions and behaviour. This should also be extended to a collective sense that people belong to a group that can experience positive outcomes (Hobfoll, 293). A community development approach would provide support for both local community people, and for professional workers, encouraging interconnectedness and social support in their work roles and identities.
6. **Hope meaning coherence:** Focusing on a community development model over responses to individual needs means groups can work together to help others, investing in early childhood programs, and in

schools for children and their parents; promoting youth-based creative and culture/environmental activities; for men and women, and for elders. Such programs, while providing trauma education and healing practise, grow a felt sense of hope, coherence and consistency, for capacity building in making meaning of life, while enriching cultural and spiritual identities (We Al-li 2018; Atkinson 2007; Hobfoll et al. 2007; Silove 2007).

Problem-posing education affirms men and women as beings in the process *of becoming*. While education consists of acts of cognition, problem-posing education involves a constant unveiling and response to Fanon's documentation of colonisation as dehumanisation on individuals and the collective, a world in transformation is also a reclaiming the self in the collective. Problem-posing education bases itself on creativity and stimulates true reflection and action upon reality, thereby responding to the vocation of persons as beings who are authentic only when engaged in enquiry and creative transformation. Such education is revolutionary and hopeful. When a woman returns home and demands to speak to the council, to tell them what she has learnt (while in prison), and demands they support her to tell others what she has learnt, she is moving into radical activism. The tension is a disconnect between the theory and practice of recovery from historic trauma. The women, given opportunity, show insight and intention for change while also seeing that the colonial system—law, health, social services, education—continues to imprison and oppress them in body, mind and spirit.

Listening to the women and understanding their pathways to prison, forced me to acknowledge what I did not know to understand what I was learning from them. I saw and began to understand more deeply, *Symptom as History* (Mollica 2006). The historical factors of a penal colony and the building of more prisons to house those who have been dispossessed and marginalised through enforced poverty and oppression, continues the colonial past in the present. The women's behaviour was the only language they had to communicate their distress in an unjust world. However in this instance, the women's behaviour (in the course and its influence on me) was the language of more than survival. They demonstrated the possibility for post-colonial redemption.

References

Aboriginal and Torres Strait Islander Social Justice Commissioner. (2009). *Social Justice Report of 2008*. Canberra: Australian Human Rights Commission.

Atkinson, J. (2002). *Trauma Trails, Recreating Song Lines: The Transgenerational Effects of Trauma in Indigenous Australia*. North Melbourne: Spinifex.

Atkinson, J. (2007). Indigenous Approaches to Child Abuse. In J. Altman & M. Hinkson (Eds.), *Coercive Reconciliation. Stabilise, Normalise, Exit Aboriginal Australia*. North Carlton: Arena Publications.

Atkinson, J. (2014). Negotiating Worldviews: Indigenous Place in Academic Space. In C. Mason & F. Rawlings-Sanaei (Eds.), *Academic Migration, Discipline Knowledge and Pedagogical Practices*. Singapore: Springer.

Australian Broadcasting Corporation. https://www.abc.net.au/news/2018-07-27/map-of-indigenous-massacres-grows-to-include-more-sites/10040206.

Australian Bureau of Statistics. (2015). *Prisoners in Australia, 2015*. Cat. No. 4517.0. Canberra: Australia Government.

B2M: Song *Mistake,* album *Home.* (2015). Skinny Fish Music. Darwin.

Baker, D. G. (1983). *Race Ethnicity and Power*. London: Routledge & Kegan Paul.

Bevis, M., Atkinson, J., McCarthy, L., & Sweet, M. (2020). *Kungas' trauma experiences and effects on behaviour in Central Australia* (Research report, 03/2020). Sydney, NSW: ANROWS

Carnes, R. (2015). *Applying a We Al-Li Educaring Framework to Address Histories of Violence with Aboriginal Women: An Evaluation Prepared by Dr Roslyn (Rose) Carnes Deakin University, School of Law Centre for Rural Regional Law and Justice*. Geelong: Deakin Law School.

Curtis-Wendlandt, L. (2016). Corporal Punishment and Moral Reform at Hermannsburg Mission. *History Australia, 7*(1), 07.1–07.17. https://doi.org/10.2104/ha100007.

Duran, E., Duran, B., Yellow Horse Brave Heart, M., Horse, Y., & Davis, S. (1998). Healing the American Indian Soul Wound. In Y. Danieli (Ed.), *International Handbook of Multigenerational Legacies of Trauma*. New York: Plenum.

Erikson, K. (1976). *Everything in it Path*. New York: Simon and Schuster.

Evans, R. (1992). A Gun in the Oven. Masculinism and Gendered Violence. In K. Saunders & R. Evans (Eds.), *Gender Relations in Australia. Domination and Negotiation*. Sydney: Harcourt Brace Jovanovich.

Fanon, F. (1963). *The Wretched of the Earth*. New York: Grove Weinenfeld.

Freire, P. (1973). *Education for Critical Consciousness*. London: Sheed and Ward.

Freire, P. (1998). *Pedagogy of Freedom: Ethics, Democracy and Civic Courage.* Lanham: Rowman & Littlefield Publishers.
Giddens, A. (1989). *Sociology*. London: Polity.
Harr'e, R. (1993). *Social Being*. Oxford: Blackwell Publishing.
Hobfoll, S. E., Watson, P., Bell, C. C., Bryant, R. A., Brymer, M. J., Friedman, M. J., et al. (2007). Five Essential Elements of Immediate and Mid-term Mass Trauma Intervention: Empirical Evidence. *Psychiatry, 70*(4), 283–315; discussion 316.
Human Rights Law Centre & Change the Record. (2017). *Over Represented and Overlooked: The Crisis of Aboriginal and Torres Strait Islander Women's Growing Over-imprisonment.* Retrieved on 6 Dec 2017 https://www.hrlc.org.au/reports/
Kerr, J. (2016). *A Descriptive Analysis of the Characteristics, Seriousness and Frequency of Aboriginal Intimate Partner Violence in the Northern Territory, Australia: A Strategy for Targeting High Harm Cases.* Master's thesis, Applied Criminology and Police Management, Cambridge University
Kidd, R. (1997). *The Way we Civilise*. St Lucia: University of Queensland Press.
Krieg, A. (2009). The Experience of Collective Trauma in Australian Indigenous Communities. *Australasian Psychiatry, 17*(1), 28–32. https://doi.org/10.1080/103985609029486.
Lederach, J. P. (2005). *Moral Imagination the Art and Soul of Building Peace*. Oxford: Oxford University.
Leeson, S., Rynne, J., Smith, C., & Adams, Y. (2016). Incarcerating Aboriginal and Torres Strait Islander Women in Australia: Finding a Balance in Defining the 'Just Prison'. *ALIR, 19*(2), 76–96.
Levine, P. (2007). *Waking the Tiger: Healing Trauma*. Berkley: North Atlantic Books.
Mehl-Madrona, L. (2005). *Coyote Wisdom: The Power of Story in Healing*. VT. Bear and Company: Rochester.
Mehl-Madrona, L. (2010). *Healing the Mind Through the Power of Story. The Promise of Narrative Psychiatry*. Rochester, Bear and Company.
Memmott, P. (1990). *Aboriginal Cultural, Social Problems and DIC Victims,* a Report to the Royal Commission into Aboriginal Deaths in Custody (unpublished), University of Queensland.
Mollica, R. (2006). *Healing Invisible Wounds – Paths to Hope and Recovery in a Violent World.* Nashville: Vanderbilt Uni.

Muid, O. (2006). *Then I Lost My Spirit: An Analytical Essay on Transgenerational Theory and Its Application to Oppressed People of Color Nations.* Ann Arbor: UMI Dissertation Services/ProQuest.

Petrie, C. C. (1904). *Tom Petrie's Reminiscences of Early Queensland.* Brisbane: Watson & Ferguson and Co..

Price, G. A. (1963). *The Western Invasions of the Pacific and its Continents.* Oxford: Clarendon.

Queensland Government. The Aborigines Protection and Restriction of the Sale of Opium Act 1897.

Queensland Government. The Community Services Act of 1984.

Ralph, N., Hamaguchi, K., & Cox, M. (2006). Transgenerational Trauma, Suicide and Healing from Sexual Abuse in the Kimberley Region, Australia. *Pimatisiwin, A Journal of Aboriginal and Indigenous Community Health, 4*(2), 118–136.

Robinson, S. R. (2002). *"Something Like Slavery" The Exploitation of Aboriginal Child Labour in Queensland 1842–1945.* UQ unpublished PhD thesis, Brisbane.

Roth, W. E. (1984). *The Queensland Aborigines Vol 11 Bulletins 1-8 North Queensland Ethnology from the Home Secretary's Department- Brisbane 1901–1908.* Melbourne: Hesperian.

Royal Commission into Aboriginal Deaths in Custody. (1991). *National Reports Volume 1–5.* Canberra: Australian Government Publishing Service.

Ryan, L. (2018). Australian Broadcasting Commission. https://www.abc.net.au/news/2018-07-27/map-of…massacres…to…sites/10040206

Salzman, M. B., & Halloran, M. J. (2004). Culture, Meaning, Self-esteem and the Re-construction of the Cultural World-view. In J. Greenberg, S. L. Koole, & T. Pyszczynski (Eds.), *The Handbook of Experimental Existential Psychology.* New York: Guildford.

Silove, D. (2007). From Trauma to Survival and Adaption: Towards a Framework for Guiding Mental Health Initiatives in Post-conflict Societies. In D. Ingleby (Ed.), *Forced Migration and Mental Health* (pp. 29–52). New York: Springer.

Townsend-Cross, M. (2004). *Indigenous Australian Perspectives in early Childhood Education,* Pacific Early Childhood Education Research Association 5 Annual International Conference and Meeting, Identities and Innovations: Shaping Better Worlds Through Early Childhood Education. 16–19 July 2004, Melbourne.

Ungunmerr-Baumann, M. R. (1993). The Spirit of the Bush. In J. Hendricks and G. Hefferan (Ed.), *A Spirituality of Catholic Aborigines and the Struggle for*

Justice (pp. 37–38). Brisbane: Aboriginal and Torres Strait Islander Apostolate Catholic Archdiocese of Brisbane. http://www.miriamrosefoundation.org.au/about-dadirri
Van De Kolk, B. A. (1987). *Psychological Trauma*. Washington: American Psychiatric Press.
We Al-li. (2018). *Responding to Potential Triggers During Orientation Visits – Self Care for Staff*. Goolmangar.

13

Representing Collective Trauma of Korean War: Creative Education as a Peacebuilding Strategy

Borislava Manojlovic

1 Introduction

This chapter examines representations of collective traumas and their implications for the sustainable peace in post-conflict societies. The representations of collective traumas are key ingredients of the collective identity, historical memory and nationbuilding narrative, which shape the views of the future generations. They can lead to more division, tension and conflict, but they can also become a unifying mechanism for societies that need healing and reconciliation. The first aim of this chapter is to examine how the collective trauma of Korean War is represented through official narratives of the past and how it affects North and South Koreans' views of each other. The second aim is to explore if collective trauma can be presented in such a way that it properly acknowledges the victims and the horrific crimes, while at the same time providing a space

B. Manojlovic (✉)
School for Conflict Analysis and Resolution, George Mason University Korea, Songdo, South Korea
e-mail: bmanojlo@gmu.edu

K. Wale et al. (eds.), *Post-Conflict Hauntings*, Palgrave Studies in Compromise after Conflict, https://doi.org/10.1007/978-3-030-39077-8_13

for co-existence, healing and reconciliation. The study concludes with an outline of the innovative strategies that can counteract the negative impacts of divisive past and promote critical thinking and accountability as an antidote to toxic memories that challenge peace.

The case of two Koreas is examined through the prism of the narrative identity theory and Vamik Volkan's chosen trauma concept. Volkan's *chosen trauma* provides insight into the internal processes of people's coming to terms with collective traumas. Trauma is indeed embedded in one's mental framework, which explains individual and group's emotional attachment and solidarity with the ancestral pain and suffering. The narrative approach to identity illuminates the understanding of meanings that are ascribed to collective traumatic events. The effect of a traumatic event on a social group arises from the collective meanings ascribed to the event rather than the actual facts. The meanings that are attached to certain events matter and the way they are constructed shape people's identity and behavior. Such claim can be seen as an entry point for intervention because if representations of collective traumas can be framed to promote differentiation, there is a possibility that they can also be reframed and represented in a way that promotes openness, critical thinking and accountability. Therefore, this chapter argues for closer attention to the structure of historical narratives as meaning making tools and proposes the spiral model of time and narrative to illuminate such structure. It also discusses the impact of historical narratives on the intergroup views and identity formation in the case of two Koreas. Subsequently, it proposes the creative educational strategies that would open the space for "better" narratives (Cobb 2013) whose structure and representation may contribute to reconciliation and sustainable peace.

2 The Case of Two Koreas

Official narratives of the past are formed around matters of memory, most notably around representations of the past traumatic events which are used to construct a sense of shared purpose and identity. Both South and North Korea have constructed their sense of national identity around a particular view of the past and especially around a distinct traumatic event: the Korean War. These views stand in sharp contrast to each other, generating tensions and conflict. While scholars have written extensively about the politics of Korean War (Cumings 1981; Merrill 1989; Park 2012), little has been done to examine the human suffering and the consequences of past traumas. In the wake of the renewed peace process in 2018 and even the possibility of unification of two Koreas, the question of coming together as a nation has become relevant, and, with it, the issues of healing, recognition of past suffering and acknowledging the past.

The Korean War was a devastating conflict which split the nation along the ideological line for almost 70 years. The war of 1950–53 resulted in almost 1.6 million civilian deaths and almost 1.3 million combat deaths, the destruction of eco-system and deep intergroup divisions (Millett 2019). Korea had once been a unified nation ruled by Chosŏn dynasty for more than five centuries until the 1910s occupation by imperial Japan. The Japanese have colonized the peninsula for 35 years. After the defeat of the Axis powers in 1945, the peninsula became split into the two blocs: the Soviet-controlled North which became known as the Democratic People's Republic of Korea and the US-controlled South which adopted the name of the Republic of Korea. In an attempt to unify the Korean peninsula under his communist regime, North Korean leader Kim Il-Sung, supported by the Chinese and the Soviets, crossed the 38th parallel with an aim to recapture the South in June 1950. South Korea and the United States, backed by the United Nations, started a counter-offensive, which led to what is known today as the Korean War (MacDonald 1986). Despite the armistice agreement which ended hostilities in 1953, the peace agreement has never been signed. The Korean War had earned a title of being one of the deadliest wars in modern history. The trauma of such a destructive conflict has had a great impact on Koreans' sense of identity, national pride and the feelings of shame and grief.

The examination of South Koreans' views toward the North Korean defectors in South Korea provides insight into the workings of the collective trauma of the Korean War today. It is important to acknowledge the dynamic nature of the North and South Koreans' views of each other as they are constantly changing and will change even more if the reunification moves forward. Volkan argues that collective traumas become reactivated when faced with a reminder of a stressful and anxiety-inducing circumstance (Volkan 2001). The defectors are the living reminders of this difficult period of Korean history and their treatment may be explained by the Volkan's concept of transgenerational trauma which causes groups to view the descendants of their former enemy as their extensions.

Only a decade after the Korean War, South Korea started experiencing rapid success and growth due the liberalization of market and support of the United States. It became the fourth strongest economy in Asia and thirteenth largest in the world (Seth 2017). Unlike their neighbors, who lagged behind, South Korea has become a technological giant. Poverty and lack of opportunity made many North Koreans defect and flee to South Korea. According to the South Korean Ministry of Unification, there was a total of 31,093 defectors registered within South Korea and 1127 people had defected in 2017 alone.[1] The long-standing ideological divide has contributed to the rift in social and cultural values, which is evident in the attitudes toward North Korean defectors and their families. For many South Koreans status and economic well-being are the top priorities and they put emphasis on success and education. The average school day in South Korea, for example, begins at 6:30 am and ends at 5:30 pm. However, almost every student within South Korea attends a private crammer (or hagwon) after their studies at school, where lessons take place from 6 pm until 10 pm (Chakrabarti 2013). Those who fall behind face the dangers of unemployment and instability. Although South Korea has given significant support to defectors to build new lives in the South, North Koreans often lag behind due to the lack of educational and social skills to compete within such a market. They often end up doing low-paid jobs that most South Koreans do not want to do. According to Seoul's Ministry of Unification, the government agency that handles refugee resettlement policy, the unemployment rate among the defectors is six times higher than the South Korean average (Ministry of Unification 2017).

Due to their links to North Korea, the defectors face the challenge of integrating into South Korean society. Few South Koreans are eager to associate with defectors, who are at times stereotyped as lazy or unsophisticated (Borowiec 2018). They are often distrusted and viewed as enemies and spies. As a result, they are deemed as outsiders and not belonging to the same nation. This view is exacerbated by the fact that the two Koreas have never had an opportunity to engage in a substantive dialogue on the issue of contentious past and particularly the trauma of Korean War. As Volkan (2001) argues: "Within large groups there exist a shared mental representation of a traumatic past event during which the large group suffered loss and/or experienced helplessness, shame, and humiliation in a conflict with another group." Such distrust is transmitted to the new generations through the representations of collective trauma, which serve to perpetuate cultural biases and mental representation of another group. For North and South Koreans, it is the traumatic event of the Korean War that caused a deep injury, creating both a physical barrier and a social barrier that continue to separate them.

It is worth mentioning that many of the South and North Koreans think of themselves as one people (*danil minjok*) connected by a common bloodline but divided by ideology. The idea of one nation has been important for national survival during some of the most difficult periods of Korean history, particularly Japanese invasion. Today, *minjok* seems a somewhat outdated abstraction which has been used in the past to promote ethnocentric and nationalist ideals keeping the group closed off from the outside influences and maintaining its sense of superiority and purity. This overarching ethnic identity may be a common ground that the North and South Koreans can explore further in their quest for unity, but it can also be an obstacle to peace and reconciliation if one group, for example, considers itself to be the true bearer of purity and nationhood.

While living in Songdo, I heard many young South Koreans saying that they felt as if they lived on an island detached from the mainland by North Korea whom they perceived as the hostile Other set out to disrupt their success story. The injured self-images of the older generation associated with the mental representation of the shared traumatic event are "deposited" into the developing self-representation of children in the next generation as if these children will be able to mourn the loss or reverse the humiliation (Volkan 1997). Such representations of collective trauma lead group members to view the descendants of their ancestors' perpetrators and/or enemies as their extensions (Volkan 1997). As Borowiec (2018) states: "The older generation view North Korea as an enemy, which means North Korea and South Korea have equal status. But young people view North Korea as dependent or a country that can't sustain itself, as beneath South Korea." Many young South Koreans view North Korea as a threat not only to their physical existence but also to their economic and social stability in case of unification. Unlike their forefathers, the young South Koreans did not experience the war but their views have been conditioned through the stories of the past. They are concerned with their education and employment opportunities which may be challenged by the unification and the influx of people willing to work for much lower wages. The young generation has become somewhat distant and apathetic toward the Northerners, and such attitude has been reinforced by the historical portrayal of North Korea, lack of interpersonal interaction and opportunity to learn more about each other. That is why education could play an important role in raising awareness and creating spaces for these two groups to learn about each other's concerns and experiences.

Despite the efforts of the Ministry of Unification, Christian and social welfare organizations assisting North Korean defectors to integrate into South Korean society, the cultural and social biases rooted in the narrative of the Korean War continue to hamper their integration into the South Korean society. Narratives of victimhood based on collective trauma serve different generations as justifications for the legitimacy of their grievances. This may be an indicator of the social dynamics and conflicts that could emerge after the unification. The memory of the Korean War, incessant threats of nuclear missiles and suspicion about the unknown and potentially hostile Other have contributed to the cautious and negative attitudes of South Koreans toward their North Korean counterparts. This study suggests that through innovation in education, learning from the past and increased interpersonal interaction, new meanings and common social identities can be created. The next section examines the structure of South and North Korean historical narratives about the Korean War in education, and more specifically in history textbooks, analyzing the roots of division as well as potential for addressing them.

3 The Representation of Collective Trauma in Education: Two Opposed Narratives

Education systems are an important locale where contentious past is taught to the new generations shaping their views, identities and sense of belonging. Education can be a part of the peacebuilding efforts, but it can also challenge the peace and reconciliation processes perpetuating Us versus Them dynamics and stereotypes about the Other. As Zamponi (2018) argues: "All memories, even the memories of eyewitnesses, only assume collective relevance when they are structured, represented, and used in social setting." Educational settings are, therefore, prone to becoming political as they are the milieu where views of diverse groups and individuals become emphasized, denied or contended. The issue of which or whose version of history is taught in schools may become, for different communities, a matter of their cultural and social survival, as well as the key issue for the preservation of their identity. Education systems, therefore, become the sites for difficult conversations about the past and for exploring the possibilities for sustainable peace.

Representations of the collective past feature prominently in history classes, and the way they are presented has an impact on how the future generations will make sense of themselves and the Other. This study focuses primarily on the representations of the Korean War in North and South Korean history textbooks. The history textbooks are the best sources to learn about the official historical narrative since they are approved by the Ministries of Education and regulated by the government. The state elites are keen to control historical narratives since they are considered an important part of the cultural capital and collective identity of a society. They serve as a nationbuilding tool that unifies the "ingroup" by glorifying its actions, while excluding the "outgroup" through the silencing and omission of certain storylines whether they be fact or fiction (Korostelina 2008, Tajfel and Turner 2004). In the case of two Koreas, history textbooks are an excellent locale to explore the narratives that divide the nation, which are deeply rooted in the trauma of the Korean War.

The story of the Korean War, which is the focus of this chapter and which will be referred to as historical narrative of the Korean War, is an integral part of the humanities curriculum taught in history, language, ethics and culture classes. If we examine the South and North Korean textbooks, we can find different and opposed narratives on who started the Korean War, how and why it started, and how it ended. South Korean narrative puts the blame on Kim Il Sung who invaded South Korea with the help of Russians and Chinese, while North Korean narrative goes to say that North Korea initiated peace talks but it was South Korea that rejected their peace offer and attacked North Korea first (Bleiker and Hoang 2006). Lin et al. (2009) in their analysis of South Korean textbooks point out the necessity of South Korean and the UN/US counter-offensive in the hope of reuniting both Koreas and defending their freedom. The Us versus Them dichotomy is evident in the textbooks which reinforces separation of the heroic, proud and victimized ingroup and the aggressive, hostile and treacherous outgroup. Such contentious interpretations of collective traumas feed into the sectarian sense of belonging to an identity which is constructed in opposition to the identity of the relevant Other. The Us versus Them dichotomy is a key ingredient of the stories told by different (adversarial) parties about the conflict that shape their versions of reality and produce separate socio-cultural entities. Thus, one of the main challenges for sustainable peace is that different groups seek to legitimize their own views of the past and present, through which they affirm their identities and position themselves on a higher moral ground in relation to the Other. As a result, members of a group start to diminish the Other, while glorifying themselves which in turn leads to the reemergence of tensions.

In North and South Korean textbooks the blame for starting and causing the conflict is placed on the Other (National Institute of Korean History 2006, 305), but what the textbooks fail to discuss are the war victims, suffering, atrocities and destruction on both sides. The total number of civilian deaths is estimated at around 1.6 million people; there were thousands of orphans and millions of displaced. Bringing to the forefront the facts about human suffering and tragedy of the fratricidal war may be an entry point for a new peacebuilding strategy—the strategy that would introduce into education a complex historical narrative about the pain of civilians and ordinary people on both sides caused by the war. This is not to deny the responsibility for atrocities committed on either side in the conflict, which needs to be acknowledged. The point for such a strategy is to put more emphasis on the suffering civilians which would make the narrative more humane, universal and recognizable for both South and North Koreans. The famous historian of the Korean War Bruce Cumings (2010) emphasized that the responsibility for the Korean War could not be attributed to one side and that narrative is much more complex.

In contrast to dichotomous simplified narrative currently presented in history textbooks, a "better" narrative is a complex narrative that incorporates alternative views about the war and emphasizes the universality of human suffering. The awareness of the complexity can broaden the space for analyzing, representing and adopting the Korean War narrative among new generations. The complexity and the cyclical and changing nature of historic narratives are keys to understanding their potential to impact peace and reconciliation processes which I discuss next.

4 Nature of Historical Narrative and Representation of Collective Trauma

Historical narratives or stories about past conflicts are constantly in flux. Their constant fluctuation is influenced by the conditions in the present moment. They are a good indicator of current underlying problems affecting the community, such as economic uncertainty, unemployment, discord between expectations and reality, exclusion, nationalism and structural violence (Manojlovic 2017). The awareness of the flexible, ever-changing nature of narratives can be an important realization for all involved in the processes of conflict transformation.

To demonstrate how changing historical narratives affect memorialization processes and how they are influenced by time and context, I have developed a visualization called the "Spiral Model of Time and Narrative." This model enables examination of the complexity and perpetually

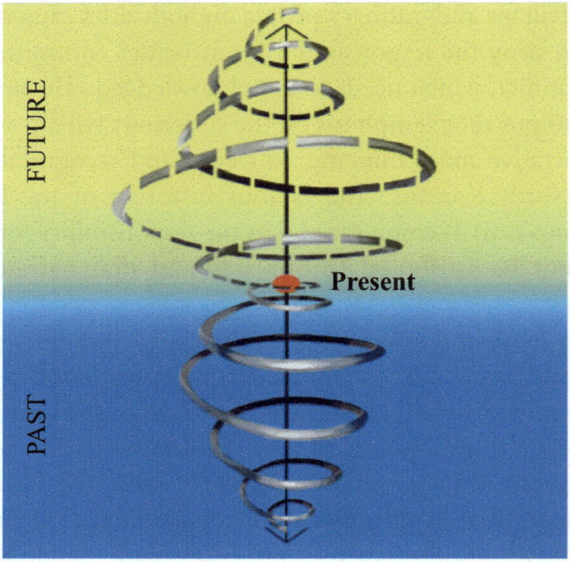

Fig. 13.1 Spiral model of time and narrative developed by Borislava Manojlovic (2013)

changing cyclical nature of historical narrative which situates the narrative in a four-dimensional space (see Fig. 13.1).

The spiral model is helpful by showing the function of historical narratives in connecting the past, present and future. The narratives about past events are always connected to the speaker's present conditions and future orientations. The cyclical construction of historical narratives takes place around the axis of time, and as such it is fluid and in traces because the initial narrative does not fully preserve its content but rather changes with the progression of time.

When we say that "history repeats itself," we are only partially right. While recurrent practices, behaviors and language constructs can certainly be traced throughout history, even the most resilient narratives change over time. The narrative contracts and widens based on the present orientations of agents. It contracts when there is less space for individual agency, openness and curiosity, leading to the creation of a uniform, dichotomous and simplified narrative. Morton Deutsch suggests that destructive conflicts are characterized by their tendency to expand and escalate in terms of issues, motives, costs, negative attitudes toward adversary and so on (Deutsch 1973, 351). At the same time, "the processes involved in the intensification of conflict result in the harmful and dangerous elements driving out those which would keep the conflict within bounds" (Deutsch 1973, 352). During a period of conflict, the number of adversarial events increases exponentially, while narratives and their diversity contract, thereby implying that historical time becomes denser during conflict. Voices of dissent are subdued and individuals are drawn toward more simplified, Us versus Them narratives.

During the time of peace, the space for narrative construction widens, as people become more open, curious and ready to engage with the stories of others. The spiral model of narrative also shows that individual narratives are always in flux, dynamical and adjusting to constant challenges. In such a world, time is not linear, but axes of the past, the present and the future interact, creating a complex and dynamical system. Heine describes "the historical continuity of past and future in terms of an ever-renewable cyclicality and reversibility of time" (Heine 1994). It can be argued that the concept of historical continuity, in a way, emphasizes the present as an intersection of the past and the future. The present is a crucial locale for understanding the past and imagining the future.

Negative evaluation of the Other, as we saw in both North and South Korean textbooks, leads to the feeling of being threatened and increases the need for positive portrayal of the ingroup. Historical representations of collective traumas are based on Us versus Them dichotomy which only exacerbates conflict. Identity threat, for example, very often arises from people's perceptions that the collectives to which they belong are being evaluated negatively. According to Korostelina (2007) the members of the ingroup use defense mechanisms embedded in their mind through either socialization or transgenerational transmission of a negative experience, such as collective trauma, to cope with this perceived threat.

This chapter claims that some of the key challenges to peace and reconciliation are fundamentally connected to the problem of representations of collective traumas, their use and role in shaping the views of the future generations. Underlying the emergence of the perception of an identity threat is the presence of opposite meaning systems that have at their core the idea of a positive, morally pure and superior "Us" and an evil, vicious and negative "Them" (Rothbart and Korostelina 2006). The implication this presents is that conflict arises and is perpetuated when narratives based on Us versus Them become so important to communities that they are central for their group identity (Smith 2003; Wertsch 2008).

The narrative theory of identity is helpful in examining the Us versus Them dichotomy as an underlying structure of contentious historical narratives. According to this theory, identity is not seen as a part of cognitive structures but is instead seen as an analyzable ingredient of narratives that include hidden scripts and overarching discourses about others and ourselves. These narratives are drawn from the knowledge stored in ingroup's "cultural memory" which is "characterized by sharp distinctions made between those who belong and those who do not" (Assmann and Czaplicka 1995). Narratives are a mixture of master collective narratives, such as stories of victimhood, aggression, domination and unity on the one hand, and individual stories, on the other. This mixture of collective and personal narratives not only influences the development of personhood and identity of individuals but also regulates the relationships within the ingroup as well as with the outgroup.

According to the narrative theory of identity, identity does change and it is constantly reclaimed through narratives that bridge the horizons of past experiences and future expectations (Hall 1992). The narrative identity approach "assumes that people act in particular ways because not to do so would fundamentally violate their sense of being at that particular time and place" (Somers 1994, 624). Within this framework of analysis, people's identities cannot be understood unless situated in a historical period, place and set of relationships. Moreover, an individual sense of Self cannot exist without the presence of Others. We need the relationship with the Other to make sense of ourselves and to open to the possibilities of life, freedom and the inevitability of living in a community of similar, yet different, individuals.

The most compelling cases through which to study the uses of historical narratives are collective traumas. Collective trauma of Korean War is based on traumatic events that have left a lasting mark on the collective consciousness of both South and North Koreans. The stories about major atrocities, victories, defeats and bombings are mythologized and framed to invoke national unity, solidarity, emotions, sense of victimhood and call for justice and reparation. The Korean War is a complex collective trauma of South and North Korean people that has been interpreted differently by the two groups. The Korean War trauma has never been addressed by either side in a substantive way and victims' claims for justice have only been partially answered. Atrocities such as killings of the civilians in No Gun Ri (Choe et al. 1999) or horrendous bombing of Pyongyang (Eperjesi 2015) continue to live in collective consciousness of the divided nation as reminders that the justice has not been done. In the absence of justice, groups tend to consolidate the narrative of collective trauma around the idea of victimhood, so that they can mourn their loss, identify the shared source of suffering, and adopt moral responsibility and solidarity with the members of the ingroup. At the same time groups tend not to recognize the suffering of the others, which leads to the continuation of divisions and conflict.

The problem with representations of collective traumas in post-conflict settings is that they are troublingly divisive, but at the same time they are essential for the collective and individual's view of reality. They acquire great potency in educational systems, in which the politics of memory and history have very concrete goals and a significant impact on how the new generations perceive the past. The takeaway point of this section is that educators and practitioners of conflict resolution and peacebuilding need to advocate for an awareness of the workings of contentions stories or, more accurately, historical narratives in shaping identities, perceptions and behaviors. In the spirit of progressive humanism, this chapter posits that raising consciousness about human suffering caused by war and educating about the misuses of contentious past may be some of the key ways for building and sustaining peace.

5 Creative Education for Peacebuilding

In societies that deal with difficult past, such as the two Koreas, people may share a common historical experience and, at the same time, they can have completely different interpretations of what had happened. The awareness that there is often a disconnect in the portrayal of history, as evidenced by representations of collective trauma in the South and North Korean history textbooks, speaks for the necessity of a different approach to learning contentious history. How the new generations understand the history of their country, particularly its most contentious aspects, may have far-reaching implications for the sustainability of peace and the emergence of violence in the future. This chapter posits that when educating about contentious past, the focus should not only be on the content of the stories, but also on how those stories are told, which medium of representation is used and who is telling the story. Moreover, there is a need for creative approaches that can increase awareness of different perspectives about conflict and encourage critical thinking. If we take the example of the historical narratives of Korean War being taught in history classes, it is evident that the new generations that do not have an actual memory of the conflict are socialized into certain culturally accepted frameworks of thinking and acting that are fundamentally prejudicial and one-sided. Therefore, it is important that students are given tools for critical thinking which would enable them to become aware of the prejudice and flaws within historical narratives.

Creative and artistic approaches to education such as intercommunal painting workshops, experiential learning exercises, reflective practices, photography, poetry, improvisational theater, dance and music both influence people's experience of conflict and reveal new and unique ways of addressing the challenges (C. Cohen 2004). Art encourages people to gain fresh perspective about conflict, to confront pain and loss and transform them through movement, creative expression and embodied experience. Artistic and creative approaches can open up a space for a more complex historical narrative that stresses consequences of war and human suffering.

What if history classes would start with a discussion about a painting? Great pieces of art are there to awaken the spirit and provoke reaction, thinking, critique. The worst reaction to an artistic creation is indifference. Let us consider Picasso's *Massacre in Korea* which he painted in 1951, just after the Korean War had started. The painting was a political act of protest against the American intervention in Korean Peninsula as the news of atrocities committed by US forces became widely publicized (The Seoul Times 2004). This anti-war painting did not receive as much attention as Picasso's earlier masterpiece *Guernica*, which has subsequently been used by people all over the world to protest war, violence and oppression (Jones 2003; Keene 2017). *Guernica* was an inspiration for anti-war activists from the time it was painted (Candy Bedworth 2018): from 1939, when it toured European capitals promoting the anti-fascist cause to becoming a symbol of protest against the Vietnam War (D. Cohen 2003). The impact of *Guernica* in the most recent times, according to Hoberman (2004), is unquestionable:

> *Guernica's shrieking horse, dead children and terrorized wraiths were held aloft on placards at antiwar demonstrations in the streets of New York and plastered across a Hollywood Boulevard billboard. Sophie Matisse, great-granddaughter of the French painter, exhibited her colorized appropriation of Picasso's most famous painting–inspired, she explained, by the destruction of the twin towers.*

Massacre in Korea[2] is a more obscure expressionist painting exhibited in the Musée Picasso in Paris. The art critics have divided views about the event it portrays. Some claim that the painting is a portrayal of the No Gun Ri massacre from July 1950, when a few hundred South Korean refugees were killed by US forces, while others argue it represents the Sinchon massacre, an alleged mass killing of Korean civilians carried out by the American forces in the county of Sinchon, South Korea (Redmond 2018). The painting has been somewhat forgotten due to censorship, but it became relevant again with the recent revelations on No Gun Ri Massacre. Although the stories of survivors of the No Gun Ri massacre were not widely known, in 1999 Associated Press wrote a report about the US veterans who confirmed the massacre story (Becker 2001). As the story about the No Gun Ri massacre in Korea became controversial in early 2000s, its pictorial representation by Picasso became relevant again. The narrative that was developed around the painting integrated its visual and symbolic meaning into universal and mythological collective reservoir through which the painting became a representation of human protest against war as well as its search for dignity and freedom. Picasso helped us to understand and respond to trauma on a deeper, emotional level. He was able to combine images of pain and death with the political statement of protest and empathy for the universal human suffering. This ability of art to incorporate multiple narratives, feelings and meanings is what makes this painting a universal symbol of protest against the war that speaks to people from all over the world. Conversely, the art can be seen as an innovative tool for teaching contentious and divisive history. Its universality and symbolism provoke discussion, dialogue and different interpretations, which can help people move from their entrenched positions and challenge their uniform one-sided interpretations in a creative way.

The universality as well as its thought-provoking qualities make art an educational tool that is politically and socially engaged. The strength of Picasso's painting is in its juxtaposition of destruction and creativity that draws the attention to the futility and senselessness of war. Painting as well as other art forms can encourage reflexive processes and critical engagement with plurality and difference. Art tackles different socio-political issues through symbols and metaphors which speak to our collective consciousness. It provides a wide canvas used to convey a universal message about the values of social justice, common humanity and interconnectivity, which are all characteristics of peaceful societies.

Representations of collective past do not only exist in the history textbooks, but they are also located in cultural artifacts as reference points. Performance art, painting, documentary film and archival photographs can all serve as creative educational tools to break the silence about the Korean War trauma and foster healing. On the other hand, artistic representations of collective traumas can also be problematic as they can be perceived to diminish the experience of the victims. Theodor Adorno argues that "after Auschwitz it is barbaric to write poetry" (Adorno 2003). The concern reflected in Adorno's idea is that the Holocaust is an event that cannot be understood and transmitted through artistic means. According to Adorno, art cannot emulate the reality of the events because the reality is beyond comprehension because of its the magnitude and horror. The other side of the coin is that art can be a key approach to uncover and start a discussion about the past that everyone but victims wants to forget. Despite the magnitude of human suffering, Korean War has largely been forgotten possibly because of censorship and inconvenient facts such as that the war never really ended and that there were no clear winners and losers. However, unaddressed trauma of Korean War continues to haunt the present. Recently, artists have found a way to break a 50-year silence by telling stories of the Korean War from the perspective of Korean War refugees in the United States. The documentary *Memory of Forgotten War*[3] and the multimedia exhibit "Still Present Pasts: Korean Americans and the Forgotten War"[4] deal with the trauma of the Forgotten War by allowing victims to voice their pain and claims for justice.

The representation of collective trauma through art shows the power of symbolic and allegoric expression in illuminating deeper and universal knowledge of humanity, knowledge that war is fundamentally evil and that there must be better ways of dealing with differences and conflict. With symbolism, story-telling, film, theater, role-playing, dancing and painting, art has the potential to send a strong message in conflict and post-conflict settings. Art as an integral part of education can be seen as communicative action, a type of social action geared toward communication and understanding between individuals that can have a lasting effect on the spheres of politics and culture as a true emancipatory force (Habermas 1987). Furthermore, art can be used to promote democratic and humanistic values in societies shattered by conflict by disrupting and reconfiguring roles, places and patterns of communications within a community (McDonnell 2014). It can put one in others' shoes, bring people together through stories and images, enable catharsis and dealing with the pain, and eventually help societies imagine a peaceful future. That is why creative education suggests incorporating art as a key approach to learning about difficult past.

6 Conclusion

One of the key challenges that post-conflict societies face is a lack of a more creative and holistic approach to education that would enable an exploration of the dynamical nature of historical narratives and raise awareness about their uses. As seen in South and North Korean history textbooks, narratives about the collective past taught in schools tend to be one-sided and monochromatic. This chapter argues for education which incorporates art and other creative approaches that enable emergence of complex historical narratives and contribute to the development of innovation and critical thinking among students. According to Montessori, children need to learn and understand the roots of the conflicts, which are often located in the traditional forms of education (Bogen 2017). She calls those traditional forms control-model education: "The child who has never learned to act alone, to direct his own actions, to govern his own will, grows into an adult who is easily led and must always lean upon others" (Montessori 1943). Montessori suggests that blind obedience leads to everything that is wrong in our society. It enables ignorance, bias and non-informed responses to different situations, and leads people to blindly follow authority figures without questioning their words and actions.

The contentious historical representations speak to the need for a more meaningful involvement in education of not only parents and teachers but also other educators and mediators of meaning such as artists, curators, historians and activists. Whether we talk about schools, museums, clubs, community centers, places of worship or online spaces, learning becomes active and operative only through interaction with others. As Paolo Freire argued: "To be is to engage in relationship with others and with the world." Creative education is about relationship building, openness, social justice, equality and diversity. Learning is not a linear, direct and automatic outcome of teaching or reading textbooks. Instead, the attention should be placed on the mediating effects of students' prior knowledge, sources of information, beliefs, values and biases as well as the role that different educators play as key mediators of meaning.

How new generations understand the history of their country, particularly the most contentious aspects of its history—collective traumas—may have far-reaching implications for the future of the peace. Creating learning communities where mediators of meaning can agree on specific guidelines for teaching collective trauma centered around creativity, critical thinking and common humanity and where youth, parents and other educators are actively involved are the two key strategies in combatting contention through education. Change in the conflict system can be introduced through creative approaches such as art that foster values of trust, empathy and views of one's identity as equally valued and relevant as the identity of any other group or individual. Such humanistic values can gain traction and can be fostered relationally and collaboratively.

Sustainable peace is a work in progress and it is defined as a condition in which all members of a society can enjoy social and economic justice, equality and self-actualization. As seen in the case of North Korean defectors and the challenges they currently face, a lot of work on sustainable peace needs to be done as the two societies proceed with unification process. To that end, more research is needed into the impact of the collective trauma representations on the identities of different groups and their views of the Other so that the contentious past can be dealt with constructively. In conclusion, I would like to refer to Freire's idea that the people can change their circumstances only through *praxis*—reflection and action—and that to do that, they must learn to analyze their lives and throw aside internalized oppression. We can easily adapt Freire's ideology to the case of two Koreas in which *oppressed* communities are communities constrained by the historical enmity system (Freire 2000). To liberate communities locked in an "Us versus Them" way of thinking is to empower them to think critically and creatively and to learn how to overcome the distrust and divisions that are products of the "Us versus Them" narrative. People can heal from false and/or biased information and change their perceptions as they learn from, understand and care for the Other.

Notes

1. See: https://www.unikorea.go.kr/eng_unikorea/relations/statistics/defectors/
2. Picasso, Pablo. (1951). Massacre in Korea. Painting exhibited in the Musée Picasso in Paris. Source: https://www.pablopicasso.org/massacre-in-korea.jsp
3. http://www.mufilms.org/films/memory-of-forgotten-war/
4. www.stillpresent pasts.org

References

Adorno, T. (2003). *Can One Live After Auschwitz?: A Philosophical Reader* (R. Tiedemann, Ed. & R. Livingstone, Trans.) (1st ed.). Stanford: Stanford University Press.

Assmann, J., & Czaplicka, J. (1995). Collective Memory and Cultural Identity. *New German Critique, 65*(Spring-Summer), 125–133. https://doi.org/10.2307/488538.

Becker, E. (2001, January 12). Army Confirms G.I.'s in Korea Killed Civilians. *The New York Times*. https://www.nytimes.com/2001/01/12/world/army-confirms-gi-s-in-korea-killed-civilians.html

Bedworth, C. (2018, May 10). War, What Is It Good For? Absolutely Nothing! A Protest Art Story. *DailyArtMagazine.Com – Art History Stories* (blog). http://www.dailyartmagazine.com/protest-art-story/

Bleiker, R., & Hoang, Y.-J. (2006). Remembering and Forgetting the Korean War: From Trauma to Reconciliation. In D. Bell (Ed.), *Memory, Trauma and World Politics: Reflections on the Relationship Between Past and Present* (pp. 195–212). New York: Palgrave.

Bogen, M. (2017). Growing Peace: Gandhi, Montessori, and What It Means to Begin with the Children. *Ikeda Center For Peace, Learning, and Dialogue*. http://www.ikedacenter.org/thinkers-themes/themes/humanism/bogen-gandhi-montessori

Borowiec, S. (2018). In South Korea, Resentment of Refugees from the North. This Week in Asia. *South China Morning Post*. https://www.scmp.com/week-asia/politics/article/2178587/south-korea-resentment-refugees-north

Chakrabarti, R. (2013, December 2). South Korea's Schools: Long Days, High Results, sec. Education & Family. https://www.bbc.com/news/education-25187993

Cobb, S. (2013). *Speaking of Violence: The Politics and Poetics of Narrative Dynamics in Conflict Resolution*. Oxford: Oxford University Press.

Choe, Sang-Hun, Charles J. H., & Mendoza, M. (1999, September 30). U.S. Massacre of Civilians in Korean War Described. *Washington Post*. https://www.washingtonpost.com/archive/politics/1999/09/30/us-massacre-of-civilians-in-korean-war-described/2676ee55-71fa-4d8c-8db0-506e142a3081/

Cohen, C. (2004). *Creative Approaches to Reconciliation*. Boston: Brandeis University Press.

Cohen, D. (2003, February 6). What's Behind the U.N. Cover-Up of Picasso's Guernica? *Slate Magazine*. https://slate.com/news-and-politics/2003/02/what-s-behind-the-u-n-cover-up-of-picasso-s-guernica.html

Cumings, Bruce. (1981). *Origins of the Korean War, Liberation and the Emergence of Separate Regimes, 1945–1947*. (Vol. 1) Limited edition, Princeton University Press.

Cumings, B. (2010). *The Korean War: A History* (1st ed.). New York: Modern Library.

Deutsch, M. (1973). *The Resolution of Conflict: Constructive and Destructive Processes*. New Haven: Yale University Press.

Eperjesi, J. R. (2015, April 15). The Unending Korean War: W.E.B Du Bois, Ko Un, and the Women's Peace Walk. *Huffington Post* (blog). https://www.huffingtonpost.com/john-r-eperjesi/the-unending-korean-war-w_b_7048634.html

Freire, P. (2000). *Pedagogy of the Oppressed*. New York: Continuum International Publishing Group.

Habermas, J. (1987). *Theory of Communicative Action: Life, World and System: A Critique of Functionalist Reason*. Boston: Beacon Press.

Hall, S. (1992). The Question of Cultural Identity. In T. McGrew, S. Hall, & D. Held (Eds.), *Modernity and Its Futures: Understanding Modern Societies, Book IV* (pp. 274–326). Cambridge: Polity.

Heine, S. (1994). History, Transhistory, and Narrative History: A Postmodern View of Nishitani's Philosophy of Zen. *Philosophy East and West, 44*(2), 251–278.

Hoberman, J. (2004, November 24). *Pop and Circumstance*. https://www.thenation.com/article/pop-and-circumstance/

Jones, J. (2003, October 25). Was Violence Picasso's Greatest Theme? *The Guardian*, sec. Culture. https://www.theguardian.com/culture/2003/oct/25/1

Keene, J. (2017). Framing Violence, Framing Victims: Picasso's Forgotten Painting of the Korean War. *Cultural History, 6*(1), 80–101. https://doi.org/10.3366/cult.2017.0136.

Korostelina, K. (2007). *Identity, Morality, and Threat: Studies in Violent Conflict*. Lanham: Lexington Books.

Korostelina, K. (2008). History Education and Social Identity. *Identity, 8*(1), 25–45. https://doi.org/10.1080/15283480701787327.

Lin, L., Zhao, Y., Ogawa, M., Hoge, J., & Kim, B. Y. (2009). Whose History? An Analysis of the Korean War in History Textbooks from the United States, South Korea, Japan, and China. *The Social Studies, 100*(5), 222–232.

MacDonald, C. A. (1986). *Korea: The War Before Vietnam*. New York: Springer.

Manojlovic, B. (2013). *Search for Positive Peace in Eastern Slavonia: Contentious Historical Discourses and School Communities*. Doctoral dissertation. George Mason University, Fairfax, USA.

Manojlovic, B. (2017). *Education for Sustainable Peace and Conflict Resilient Communities*. New York: Palgrave Macmillan.

McDonnell, J. (2014). Reimagining the Role of Art in the Relationship Between Democracy and Education. *Educational Philosophy & Theory, 46*(1), 46–58.

Merrill, John. 1989. *Korea: The Peninsular Origins of the War*. Newark, DE: University of Delaware Press.

Millett, A. R. (2019). Korean War | Combatants, Summary, Facts, & Casualties. *Encyclopedia Britannica*. https://www.britannica.com/event/Korean-War

Ministry of Unification. (2017). *Policy on North Korean Defectors*. https://www.unikorea.go.kr/eng_unikorea/relations/statistics/defectors/

Montessori, M. (1943). *Peace and Education* (5th ed.). India: The Theosophical Publishing House. http://archive.org/details/Peace_And_Education_

National Institute of Korean History. (2006). *Korean history. Ministry of Education and Human Resources Development*. http://www.history.go.kr/en/contents/contentsPage.do;jsessionid=BED0956DD58F2C939ABEA7ED7D28E907?groupId=000000000607&menuId=000000000871&pageId=000000000249

Park, Tae Gyun. 2012. *An Ally and Empire: Two Myths of South Korea-United States Relations, 1945–1980*. (trans: Ilsoo David Cho). Sl: The Academy of Korean Studies Press.

Picasso, Pablo. (1951). *Massacre in Korea. Painting Exhibited in the Musée Picasso in Paris*. https://www.pablopicasso.org/massacre-in-korea.jsp

Redmond, C. (2018, October 1). Did the U.S. kill 35,000 Innocents in One Korean War atrocity – Or Is It North Korean Propaganda? *All That's Interesting*. https://allthatsinteresting.com/sinchon-massacre-united-states

Rothbart, D., & Korostelina, K. (Eds.). (2006). *Identity, Morality, and Threat: Studies in Violent Conflict*. Lanham: Lexington Books.

Seth, M. J. (2017, December). South Korea's Economic Development, 1948–1996. *Oxford Research Encyclopedia of Asian History*. https://doi.org/10.1093/acrefore/9780190277727.013.271.

Smith, R. M. (2003). *Stories of Peoplehood: The Politics and Morals of Political Membership*. New York: Cambridge University Press.

Somers, M. R. (1994). The Narrative Constitution of Identity: A Relational and Network Approach. *Theory and Society, 23*(5), 605–649. https://doi.org/10.1007/BF00992905.

Tajfel, H., & Turner, J. C. (2004). The Social Identity Theory of Intergroup Behavior. In J. T. Jost & J. Sidanius (Eds.), *Political Psychology: Key Readings* (Key Readings in Social Psychology) (pp. 276–293). New York: Psychology Press.

The Seoul Times. (2004). Massacre in Korea' to Make Seoul Debut, Picasso Depicts Civilian Killings by U.S. Soldiers. Online article. http://theseoultimes.com/ST/?url=/ST/db/read.php?idx=480

Volkan, V. D. (1997). *Bloodlines: From Ethnic Pride to Ethnic Terrorism* (1st ed.). New York: Farrar, Straus and Giroux.

Volkan, V. D. (2001). Transgenerational Transmissions and Chosen Traumas: An Aspect of Large-Group Identity. *Group Analysis, 34*(1), 79–97. https://doi.org/10.1177/05333160122077730.

Wertsch, J. V. (2008). Collective Memory and Narrative Templates. *Social Research, 75*(1), 133–156. https://doi.org/10.2307/40972055.

Zamponi, L. (2018). *Social Movements, Memory and Media: Narrative in Action in the Italian and Spanish Student Movements*. New York: Springer.

14

Monuments of Historical Trauma as Sites of Artistic Expression, Emotional Processing and Political Negotiation

Andrea Bieler

1 Introduction

This chapter reflects on the phenomenon whereby the aftermath of atrocious violence frequently becomes a space of cultural and religious creativity insofar as artists and architects experience the freedom to develop, publish, perform, or display their works publicly. Accordingly, we can observe that, in many cases, collective trauma not only entails silence, loss, and disorientation but rather holds the potential for creativity and aesthetic response to the experience of shattered worlds. This creativity is embedded in an aesthetic "memory boom" that has been unfolding in recent decades in the arts as well as in the world of museums and public memorials. It reflects a transnational and transcultural response to the memory imperative "never again" first powerfully articulated in the aftermath of the Shoah. We can identify a large number of memorials,

A. Bieler (✉)
University of Basel, Basel, Switzerland
e-mail: andrea.bieler@unibas.ch

K. Wale et al. (eds.), *Post-Conflict Hauntings*, Palgrave Studies in Compromise after Conflict, https://doi.org/10.1007/978-3-030-39077-8_14

museums, and works of visual art that were created in different proximity to the originating atrocities.[1] Some of these artworks grapple with religious questions or imply a spiritual dimension; others do not. These artistic responses follow a different logic than political and legal interventions; however, they might share some sort of overlap.

In what follows, I will engage three interrelated issues that are relevant for memorial sites and art projects, namely: how contestations in the realm of aesthetic commemoration unfold, how ambivalences that are engrained in mass violence are reflected, and how unresolvable dilemmas are negotiated. I will discuss these issues by focusing on selected examples. I will point to similarities and convergences as well as to distinct differences in order to identify ways that haunting memories of a violent past are attended to in particular contexts. In the concluding paragraph I will ask how cognitive and affective dimensions are intertwined in educational concepts that undergird memorial sites and artworks. It will become clear that the concept of travelling memory that focuses on the aesthetic similarities of commemorative practices needs to be nuanced in light of particular contexts. Finally, I will pick up the overarching question of what we can learn from these artistic examples in terms of memorialising past violence. What are the pitfalls? What are the possibilities? What does it take to work aesthetically with haunting memories in anticipation of a more peaceful future?

I have chosen memorials, museums, and an installation that reframe public spaces residents dwell in, tourists visit, or survivors, families, and friends approach. Special attention will be given to a new hybrid genre that emerged in the wake of the memory boom, namely the memorial museum. It embraces the classic purpose of archiving and documenting as well as offering a space for grief and empathy (Sodaro 2018; Williams 2007; Alba 2015).

I distinguish between two genres. The first consists of official national memorials and museums that commemorate state-sponsored violence and which required governmental approval. Examples of these have been chosen from Argentina, the United States, Rwanda, and Cambodia. These sites are frequently placed at historic locations marked by previous violence. Various political and cultural agents played a significant role in the debates prior to the construction of these memorial sites. Inevitably, conflicting interests came to the fore and influenced the aesthetic process.

As contrasting examples to the first genre, I have chosen the work of the German artists Benita Joswig, Jochen and Esther Gerz. Joswig created a series of installations under the overarching motto *Archaeology of the Present*, Gerz and Gerz designed a self-dissolving monument.

Both of these art works had ephemeral forms that functioned as aesthetic interventions in public spaces. Their work will be introduced as examples of a different aesthetic approach in terms of the participation and interaction of visitors as well as the ephemeral character of the displayed objects. Both artists experimented with more dynamic practices of commemoration.

In what follows I do not intend to do a close interpretation of individual sites. Nor do I aim at making substantial comparisons regarding the political and historical nature of these events and circumstances. Instead, I would like to highlight shared challenges as well as distinct differences that come to the fore in very different contexts with regard to the aesthetic, formative, and performative questions embedded in larger political debates.

2 Memorials, Museums and Art Works as Contested Terrain

Many artworks and memorials reflect the fact that remembering violence is a contested terrain. This terrain is shaped in three ways: by conflicting political narratives and the politics of voice, namely who is allowed to speak and whose perspectives are depicted, by diverging aesthetic approaches and convictions, and finally by the aspect of time in the intergenerational transmission of memories (Achugar 2016; Argenti and Schramm 2010). The latter also includes changing patterns of interpretation that dominate public discourse in relation to a violent past.

Many conflicts deal with aesthetic issues and grapple with the question of how works of art and museum designs relate to past atrocities that have powerful repercussions in the present.

In order to explore this field of contestation more satisfactorily, a theoretical approach is needed that moves beyond the alternative between a presentist and an essentialist approach. A presentist approach comprehends works of art as mere constructions that serve certain purposes for the present. An essentialist approach understands them as straightforward representations of a past that can be "reproduced" by those who remember it. The sociologist Jeffrey K. Olick suggests as an alternative a process relational approach for the analysis of commemorative practices that is also useful for the analysis of the arts (Olick 2007). Olick's theory focuses on collective remembering as a thoroughly interactive phenomenon in which the connections between the present and the past are constantly negotiated. In this vein, collective memory can be understood as a field of contestation which exists in constant flux. In this field, official and vernacular memory is navigated and diverging narratives of a violent past are both shaped and contradicted by the arts. These narratives are shaped by different groups within a society, such as politicians, human rights organisations that represent victims and survivors, artists, and educators. In this vein, controversies around memorials and artworks can also have an impact on public discourse. By analysing examples from Germany, Argentina, Rwanda, and Cambodia with a process relational approach, a more nuanced understanding of how memorial sites reflect struggles and negotiations in the field of memory politics is possible.

2.1 Conflicting Political Narratives and the Politics of Voice

In particular, official national memorial museums have been steeped in deep controversies, as they carry the weight of atrocious violence caused by preceding governments. Accordingly, the question of how stories of violent conflicts, genocide, and enduring structural violence are depicted and interpreted becomes an issue of political identity formation in the present.

The Memorial to the Murdered Jews of Europe, which is situated in front of the German Reichstag (the parliament) in Berlin, is a classic example of the heated debate in which different actors struggled with the question what kind of memorial is needed and appropriate (Fig. 14.1).

Fig. 14.1 Memorial to the Murdered Jews of Europe © Ralf Bieler, used with permission

Twelve years of conflict and controversies preceded the inauguration of the memorial in 2005. During this time period a contentious point of discussion was whether the memorial should focus solely on the murder of Jewish persons and thus leave out other groups of victims who were persecuted and killed under the Nazi regime. Furthermore, the architect Peter Eisenman, who had won the design competition, proposed a very non-didactical approach. He deliberately rejected any explanatory framing of his work. He also refused to make suggestions on how the memorial could be used for public commemoration ceremonies. The issues of the vastness of the field of stelae, its location in front of the *Reichstag*, and the aesthetic concept were all constantly under debate. A year after its inauguration one of the promoters of the project, the journalist Lea Rosh, caused another upheaval by suggesting that a tooth that she had found in the Bergen-Belsen concentration camp should be inserted in one of the stelae as well as a star of David that a Jewish person had worn during the Nazi dictatorship (Wefing 2005).

In January 2017, with the resurgence of right-wing populist parties all over Europe, the debate took a new, uncanny turn. One of the leading figures of the *Alternative für Deutschland* (Alternative for Germany),

Björn Höcke, insisted on a radical change to the German memorial culture, calling *The Memorial to the Murdered Jews of Europe* a *Mahnmal der Schande,* a memorial of dishonour, in the midst of Berlin. He claimed that Germans were the only people in the world that would have erected such a memorial in the centre of their capital.[2] Since then, such provocations have become a political strategy for neo-fascist protagonists to establish their agenda in the political arena. One way to speak freely again in *völkisch,* racist, terms about German identity is to attack such sites of commemoration. These statements were obviously inacceptable for many citizens and faced a huge opposition.

Yet problems also arise when controversies around questions of how to remember a violent past are suppressed. *The Kigali Genocide Memorial Centre* is an example of a memorial site that takes its mission to provide moral education after the Rwandan genocide against the Tutsi very seriously. It seeks to be part of the efforts to promote peace and reconciliation with the intention of preventing future ethnically motivated violence.

At the same time the centre works in the climate of a regime that does not allow an open debate about the past, but rather criminalises anyone who does not follow the official government narrative. It is troubling to see that under the powerful leadership of President Kagame it is still not possible to have an open debate (Reyntjens 2015). In particular, the mention of the human rights abuses of the Rwandan Patriotic Front is characterised as "divisionism" and subject to punishment. The imposed constraints are reflected in the memorial's permanent exhibit. It is composed of three parts: one part is entitled *Wasted Lives* and attends to genocides around the world, the second section *Genocide* tells the story of the Rwandan genocide, and the third section *Our Future Lost* is dedicated to the memory of killed children.

The section *Genocide* chronologically outlines the conditions and developments that led to the genocide. It begins with the time before colonisation in which a peaceful coexistence of eighteen tribes is portrayed. Harmony and unity are the main metaphors through which this era is depicted. The undergirding narrative that the exhibition creates is one of collective victimisation, although the atrocious activities of the Hutu paramilitary organisation, *Interahamwe*, are obviously mentioned. The major blame, however, is directed towards external forces, mainly the pervasive colonial ideology of ethnic division that planted the seeds of hatred. This one-dimensional explanation paradoxically obscures the agency and responsibility of the Rwandan population and the government at that time. It matches well, however, with President Kagame's ideology of national unity which brushes over and suppresses an open discussion about the repercussions of ethnic division immediately after the genocide and into the present. Accordingly, the memorial centre becomes complicit in activities that instrumentalise genocide memory. Amy Sodaro states it in this way:

> Rather than a fragmentation of memory and narratives—including those that look critically at the causes and effects of the genocide, as proposed in theories like Olick's politics of regret ... in the Kigali Centre the genocide memory appears consolidated into the single dominant version that supports the goals and dogma of the government. This consolidation threatens to usurp for political purposes the memory of those who most need remembrance and acknowledgment and potentially undermines the Kigali's Centre's goals of learning from the past, preventing genocide and human rights abuses in the future, and healing this country that is still deeply wounded. (Sodaro 2018, 109)

2.2 Fearing the Closure of an Open Wound

Another dimension in the field of contested collective memory culture is found in two questions. Under which circumstances do memorial sites numb political conflicts that are still unresolved? And do memorial sites have a tendency to disempower the productive side of memory that takes into account the haunting quality of memories?

For instance, conflicts arose in Argentina about the erection of an official memorial that reflected the human rights abuses during the Argentinian dictatorship. In Buenos Aires, ten human rights organisations made a proposal to local officials of the city to allocate a site and a public memorial park that would include the names of the disappeared ones, the *desaparecidos* (Sion 2008, 25f). In 1998 a law was passed by the local officials that included plans for the realisation of the proposed site of commemoration. This plan, however, was opposed by some human rights groups that represented the families and friends of the *desaparecidos*. They were concerned that an official memorial site would create a kind of closure and that such institutionalised memory would brush over the still unresolved murder cases and the open wounds attached to them.

These organisations raised a political and aesthetic issue that became pertinent in other countries as well. The suspicion that memorials could paradoxically create amnesia instead of historic attentiveness, political alertness, and productive restlessness, is a debate that also emerged in Germany in the 1980s. James E. Young discusses, in his work on Holocaust memorials, the rise of counter monuments that critically engaged the aesthetic and political premises of their very existence (Young 1993, 27).

Artists like Jochen and Esther Gerz, Norbert Rademacher, and Horst Hoheisel shared a deep mistrust in monumental forms as they had been systematically exploited by the Nazis:

> To their minds, the didactic logic of monuments, their demagogical rigidity, recalled too closely traits they associated with fascism itself. Their monuments against fascism, therefore, would amount to a monument against itself: against the traditionally didactic function of monuments, against their tendency to displace they would have us contemplate—and finally, against the authoritarian propensity in all art that reduces viewers to passive spectators. (Young 1993, 28)

For example, in 1986, Jochen and Esther Gerz designed a self-consuming monument entitled *Gegen-Denkmal*. This counter monument was placed in a fairly ugly spot in the centre of a shopping street in Harburg, at that time a run-down suburb of Hamburg. The monument consisted of a 12-metre-high, hollow aluminium pillar covered with a layer of soft, dark lead. An inscription close to its base read in German, French, English, Russian, Hebrew, Arabic, and Turkish:

> We invite the citizens of Harburg, and visitors to the town, to add their names here to ours. In doing so, we commit ourselves to remain vigilant. As more and more names cover this 12 meter tall lead column, it will gradually be lowered into the ground. One day it will have disappeared

completely, and the site of the Harburg monument against fascism will be empty. In the end, it is only we ourselves who can rise up against injustice. (Young 1993, 30)

And indeed, this self-consuming memorial finally disappeared in 1991, leaving behind only those who remembered it and their memory of the memorial. According to Jochen and Esther Gerz, the visitors who left their names and messages became the "invisible sculpture" in society. The artists had the hope that one day physical memorials would no longer be necessary; instead, the internalised memories and images of the monument would inspire a vigilance now locked in the mind's eye (Young 1993, 33). Such memories without physical objects would finally correspond to the invisible hauntings of past atrocities that cannot be contained in particular times and places.

Artists who are aware of the ambiguities of aesthetic expressions in remembering a violent past are often keen to reflect on haunting memories, not only as a destructive but also as a productive force that provides a necessary unsettling drive for dealing with the past. There is an apprehension that if one gives those haunting spirits a place by erecting memorials set in stone or by building a memorial museum, one might paradoxically create more oblivion or apathy that could silence the quest for truth and justice.

In that sense, the arts can make a different contribution than what we would expect in other arenas of social life. For instance, in trauma therapies that work with a resource-oriented approach, the focus is to calm down and disempower haunting memories that are out of control and causing pain in order to create a safer environment for the patient.[3]

On a related note to the aesthetic debate, the philosopher Jacques Derrida calls for a "hauntology" that rejects a clear-cut, linear understanding of past, present, and future. Instead, hauntology calls for an attentiveness to the "non-contemporaneity of the living present" (Derrida 2006, XIX). In *Specters of Marx*, Derrida proceeds from the assumption that the possibility of a just future depends on our readiness "to learn to live *with* ghosts." He insists on an obligation to live not solely in the present but "beyond all living present," aware of and attentive to those already dead or not yet born. According to Derrida, being neither fully present nor fully absent, ghosts belong to a liminal *hauntological* domain (Derrida 2006, XVIII). This domain opens up the possibility for practices of commemoration that do not offer false consolation but provide a sense of an unsettling awareness that neither closure nor the continued cultivation of hate-filled memories is an option.

In the Argentinian example, we can argue that those who were in favour of the proposal for the *Parque de la Memoria* issued a mission statement that included a hauntological perspective:

> The monument to the Victims of State terrorism is going to be erected on the river banks because it is in its waters that many of the victims were thrown. It is not the intention of this memorial to close any wounds that cannot be closed or replace truth and justice. Nothing will restore real peace to the relatives that have not been able to know the final fate of their loved ones, savagely tortured and murdered, and nothing will ever replace the social emptiness created by their absence. (Sion 2008, 26)

As the Argentinian case shows, it is not as easy to judge from the intentions of political agents and artists or from the actual effects a memorial site has on visitors, if such art works indeed provoke amnesia or suppression.

The *Parque de La Memoria* that was finally built was dedicated to victims of state-sponsored terrorism during the military dictatorship between 1976 and 1983. It was placed along the Rio de la Plata in the Belgrano close to Buenos Aires. The park was also deliberately selected as it is in close proximity to a detention centre where inmates who had been accused of being enemies of the state were tortured. It is also close to the airport from which prisoners were taken up into the air and dropped into the river or the ocean. Hundreds of civilians were killed in this way and "disappeared" under governmental terrorism.

The final memorial was designed to cut into the landscape like an open wound. The architect who conceptualised the design was inspired by the work of Maya Ying Lin, who created a similar design effect.[4] In Buenos Aires, a wall was erected as the centre piece that contains the names of 9000 murdered victims as well as empty plaques for the *desaparecidos*. It is surrounded by eighteen different sculptures that have been installed in the park. The empty plaques, symbolising the cruel logic of letting people disappear, were of major importance for critics who were fearful that the memorial would close the case and disempower the voices of those speaking on behalf of the *desaparecidos*.

2.3 Changing Patterns of Remembering Through the Generations

The contested field of aesthetic commemoration is also in constant flux due to changing narratives as history is transmitted from one generation to the next. These changes effect the experiences of younger visitors at memorial sites who were born after particular atrocities happened and who "represent" the perspective of either the perpetrator or the victim groups. In many contexts, identity formation through the politics of representation becomes increasingly difficult for subsequent generations. Accordingly, understanding collective memory as a field that is in constant flux acknowledges the factors of time and intergenerational transmission as shaping collective memory.

Narratives of a violent past that were perceived as common-sense paradigms in one generation might change in the succeeding generation. For example, for many decades after World War II it was very difficult to talk about the victimhood of German civilians in a nuanced way in the public. Often, those who had brought up the subject were right-wing politicians who wanted to downplay the devastating role Nazi Germany played during the war. In the mid-1990s things changed and it became possible to talk about the destruction of German cities by the Allied Forces that caused the death of thousands of inhabitants, mainly in urban centres. This change was also reflected in the work of artists.

Benita Joswig's installation *altäre* serves as an example of this shift in interpretative patterns. She designed this art work in the mid-1990s for the *Messeplatz* in Kassel, Germany, a city that was entirely destroyed. Approximately 10,000 inhabitants died during the fire storm which lasted through two nights.

Joswig's installation was part of a larger cycle of temporary projects that she entitled *Archaeology of the Present*. Through archival research of historic maps and photo material, she reconstructed where the houses at the *Messeplatz* once stood and where the streets were previously located. She invited one hundred inhabitants of Kassel to participate in the installation by asking if they would donate a table that they currently used in their kitchen or dining room. The table would be placed at the *Messeplatz* in the locations where people once met over common meals (Joswig 2003) (Fig. 14.2).

This installation was, by its very nature, only temporary. Joswig's work had the character of an ephemeral intervention. It brought traces of the past into the present by creating an effect of alienation. By asking inhabitants of Kassel to give away a table they were using in their ordinary lives, they were also asked to put themselves into the scene. The installation, which was up for three days, created a space for conversation between residents who had survived the fire storm and those who had no idea that the parking space they were using was built on the rubbles of the inner city.

Ten years earlier such an art project would have probably fallen under the suspicion of being a right-wing activity of revanchists intent on denying German aggression during World War II and emphasising only

Fig. 14.2 Installation "altäre" © Michael Moll, used with permission

German victimhood. Yet in the mid-1990s the topic gained greater credibility in the wider society. A space opened up to talk about victimhood in times of war in more nuanced ways including the entanglement of aggressive foreign policies and warfare and the simultaneous suffering of civilians in Germany. In this environment, it was possible for Joswig to use her work to draw attention to the destruction of a German city during World War II and to enrich the conversation about commemorative practices. She opened up a space for citizens of different generations to share their experiences and knowledge about that time period. In particular, those who experienced the bombing had the opportunity to share how these two nights had shaped their lives in the decades that followed.

There was, however, another layer to this work. It can also be understood as an embodied practice of hauntology. By placing tables where once houses stood, the void created by the destruction became visible. For a few days, people mingled and walked through this void filling it with conversations, walking in silence, and listening to a jazz trumpetist who played sounds reminiscent of the sirens that had alerted residents of the coming attacks. This intervention had a temporal character. It offered a window for unexpected conversations as well as an aesthetic experience of a place that had once been the vibrant centre of a medieval town.

And finally, it touched upon a deeply human experience: what does it mean to enjoy a meal together or to lose that fellowship around a table? By posing the question: "Could you imagine your table as an altar?" Joswig also hinted at the religious connotation implied by sharing a meal around a table. The term "altar" refers also to the sacralisation of the table. This reference has multiple ambiguous layers. It hints at the altar as the object and the place where people commune, not only with each other, but also with God. Thus, the notion of the altar also potentially denotes redemptive communion or community. Yet it also implies the contested subject of sacrifice found in civic religious discourse about war around the globe. This discourse entails the interpretation of soldiers' deaths as a sacrifice given for the sake of a nation's freedom.

Joswig's approach to installations as aesthetic interventions in public spaces resonates with Joseph Beuys' concept of the social sculpture (*Soziale Plastik*) which allows ordinary citizens to engage in highly relevant social and cultural issues by means of collective aesthetic practice

(Harlan et al. 1986). The social sculpture blurs the distinction between artists and visitors and opens up a space of shared participation. Within the selected location, the installation *altäre* enabled multi-layered interactions that unfolded in a limited span of time. The aesthetic process created an ephemeral commemorative space for various groups of people that evoked diverging memories and questions.

2.4 Negotiating Aesthetic and Political Ambivalence

Another issue arising in conflicts around memorials is the aesthetic and political negotiation of ambivalence, especially with regard to war memorials. Some memorials reflect the ambivalent ways in which historical events are remembered. On the one hand, the ambivalence arises from the historical events themselves. For instance, in many wars individual soldiers have been both perpetrators and victims during their time of service in the army. Many veterans have to grapple with both experiences. And when the wars that were supposed to turn them into heroes are lost, they come home as part of a defeated army and feel welcomed back home in ambiguous ways. On the other hand, in most cases war memorials attempt to erase this ambivalence; war memorials are deliberately one-sided with regard to who and what is supposed to be remembered. This erasure, however, holds the potential for new conflicts to emerge. At the same time, such memorial spaces are important for the social recognition of veterans who feel devalued, betrayed, or abandoned when they return home.

In order to discuss the issue further, I have chosen the *Vietnam Veterans Memorial* in Washington DC. It is the official national war memorial dedicated to the US-American soldiers who died in the Vietnam War. The American War, as it is called in the view of the Vietnamese people, resulted in an enormous death toll. The US-American involvement in this war lasted from the mid-1950s until 1975. Approximately five million Vietnamese people were killed or wounded; another twelve million were displaced and had to flee from their homes. An estimated 58,000 US-American soldiers were killed or reported missing in action (Herring 1986). Most of them died at the average age of twenty-one due to the compulsory military draft that the US government exercised at that time. The returning soldiers became highly ambiguous figures in US society; many protesters of the war saw them as agents of merciless killing. The senseless devastation of the Vietnamese village of My Lai, where 400 civilians were killed, became a gruesome point of reference. From the point of view of the promoters of the war, the returning soldiers had failed their mission since the US-American army did not win. Many of the returning veterans perceived themselves as walking dead, as living shadows in a society that did not receive them back in respectful ways. About one third of the returning veterans were diagnosed with post-traumatic stress disorder and many of them experienced a profound disorientation as they were not able to continue the lives they had led before Vietnam (Kulka et al. 2013).

There are various layers of ambivalence related to the memory of this war. One layer is the complicated perception of the returning soldiers. On a political level the majority of the US-American population severely opposed the war in the end, although many had embraced it in the beginning. The way the war ended in loss had smashed the myth of American invincibility. Against this background, conflicts arose around how to publicly remember the Vietnam War and the human beings who died in it.

The US government at that time was not willing to create a public space of remembrance and learning that would embrace these complexities. Instead, it was determined to push for a memorial that would entirely leave out the atrocities that were done to the Vietnamese people.

During the early 1980s it was still difficult to publicly discuss why this war had been waged in the first place and what interests it had supposedly protected. Finally, the political decision was made to create a war memorial as a space that would exclusively remember the American soldiers who had died in the Vietnam War. For one of the initiators of the memorial initiative, Jan Scruggs, this space of commemoration was supposed to help veterans gain social recognition and offer them the opportunity to connect and build networks of support amongst themselves. The involvement of the veterans hints at another layer of ambiguity in this process. Many soldiers had to suffer from the consequences of the war psychologically and physically. Many suffered not only from post-traumatic stress disorder but also from moral injury that included a profound shattering of their value systems. These soldiers who had to live with these hardships were looking for a place where they could gather and leave their social isolation behind—at least for a moment.

In 1981, in the midst of these controversies, a design competition for an official national war memorial took place. Maya Ying Lin's proposal was chosen out of a pool of 1421 submissions. She designed a black stonework with the names of 57,661 soldiers who died in Vietnam (Goldman Rubin 2017). Their names were etched in the surface of the masonry. Over time more than three hundred additional names were added. The stonework consisted of a dark grey granite wall shaped as a V, with one side pointing to the Lincoln Memorial and the other to the Washington Memorial, placing it amid the historic narrative of the founding fathers of the Unites States.

Lin's intent was to symbolically create a wound-like opening in the earth as a gesture towards the enormous loss of soldiers. From a bird's-eye perspective, the design looks like a huge scar cut in a zigzag shape into the earth. This design was an inspiration for further memorials and museums to come. The wall of names situated in the Memorial Parque in Buenos Aires, Argentina, has a similar V-shape. Also, the main structure of the Jewish Museum in Berlin is a shattered Star of David whose V-shaped ends perforate the surrounding *Topography of Terror* (Fig. 14.3).

As visitors enter the *Vietnam Veterans Memorial*, they walk on a pathway that goes slightly down into the "wound". The material Lin used for the wall of names has a reflective quality. Those who are reading or searching for names can recognise the reflection of their own face in the wall. In this way they also become visible in the commemorative scene. In some spots the sky with its moving clouds is also reflected.

This memorial grapples with the tragedy of young lives lost, but it does not turn them into heroes or sacrifices for the nation. Lin deliberately wanted to move away from the sculptural tradition of war monuments depicting military generals on rushing horses surrounded by a group of unified and determined soldiers. In the same way, no figurative allegories appear in the design, such as angel-like figures, that symbolise peace or justice.[5] Lin's memorial explicitly breaks away from this European and North American tradition of heroic war monuments that radiate a triumphant ethos. Since it withholds itself from any victorious symbols, it

Fig. 14.3 Vietnam Veterans Memorial © Oliver Sallet, used with permission

instead displays a stunning simplicity that gestures towards deep sorrow, grief, and tragedy.

The memorial has since become a location where family members, friends, and veterans go in order to commemorate the US-American soldiers who died in Vietnam. One can see visitors searching for names, touching names on the wall, and laying down personal items or flowers. In the midst of the vast number of names carved into the wall, moments of intimacy are created. People stand in silence; sometimes they cry.

Since its inception there have been lots of controversies around this memorial (Reston 2017). Some disapproved of its abstraction. Other critics complained that it did not honour the surviving soldiers because it did not portray the death of these young men as a worthwhile sacrifice given for the glory of the American nation. And some opponents expressed the opinion that Lin's proposal reflected mainly disgust towards the Vietnam War.

These accusations were addressed by reinserting the traditional war monument aesthetics into the scene—a move Maya Ying Lin certainly was not fond of. A 50-foot-high flagpole with the American flag accompanied by an 8-foot-high statue entitled *The Three Soldiers* were added to the outlet of the memorial to placate fierce critics. The statue depicts three soldiers in uniform, a White Anglo-American soldier standing slightly in the leading position, accompanied by an African-American and a Latino soldier. The sculptor, Frederick Hart, intended to depict a sense of togetherness among comrades as well as individual strength and determination (Reston 2017).

These additions need to be understood as the result of the political as well as the aesthetic conflicts that Maya Ying Lin's memorial provoked from the time of the design competition up to its inception. They stand in contrast to her design and certainly damaged its consistency. The statue *The Three Soldiers* installed next to Maya Ying Lin's memorial reflects the contestations of the time period. These tensions produced aesthetic inconsistencies and new ambivalences. They reflect a very ambiguous past of atrocious warfare and its challenges for the present. Even today, the United States is a country divided around the questions of how to remember the US-American soldiers who died in Vietnam and how to commemorate the devastation caused by the Vietnam War.

2.5 Dealing with Dilemmas

Finally, many memorials and art works need to grapple with unresolvable dilemmas. Artists and architects have to choose between alternatives that all seem inappropriate for certain reasons. Relating aesthetically to the memory of mass killings with their overwhelming death tolls creates huge challenges. A striking example of what causes such predicaments is the absence of dead or identifiable bodies, a direct result of the erasure of the singularity of human lives perpetrated in mass killings. In many cases, the remains of the dead are unidentifiable or the bodies of victims cannot be found. This erasure makes it impossible to remember each victim with respect and attention to his or her individual live story. This unresolvable dilemma is a challenge to the aesthetic, cultural, and religious collective memory culture.

In various contexts the logics of annihilation and genocidal erasure have created deep psychological and spiritual damage for family members, friends, and survivors as they amplify often unaddressed issues of unresolved grief. The absence of bodies is deeply complicated in many cultures and religious traditions. The human need to find some form of consolation by accompanying the deceased on a journey from the land of the living into the realm of the dead has become impossible. Consequently, problems arise when the living are denied these ritual and symbolic journeys which are supposed to help them to return to their own lives in transformed ways. Since performing the necessary rites is not an obtainable option, the deceased as well as the mourners are trapped in an in-between place.

In the aftermath of massive collective violence, relatives often claim that the remains of their loved ones should be found and buried properly. These claims are understood as a crucial form of symbolic reparation. These claims point to the significance of a basic human need.

This urgent desire to find a place of rest for the deceased has a religious or spiritual dimension as well. Burial rites in Judaism, Christianity, Islam, and Buddhism normally require the individual remains, in the form of either corpses or ashes, in order for the symbolic rituals of their respective burial rites. These are rites related to soul release, hope for resurrection, or peaceful rest for the dead.

A striking example of how the absence of identifiable bodily remains is highly problematic is the memorial in Choeung Ek, Cambodia. This memorial is closely located to one of the infamous killing fields of the Khmer Rouge regime. At Choeung Ek, 9000 bodies were merciless thrown into mass graves. Performance studies scholar Brigitte Sion, who researched this site thoroughly, describes it as follows:

> Between 1975 and 1979, the Khmer Rouge regime, under the leadership of Pol Pot, caused the death of about 1.5 million people, or a quarter of the population. Thirty years later, memorialization of the genocide stands at the center of conflicted interests – the government's politics of reconciliation, Buddhist beliefs in Karma, economic development, mass tourism opportunities, international law, and national historical narratives. Located ten miles southeast of Phnom-Penh, Choeung Ek is described, on the offi-

> cial flyer, as 'hell on earth in the 20th century'. A former orchard and Chinese cemetery, it was the main killing field where prisoners from Tuol Sleng prison were transported to be murdered between 1977 and 1978. When Vietnamese troops discovered the site, they found about 9,000 bodies in mass graves; many were headless, their hands tied and naked; the separated heads were blindfolded. The skulls and bones showed traces of bullets, knives, and other forms of violence inflicted upon men, women, and children. Babies were thrown against trees and instantly killed. (Sion 2011, 71f)

At the memorial site a monumental stupa was erected as a centre piece: a translucent tower that preserves about 5000 skulls and further remaining bones. These remains are displayed for the visitors who are almost exclusively tourists. In Khmer Buddhist belief, a stupa is a sacred object that contains the remains of revered individuals. Remembering the dead as respected people who have names, and are thus identifiable, serves to increase the merit of those who remember (Hughes 2006, 261). Without identified bodies, this practice is not possible and the stupa is not warranted.

Sion points to the fact that the erected stupa, however, is a rather frightening object for the local population. In Khmer Buddhist belief, human beings who die a violent death have to be cremated or buried as quickly as possible; otherwise, the spirits of those victims will haunt the surviving community. A speedy cremation also helps the spirit of the deceased move successfully into the next karmic realm. The stupa at Choeung Ek, however, is a desacralised and senseless object for the locals, since a stupa is not meant to keep unidentifiable remains of ordinary people (Sion 2011, 76f).

This particular commemorative practise seems inadequate, even harmful, for the local population. It points to a larger spiritual issue for Khmer Buddhists who feel they have to live with restless spirits since the mass killings of the Khmer Rouge dictatorship left millions of bodily remains unidentified up until this very day. Therefore, Cheong Ek attracts mainly tourists who visit from abroad and want to learn about the atrocities committed by the Khmer Rouge regime. It failed in its attempt to create a site of remembrance, grief, and reverence to the dead for the local population due to its cultural and religious insensitivity.

3 Conclusions

My journey into various memorial sites concludes by addressing the cognitive and affective dimensions in prosthetic memory and further learning processes. In a second step, I will revisit the concept of travelling memory and finally I will summarise my deliberations by asking what can we learn from this analysis for future aesthetic works that commemorate atrocious violence.

3.1 Memorial Museums and Art Projects as Sites of Learning? How Cognitive and Affective Dimensions Intertwine

In regard to memorial museums, the question often arises as to what visitors are expected to learn and whether an undergirding core message shapes particular exhibitions. These questions are reflected in how artefacts and visuals are displayed, how mnemonic devices are introduced, and how historical narratives are formed. If the focus is on documentation, one will likely find a narrative presented, for example, through texts, photos, videos, or artefacts that seek to create a consistent story line or message for visitors. If there is an emphasis on the creation of affective impulses, such as empathy with victims, particular aesthetic means are employed. For instance, documenting the time line of how a genocide was painstakingly planned and purposefully exercised might evoke a sense of shock in someone who studies it for the first time. In this case, the cognitive dimension of conveying facts is emphasised in the display while at the same time emotional responses are expected to be released. However, if a visitor enters a room filled with bones and skulls, a different kind of response is produced. The display of human remains is limited in its ability to explain complex historical events. It points instead to the gruesome gravity of atrocious killing. In this vein, remains are intended to create an affective response. Consequently, learning processes occur on both the cognitive and the affective levels and are constantly intertwined. Displays in memorial museums shift their focus in one single exhibition in order to provide a multi-layered experience.

Another layer within the affective dimension is the interrelation between public grief messages and private mourning. For instance, the *Kigali Genocide Memorial Centre* in Rwanda seeks to attend to both dimensions. The website of the memorial introduces the intention of providing a space for grieving and learning:

> The centre was officially opened on 7 April 2004 to mark the tenth commemoration of the 1994 genocide against the Tutsi in Rwanda. The memorial is the final resting place for up to 259,000 victims of the genocide and serves as a place where people can grieve for their lost loved ones and remember them. It also serves as a museum where both local and international visitors can learn about the history, implementation and consequences of the genocide. (Kigali Genocide Memorial Centre)

The structure of the memorial consists of two distinct spaces, namely a documentation centre and the grave site, which consists of concrete surfaces placed in a terraced park leading down the hill. The graveyard has three purposes: it is the place for commemoration ceremonies, it is considered to be a resting place for the dead, and it is designed to be a place of intimate mourning and expressions of grief. One can observe from time to time a few individuals remaining in silence at this site and flowers are placed on the concrete surfaces.[6] Particularly tourists, who do not have lost loved ones, are instructed by museum guides to dwell in the place in a silent and respectful manner and to respect the calm of the dead.

The educational framework of the documentation centre has a clear, yet constrained, focus. It is geared towards an international as well as a local visitorship. It focuses on the genocide against the Tutsi by giving a historical explanation, introducing the colonial legacies involved, and describing the various waves of "ethnic cleansing" that happened since the 1950s. It offers a detailed documentation of the massive atrocities that occurred in 1994. It is also clear about the failure of the United Nations and its troops and political entities, since they did not help to prevent or stop the violence of the genocide.

It focuses on the genocide against the Tutsi by also including the Hutu victims who had resisted the violent political developments. The exhibition, however, does not mention the counter aggression against the Hutu that finally stopped the genocide and simultaneously unleashed an enormous amount of revengeful killing. Since the public message of the museum does not leave room for this complicated part of Rwanda's history, it does not offer a space for all visitors. This includes the current youth as well as the remaining relatives who come from Hutu families and whose fathers, who might have been perpetrators, were also killed. This is a missed opportunity to deal with complicated grief and ambiguous loss in this particular narrative. The Kigali Centre demonstrates how affective and formative aspects can also be intertwined in problematic ways.

Furthermore, the affective dimension of learning processes is visible in the phenomenon of prosthetic memory that is particularly at work in memorial museums.

By displaying graphic images that depict violence, listening to video testimonies of survivors that lift up intimate moments of affection or loss, or by exhibiting human remains that point to the raw facts of violent death, visitors who have no personal relationship are invited into a space of deeply felt connection to a past they did not live through. Alison Landsberg coined the term *prosthetic memory* in order to describe affective learning processes in which an individual is placed in the proverbial shoes of another who has experienced a traumatic event (Landsberg 2004, 4). The hope is to instil the ethical imperative of "never again" in memorial museums visitors by inviting them to empathise with the victims' perspective. These learning processes are called prosthetic memory because they derive from engagement with mediated representations and not from immediate personal experiences. In this vein, walking through an exhibit that depicts the history of a particular genocide can evoke prosthetic memory. According to Landsberg, these memories can be useful in moral learning processes. Since they "feel real," they can potentially nourish a constructive political commitment. We might argue, however, that they transform a haunting sense of moral helplessness too easily into an educational programme. This kind of programme can foster the illusion that learning from past wrongs will automatically create a better future by enhancing moral sensibilities of the visitors.

3.2 Travelling Memory?

The transnational memory boom, mentioned in the introduction, spread across all continents, bringing forth striking similarities in sites of commemoration.

This phenomenon can be discovered, for example, in memorial museums around the globe in regard to their use of mnemonic media, such as the display of bones, skulls, and children's photos, or through walls with names of killed persons. There are also similarities in the ways individual narratives and testimonies are used in the context of video installations or in relation to visual material documenting atrocities. These observations point to the fact that a global aesthetic memory culture has developed in the second half of the twentieth century in which the imperative "never again," first powerfully articulated in the aftermath of the Shoah, found a material gestalt. Some scholars have captured this development with the concept of *travelling memory* (Erll 2011). In particular, Holocaust memorials and memorial museum were inspirational examples of this concept in different parts of the world. For instance, we can trace direct influences in how the Kigali Centre was inspired by the Beth Shalom Holocaust Centre in the United Kingdom. The Rwandese government entrusted James and Stephen Smith, two architects with extensive experiences in constructing Holocaust memorial centres, for example, in Cape Town, with designing the Kigali Centre. Both had been very impressed with the British example. Maya Ying Lin's Veterans Memorial, particularly the wall of names, also served as a model in various places, for example, in the *Parque de La Memoria* in Buenos Aires.

The discussed examples, however, show that a closer look at exhibits and art works reveal that similar displays can create differing results, largely due to nationally bound agendas, as seen in memory politics in Rwanda. The display of human remains, for instance, does not speak for itself but is in need of further narrative framing. Similar displays can provoke different meanings due to religious and cultural beliefs, as in the example of the display of skulls in the stupa in Choeung Ek.

3.3 Transforming Haunting Memories?

What can we learn from the introduced memorial sites and artworks with regard to the difficulties and the prospects of transforming haunting memories?

First of all, it needs to be highlighted that we cannot make the general claim that engaging memorial sites automatically leads to resistance to the rise of authoritarian regimes, right-wing populism, and practices of exclusion. There exists no causal relationship between remembering past violence and preventing it in the future.

The ethics of "never again" that undergirds many sites of commemoration is articulated in a world in which genocide and structural political violence do not cease to exist. This is the context in which we visit sites, engage with artworks, and develop practices of commemoration. These practices are in need of critical reflection, since many of them say as much about present political agendas as they do about the relation to past atrocities. Especially "memorial museums reveal the political priorities and goals of the regimes that build them, reminding us that memory remains very much in the domain of the nation-state, with the past being simply another arena for enacting present politics" (Sodaro 2018, 11).

In that vein, it is crucial that debates around memorial sites and artworks leave room for contestation, for minority voices and for the perspectives of different generations. Notably, installations that do not have the intention of creating "eternal messages" allow for this kind of multi-perspectivity.

In a time of global exchange and of "travelling memory" the question arises if there are art forms that express more indigenous ways of attending to a violent past. It might be questionable if in the future European and North American examples of Holocaust memorials will serve as aesthetic blueprints with regard to different geographic contexts and different atrocities.

And finally: There seems to be a productive side to the phenomenon of haunting memories in relation to artworks insofar as they give room for the complexities of mixed emotions and the remembrance of ambivalent constellations between perpetrators and victims. Also, artwork that has a productive haunting quality will not seek to create numbing and superficial closure but will inspire a sense of openness and commitment in those who engage with it.

Notes

1. Artistic responses also developed in the areas of autobiographical and fictional writing, musical compositions, dance, and theatre. While it is pivotal to explore these artforms as commemorative practices in the aftermath of atrocious violence as well, they will not be discussed in this chapter.
2. https://www.youtube.com/watch?v=U8lFEy5QTko. Accessed 20 November 2018.
3. This is at least true for therapeutic approaches that seek to activate resources in patients rather than aim for exposure therapy. An example hereof can be found in the work of Reddemann (2011).
4. See further the discussion of Lin's work in this chapter.
5. See Smart History. Khan academy video on Maya Ying Lin's concept: https://www.youtube.com/watch?v=wuxjTxxQUTs. Accessed 4 November 2018.
6. More ethnographic work is needed in order to assess if this site is vital for many survivors and family members who have had to deal with the loss of loved ones due to the genocide.

References

Achugar, M. (2016). *Discursive Practices of Intergenerational Transmission of Recent History. (Re)making our Past*. New York: Palgrave Macmillan.

Alba, A. (2015). *The Holocaust Memorial Museum. Sacred Secular Space*. New York: Palgrave Macmillan.

Argenti, N., & Schramm, K. (Eds.). (2010). *Remembering Violence. Anthropological Perspectives on Intergenerational Transmission*. New York: Berghahn Books.

Derrida, J. (2006). *Specters of Marx* (Routledge Classics). New York: Routledge.

Erll, A. (2011). Travelling Memory. *Parallax, 17*(4), 4–18.

Goldman Rubin, S. (2017). *Maya Lin: Thinking with Her Hands*. San Francisco: Chronicle Books.

Harlan, V., Rappmann, R. & Schata, P. ([3]1986). *Soziale Plastik. Materialien zu Joseph Beuys*. Krefeld: Achberger Verlag.

Herring, G. C. (1986). *America's Longest War: United States and Vietnam, 1950–1975*. New York: McGraw Hill.

Hughes, R. (2006). Memory and Sovereignty in Post-1979 Cambodia, Choeung Ek and Local Genocide Memorials. In S. E. Cook (Ed.), *Genocide in Cambodia and Rwanda: New Perspectives* (pp. 257–279). New Brunswick/London: Transaction Publishers.

Joswig, B. (2003). *altäre. Theologie und Kunst im urbanen Raum. Ein Tischprojekt*. Gütersloh: Gütersloher Verlagshaus.

Kulka, R. A., et al. (2013). *Trauma and the Vietnam War Generation: Report of Findings from the National Vietnam Veterans Readjustment Study*. New York: Routledge.

Landsberg, A. (2004). *Prosthetic Memory: The Transformation of American Remembrance in the Age of Mass Culture*. New York: Columbia University Press.

Olick, J. K. (2007). *The Politics of Regret: On Collective Memory and Historical Responsibility*. New York: Routledge.

Reddemann, L. (2011). *Psychodynamisch imaginative Traumatherapie PITT – Das Manual. Ein resilienzorientierter Ansatz in der Psychotraumatologie*. Stuttgart: Klett Cotta.

Reyntjens, F. (2015). *Political Governance in Post-Genocide Rwanda*. Cambridge: Cambridge University Press.

Reston, J., Jr. (2017). *Rift in the Earth: Art, Memory, and the Fight for a Vietnam Memorial*. New York: Arcade Publishing.

Sion, B. (2008). *Absent Bodies, Uncertain Memorials. Performing Memory in Berlin and Buenos Aires*. Ann Arbor: Proquest LLC.

Sion, B. (2011). Missing Bodies, Conflicted Rituals: Performing Memory in Germany, Argentina, and Cambodia. In A. Bieler, C. Bingel, & H.-M. Gutmann (Eds.), *After Violence. Religion, Trauma and Reconciliation* (pp. 61–81). Leipzig: Evangelische Verlagsanstalt.

Smart History. Khan Academy Video on Maya Ying Lin's Veterans Memorial in Washington, DC. https://www.youtube.com/watch?v=wuxjTxxQUTs. Accessed 4 Nov 2018.

Sodaro, A. (2018). *Exhibiting Atrocities. Memorial Museums and the Politics of Past Violence*. New Brunswick: Rutgers University Press.

Kigali Genocide Memorial Genocide. http://www.genocidearchiverwanda.org.rw/index.php/Kigali_Genocide_Memorial. Accessed 5 Nov 2018.

Wefing, H. (2005, May 4). Das Holocaust Mahnmal. Wider alle Erwartungen. *Frankfurter Allgemeine Zeitung*, p. 37. https://www.faz.net/aktuell/feuilleton/debatten/das-holocaust-mahnmal-wider-alle-erwartungen-1189880-p3.html. Accessed 24 June 2019.

Williams, P. (2007). *Memorial Museums. The Global Rush to Commemorate Atrocities*. Oxford: Berg.

Young, James E. (1993). *The Texture of Memory. Holocaust Memorials and Meaning*. New Haven and London: Yale University Press.

Index[1]

[1] Note: Page numbers followed by 'n' refer to notes.

K. Wale et al. (eds.), *Post-Conflict Hauntings*, Palgrave Studies in Compromise after Conflict, https://doi.org/10.1007/978-3-030-39077-8

The manufacturer's authorised representative in the EU is Springer Nature Customer Service Centre GmbH, Europaplatz 3, 69115 Heidelberg, Germany. If you have any concerns regarding our products, please contact ProductSafety@springernature.com

Printed and bound by CPI Group (UK) Ltd, Croydon, CR0 4YY
30/09/2026
02225456-0011